Hitler's Last Bastion

Hitler's Last Bastion

The Final Battles for the Reich 1944-1945

Franz Kurowski

Schiffer Military History
Atglen, PA

Book Design by Robert Biondi.
Translated from the German by Joseph G. Welsh.

This book was originally published under the title,
Endkampf um das Reich 1944-1945,
by Podzun-Pallas Verlag, Friedberg.

Copyright © 1998 by Schiffer Publishing Ltd.
Library of Congress Catalog Number: 97-81429.

Printed in the United States of America.
ISBN: 0-7643-0548-4

We are interested in hearing from authors with book ideas on related topics.

Published by Schiffer Publishing Ltd.
4880 Lower Valley Road
Atglen, PA 19310 USA
Phone: (610) 593-1777
FAX: (610) 593-2002
E-mail: Schifferbk@aol.com.
Please write for a free catalog.
This book may be purchased from the publisher.
Please include $3.95 postage.
Try your bookstore first.

Contents

INTRODUCTION

The Beginning of the End in the West

After the Allied troops broke out from the Normandy beachhead they first advanced to the south, then, however, they advanced to the southeast and east, through France to the German border.

Hitler's instructions, sent through General Warlimont on 2/8/1944 to the commander on the Normandy front, Generalfeldmarschall [GFM] von Kluge, read:

> "Re-establish the front! The enemy breakthrough is to be parried by a strong counterattack. Moreover, several panzer divisions committed on the front are to be removed and replaced by infantry divisions. In this manner at least four panzer divisions must be made available for a German breakthrough near Avranches to the coast – without regard for the enemy forces that have already broken through into Bretagne."

On the following morning GFM von Kluge declared to his guest that, after U.S. troops captured Martain and because of the fact that the II SS

Panzer Corps was tied up by British forces, there was no question of a German attack, but only a retreat.

When Warlimont gave Hitler the GFM's reply the Fuehrer could not be deflected from the idea of a major offensive. There were still intact panzer divisions being represented on the situation map in the Fuehrer Headquarters, which in reality were only, at the most, in regiment strength.

On 6/8 Vire was lost. U.S. troops reached Le Mans and on 8/8 the Loire.

General Buhle, the Chief of the Heeres Staff, flew from the Fuehrer Headquarters and informed von Kluge of the Fuehrer Order to conduct an attack under all circumstances (even if two days later). Von Kluge immediately ordered the execution of Operation "Luettich." The four German panzer divisions that were committed had only 185 tanks, instead of the 800 tanks they were supposed to have on paper. The 2nd Panzer Division was able to advance 12 kilometers in the direction of Avranches on the early morning of 7/8. However, then they were stopped by battle commandos of the 3rd U.S. Armored Division. Mortain was re-captured by German panzer formations.

However, when at midday on 7/8 the fog lifted and U.S. fighter-bombers were able to take off again, the lead formation, the 1st SS Panzer Division, was smashed. The attack of the 116th Panzer Division also did not succeed. Fighter-bombers and medium bombers decimated them and the 2nd Panzer Division to the point where they had to suspend their attacks one hour after noon.

After receiving these reports, GFM von Kluge wanted to suspend these attacks, because they could only end with the complete destruction of the last German tanks. He was ordered by the Fuehrer Headquarters to remove another two of the four panzer divisions committed against the British front and, therefore, renew the attack. Thus the captured terrain could, indeed, be held by mobilizing all of their forces, however, they could not achieve any further ground gains.

GFM von Kluge drove to the front and got the impression that no further success was possible here. The German forces were exhausted, while the enemy was constantly reinforcing.

While the German commander was still underway, General Montgomery had ordered the execution of the Operation "Totalize" on the morning of 8/8/1944, which was to lead to the destruction of the 7th German Army. An enormous avalanche of tanks set in motion. The first strike hit the 272nd and 89th German Infantry Divisions. The latter had just arrived from Norway and was unable to hold up against this pressure. Both divisions were already heavily exhausted when the 2nd phase of this operation kicked in: 500 Allied combat bombers took off to attack. They circled over the infantry positions in attack, dropping rocket bombs and firing from all on-board weapons.

An hour later they were followed by a large formation of 700 heavy bombers from the USAAF. Only thanks to the fact that the 1st Polish and 4th Canadian Armored Divisions did not follow the Americans immediately at the end of this two-phased bombardment and the radical commitment of the 101st Heavy SS Panzer Battalion (the later 501st Corps Tiger Battalion) and a handful of tanks from the 12th SS Panzer Division "Hitlerjugend", did the situation not deteriorate completely.

While in combat against the 4th Canadian Armored Division, the German tanks, including the Tiger battalion of the unforgettable Michael Wittmann, were covered by a large-scale bombardment. Nevertheless, the enemy advance was halted, Obersturmfuehrer Wittmann had fallen.

On the following evening and during the upcoming night the 1st Polish Armored Division attacked. They were repulsed. The 12th SS Panzer Division was located here until their destruction on 11/8.

Enemy elements attacked through Le Mans, which fell into their hands again on 10/8, in the direction of Alencon. The main supply installations of the 7th Army were located here. At the head of the attackers rolled the XV U.S. Corps under Lieutenant General Haislip, it was subordinate to the 3rd U.S. Army. On 12/8 Alencon was lost to this corps.

On the evening of 13/8 GFM von Kluge reported that the enemy was not only about to encircle the 7th Army, but that their attack indicated that they wanted to encircle the 5th Panzer Army also. The withdrawal ordered by the commander was, 24 hours later, prohibited by Hitler. During this time, the enemy was able to reach Falaise on 14/8 and, several days later, reinforce the pocket. On 18/8/1944 nothing else happened here. What now followed was the fatal attempt of the remnants of the 15 German divisions encircled in the Falaise pocket to force a breakout. Of the 100,000 German soldiers encircled here, 10,000 were left behind in the pocket dead and 50,000 were left as prisoners. The rest were able to escape, if, for the most part, wounded.

The defeat at Falaise was, for the German Wehrmacht, a catastrophe. The struggle to obtain the open area was over. Now Generals Bradley and Montgomery regrouped. On 1/9/1944 Monty was promoted to Field Marshal.

The next objective of the Western Allies, the reconquest of Paris, was realized very quickly, even though Hitler, on 18/8, had entrusted the more tenacious Model with the command of the Western Front, after GFM von Kluge committed suicide. GFM von Rundstedt was assigned as OB West, a position he held earlier, on 6/9/1944, while GFM Model took command of Army Group B.

General Eisenhower took command over all Allied forces in Western Europe on 1/9/1944 in Granville. To him were subordinated:

The 6th Army Group under Lieutenant General Devers.
The 12th Army Group under General Bradley and the 21st Army Group under Field Marshal Montgomery.

The assault through France to the West Wall could now begin.

Now the absence of the 15 divisions, which were lost in the Falaise pocket, made itself felt. The German panzer and panzergrenadier divisions were only at regimental strength. Each of these exhausted divisions had only five to ten tanks left, as GFM Model reported to Hitler on 29/8/1944. The Allies assaulted forward, pursuing the withdrawing German divisions and captured Antwerp on 4/9.

Now the German defensive line ran from Antwerp across the Albert Canal and Maas to the West Wall, along the West Wall to the Swiss border. In order to hold this defensive line, according to the words of GFM Model, 25 fresh infantry divisions and five to six panzer divisions were needed.

"Otherwise", according to Model, "the gate to western Germany will lay open." (See Wilmot, Chester: The Battle for Europe).

On the early morning of 11/9/1944 a U.S. scout troops was first to cross the German border unnoticed near Pruem. Therefore, the formations of the Western Allies reached the gate to the Reich. The march into Germany could begin.

The Beginning of the End in the East

Not three weeks after the beginning of the Allied invasion in the west the Red Army unleashed its major offensive "Bagration" on 22/6/1944, the third anniversary of "Barbarossa."

The fighting in Belorussia was equivalent to that with the Anglo-Americans. The Red Army, which attacked the 500,000 soldiers of German Army Group Center with 2.5 million soldiers in 185 divisions, advanced into an area completely devoid of tanks. The panzer formations of Army Group Center had shortly before been transferred to the south into the Army Group South Ukraine area of operations, where the Soviets had simulated strong deployments. The OKH's Fremde Heere Ost [Foreign Army East] was not in a position to uncover this large-scale deception. Thus, an offensive began against which the Germans had no corresponding defensive forces. It ended with the destruction of Army Group Center and brought the Red Army within a few weeks to the East Prussian border.

The Red Army assault pushed 600 kilometers further to the west. They had achieved victories which Marshal Stalin had not dreamed of.

In the deadly assault of 45,000 guns and in the hail of bombs of 4500 aircraft committed on the opening day the steel attack wedges of 6100 tanks and assault guns destroyed an entire German army group, 28 German divisions with 350,000 men wallowed in the dust.

A timely regrouping and the evacuation of the fortified places designated by Hitler could have hindered such a grievous disaster. Instead, 350,000 German soldiers were sacrificed and the enemy was allowed to advance to the west up to the East Prussian border.

On 20 June neither Hitler nor his advisors believed that a new Soviet offensive would take place in the Army Group Center area of operations. The reports coming from the front about enormous troop movements were taken to be "diversionary attacks" and "diversionary deployments."

They were unwaverable in their conviction that a new Russian offensive would only occur in the Army Group South Ukraine area of operations. However, this was only a Russian faint, a deception involving a great number of empty trains to simulate a railroad deployment.

Thus, ultimately, on the basis of a proposal by Feldmarschall Model, the commander of Army Group North Ukraine, strong panzer formations were removed out of the Army Group Center sector and transferred to the south with the objective of straightening out the situation in the Kovel area by a strong attack. A total of eight panzer and panzergrenadier divisions were transferred into the Army Group North Ukraine area of operations so that the enemy would be prevented from "attacking through Lvov and Warsaw to Koenigsberg and cutting off Army Group Center, as well as Army Group North, from their rear area communications."

The German military made a big mistake in believing Marshal Stalin and the Red Army incapable of such wide-ranging and far-reaching operations. (On their part, Operation "Bagration" was to be conducted in the Army Group Center area of operations with the objective of "gaining approximately 150 kilometers.")

Therefore, on the basis of an incorrect situation assessment, Army Group Center was relieved of almost all of its panzer troops and a third of its Heeres troops.

GFM Busch, the commander of Army Group Center, declared that he could frustrate the enemy from establishing a main effort in front of his sector by promptly inserting his mobile forces.

On 4/6/1944 Army Group Center reported in its enemy assessment that the local Red Army force concentrations facing it could be increased at any time by the insertion of considerable enemy forces. Therefore, they had to anticipate that the enemy would conduct operations at numerous locations on the Eastern Front, varying the main efforts, "in order to fix the German forces."

On 19/6 the leadership of Army Group Center reported that the enemy was deploying strong reserve forces in front of the 9th Army, including armored formations. Thus, the 33rd Guards Army was noted near Ryassna and the 11th Guards Army was located on the highway southeast of Vitebsk, while the V Rifle Corps was found on the Sukhodrovka front. Moreover, the 5th Guards Tank Army was established in the Smolensk area. All of this signified that the enemy did not intend to conduct any fixing attack in front of Army Group Center, but that he was planning an enormous offensive. That the Russian Air Force was reinforced with 4,500 aircraft in front of Army Group Center was an unmistakable sign that the Russians were planning a large-scale offensive.

Still the situation assessment at OKH reflected the opposite. The Chief of Operations at OKH, Oberst Heusinger, had the impression on 14/6 that the "main enemy attack would occur in the Ukraine." The advances against Army Groups South Ukraine and Center would only be secondary or fixing attacks. GFM Keitel declared on 20/6/1944 to the NSFO Conference (Nationalsozialistischen Fuehrungsoffiziere) in Sonthofen:

"The Soviets will attack after the Western Allies have achieved an operational breakthrough with their invasion forces in Normandy. The main effort of the Soviet offensive would again be in the south, in Galicia."

Thus, Army Group Center stood with a total of 38 divisions, including not one single panzer division, on a long bend on the front in thin positions. Six of these divisions were assigned by Hitler to fight to the death in cities he designated as fortified places: in Vitebsk there were three divisions, in Orsha, Mogilev and Bobruisk there were one apiece.

However, what had the Abwehr and Fremde Heere Ost, who were directly subordinate to the OKH to say? What of their master spies that were supposed to be swarming in the Russian staffs?

As they were before the Allied invasion, the OKH Fremde Heere Ost was in no position – or were not willing – to recognize the large-scale changes in front of Army Group Center. This was not just the shifting of one division, or even a corps. Entire armies were being brought up; enormous concentrations of aircraft from various air armies were transferred into the neighborhood of the front, and this was done completely unnoticed?

What were the 12,000 soldiers of the German radio reconnaissance troops doing? Ten communications detachments, ten long-range communications reconnaissance companies and just as many short-range communications reconnaissance companies were committed. There were also five short-range reconnaissance companies. Did they not hear one "dit [morse code bit – dit – dah]" from the enormous radio traffic of four Russian fronts and between the air armies?

And what impression did the 240,000 Russian partisans make, who on the night of 20 June conducted 10,500 sabotage missions between the Dnepr and Beresina, paralyzing rail lines and telephone communications in the Army Group Center sector?

In the combat diary of the German Wehrmacht there are no indications that any such reports were passed on. On a frontal sector of 700 kilometers on the morning of 22/6 (and within a time range of 48 hours) 2.5 million Russian soldiers attacked, 45,000 guns fired, 6100 tanks and assault guns rolled, 4500 aircraft attacked. Within a few days entire divisions were destroyed in the marsh region between the Dnepr and Beresina.

Vitebsk and Bobruisk, Minsk and Baranovichi fell to the assaulting troops of the Red Army. Three weeks after the beginning of the attack the Red Army had recaptured Brest Litovsk. Shortly thereafter the lead Russian formations stood on the Memel and the Vistula. At the end of July 1944 they had already reached the East Prussian border.

Therefore, the enemy in the east also stood at the threshold of the Reich. Four Russian army groups advanced 600 kilometers in one assault.

At the end of August 1944 German troops on the southern flank of the 3rd Panzer Army were in defensive combat in the Lake Wystiter hills up to the Memel.

Koenigsberg was attacked for the first time by 200 British bombers during the night of 17/8/1944. During the night of 30/8 the second attack occurred. This time the British pilots tested the first incendiary bombs.

They hit the residential quarter of the city, this was the plan. The cathedral, the Schlosskirsch, the university and the historical district were destroyed by fire. 50 percent of all of the houses in Koenigsberg were turned to ashes. The number of killed during the two attacks totaled 3,500; 150,000 Koenigsbergers were homeless.

On 2/9/1944 when Finland withdrew from the war, additional Russian troops were freed-up by the withdrawal of the Lappland Army in the north, they could now be utilized against the Reich.

On 15/9/1944, at approximately the same time as in the west, the Leningrad Front and the 1st, 2nd and 3rd Baltic Fronts fell on Germany.

Fortified places and fronts were also formed here, often decisively, as will be described in the second part of this work.

1

BEFORE THE GATES OF THE REICH

The Battle of Aachen – Preliminary Remarks

Long before the battle for the Reich reached its last decisive phase, a German border city stood under the hail of shells from Allied weapons and had to be defended. It was the old imperial city of Aachen. The order of the Commander-in-Chief of the Wehrmacht to defend it ran:

> "The West Wall is to be defended and Aachen is to be held under all circumstances as the first German city to be attacked by the enemy."

The German imperial city, which had symbolic significance, could not be allowed to fall into the hands of the enemy. Nevertheless, the means available to defend Aachen were too limited to hold the city as a fortress.

At the beginning of September 1944 the entire area around Aachen was still unprotected. In the city itself were the 453rd Replacement and Training Battalion under Oberst Osteroth and the 34th Fortification Machine-gun Battalion, as well as a panzerjaeger battalion. Generalleutnant Mahlmann took command of these hastily thrown together formations with the 353rd ID staff.

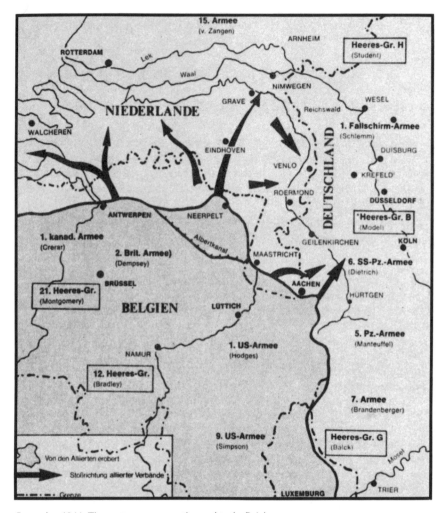

September 1944: The western enemy on the road to the Reich.

Up to this point in time, Aachen had a little experience with Allied terror bombings. Thus British bomber formations hit the city during the night of 12/4/1944 with 4000 high explosive bombs, 34,000 fire bombs and 8,600 phosphorus bombs, in order to smoke it out. 1,252 registered dead were the result, over 1000 wounded were admitted to hospitals.

When the VII U.S. Corps under Lieutenant General Collins, known to his friend as "Speedy Joe", attacked on a front 50 kilometers wide on 11/9/1944 out of the area west of Aachen, in order to reach their objective, the

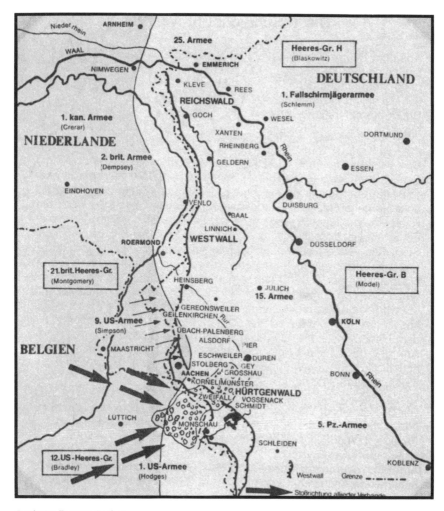

Battle for Fortress Aachen.

German imperial city, the men at Allied Headquarters believed that the Stolberger Corridor was relatively free of enemy forces. Collins and his troops were, therefore, committed there. He selected the 1st Infantry Division [ID] under Major General Huebner and the 3rd Armored Division [AD] under Major General Rose.

    The objective of this new attack of the 1st ID was Aachen, which was to be captured in a raid. At the same time, therefore, the tanks of the 3rd AD were to roll past Aachen in the direction of Dueren and capture this city.

The Germans, as the Anglo-American commanders "knew", no longer had any guts after their rapid retreat through France and Belgium, after they lost the battle of France. All that was necessary was to continue the advance and they would continue to run from the Allied divisions. All they had to do was to advance quicker then they and overtake them and cut them off. Within a few weeks the Second World War would be over.

Agents and scouts had reported long ago that the West Wall was no more than a mockery, it even lacked guns.

Later this would be confirmed by the words of the German General der Kavallerie Siegfried Westphal, Chief of Staff of OB West, and GFM von Rundstedt:

> "The much touted West Wall had only symbolic value in the sixth year of the war. At the end of September/beginning of October 1944 the road to the interior of the Reich lay open." (See Westphal, Siegfried: Report to the author)

Lieutenant General Hodges, commander of the 1st U.S. Army, an energetic soldier who rose from a private to a three-star general, was not convinced of the ineffectiveness of the West Wall. Through his field glasses he viewed forward observers in bunkers and he warned his three corps commander, Corlett, Gerow and Collins. They were not to advance too quickly and, above all, they were to allow the supplies to catch up before they took any decisive steps forward. However, Lieutenant General Collins raised a protest:

> "When we get started, we can't stop!"

Collins said further: "let us first take Aachen. Then we can rest and let the supply catch up."

Therefore, General Hodges turned Collins loose. However, it was only to be a "reconnaissance in force!" The objective of this reconnaissance in force was to knock at the West Wall before the German troops could occupy these bunkered positions. At the time, these bunkers were essentially vacant. The start of the attack of the divisions of the VII U.S. Corps was 12/9/1944.

The 1st Battle of Aachen

The two above mentioned divisions from the VII U.S. Corps attacked out of the Eupen area to the northeast on the morning of 12/9. The direction of attack for the 1st ID was Aachen, the 3rd AD to the south of there, from Kornelimuenster to Roetgen and Rott.

The U.S. combat formations advanced very quickly and within a few hours approached the southwestern edge of the city of Aachen with little resistance.

The commander of the German LXXXI Army Corps, Generalleutnant Schack, to whom this frontal sector was subordinated on 5/9/1944, named Oberst Osteroth as combat commandant, as soon as he received reports that the Americans had advanced to the southeastern edge of Aachen, and dispatched the 34th Machine-gun Battalion north of Aachen on the road to Maastricht. The two grenadier battalions were transferred into the city forest, where the Americans had, in the meantime, advanced and had penetrated lead formations into the West Wall.

The soldiers of the 1st U.S. ID assaulted the large 113 Bunker and overcame the first bunker line through the existing gap, without being able to crack the additional bunkers to the left and right of this gap. The second bunker-line in the southeast of the city, with the 161 Main Bunker, was lost 48 hours later.

On 10/9 the Reichsfuehrer SS, Heinrich Himmler, visited Aachen and appealed to the defensive will of the residents and soldiers. He drove it into them that the city had to be defended with all means. Generalleutnant Schack, whose LXXXI Army Corps was subordinate to the 7th Army and who had four divisions available, to which only a handful of tanks belonged, immediately ordered his most intact 116th Panzer Division [PD], which, however, had suffered severely in France, to secure the imperial city.

On Wednesday morning, 13/9/1944, Generalleutnant Graf von Schwerin, took command in Aachen. He set up his command posts in

Laurensberger Schloss and in the Hotel Berliner Hof on Bahnhofstrasse.

The 116th PD entered Aachen. The "Windhunde", as this division was referred to, occupied the decisive defensive positions on the edge of the city. The civilians were evacuated by the Party leadership on the previous day. On 13/9, as the residents struggled through the streets of Aachen with carts piled high, Generalleutnant Graf von Schwerin issued an order forbidding all unplanned evacuations. Only those people would be allowed to leave the city whose transport was secured to the east.

On the early morning of 13/9/1944 the Americans initiated Operation "Leander." Lieutenant Colonel Leander Doan, commander of Battle Group X of the 3rd U.S. AD received orders to test the defensive strength and the will to defend of the Aacheners. Doan attacked the German machine-gun positions near Oberforstbach with his tanks, which were followed by infantry.

His battle group, in all 1600 men with heavy weapons and tanks, attacked through these German outpost positions and penetrated through the armored obstacle, after blowing one of the notorious dragon's teeth of the West Wall, and reached high ground from where Doan and his staff could view the German defensive positions around Aachen.

The Sherman tanks rolled further. Here and there groups would stop to fire at the few targets that presented themselves.

The German eighty-eight flak returned the fire as soon as the tanks had worked their way to within range. The lead enemy tanks were stopped with damaged tracks and destroyed turrets. Nevertheless, the battle group continued to advance.

From a bunker, which had already been bypassed by the tanks and flanked by infantry units, the "Hitlersaegen", as the new rapid firing MG 42 was called, fired. Men collapsed. There were calls to medics throughout the day, the advance came to a standstill, the tanks rolled on by themselves and were attacked and knocked out by close combat troops with explosives and magnetic anti-tank hollow charges.

A platoon of U.S. infantry under the leadership of a lieutenant advanced against the bunker, from which the destructive fire was coming, from two sides. Several tanks fired on it from two sides. When the platoon leader fired a flare, which indicated to the tanks that the infantry was at the objective, the fire turned again to the east.

Engineers brought their explosives and the officer in charge ordered the bunker defenders to come out, without weapons and with their hands raised over their heads.

"Go to Hell!" was the reply from the bunker.

Seconds later the fuses were set to the explosives. After being covered by a thick mantel of flame and smoke, this bunker was silenced forever.

The battle group advanced gradually and, as midday approached, it became clear to Lieutenant Colonel Doan that it would not be so easy to breakthrough into the city.

After a scout troop found a narrow, but passable for tanks, lane through the dragon-toothed bunker-line, Doan saw his chance. He ordered the threshing tanks to advance and neutralize the mines.

However, this passage was not mined. It appeared that the Germans had simply forgotten to mine it.

The threshing tanks paved a way through this aisle. The steel balls on the ends of the long tacks, that penetrated the ground in random patterns, found no mines. However, one of the steel balls lodged in a concrete hump and became stuck. The tank maneuvered back and forth. Thick smoke came out of its exhaust, which drew the attention of the Germans to its position. The crew abandoned the tank and the "Scorpion" was left as an additional obstacle in this narrow aisle.

Therefore, Battle Group X blocked its own way to the city.

The U.S. infantry also experienced many difficulties on this day of combat. The 16th Infantry Regiment [IR] from the 1st U.S. ID, during its attempt to penetrate directly into the city from the west, was stopped several times. Finally, the 1st Battalion achieved a penetration into the city forest. The advancing infantry vehicles advanced up to the Pelzerturm. Here they stalled.

The report of a penetration into the city forest was passed on by Generalleutnant Graf von Schwerin only minutes later to the LXXXI Army Corps. Generalleutnant Schack ordered the 116th PD to attack and throw back the enemy forces that had penetrated into the forest.

The commander of the 116th PD issued the attack order to his trusted panzergrenadiers. At the same time he ordered the first elements of the 394th Assault Gun Brigade, which had just arrived at the Aachen main railroad station, to quickly drive directly from the railroad unloading ramps and provide the panzergrenadiers with the necessary heavy weapons support. Two couriers were hastily dispatched to direct the assault guns to the commitment area.

These troops were able to drive the enemy from the forest. Wherever small groups of Americans had established themselves, the assault guns rolled up and destroyed these nests of resistance. Here once again they gave evidence of their worth and helped the panzergrenadiers.

The gap was closed. Only a few groups of the U.S. infantry with anti-tank guns and mortars were able to entrench themselves in the city forest. They were overwhelmed during the coming night in attack.

After Lieutenant Colonel Doan had reported that the passage they had found was blocked by an American tank Major General Rose ordered a second attack. First the stalled threshing tank was to be made operational and advanced. As soon as the gap was open, tanks were to follow, secured by infantry, and resume the attack.

This venture succeeded. The Scorpion was still operational, the engineers freed the track and the tank rolled forward and veered off to the side after negotiating the passage.

The 20 Shermans following rolled through the gap in the West Wall one behind the other. The flames from their exhausts darted through the night and signaled their approach to the German infantry, who waited in their close combat fox-holes. When the Shermans had passed over the covered trenches the first panzerfausten were fired. Their flaming trails drove through the darkness. Explosives cracked, tanks exploded, ammunition illuminated this eerie picture in a hellish Breughelian symphony. The lead American vehicles lay destroyed. A follow-on combat vehicle ran in circles on a broken track, firing helplessly into the night.

In between the thuds of the panzerfaust rounds their were the explosions of shells and the following detonations. Flames rose into the night sky. Thick black smoke spiraled up from the stalled steel boxes.

The surviving crew members abandoned ship and attempted to take cover from the bellowing machine-gun fire. The enemy armored attack was stopped.

In the meantime, the main body of the assault guns of the 394th Brigade had unloaded from the Aachen main railroad station. They formed up and dispatched to where Battle Group X under Lieutenant Colonel Doan had stalled.

After its commitment in Normandy and its destruction in the Falaise pocket, this brigade, under the leadership of Hauptmann Schmock, received new guns and had arrived on the battlefield in time for the defense of Aachen.

Moving quickly, stopping to fire and then moving quickly again, the experienced gun commanders were able to destroy seven additional U.S. tanks during this night combat. The rest finally turned around and rolled back they way they had come. It was now evident that Aachen would not be captured in a quick raid.

The raid on Aachen, which went down in the history of the war as the 1st battle of Aachen, was over. It was indecisive. The troops of the 1st U.S. Army were ordered by the commander of the 12th Army Group, General Omar N. Bradley, to remain in their achieved positions and wait for their supplies to catch up.

Allied and German Formations Before the West Wall

The Allied deployment on the German border after the victory during the battle of France ran from the area northwest of Luxembourg in a wide bend to the north and northwest through Aachen and Maastricht to Neerpelt and Antwerp. The major U.S. and British formations committed here were:

The 9th U.S. Army under General Simpson, the 1st U.S. Army under General Hodges, the 2nd British Army under General Dempsey and the 1st Canadian Army under General Crerar. The U.S. armies belonged to the 12th Army Group, while the two British armies were subordinate to the 21st Army Group, Field Marshal Montgomery.

Opposite them from the southeast to the northwest lay the following German formations:

The 7th Army under General Brandenberger, the 5th Panzer Army under General von Manteuffel, the 6th SS Panzer Army under General Dietrich, the 1st Fallschirmjaeger Army under General Schlemm and the 15th Army under General von Zangen, which was located in the Netherlands.

German Army Group B with its headquarters in Duesseldorf and Army Group H under Generaloberst Student north of Wesel were subordinate to OB West, GFM von Rundstedt.

In the northern sector of the German Western Front the Allies had captured Antwerp on 4/9/1944.

The German troops, which had fled out of France, had stopped at the West Wall at the beginning of September. The German front-line now ran from Antwerp on the Schelde Estuary (the city and the harbor itself were lost, however, the front held on the far side) in a bend up to the area south of Aachen, where it made contact with the West Wall. From there the defensive line corresponded with the West Wall up to Trier. The defensive front continued on through Metz and Belfort to the Swiss border.

On Monday, 11/9/1944, the British 2nd Army under General Dempsey advanced out of Belgium to Holland. On the same day at 1855 hours U.S. scout troops from the 1st U.S. Army crossed the German Reich border unnoticed north of Trier near Stolzenbourg in Luxembourg. These were the first Allied soldiers to step foot in the German Reich in the west. After this short explanation, we return to the situation in September 1944 in the greater area of Aachen.

There in front of the city from the south to the north stood the 275th ID under Generalleutnant Schmidt, the 49th ID commanded by Generalleutnant Macholz and the 116th PD under the command of Generalleutnant Graf von Schwerin.

The latter received the 165th Panzer Brigade. Ultimately the 12th Volksgrenadier Division was rushed forward, in order to hold the front, which was threatened with collapse.

Generalleutnant Schack commanded the LXXXI Army Corps under the 7th Army in the vicinity of Aachen. The second large formation available to General Brandenberger was the LXXIV Army Corps under General der Infanterie Straube.

In the Fortress – The "Fall" of Schwerin

In Aachen itself Gauleiter Grohe refused to obey the order to stop the evacuation, which General von Schwerin had issued, so that the civilian population would not be left leaderless and to signal the enemy that Aachen could be surrendered.

Instead, Gauleiter Grohe announced the "explicit will of the Fuehrer to completely evacuate Aachen." In addition, he hung his announcements at all public squares:

> "We must, therefore, consider that the town will soon become part of the western combat zone. Therefore, the Fuehrer has ordered the evacuation of all towns and cities laying in the foreground of the combat zone, in order to secure German lives and important war material. Men between the ages of 15 and 60 that are not incapable of working will not be withdrawn first, but will be committed to constructing fortifications."

Of the approximately 25,000 civilians still in the city, about 20,000 set out to the east. 5000 citizens of Aachen, and these were not only men capable of working, remained in the city and managed to live in cellars and bunkers.

After their setback during the night of 14/9/1944, the American troops did not launch a new attack. Even 15/9 passed quietly, except for some sporadic artillery fire. Only enemy scout troops probed up to the bunker-line, looking for weak spots.

On the morning of 16/9 Generalleutnant Graf von Schwerin received a summons from the commander of the LXXXI Army Corps. When von Schwerin reported to him over the telephone, Generalleutnant Schack informed him:

"Listen, Schwerin, you will be relieved of command within the hour. Make yourself available."

Generalleutnant Graf von Schwerin immediately realized that this referred to a letter he had written to the commander of the American troops facing his troops.

In this letter he, Schwerin, said that he prohibited the evacuation of the residents of Aachen and he requested that they [the Americans] take notice of this. The contents of this letter were enough to bring him up before a court-martial, especially since he raised the possibility of surrendering the city.

All of 14 September General Graf von Schwerin awaited an answer to his letter. In his command post near the Maahsen Farm the commander of the Windhund Division asked what would happen if the Allies bombarded Aachen again.

Shortly after 1630 on this 14/9 General von Schwerin received the order from Generalleutnant Schack that the civilian population of the city must be evacuated under all circumstances and that only combat formations were to remain in the city, because Aachen was to immediately be declared a fortress.

On the following day, 15/9, the political leadership returned to the city, "in order to enforce the Fuehrer Order."

But what happened to Generalleutnant von Schwerin's letter? This letter had fallen into the hands of the political leadership, who had immediately reported the "betrayal of a German General."

Thus, on the morning of 16/9 – as already described – Generalleutnant Schack called the command post of the 116th PD and informed Generalleutnant Graf von Schwerin of his impending arrest. An hour after the call from Generalleutnant Schack Generalleutnant Graf von Schwerin was ordered to turn command of the 116th PD to the senior regiment commander and immediately report to the LXXXI Army Corps. There he was to be arrested for the upcoming military court-martial.

Immediately after the division commander learned of the serious charges, General Mattenklott, the commander of Wehrkreise 6, Muenster, appeared at the 116th PD command post. He informed Graf von Schwerin of an order from the Reichsfuehrer SS, Heinrich Himmler, that the police were to be immediately committed with panzerfaeusten, in order to shoot the enemy tanks that penetrate into the German defensive line and that "the remnants of the 116th PD, because of the treachery of its leader, had to be regrouped."

General Mattenklott, an old Russia fighter who had received the Knight's Cross in 1941, felt duped by these false accusations from the Reichsfuehrer SS and asked Schwerin if he could use his telephone. He then reported to the Reichsfuehrer SS:

"The 116th Panzer Division is fighting in its positions. The front will be held by them as before. There is no trace of flight, Herr Himmler!"

General Mattenklott now knew that the commander of the 116th PD did not commit any crime.

On the morning of 17/9 he [von Schwerin] reported to the Generalleutnant Schack at the LXXXI Army Corps command post. He reassured him that the 116th PD had taken all measures for the defense of Aachen and had even repulsed the initial enemy attack.

While Generalleutnant Schack was being reassured, a radio message arrived from GFM Model, which ordered him to arrest Generalleutnant Graf von Schwerin and turn him over to the Peoples' Judge, as soon as he arrived at the Fuehrer Bunker near Muenstereifel.

This indicated to Generalleutnant von Schwerin that he had a problem. He requested Generalleutnant Schack relieve him of his division's command. This was granted.

During the evening of this gloomy Sunday von Schwerin arrived at his command post on the farm in Berenberg. Here there was already a kradschuetzen platoon waiting for him. When Graf von Schwerin reported to the commander of the 7th Army, General Brandenberger, at the Fuehrer Bunker in Muenstereifel, he was taken prisoner. He was driven under guard by a major, who was ordered to shoot him if he tried to escape, to OB West,

GFM von Rundstedt. An armored scout troop followed the vehicle he was riding in as extra security.

The various parties presented their cases for and against the commander of the 116th PD. The charges that the General had conspired with the enemy did not stand up. The judge proposed to GFM von Rundstedt that these silly proceedings be terminated as quickly as possible.

The proceeding finally ended on 13/11/1944, as the 116th PD had proved itself in further combat and Generalleutnant Graf von Schwerin was again assigned a command, this time as commander of a corps in Italy.

However, what had happened in the Aachen area in the meantime?

The 2nd Battle of Aachen

After the easy victories during the retreat of the German Wehrmacht from France, the soldiers of the 3rd U.S. AD were surprised by the decisive resistance they ran up against in front of Aachen. For them and all of the rest of the divisions of the American Expeditionary Forces in Europe the war had appeared to be a pleasure trip, and now this!

When the soldiers in the divisions committed near Aachen at the end of September held the "Stars and Stripes" – their front newspaper – and read the reports from the front, they did not believe their eyes. There stood the German troops like a band of "cripples with wooden legs and glass eyes, dispeptic grandfathers and young brats."

Major General Rose, the son of a New York rabbi, gave expression to his wonder: "I don't give a damn whether the fellow laying behind the rifle or machine-gun is 50 or 100 years old, so long as he can still pull his trigger finger. Ultimately he can still sit behind a meter thick concrete wall and cause us great concern."

On the morning of 15/9 Rose ordered Lieutenant Colonel William Lovelady: "Break through into the Stolberg Corridor, Bill!"

Lieutenant Colonel Lovelady clambered into his command tank a half hour later and gave the signal for his Sherman tanks to roll. They followed him in the assigned direction.

South of Stolberg these 30 ton colossi crossed the Bichtbach over an undamaged bridge, several hours after that they reached a line approximately three kilometers on the far side of this stream and stood in front of the German main combat line. However, these shelters and bunkers proved to be empty.

The tanks now rolled further on the Mausbach – Gressenich road. When they had reached the approximate mid-point between these two towns they came upon six German tanks in a depression to their left. They advanced several dozen meters further until they had an open field of fire and then the German tanks opened fire from their heavy cannon.

The forward-most Sherman received a direct hit. Thick, dark smoke rose through the flames above this Sherman tank. The surviving crew members abandoned ship and took cover in the ditch by the side of the road.

The second U.S. tank was hit in the left track. It fired blindly into the terrain until the next shot set it afire. Then a shell hit the ambulance vehicle, which accompanied the group of tanks. The vehicle splattered like a ripe fruit. The wounded were thrown about and lay screaming on the road. One of them was run over by an American tank, crushed into the dirt.

Three to four additional U.S. tanks were eliminated in this manner before they returned fire. However, Lieutenant Colonel Lovelady now gave the order to withdraw toward Mausbach, where the tanks could find shelter behind the houses. When Lovelady reported to Major General Rose he had only thirteen tanks left, some of which were still operational but could not fire.

Rose ordered him to hold the town and repair the lightly damaged tanks. He would dispatch replacements.

On the morning of this day Generalleutnant Schack ordered the 9th PD to attack the forces of the 3rd U.S. AD and throw them back behind the West Wall.

The 9th PD under Generalmajor Elverfeldt were the ones that had stopped Battle Group Lovelady. Now, as Elverfeldt's tanks tried to throw the enemy out of Mausbach as ordered, the Americans opened a powerful blocking fire. Three times the dismounted panzergrenadiers of the 9th PD attacked Mausbach and the American line there and three times they were repulsed with heavy losses by the ravaging barrage fire.

This weakened the 9th PD so that they could now hold their departure positions only with difficulty. There was one bright spot on the morning of 16/9, as General der Kavalerie Westphal reported from Vallendar, the command post of OB West, and informed the LXXXI Army Corps that it could count upon receiving the 12th Volksgrenadier Division soon. "Until the Twelfth gets there, you must hold the front, Schack", explained the Chief of Staff of OB West.

The first elements of this division, which was created from the glorious 12th ID, were to arrive in Juelich and Dueren on the evening of 16/9. The rest were to make into the combat area within the next 36 hours.

The 12th ID was severely decimated during the collapse of Army Group Center in summer 1944 and returned to the Reich for reconstitution and reorganization. From here it emerged as the 12th Volksgrenadier Division and was now under the leadership of Oberst Engel, the personal adjutant of the Fuehrer, and thrown into the fighting around Aachen. It had a total strength of 14,800 men and received a group of 17 assault guns. It had considerable combat strength with its panzerjaeger battalion.

From the unloading railroad station the 27th Fuesilier Regiment under the leadership of the Oak Leaf winner, Major Lemm, was set in movement in the direction of Eschweiler – Stolberg. Both cities were already occupied by U.S. troops, which were again driven out.

Under the trusted Russia veteran Lemm and the core of old soldiers they were able to quickly penetrate to Eschweiler and recapture the city in a raid. After that the battle group turned toward Stolberg. This city was also freed from the enemy within a few hours. The 48th Grenadier Regiment of the division under Major Osterhold joined in the fighting and completed the over-powering of the withdrawing enemy forces.

Troops of the 3rd U.S. AD, which had resumed the attack against the Aachen bunker-line on the morning of 16/9, stalled against the thick enemy fire coming from all of the bunkers. The engineer assault troops, which were to crack the bunkers, were in a difficult situation, because the bunker defenders were able to cover each other with machine-gun fire. Nevertheless, they were able to break the chain of bunkers at several locations, so that the intersecting German covering fire was eliminated. Still this new attack came to a halt quickly. The men returned to their departure positions.

The advancing front of the VII U.S. Corps was finally halted. Stolberg and Eschweiler to the rear of Aachen were again free of enemy forces. The fighting had lasted a week, and Aachen was still holding. The 9th PD under Generalmajor Freiherr von Elverfeldt was now inserted to the left of the 12th Volksgrenadier Division and reinforced the front. Both formations held up to each American attack. On 17/9 the enemy finally regrouped. On the next day they attacked with their 3rd AD, as well as the 1st and 9th Infantry Divisions in the direction of Stolberg. However, in Stolberg stood the fuesiliers and panzergrenadiers of the 12th Volksgrenadier Division. They conducted fierce street fighting against the penetrating enemy forces. By 21 September they were still standing like iron.

General der Infanterie Koechling, who had, in the meantime, replaced Generalleutnant Schack as the commander of the LXXXI Army Corps, received the following order from the OKW on 17/9:

"The West Wall is to be defended, and Aachen is to be held, as the first large German city to be attacked by the enemy, under all circumstances."

The 116th PD, which had still not been reconstituted since its retreat from France, fought with its last ounce of strength. This division was continuously bloodied since the very first hour of the defense. Finally, on 28/9, it was relieved by the 246th ID under Oberst Wilck, which had just arrived in the Aachen area.

This division consisted of combat inexperienced formations, approximately a third of it was composed of members of the Navy, Luftwaffe and new recruits. The division was assigned the mission of defending the city of Aachen.

General der Artillerie Brandenberger, as commander of the 7th Army, issued an order, right after Oberst Wilck took command of the fortress of Aachen, tasking the 12th Volksgrenadier Division with recapturing the first bunker-line. In the staff headquarters of the division, which was located in

Goering Kaserne in Eschweiler, Oberst Engel planned this counter-strike as on 17/9/1944 in the greater Arnheim, Nijmwegen and Eindhoven area Montgomery's plan was set in motion to breech the West Wall with a combined Anglo-American airborne army, land on the far side of the Maas and Niederrhein and advance from there directly into the heart of the German Reich, the Ruhr area.

This ingenious plan, the most bizarre during the Second World War according to General Omar N. Bradley, bore the code-word "Market Garden." It was conducted by the 82nd and 101st U.S. Airborne Divisions and the 1st British Airborne Division. It required reinforcements and General Eisenhower, the Supreme Allied Commander in the west, gave Monty the reinforcements.

The hopes the Brit hung on this spectacular operation were not realized. The air landings ended in complete destruction.

This event inspired Lieutenant General Collins on the Aachen front. In his own words: "this was a sign for my corps to resume the attack on Aachen." He ordered Major General Rose to set out again with his tanks.

The tanks of the 3rd U.S. AD rolled again on the morning of 18/9 toward Weissenberg and Donnersberg, as well as Eschweiler. The two hills were defended by a thin line of infantry with a few mortars. By the following day the Americans were able to capture these two hills after three artillery barrages.

Exactly 36 hours later panzergrenadiers and fuesiliers from the 12th Volksgrenadier Division conducted simultaneous counterattacks on both hills. During the night they were able to penetrate unnoticed into the American positions. They assaulted shouting "Hurrah!", threw hand-grenades, fired their machine-pistols and liberated both hills. Killed and wounded covered the positions on the hills. Therefore, Lieutenant General Collins quit for the time being. He did not believe that he could launch a new attack without additional reinforcements.

The fighting, which lasted from 17 to 23/9 and ultimately only consisted of nightly raids by small units reduced the combat strength of the 12th Volksgrenadier Division and the 9th PD by half. The 9th PD had lost two-thirds of its tanks.

Lieutenant General Hodges, the commander of the 1st U.S. Army, now ordered the 30th ID forward. This division had distinguished itself as the "Victor of Mortain" in Normandy. Under the leadership of Major General Hobbs they were to launch the next attack on Aachen from the north, advancing as far to the south as possible, while the 1st U.S. ID was attacking from the south to the north. This should break the necks of the Krauts, then when the two divisions meet somewhere to the east behind Aachen the city would be cut off from all supply.

The date of the attack was set for 1/10, in the meantime, both divisions had to regroup. During the days prior to the beginning of this attack the U.S. artillery conducted heavy fire on the city. U.S. bombers flew at Aachen during the day, at night came bombers from the RAF, so that the city would be forced to endure round-the-clock bombing.

With this transfer of the main effort of the fighting into the area north and northeast of Aachen, General Hodges also committed the XIX Corps of the 1st U.S. Army in movement on a wide front. Their objective was Geilenkirchen.

The two German divisions fighting northwest of Wuerselen, the 49th and 183rd Infantry Divisions, desperately opposed this attack, however, they could not prevent the enemy from gradually advancing on Geilenkirchen.

On 28/9/1944 the commander of the 12th Army Group, General Bradley, was presented with a bust of Hitler from a Eupener Party office. General Hodges then promised that his 1st Army would "produce the real thing within 30 days."

This was only wishful thinking, as the next few days would prove. A decisive battle would occur here near Aachen, it would delay the end of the war for months and give Hitler the opportunity to play the last German trump and prepare for the "battle in the Ardennes."

On the early morning of 2/10/1944 the 30th U.S. ID was ready for commitment. Its commander, Major General Leland Hobbs, stood in his command post near Rimburg directly west of the German border, which ran near Uebach – Palenberg, and waited for the appearance of the promised bomber formations, which were to plow-up the battlefield. It was 0900 hours before approximately 300 flying fortresses flew over the forward-most forces of the 30th ID with their enormous bomb loads. They were to batter the German bunkers on the West Wall.

When they dropped their bombs, they were located a distance from their targets. One element had even bombed the Belgium village of Genk, 55 kilometers further to the west of the German – Dutch border. The result of this mistake was the death of 34 civilians and the wounding of another 45. Here in Genk was also a Polish ditch digger, Eduard Gierek, who was working on the Genk – Waterschei mine. He was not injured during this attack and, in 1948, returned to Poland, where he became the First Secretary of the Central Committee of the Polish Workers' Movement.

When the air bombardment ended at 1000 hours, the men of the 30th U.S. ID advanced to attack. Over their heads screamed artillery salvoes, which were to eliminate a two kilometer wide German frontal sector.

However, this fire was also poorly placed and resulted in little loss. When the U.S. infantrymen approached west of Wurmtal, they faced a counter-fire. Each man was ordered to carry a board, in order to make the marshy meadow trafficable for vehicles and also to overcome the stream.

The German artillery opened fire. Mortars joined in. One U.S. company that had been caught in the middle of a salvo suffered heavy casualties. They lost 93 killed and wounded of their 120 soldiers.

The assault troops crossed the Wurm and moved in the direction of the Aachen – Moenchengladbach rail line, in order to find cover at the railroad embankment located there.

20 tanks and 1000 soldiers attacked in the first echelon. They worked their way up to the first German bunkers. They also brought flame-throwers with them.

The long streams of flame flicked through the rifle ports of the bunkers. Thick smoke rose above. The entire bunker would suddenly be engulfed in flame. Then it would become silent.

The engineers jumped forward, inserting explosives fastened on poles and detonating them. Three to four seconds later the detonation would roar over the din of the fighting.

A few survivors came out of the first bunkers, some with burning clothing. A little later the second bunkers were overcome in this manner. Flame-throwers and explosives were weapons that no amount of bravery could withstand.

Then German assault troops appeared to the right and left. They were firing on the run, taking cover for short periods, then firing and assaulting again. Machine-guns were firing from three, four, five positions, completely covering the attackers.

The flame-thrower troops were suppressed. They were now taking heavy casualties. After that the German troops had to gradually retreat and give ground in the direction of Palenberg.

The Americans shot holes in the bunkers with their bazookas and smoked the defenders out in this manner.

The Germans also were firing panzerfaust rounds, thereby destroying advancing vehicles or troop concentrations, machine-gun nests and advancing guns.

At 1230 hours, when the forward-most battle groups of the 30th U.S. ID were south of Palenberg, they stalled there near the chapel. They were exhausted, they could not advance any further. The attack for them had ended here. However, an hour later replacements arrived to continue the fighting.

In the afternoon the 30th ID reached Palenberg. Here they also had to fight from house to house and street to street. Hand-grenades and machine-pistols, explosives and machine-guns took a heavy toll on both sides.

The fighting raged through the evening, and if the commander of the 30th U.S. ID had hoped that he would be able to breakthrough quickly as he did during the pursuit battle through France he would be disappointed here. As it grew dark and the shadows of the night covered the battlefield a total of nine bunkers on the West Wall were in American hands.

In the afternoon, as the reports made it through of the reinforcement of the enemy, operational elements of the 49th ID – just a few – were thrown into the battle. These soldiers counterattacked and were able to stop the enemy after fierce fighting.

During the evening the operational assault guns of the 1183rd Independent Assault Gun Battery arrived. They rolled out of their assembly area in Beggendorf and shot up everything that opposed them. Two of them were paralyzed by bazooka hits. One was able to continue after its tracks were repaired, the other had to be towed away by a Zgkws.

When the Americans reached Schloss Rimburg in further advance, they were in for a surprise. What appeared to be an old outlying house for the castle was in fact a camouflaged bunker from which emanated heavy machine-gun fire. In addition two 2 cm air defense guns were also firing as fast as they could.

Here, at the castle of the von Brauchitsch family, that of a Feldmarschall and highly decorated officer and General, one could not really expect otherwise.

The Americans requested tanks over the radio, in order to eliminate this strong bunker. However, the tanks did not make it to the Wurm. They got stuck in the mud on the bank and could only be freed by being towed.

After that the U.S. attack troops were able to keep the German defenders from the walls and get behind the castle's moat in a pincer maneuver, bypassing the bunker. The castle was surrounded on three sides. Then the defenders held out inside. The castle – as was later found out – was connected to another bunker 200 meters away by an underground passage.

At midnight the U.S. troops attacked again. On the seam between the 183rd and 49th German Infantry Divisions they were able to crack four bunkers.

These attackers had also heard that the bunkers of the West Wall were only a figment of their imagination. They were now convinced otherwise. Wherever bunkers were occupied by determined soldiers, who had sufficient weapons and ammunition, they could not pass, especially when they themselves did not have heavy weapons with which to engage the concrete colossi.

During the night the wounded and the dead were removed from the battlefield by the U.S. ambulance vehicles. The last defenders of the castle were overcome and vanished like ghosts. They blew up the underground passage from the castle to the bunker.

General Koechling, the commander of the LXXXI Army Corps, learned in his command bunker in Muenstereifel, that the enemy was making progress and was laying murderous fire on the German positions.

During the same night U.S. engineers threw up a bridge across the Wurm south of Marienberg, which could also be used by tanks. In the early morning hours tanks from the 67th U.S. Armored Regiment crossed the Wurm in this manner and now rolled as the lead attack elements against the bunkers still being held by German troops. These tanks were able to silence several bunkers in direct fire and make it possible for the engineers to blow them up.

They continued to advance. One of the companies advanced 100 meters. It was attacked by two strong assault troops on both flanks and almost wiped out. Therefore, this battle was decided for the time being. The attack succumbed. The 30th U.S. ID achieved a ground gain of 1000 meters from the banks of the Wurm, and this with fearful losses.

During the evening the Americans were able to penetrate into the village of Uebach from the south and the southwest and block the Aachen – Geilenkirchen road.

In the early morning hours of 3/10 Generalmajor Lange was ordered by General Koechling to launch a counterattack against the U.S. penetration at Palenberg with subordinate units and assault guns from the 902nd Brigade, as well as the 341st Battalion and the 1184th Independent Battery, which still had several tanks from the 217th Sturmpanzer Battalion left. They were to stop the enemy penetration and throw them back to their departure positions.

In addition, the attack formations received another two battalions from the 246th Volksgrenadier Division and several units of the 49th ID.

At 0330 hours the strong German counterattack began. The assault guns rolled in front of the infantrymen and shot up the enemy nests of resistance and tanks. The night was shattered by the detonations and impact of the tank cannon. They reached the first houses. The engineers and grenadiers assaulted. Hand-grenades exploded, machine-pistols rattled. Glass shattered and steel banged against steel.

Uebach was snatched away from the Americans in the first assault. However, Generalmajor Lange's men were denied the breakthrough to the Wurm. Strong U.S. artillery fire stopped the forward momentum of the tanks and assault guns, several of them were lost.

In the early morning of 4/10 the fighting continued. The Americans literally threw every tank and fighter-bomber they had into the battle. Their artillery fired without pause. And they halted the German attack. One of the U.S. battalions on the front lost two commanders within one hour.

After some additional success the German attack stalled in this wall of fire. The Americans transitioned to the counterattack, penetrated again into Uebach and again began the house to house fighting. Man fought against man, both sides sought to throw the other from Uebach.

On the following day the troops of the 30th U.S. ID under Major General Hobbs reached the line Beggendorf – Uebach. Herbach, however, which they had also attacked, remained in German hands, and there was no end to the fighting in sight after these three days of attack. After that: the 30th U.S. ID broke through the West Wall north of Aachen. Now all they had to do was capture the three key German positions at Alsdorf, Maesweiler and Waurichen, then the way to Aachen would lay open to this division. Or if the 30th ID advancing from the north joined up with the 1st ID attacking from the south, then the battle of Aachen would also be at an end, because the German imperial city would be completely cut off from supply.

A new large-scale attack was planned for 8/10. This time it was to be conducted by the 1st U.S. ID from the south and southwest. Would Aachen then fall? Of all cities this was a symbol for Germany. Would the first fortress on German territory be lost?

The Visit to the Fuehrer Bunker

On 4/10/1944 the command of the LXXXI Army Corps held a meeting with the commander of the 7th Army, General Brandenberger, to discuss the so-called blocking ammunition allocations, the amount of ammunition of all types needed to defend an encircled fortress or to declare a city a fortress. The General- quatiermeister of Army Group B refused to make special arrangements in the blocking ammunition allocation for Aachen. He would not accept the fact that within a few days Aachen would be completely encircled. Then all that would be available would be air supply and there were already dozens of examples showing the poor chances of success of such operations.

Oberstleutnant Max Layherr, commander of the 689th Grenadier Regiment of the 246th ID, who as Aachen City Commandant had taken responsibility for the defence of the city, while the division itself, under Oberst Gerhard Wilck, was responsible for the defense of the entire frontal salient, received his ammunition for the defense of the city on Thursday, 5/10. This was only the exact blocking allocation. Accordingly, the 5000 soldiers fighting in the city received a total of 45,000 rounds of pistol ammunition, 105,000 rifle shells, approximately 1000 steel hand-grenades, 1600 egg hand-grenades, 300 panzerfaeuste, 272 anti-tank rounds, 1800 8 cm mortar rounds and 300 infantry shells.

That was all. If things got rough this supply would be exhausted within 48 hours. On 6 and 7/10 approximately the same amount of ammunition would come into the city.

The day before, on 5/10/1944, Reichspropagandaminister Dr. Goebbels visited the Fuehrer Bunker in Muenstereifel in the company of actress Marianne Hoppe.

The minister, who originally came from Rheydt, gave the men on the staff a fiery speech and explained that besides the V 1, which had already been flying against the enemy since September, the V 2 would also soon be ready for commitment. They would destroy the enemy.

When Dr. Goebbels and his entourage disappeared, the men breathed a sigh of relief. Instead of speeches, the great speaker Goebbels should have brought them new troops. They had heard speeches like this often enough from Goebbels. They influenced no one and did not stop one American tank.

New Attack

On the early morning of 8/10 the Americans initiated the next major attack with a hefty barrage fire. At 0745 hours the U.S. tanks rolled in the Merkstein area and broke through the weak German front. For 90 minutes the battle see-sawed, then the German defenders withdrew, and the pursuers rolled on, mounted on tanks, toward Alsdorf.

By midday 46 tanks reached the northern edge of Alsdorf. The Aachen – Erkelenz – Moenchengladbach Reichsstrasse 57, which passes by here, was, therefore, severed and blocked. By evening these tanks, in spite of considerable losses, were able to rip a 2000 meter wide gap in the German front on the southeastern edge of Alsdorf. Therefore, from this hour on, Aachen could only be reached over one road, Reichsstrasse 1, which ran from Duesseldorf via Juelich and Haaren to Aachen.

U.S. fighter-bombers continued to appear in the skies over the front, flying low over the German positions and dropping their 50 kilogram rocket bombs.

Lieutenant General Corlett, commander of the XIX Corps here, reported to the army:

"We have torn an enormous gap in the front. The army can funnel two divisions through here."

Now the 30th U.S. ID was to secure the captured area. The 1st U.S. ID under Major General Huebner was to be committed immediately from the south. However, this division was already holding an 18 kilometer sector in a half-circle south and southeast of Aachen. Nevertheless, Huebner was ready to conduct an attack out of the south through Eilendorf in the direction of Haaren. If he reached this objective, then his division would stand directly east of Aachen in the rear of the city. If his division succeeded in advancing to make contact with the lead formations of the 30th ID, which had transitioned to the defense in front of Wuerselen, then Aachen would be completely cut off from the east.

The attack was to start on Sunday, 8/10. Besides the 1st U.S. ID the 3rd U.S. AD under Major General Rose was also to be committed, they were at full combat strength after receiving armored reinforcements.

Rose's tanks rolled on the morning of the attack toward Verlautenheide, between Eilendorf and Haaren, after the artillery preparation had shifted into the rear. At midday this eastern attack wedge turned to the west and rolled against "Crucifix Hill", Hill 239, which in folklore was called Kaninberg and on whose peak stood an 11 meter crucifix.

From the West Wall bunkers the attackers were met by heavy German defensive fire. After three of the bunkers were destroyed, the defence collapsed at this location. These were soldiers of the 246th ID, who were being attacked on a 20 kilometer wide sector and who could not stand up to the enemy's superiority. The three exhausted grenadier regiments and the subordinate units of this division – such as the 19th Luftwaffen-Jagdkommando, the 34th Fortification Machine-gun Battalion and the 246th Fuesilier Battalion – were being fired on by artillery from all sides and continuously covered by swarms of fighter-bombers dropping rocket bombs and firing their on-board weapons.

The following night saw the soldiers of the 1st U.S. ID in a night attack on the Ravelsberg near Haaren. This was the first effective night attack conducted by this division. On the hill itself were only 65 German soldiers. The defenders of this hill were overwhelmed.

On the following morning, 10/10/1944, Haaren was also captured by the Americans in an assault. Therefore, the 1st U.S. ID had achieved its objective.

Things went otherwise with the 30th U.S. ID, which had resumed its attack in the north. They were stopped by the 49th ID under Generalleutnant Macholz. 15 enemy tanks, which had penetrated toward Wuerselen during the fighting, were destroyed, mainly by panzerfaeusten and mines. Here the two enemies stood opposite each other at the range of a hand-grenade throw. When SS Battle Group Bucher finally was able to be inserted into the enemy's flank between Wuerselen and Bardenberg, the 30th U.S. ID stalled.

In the morning on this 10/10 Major General Huebner demanded that the defenders of Aachen surrender in pamphlets that he had dropped over the city. Oberstleutnant Leyherr turned down this demand, even though Party members were, at this time, begging that the fighting be brought to an end. By midday on 10/10 the enemy had approached to within 3000 meters of the city.

The Germans in the Defense

On the morning of 9/10/1944 the commander of Army Group B, GFM Model, reported the following to OB West, GFM von Rundstedt:

"The situation near Aachen is becoming more critical. If no rein-forcements are deployed, further withdrawal will be unavoidable."

This report led to hectic troop displacements. On the same day the 7th Army received instruction to set the 3rd Panzer- grenadier Division [PGD] under Generalmajor Denkert in march to Aachen. This division, together with battle groups of the 116th PD, which were again thrown into the battle for Aachen, was to attack through the positions of the 12th Volksgrenadier Division to widen the passage to Aachen. However, the passage was still not very wide. At first only the 1st Motorized Assault Engineer Regiment and Battalion Rink from the SS PGD "Leibstandarte Adolf Hitler", com-manded by Obersturmfuehrer Rink, arrived.

In spite of his turning down the surrender demand, Oberstleutnant Leyherr, the son-in-law of Generaloberst Halder, who was arrested after the assassination attempt on Hitler, was relieved on the evening of 12/10/1944. On the morning of 15/10 Oberst Wilck, the commander of the 246th ID, took over as combat commandant of Aachen. His division was to de-fend the city directly. Oberst Wilck set up his command post in the high bunker on the Foerster Ritscher Strasse and issued a fortress order:

"We soldiers have the duty of defending German territory and we will fulfil this duty as have thousands of our comrades, our fathers, brothers and sons, who have already given their lives...

Aacheners!

In this hour verify your glorious history! God will not abandon us in this holy struggle for our homeland and our German culture. He will help us, if we remain steadfast."

In the ruins of Aachen there were still 1500 combat capable men. The majority of the 246th ID, which was outside of the pocket on the defensive points, were taken over by Oberst Koerte. Oberst Peter Koerte was an experienced officer, who had received the Knight's Cross as commander of the 26th Fuesilier Regiment on 27/9/1943.

On Wednesday evening, 11/10/1944, when the ultimatum for surrender expired, bombers from the 16th U.S. Combat Bomber Squadron appeared. They flew very deep and were able to recognize all of their targets, because the U.S. artillery had marked these targets with colored shells, so that the targets appeared in a red light.

First the bombs fell in the western quarter of Aachen, then the freight railroad station was raided, then followed the technical high school and the eastern quarter with its churches.

The groups of Lightnings and Mustangs were able to make the most use of their bombing time and flew over their objectives for as long as possible, since there were no German fighters in sight and the few air defense guns were committed to the ground battle against tanks.

In all only 63 tons of bombs were dropped, however, each of the high explosive bombs hit their target.

Simultaneous with the bombing, twelve U.S. artillery formations fired on the city, in particular the downtown area. A total of 5000 shells were lobed into the city. That was a total of 169 tons of steel. The sky over the city darkened and, at 1700 hours, a second wave of bombers flew over this target and bombed the northwest and northeast of Aachen, where they had noted German resistance.

At 2000 hours the American loudspeakers began to blare on the edge of the city. They presented a new ultimatum. It ran:

"Either the city is surrendered tomorrow morning, or a new bombing attack will occur between 1000 hours and 1700 hours."

No reply was given. The Americans made good on their promise. At 1000 hours bomber formations took off and dropped their bombs on new targets. While this was going on, the U.S. formations tried to close the gaps that were still open near Wuerselen. The 1st and the 30th U.S. Infantry Divisions slowly moved toward one another. On 14/10 the 30th U.S. ID reported the loss of 2000 fighting troops, that was a third of the total combat strength of this division.

In the meantime, the German SS Battle Group Rink, which had arrived on 10/10 and destroyed ten of the 15 Sherman tanks that had penetrated toward Wuerselen and, thereby, recaptured a portion of the town, advanced again. They destroyed two more Shermans with panzerfaeusten and penetrated into Aachen. Nevertheless, this battle group, which had set out with 311 soldiers and five officers, had lost 139 soldiers and all five officers.

This SS battle group and a second, which was led by Obersturmfuehrer Bucher, gave no quarter after they had seen the city that had lay in the hail of bombs from the American combat bombers.

A participant and eyewitness reported:

"It was a frightful, horrible sight, and we were beside ourselves. Because dead children and dismembered women lay everywhere." (See Whiting, Charles and Trees, Wolfgang: *The Amis [Americans] are Here!*)

On the early morning of 12/10 these two battle groups had the opportunity of seeing the Americans up close near Birk. Out of a thick fog stormed Obersturmfuehrer Rink and his men into the front-lines of the 30th U.S. ID. Supported by several assault guns and tanks, which fired on the enemy tanks, machine-gun nests and mortar groups, they were able to exhaust the Americans in a three-hour battle. After additional Sherman companies showed up, the tide turned. Five German tanks and three assault guns were shot up. Nevertheless, the panzergrenadiers continued to advance for the time being.

Only by committing all reserves could the U.S. leadership stop this attack wedge. Major General Hobbs reported that the enemy was heavily pressuring his lines at all corners, however, the feared major German attack did not materialize.

On 13/10 when a U.S. battle group, in the strength of 300 men supported by five Shermans, attacked through from the Aachen cemetery up to the Quellenhof in the vicinity of the combat commandant's command post, SS Battalion Rink was summoned. This combat group was supplied with several additional assault guns and tanks. In the Quellenhof itself defended clerks and communicators, fourieres and cooks. They defended the command post and repulsed the U.S. raid.

Nevertheless, the U.S. troops continued to approach closer and closer to Aachen and they penetrated into several suburbs. They formed their own combat lines in the streets of the city and tried to continue the advance from these locations. During the night before 14/10 the Germans were able to bring fuel and ammunition into the city. The unloaded wagons were fully loaded with wounded and returned through the narrow gap on the following night, Sunday, 15/10/1944. They made it through the passage and reached the main first aid stations and hospitals in the east.

A series of small formations, which were, however, combat capable and combat experienced, continued to help at the various crisis points during the battle for Aachen.

One of these was the 506th Heavy Panzer Battalion under Major Lange. From 20/8 to 12/9/1944 this battalion was assigned 45 new King Tigers – the heaviest tank in the Wehrmacht. The training of the crews was conducted to take into consideration the combat situation on the Western Front, concentrating on protecting the tanks from air attack.

From 22 to 24/9 this battalion was up-loaded and transported by rail through Cologne and Wesel to Holland. There it was subordinated to the 1st Fallschirmjaeger Army and committed against the enemy's air landings in the greater Arnheim area, while also providing defense against the enemy's rolling armored formations.

Within a few days the King Tigers of the 506th Heavy Panzer Battalion, which had stopped the advance of the enemy from out of the south, who were hurrying to the aid of the air landed troops, destroyed the encircled paratroop and airborne formations. At this time, all of the officers in the 1st Company fell.

At the beginning of October the King Tigers went to rest in Apeldoorn and Zutphen, and then to Bocholt, in order to replace the losses suffered and repair damages. However, soon after this combat capable formation was thrown into a new commitment in the defensive battle for Aachen.

Between Geilenkirchen and Eschweiler the King Tigers stood during the 2nd Battle of Aachen in bitter defensive combat. They shot-up a number of enemy tanks and proved that they were far superior to all enemy tanks. Nevertheless, they were not in a position to change the fate of Aachen and prevent Aachen from falling on 21/10/1944.

After that this battalion, whose commitment served as an example for all other small formations, was committed several kilometers west of the Roer in the Gereosweiler – Freialdenhoven defensive front and, during the 3rd Battle of Aachen, stood on a critical point of the defense and was able to participate decisively in the fighting. However, back to Aachen.

On Saturday, 14/10/1944, the commanders of the Allied forces gathered together in the small Ensival castle near Verviers, just 40 kilometers west of Aachen, in order to celebrate the victory in the battle near Aachen. Among those gathered was King George VI of England. The inhabitants of the castle, the industrial family of Zurstraaten, were not at home, therefore, General Hodges, the commander of the 1st U.S. Army and, therefore, the master of the house, saw to his guests.

King George VI arrived in the accompaniment of his personal staff and with U.S. General Hart. Under the cover-name of "Master" Eisenhower also arrived at Ensival. Generals Bradley and Patton followed Eisenhower.

There were many speeches and toasts: to the victory in Aachen in general and the victory over Germany in particular. Many war-stories were enumerated. Thus General Patton told King George of England that during his commitment in Tunisia he had to "personally shoot a dozen Tunisian pick-pockets."

King George VI appeared shocked, therefore, Eisenhower intervened in the conversation and after intensively pressing Patton, he [Patton] softened his reply:

"Well, perhaps it was not so many; perhaps I did not shoot any Tunisians, however, near Gafsa I kicked at least two of the thieves in the ass."

The victory celebration was splendid. However, they would have to wait longer for the victory over Aachen.

The Last Phase of the Battle of Aachen

In the meantime, on the evening of 14/10/1944, SS Battle Group Rink had fought its way through the U.S. lines and the encirclement ring of the Americans, up to the Quellenhof. These soldiers presented themselves to the city commandant with assault guns and tanks. They had fought their way forward slowly. The enemy moved aside as soon as the assault howitzers and assault guns, which Rink had available, blasted away.

Several U.S. tanks, which had moved forward and opened fire, were sacrificed to the assault guns.

By 2000 hours the men of this battle group had already reached Monheim Allee. From here they moved gradually, but continuously. In a small wedge the assault guns rolled through the side streets and shot up the enemy's nests of resistance.

In this manner they reached the Quellenhof and formed a welcome reinforcement with their assault guns for the defenders of the command post.

On 15/10, while U.S. troops continued to try to penetrate deeper into Aachen and the lead groups of the 30th and 1st U.S. Infantry Divisions, advancing from the north and the south, had approached to within eyesight of each other on the afternoon of this day, the gap was reduced to only 1000 meters. In the meantime, however, the large bunker was still on Ravelsberg. This bunker was defended by Leutnant Zillies. He and his men of the 10th Company of the 8th Motorized Grenadier Regiment were in Bunker 170 and entrenched around it in a circular defense. Bunker 167 and Bunker 168 were being defended by the neighboring companies of this regiment. Bunker 165, an observation position, was captured by the Americans no less than sixteen times between 14 and 19/10; as many times as they were removed by a German counterattack. Other bunkers also changed occupiers several times. Only Bunker 170 held like iron. Leutnant Zillies was awarded the Knight's Cross on 11/12/1944 for this defensive effort. No enemy entered his bunker. His system of trip wires and remotely detonated mines and other explosives, machine-gun trenches and tank destroyer troops was insurmountable. Expended mines and other explosives were replaced by the engineers during the night.

On Monday, 16/10/1944, at 1615 hours the troops of the two above mentioned U.S. divisions met after overcoming the last resistance on the Ravelsberg. Therefore, in spite of the few bunkers still holding out, Aachen was hermetically sealed from the outside world.

On 16/10 the Germans began their attack from the east to break into the fortress. It was led by SS Gruppenfuehrer Priess with the divisions of the I SS Panzer Corps. The corps committed the 1st SS Panzer Division "Adolf Hitler", which was divided into two battle groups.

The attack of Battle Group Diefenthal under Hauptsturmfuehrer Diefenthal with elements of the 2nd SS Panzergrenadier Regiment "Leibstandarte Adolf Hitler" was successful. Unfortunately, the attack by Battle Group Wegelein was unsuccessful, because in the middle of the effort they were diverted to another commitment. This formation veered off and rolled from the battlefield in the direction of Huertgenwald, where a heavy enemy penetration was noted.

Therefore, the counterattack stalled. It could not get through and, on the morning of 19/10, it had to be suspended.

In the meantime, U.S. troops were penetrating into the city from three sides. Assault troops were advancing into the center of the city. The last defenders were holding out only in a narrow area between Lousberg – Ponttor – the west railroad station and the Guten Hirten Monastery.

On 20/10 Oberst Wilck transmitted the last radio combat message, in which he reported to LXXXI Army Corps that the last defenders of Aachen, compressed into a narrow area, were engaged in the final battle. The Americans had introduced a new weapon into the city, the accurate 15.5 cm "Long Tom" gun, which was able to direct point fire at individual nests of resistance.

A day earlier Oberst Wilck had already informed the 7th Army over radio that the breakout of the last forces was only possible through Soers and that if this was to take place, a decision had to be made immediately. Such a breakout order was not forthcoming, Hitler had decided weeks ago that:

"Aachen will be held to the bitter end. It is the first fortress on German territory and it will not give up!"

The U.S. soldiers under Colonel Corley, who were to attack through to Lousberg after the "Long Toms" suppressed the last resistance, ran into the men from Battle Group Rink, who had been reinforced. They [BG Rink] were attacking into Farwickpark, supported by the last operational assault guns, and suppressed the enemy forces advancing here. An assault gun put an American machine-gun position out of commission with a well placed shot. Then two assault guns, which had been repaired in the meantime, rolled forward and fell under fire. They conducted direct fire with high explosive shells.

The Americans left the field at this position. They fled. THe men of Battle Group Rink pursued in their camouflage jackets. The assault guns advanced on the flanks. After a short halt they had the next U.S. unit in front of them and they also threw them back.

After that, strong artillery fire erupted and within a minute it increased to a raging inferno that beat Battle Group Rink down and forced them to the ground. Nevertheless, as confirmed by the words of Eisenhower, these troops had:

"The highest morale! They were animated with courage during the attack was well as in the defense."

On Friday morning, 10/10, a radio message from LXXXI Army Corps arrived at Oberst Wilck's command:

"The LXXXI Army Corps pays highest respect to the last brave defenders of Aachen fighting for Fuehrer and people. Koechling, General der Infanterie."

On the following day the final word came out of the city. The German radio stations outside of the pocket intercepted the last radio message from the fortress:

"We defenders of the German imperial city are engaged in the final battle around the command post."

Eight minutes after that followed a last sentence:

"Aachen signing off!"

The last defenders on the Lousberg were shot out of their trenches by Sherman tanks.

Oberst Wilck now had to surrender. He informed the enemy directly in front of his command post and went to the command post of Colonel Corley with a U.S. officer. The Colonel insured Wilck that all Germans were covered by the Geneva Convention.

In a U.S. Jeep, accompanied by Major Heimann, a German-American, and two GI's, Oberst Wilck was later transported to Hergenrath into the Henri-Chapelle Prisoner of War Camp.

It was exactly 1200 hours on 21/10/1944. The battle for Aachen was over, and in the city the weapons grew silent.

In Soers, however, Obersturmfuehrer Rink's men stood in their rifle trenches and waited for the night. When it became dark they got up and fought their way in small groups through the U.S. lines to their own troops. In the early morning hours of 22/10/1944 they reached the forward-most German positions. A total of four officers and 15 soldiers from the battle group had survived Aachen.

Aachen was the first German fortress to die. The holding of this city for such a long time prevented a rapid Allied breakthrough to the east and allowed Hitler to prepare for the Ardennes offensive.

The Western Allies had placed great hopes on the rapid fall of Aachen. Now they knew that there would be "three to four Aachens", the war would have to last at least a year.

Aachen, like the disaster near Arnheim, had considerably delayed the Anglo-American advance into Germany. This was one of the reasons why the Russians were able to advance to Berlin and even reach the Elbe.

On 22/9/1944, in spite of the heavy fighting around Aachen, the Allied Supreme Command in Versailles was already establishing the instructions for a continuation of the attack to the east. Eisenhower and Montgomery were in agreement that the German troops in the Niederrhein area had to be encircled and defeated in a large-scale pincer movement. After one of the German army groups was eliminated, then the resistance in western Germany would collapse.

This Operation "Gatwick", with the advance of British troops out of the Kleve area to the southeast and the U.S. troops out of the Aachen area in the direction of Duesseldorf, was planned for 8 October. However, the fighting around Aachen did not end until 21/10.

Nevertheless, in spite of the Aachen mishap, Field Marshal Montgomery ordered the start of the preparatory attack by the RAF on 7/10/1944.

On 8/10/1944 a total of 3000 Allied aircraft were in the air and flying over Reich territory. 681 of them attacked cities on the Niederrhein. Alone the 8th USAAF dropped 1270 tons of bombs on assigned targets on this day.

335 RAF bombers participated in the attack on the Niederrhein cities on 7/10, dropping 1738 tons of bombs on the small city of Kleve. On the same day, 665 tons of bombs fell on Emmerich.

While there was still fighting going on around Aachen, the troops of the VII U.S. Corps, which had bypassed Aachen, approached a second point of resistance on the German Western Front: the Huertgenwald.

2

ON THE WAY TO THE RHEIN

The Hell in the Huertgenwald

The bitter fighting around Aachen, which hindered the planned advance of the Allies, and the bitter defeat of the British – American airborne operation near Arnheim pushed the planned Operation "Gatwick" to the back burner. Nevertheless, Field Marshal Montgomery still ordered the planned air attack be executed on 7 October.

The cities on the left bank of the Rhein were forced to evacuate in mid-September. The entire region was designated as a fortress by Hitler. Not one meter of ground was to be voluntarily given up. Thus the I Cavalry Corps under General Feldt was ordered on 18 September 1944:

> "The fighting in the west has transitioned onto the German homeland. Therefore, the combat leadership has to be extremely fanatical. Each city, each town and each bunker is to be defended like a fortress to the last drop of blood."

Therefore, for the first time in memory an entire region was declared a fortress. This would be repeated several times in the west. On the Rhein as well as in the Ruhr pocket.

What the thinking was and how the defense was to be conducted was demonstrated in Aachen.

Already at this time, because of the bitter struggle around Aachen, other regions and cities were being threatened by U.S. attack. The XIX Corps under Lieutenant General Corlett, which was also participating in the fighting around Aachen, had committed its 29th ID northwest of Geilenkirchen, while the 30th ID and the 2nd AD were tied up by the fighting around Aachen.

The VII U.S. Corps, which had already bypassed the imperial city during the 1st Battle of Aachen, stormed into the Huertgenwald, an extensive forested region between Monschau in the southeast and Dueren in the northwest. This corps now had to bear the brunt of the developing combat around the Huertgenwald.

In a bitter ten-day battle the divisions of this corps were able to advance a total of 2700 meters. This ground gain cost them 4500 men. The attack had to be suspended, because the corps had become partially combat incapable.

The defenders looked upon the Huertgenwald somewhat like a green fortress with entrenched machine-gun stands and anti-tank nests, which could not be seen until they opened fire.

This series of blocks was not easily transited as one had first believed. It denied the U.S. troops access to the Rhein, which they desired to reach between Cologne and Bonn.

The 9th AD, which had stood at the head of the attack, was no longer combat effective after these ten days of fighting. Completely exhausted and demoralized it had to be disbanded. They had only reached Roettgen.

Taking their place was now the 28th U.S. ID under Major General Cota. They were tasked with rejuvenating the stalled attack.

• • •

On 18/10/1944 the commanders Eisenhower and Bradley met with Montgomery in Brussels. The objective of this meeting was to discuss strategic plans that had caught their attention after the breakout from the greater Falaise area and the breakthrough into the open in France.

As a result of this meeting they decided to make the decisive effort to reach the Rhein before the onset of winter and establish a strong bridgehead on the eastern bank of the river, which could be constantly expanded, so that after all of their strength was assembled, they could launch the decisive major offensive into Germany from this bridgehead. The plan they worked out read:

"The attack to the Rhein will be conducted by the 1st and 9th U.S. Armies through Aachen, which must soon fall. The troops of the 1st U.S. Army located behind the Roer will cross the river and advance to the east toward Cologne and Bonn. The 9th Army will move to the northeast. Their objective is Krefeld."

These operations were to be supported by the 2nd British Army. They were ordered to attack the Reichswald out of the northern sector near Nijmegen on 10/11 and advance to the south between the Maas and the Rhein.

Through the offensive the Rhein was to be reached between Arnheim and Bonn on a front 160 kilometers wide.

After the conclusion of this first phase of the Western Allied offensive the 9th Army was to attack to the east, south of Cologne, and the 1st Army to the east, north of Duesseldorf, advance through the northern and southern Ruhr region and meet in the Lippstadt – Paderborn area in a large-scale pincer operation and then reinforce the sack around Army Group B, which would still be located back in the Ruhr region. If this army group was either destroyed or captured, then the defeat of Germany would be sealed. The Western Allies would also secure the end of the war by capturing the Reich's weapons factory.

On 18/10/1944 an exact date for the start of the attack by General Patton's 3rd U.S. Army was still not established. This army was to resume its attack as soon as the supply situation, which was strongly strained during the Arnheim operation, was restored. Nevertheless, its attack would only have a supporting nature. It was to be proportioned "to best serve the main operation in the north." (See Eisenhower, Dwight D.: *Crusade in Europe*.)

Nevertheless, the plucky Patton did not agree with this casting of the parts, and he would forget these instructions when it suited him.

Above all, what was discussed in Brussels: was the supporting attacks of the Allied bomber formations, which in a month, from mid-October to mid-November 1944, would be flown in western Germany to make the upcoming battlefield ripe for the picking.

The American Air Force in mid-October had 4700 fighter aircraft, 6000 light and heavy bombers and approximately 4000 reconnaissance, courier and transport aircraft of all types available.

The Bombers Are Coming!

To fulfil this mission, the formations of the RAF and the USAAF doubled the number of bombers committed between 15 October and 15 November against the German cities in the west, these were the strongest sorties of the entire war up to this point.

The new date for the start of the Western Allied attack was set at 16/11. By then, the Supreme Command believed that the air bombardment would have done its job.

During the night of 15/10 Duisburg had to be bombarded by 1005 Lancaster-Halifax and Mosquito aircraft, which flew out of the 1st, 3rd, 4th and 6th Bomber Groups. 711 tons of bombs fell on Mainz on 19/10. This time it was a daytime attack by the 8th USAAF. The same large formation also attacked Muenster and Hamm on 22/10. 864 and 970 tons of bombs fell on these cities respectively, these included thousands of incendiary and phosphorus bombs.

Essen was the attack target of 955 bombers of the RAF on the late evening of 23/10, they dropped 4522 tons of bombs, one of the largest numbers of bombs ever dropped. Not only military targets were hit, throughout many civilian houses were destroyed. This was done on purpose, as confirmed by Air Marshal Harris after the war, when he noted that these terror attacks were designed to convince the civilian population to end the war.

During the night of 25/10 – the work of clearing the debris was not yet completed in Essen, there were still fires glimmering among the ruins – this city was again attacked. This time "only" 3719 tons of bombs were dropped. Again the civilian population was targeted.

Homberg was covered with 967 tons of bombs on this night. During the night before 29/10 Cologne was attacked. The Cathedral City was covered with 2699 tons of bombs, which caused enormous fires.

During the night before 30/10 2746 tons of bombs rained down upon Walcheren Island and the coastal batteries located there, and during the following night Cologne was again the target of a major attack; the committed bombers dropped 3937 tons of bombs. And while the people of Cologne were roving about their destroyed city, the terror squadrons attacked their city again. Another 2383 tons of bombs rained down upon the city on the Rhein, laying thousands of residential houses in ruins or severely damaging them. Over 1000 civilians were killed. The number of injured was significantly higher. Indiscriminately were the elderly, women and children sacrificed to these terror attacks. During the following 14 days Oberhausen was hit with 1191 tons of bombs on the night of 1/11, Duesseldorf on the night before 3/11 with 4468 tons and Solingen on 4 and 5/11 with 946 and 888 tons of bombs. Thousands and thousands of people died, burned in their houses by the ignited phosphorus, buried under the ruins, or drowned in their cellars by the water hoses.

Bochum was next during the night before 5/11. 2323 tons of bombs fell on this Ruhr city, while during the same night a formation dove on the Dortmund – Ems Canal near Ladbergen with 932 tons of bombs, in order to paralyze the shipping on this important waterway.

Gelsenkirchen suffered a destructive fire-storm on 6/11, when 2634 tons of bombs fell on it, including thousands of phosphorus-incendiary bombs. Wanne-Eickel was declared a bombing target on 9/11. Here "only" 1315 tons of bombs fell.

During the night before 12/11 1122 tons of bombs rained down upon Dortmund. During the same hour a formation from the RAF dropped 913 tons of bombs on Hamburg-Harburg.

Dortmund suffered its next attack on 15/11. This time only 904 tons of bombs fell on the city, which would suffer a series of further attacks in the future, laying waste a third of the city and a portion of its industrial installations in ruins and sacrificing thousands of lives.

The Allies would never know that they accomplished the exact opposite to what they had strived for.

The 3rd Battle of Aachen

What was later called the "Forest Battle in the Huertgen National Forest" and which the Americans called "Huertgen Forest – Valley of the Crosses", began on 19 September, as the fighting around Aachen reached its decisive phase.

The 9th U.S. ID attacked to the east out of the Lammersdorf – Zweifall area, in order to cover the right southern flank of the VII U.S. Corps on a wide front and ultimately turn to the southeast.

The 4th Cavalry Group attacked in the Kalterherberg – Hoefen area. The 9th U.S. ID attacked in three assault groups. From Lammersdorf rolled a formation, with the 3-39 IR [Infantry Regiment] as its core, to the south toward Paustenbach and Hill 554, as Paustenbach Hill was known. This dominant hill had to be captured before the attack through the West Wall was conducted. The second attack wedge of this battalion was directed from Lammersdorf to the east in the direction of Kall-Talsperre and Kallbrueck.

The second assault group, consisting of the 1-39 IR and led by regiment commander Colonel Thompson, was to attack in conjunction with the 1-60 IR under Colonel Chatfield from the same assembly area out of the Zweifall area in the direction of Staatsforst Huertgen. The 1-39 IR had the final objective of Huertgen, the 1-60 IR the Todtenbruch, up to the road running from Lammersdorf to the south, which was to be severed.

The attack to Paustenbach Hill, with the German bunkers on its slope occupied by men from the 1055th IR of the 89th ID, was costly. The two bunkers on the top of the hill held out for a long time. One of the bunkers on the southern slope was defended by 38 men for twelve hours against several American combat troops, who had to use over 400 kilograms of TNT before they could crack the bunker.

The attack of the 39th IR was supported by the 15th Engineer Battalion. In the first phase of the commitment in and around the Huertgenwald the attackers had already suffered heavy casualties. Their companies, which were approximately 180 men strong, lost 100 to 120 men killed and wounded.

A main effort of the attack was on Hill 554 with the far-seeing "Eifelkreuz", the Paustenbach Hill. Here the Americans attacked six times in succession against the troops of the German 89th ID. The Paustenbach Hill did not fall until 29/9/1944 after an artillery fire-strike with smoke. Now the victors could view the villages of Rollesbroich and Simmerath, which beneath them.

The attack against the Kall-Talsperre was initiated at the beginning of October 1944, after a German counterattack on the night of 1/10 recaptured this point.

The attack of elements of the 39th IR and the 60th IR from Zweifall reached the Todtenbruch objective on the evening of the second day of the attack, because the bunkers in Gieschbachtal were unoccupied. First Bunkers 342 and 343 on the edge had to be destroyed.

When the 1-39 IR had to be withdrawn, in order to support the U.S. 47th IR near Schevenhuette, where the German 12th Volksgrenadier Division had attacked, further advance ceased. The German companies from the 942nd Grenadier Regiment under the command of Oberst Troester had, in the meantime, entrenched and repulsed every attack. They received help from assault guns from the 341st and 902nd Brigades. Nevertheless, a breakthrough would have been achieved here, had the German leadership not deployed two regiments of the 347th ID to support the defending 353rd ID here. These were the 860th and 861st Infantry Regiments.

The Huertgenwald would be the only green fortress designated by the senior German leadership at which the strength of the enemy would crash and be dashed to pieces.

At the same time, the American 1-60 IR was fighting in Todtenbruch. This battle group had more hard luck than the others, each bunker it was assigned to take was occupied. Here all of the company commanders and lieutenants were wounded or killed.

The Germans fought here under the leadership of Oberst Feind, they were the 253rd Reserve IR and units from the XX Luftwaffen Fortification Battalion. Here the attackers experienced the first level of Hell in the Huertgenwald, with an exchange of hand-grenades and hand-to-hand combat in the forest.

There was bitter fighting around Bunkers 363, 364 and 365. When the Americans were able to overcome one of these bunkers in a night attack, the Germans would reoccupy it during the following night. 49 Americans and four officers were captured, escaping the hell of the Huertgenwald. When new attacks were ordered here, the units refused to follow orders. (See: MacDonald, Charles B: *The Battle of the Huertgen Forest*, Philadelphia/New York 1946.)

The Germans established mortars and assault guns in hidden ambush positions. When they opened fire, the enemy stood directly in their sights and were disposed of.

That these efforts also took a toll on the German defenders was shown by the desertion of several "old men" from the XX Luftwaffen Fortification Battalion.

When the attack was suspended on 29 September 1944, the assigned objective was not achieved at any location. This was, as Charles MacDonald moaned, "the gloom and misery of the 9th U.S. Division."

In these days of defeat the concept of the "Huertgen Forest" appeared to the Americans for the first time. From this time on the entire area between Schevenhuette and Simmerath and from Eupen to Nideggen was simply referred to as the "Huertgen Forest."

The fighting here lasted from 19 September to 28 November, almost nine weeks before the U.S. troops achieved their assigned objectives, and all they were fighting here were "a handful of old men." (See MacDonald, Charles B: Op. cit.)

And so it continued:

Under the leadership of General der Panzertruppe von Manteuffel the divisions of the 5th Panzer Army stood against the penetrating U.S. formations in the Huertgenwald. Hasso von Manteuffel, one of the best known panzer leaders, after being directly involved in the fighting around Aachen, only had exhausted formations from the LXXXI Army Corps, the LXXXVI Army Corps, the XXXXVII Panzer Corps, the XII Waffen SS Corps and Korpstruppen Feldt available.

They were supposed to hold the Allied armored avalanche and destroy them. However, before the U.S. troops launched their planned offensive, Eisenhower again regrouped the formations at the end of October.

Now the 1st and 9th U.S. Armies were selected to breakthrough the German front in the Huertgenwald. And, indeed, the VII U.S. Corps (from the 1st U.S. Army) was to advance out of the Schmidt area in the direction of Dueren, cross the Rur there and march directly on Bonn.

The 9th Army received the instructions to advance the XXX Corps through Geilenkirchen, north of Aachen, cross the Rur and advance up to Juelich. From there they were to penetrate into the Niederrhein area and open the way to the Rhein.

On the morning of 2/11/1944 at 0900 hours the VII U.S. Corps attacked to the east in the direction of Vossenack. They advanced slowly here. This village was captured in the afternoon after house to house fighting.

The attack directed on the village of Schmidt stalled in the defensive fire of the German artillery. It was resumed on the morning of the following day. They reached Kammerscheidt and captured it, again after house to house fighting. During the further advance, supported by strong armor, the American assault formations broke into the village of Schmidt. Here again the numerical superiority of the U.S. forces proved to be an advantage in the urban fighting.

At this point of the German defensive front the 341st Assault Gun Brigade was committed. Under the leadership of Hauptmann Barkley, this brigade was refitted after the retreat from France in the greater area of Aachen. Hauptmann Barkley now led this strong combat formation, whose 1st Company under its commander Oberleutnant Hermann Wolz had already achieved great defensive success in the fighting around Aachen. These assault guns now rolled to the front out of the Kaster area near Bedburg. Hauptmann Barkley experienced a dramatic battle with this formation in the vicinity of the Huertgenwald, which had now reached its decisive phase.

The U.S. attack again bogged down after initial success and General Bradley, the commander of the 12th Army Group, ordered another regrouping. With his directive to the troops he ordered the 1st U.S. Army to attack and occupy the two valley blocks of Urftsee and Schwammenauel and breakthrough further to the Rhein.

The attack was given the code-name "Queen."

On the early morning of 16/11/1944 the RAF launched 1888 heavy and 107 medium bombers from all airfields in the vicinity of the front in France and Belgium and even from the southern coast of England, while the USAAF launched 1204 bombers and 485 fighter-bombers.

The RAF attacked the known German positions and dropped the gigantic total of 9700 tons of bombs in the Rur Valley and on the German positions behind it. The cities of Juelich, Dueren and Reinsberg, which were central to the German defense, were laid in ruins. No less than 1200 bombers dropped their loads over Juelich and laid the already heavily damaged city in complete ruin.

And still before the attack of the armored and infantry formations, the American army artillery opened a barrage fire. 45,000 shells were launched from a total of 694 guns against the German positions. Then the eight divisions set out to attack the Huertgenwald in the first wave during a pouring rain.

The XXX British Corps, whose artillery had turned the Geilenkirchen area into a moon-scape, advanced against the 15th PGD under General Rodt. An element of the central attack formation of this corps was still located in the 10th SS PD area of operations, who was defending bitterly.

The attack stalled in strong German defensive fire. German assault guns and flak battle groups shot up the advancing tanks. The eighty-eights were able to destroy the first enemy vehicles at a distance of 2000 meters. After 48 bitter hours, the attack of the XXX Army Corps had to be broken off.

On 20/11 the XXX British Corps attacked a second time. The direction of the attack was toward Geilenkirchen. The 43rd ID – followed by the 79th AD – attacked through to Geilenkirchen, which gave the appearance of a dead city.

This British attack was finally suspended on 22/11.

In the Huertgenwald, where the formations of the VII U.S. Corps were attacking, the Germans had the 89th and 275th Infantry Divisions, together with the 116th PD under Oberst von Waldenburg, and they repulsed the U.S. attack. In the meantime, winter had arrived. The U.S. soldiers, accustomed to the summer combat in France and not particularly tested during the "pursuit battle", were streaming to the hospitals with frost-bitten feet, even though they were not seriously injured.

Near Huertgen, Vossenack, near Pier and Hey, as well as in Grosshaus and also in several small hamlets, there was bitter street fighting. There was a struggle to occupy each house and each barn. According to the soldiers of the U.S. Army – this was the "Green hell of the Huertgen."

In the Huertgenwald, the adversaries often lay only a hand-grenade throw apart. They fought with cunning and trickery. Night ambushes and raids alternated with hand-grenade duels and machine-pistol fire.

Near Huertgen and Schmidt the "Windhunde" of the 116th PD again were tested and repulsed every enemy attack and then ironed out enemy penetrations in neighboring formations.

When the 112th U.S. Infantry Regiment attacked Vossenack, which had been recently recaptured by the Germans, they had to make an extraordinary effort to advance several dozen meters. Then, during the coming night, they were again thrown out of the area they had struggled so hard to conquer. The fighting then developed into a free-for-all. The Americans attacked again, within the next week, in exactly seven days, they gained 70 meters of ground, paying for this "gain" with 167 killed, 719 wounded and 663 missing and captured. In addition, they had 544 fall ill, of which the majority suffered from second and third degree frostbite. Therefore, almost the entire regiment was lost.

Things went just as badly on the morning of 16/11/1944, after the artillery fire shifted to the rear the 28th U.S. ID attacked. They constantly ran into German defensive blocks, which were bitterly defended by individual squads and platoons entrenched in their "foxholes", who would allow the attackers to roll over them and then appear suddenly in their rear. This division experienced the hell of the Huertgenwald in its unadulterated form.

The entire forest was shot up and covered by enormous craters, it was turned into one single green fortress, where each bomb crater could signify a machine-gun nest or a hidden anti-tank gun. From these bushes and craters and ruins of houses the Germans retreated only gradually, in order to regain their old positions during the night, appearing like banshees with machine-gun and machine-pistol fire, with hand-grenades and spades in hand-to-hand combat.

On the evening of 19/11 the commander of the 28th U.S. ID had to report to his commanding general that the division was no longer combat effective. Within a few days, they had suffered 6184 losses in men, 31 tanks and 16 anti-tank guns were also lost.

On the German side, the 246th ID lay in the middle of the enemy artillery fire and the later American attack. They had to stop the first enemy assault and, during the period from 16 to 19/11, they were no less exhausted than their American opponents. During these three days they lost 17 officers and 3000 soldiers of all grades. Alone the 404th Grenadier Regiment, which had stood in the center of the defensive combat, lost the main body of its fighters. On the evening of 19/11 they had a total of 100 men left. One non-commissioned officer from this regiment lost eleven of his 18 men within a few seconds during an enemy fire-strike. With his remaining seven soldiers he defended against the attacking U.S. soldiers. Several dozen panzerfaeuste helped this handful of men to resist. When after a week, the retreat began, there was only the non-commissioned officer left. All of his men were left dead on the battlefield.

The U.S. artillery continued to fire out of hundreds of tubes into the forest, the effect was to tear trees apart leaving only the trunks as if the forest were hit by a tornado. Thick branches were knocked down by the shells. They made the impassible forest even more difficult to traverse.

The Huertgenwald had been turned into a dangerous jungle. At any time, day or night, deadly fire could erupt from hundreds of machine-guns and rifles.

In his excellent report "Battlefield Rheinland", Wolfgang Trees recorded the statements of American soldiers about the hell of the Huertgenwald:

"The Germans fired without end. I began to scream; I banged my head against a tree. I heard nothing more and was unconscious for a short time. When I slowly regained consciousness, I saw one of our soldiers a couple of meters away, he was crawling from a destroyed tank, he had lost both arms. I thought I would loose my mind." (See *Trees*, Wolfgang: Op. cit.)

Schleiden, a village southeast of Vossenack and Schmidt, was captured by the Americans on 19/11. However, it lay outside of the German main combat line in the Huertgenwald. The Huertgenwald had become a nightmare for both sides. Whoever fought there was filled with wonder that he had survived this hell.

Besides the 404th Grenadier Regiment of the 246th ID, its sister regiments the 352nd and 689th had also registered heavy losses. They also fought to their own destruction. The Huertgenwald had been turned into a green fortress, the likes of which the Second World War would not see again.

The town of Huertgen was captured by the Americans much earlier. It was immediately taken back by the Germans the following night in a counterattack. This happened no less than fourteen times. The fighting was indescribable.

If the town of Huertgen was experiencing heavy fighting, it was no less so in Vossenack. There the fighting see-sawed several times per day. Individual farmsteads and hamlets, road intersections and trails through the forest were contested as if the outcome of the entire war depended upon it. In spite of the ferocity of the fighting in Huertgen and other towns, Vossenack still was an exception, it had changed hands more than 28 times. There were many instances where German soldiers, who had to leave houses or provisional bunkers, would return after a successful counterattack to find that everything was just as they had left it, because the enemy did not have time to settle in. There were some cases where they had returned to find even their bread and rations untouched.

The 30th U.S. ID, "Roosevelt's Butchers", had recovered from their losses in the fighting northeast of Aachen. They were now also committed and attacked north of the Huertgenwald toward Lohn in front of Juelich, which they captured in assault. Frenz and Lammersdorf and, above all, Inden in the Inde Valley were the next targets of their attacks, which again cost both sides a high price in blood.

A battle group from the 9th German PD was committed in a counterattack against the Americans that had penetrated to Puffendorf. The 506th Heavy Panzer Battalion – equipped with King Tigers – was committed with elements of the 352nd Grenadier Regiment against the enemy occupied village of Merzhausen. They attacked with mounted grenadiers and several groups following in SPW's [armored personnel carriers].

The fire from 30 U.S. tank cannon crashed against the attackers. The Tiger II's rolled along both sides, they abandoned their march formation, in order to obtain a better field of fire. They halted to fire by platoons and shot-up the visible enemy tanks. Their large caliber cannon destroyed the Shermans. Explosions ripped the tanks apart, turrets were torn from their undercarriages and their frontal glacis was penetrated by the hits.

Just as they had destroyed the enemy during Operation Market Garden when they destroyed the encircled Allied paratroopers, they fought here in the Huertgenwald. Their tank commanders were disciplined tank men and the new combat vehicles with their longer cannon had tremendous firepower.

The out-gunned enemy tanks withdrew. Merzhausen was again free, the village was again in German hands.

During this commitment Stabsfeldwebel Kurt Kannenberg, a platoon leader in the 3/sPzAbt 506, was shot and killed on 17/11/1944, after destroying numerous enemy tanks. For this commitment he received the Knight's Cross posthumously on 17/12/1944.

During their period of commitment from September to November 1944, the 3rd Company alone shot-up 222 enemy tanks, 189 anti-tank guns, 24 guns and 32 trucks. All of the other companies achieved similar successes.

In the Inde Valley, a large tributary of the Rur which could not be traversed by tanks, stood the infantry formations of the 246th, 340th and 363rd Infantry Divisions, along with several attached heavy weapons. Here the enemy crashed to a halt. All of the formations of the 9th PD under

Generalmajor Freiherr von Elverfeldt fought with unheard of bravery. This division destroyed 134 enemy tanks in the time period from 17 to 22/11/1944. A number of these tanks were destroyed in close combat with panzerfaeusten. On 26/11 this division was mentioned in a Wehrmacht report.

Forward observers from the various artillery regiments directed fire onto the attacking enemy from the hills east of the Rur. Besides divisional artillery, the 408th and 466th Volksartillerie Corps were also committed in the II SS Panzer Corps sector, with the 9th and 10th SS Divisions. In addition, there were also three railroad guns and the 301st Fortification Artillery Battalion.

The guns unleashed a fire-strike from all tubes. Mortars fell in crescendo. The enemy's motorized formations were severely decimated. Finally the attack grew silent, and they all returned to the forest combat with hand weapons and hand-grenades.

In spite of all defensive measures and the last efforts of the soldiers committed here, the Allies captured additional villages, after Schleiden fell on 19/11. On 28/11 they advanced in the south from Dueren up to the western bank of the Rur.

Dramatic combat took place in the church of Vossenack. While one side was hiding in the altar room, the other side was in the Sacristy – until one of the parties was discovered.

It was not until the end of November 1944 that this great obstacle, the green hell of the Huertgenwald, which was now grey and white, was overcome by the Americans. The German front now ran on a line from Bruchelen north of Linnich to the eastern bank of the Rur to Mariaweiler, from there through Guerzenich and Birgel to Untermaubach and Huertgen and from there to Brandenberg.

In Linnich, a town near Rurdorf, was located the last German bridgehead on the western bank of the Rur, near Flossdorf. It was held to allow the withdrawing German troops to cross the river. The Rur bridges were blown up at the last second in front of the pursuing enemy tanks. Finally, combat activity ceased on both sides and, by 3/12/1944, the 9th U.S. Army reached the area between Linnich and Gereonsweiler against the still bitterly resisting men of the 3rd PGD and the 12th Volksgrenadier Division. The German 393rd ID had to evacuate the exposed bridgehead around Hasenfeld.

The U.S. troops continued on toward Juelich with new forces. The 29th U.S. ID crossed the Rur between 6/12 and 8/12 and attacked Juelich in conjunction with the 30th ID and the 2nd AD.

Here the attackers ran into the hurriedly transported 3rd Fallschirmjaeger Division under Generalleutnant Schimpf, which took over the defense of the city. Troops from the LXXXI Army Corps also withdrew and established a defensive front around Dueren.

The fighting around the Huertgenwald and in the entire combat area at this time had cost the lives of 68,000 soldiers from all nations. After the war the remains of 23,000 German and 40,000 American soldiers were found in the region from Aachen to Vossenack. This was the greatest loss the American troops had suffered in the fighting in Fortress Europe.

Now the exhausted regiments of the 12th Volksgrenadier Division, the 459th, 176th, 183rd and 363rd Infantry Divisions lay in a weak defensive ring around Juelich in anticipation of the enemy attack.

The 1st U.S. Army lost 21,000 men during the past 23 days of combat. The Germans bemoaned the loss of 1133 killed, 6864 wounded and 2049 missing in this combat area.

A period of quiet and refitting arrived. Each side had reached the end of its strength. The Huertgenwald had exacted its sacrifice.

After this debacle near Arnheim and Huertgen, as well as the failed airborne operation in the greater Arnheim area, the far-reaching hopes of the Allies to reach a decision here in the west had been dashed. Indeed, they had believed that the way into the heart of Germany would be a cakewalk. However, now they had to realize that they could do no more before the outbreak of winter, they had to reorganize their supply lines and prepare for the great decisive spring offensive.

Since the beginning of the Allied invasion on the French Atlantic coast the German Army had lost 54,754 killed and 338,933 wounded and missing. Of the missing, the majority were captured.

However, on the enemy side, the Americans alone in the same period of time lost 65,000 killed, 177,000 wounded, 22,000 prisoners and 6000 missing. They could not take such high losses. Even if they were constantly being replenished with new troops replacements and weapons.

A comparison at the end of November 1944 showed the discrepancy between the combat strengths of both sides. While the Germans had committed 416,713 men in the west, the Anglo – Americans had a combat strength of 2,699,647 soldiers from all branches of service.

Nevertheless, during this first phase of the combat around the fortresses of the Reich that has just been described, Hitler had worked out a new plan that was as phenomenal as it was fantastic. This plan was based on the fact that during the crisis months of August and September 1944 the Allies had not reached the Rhein at any location while they were pursuing the German troops withdrawing from France. As soon as winter arrived, as it soon must, the Allies would loose their strongest weapon – the air forces – then, under the weight of a major decisive German attack, they would collapse.

Hitler issued the directives and Generaloberst Jodl drafted the initial plans, then he developed them with the OKW and the Wehrmacht Operations Staff under total secrecy and without informing the commanders of the Western Army. The title of this plan was:

"Wacht am Rhein [Watch on the Rhein]!"

This was the code-name of the last German offensive, which was to begin in the Ardennes.

3

BETWEEN THE ARDENNES AND THE RHEIN

Report on the Ardennes Offensive

On 10/12/1944 Hitler met with his operations staff at the Adlerhorst near Bad Nauheim. Several days later he informed the army and division commanders and their chiefs of staff in Schloss Ziegenberg of the new offensive. Accordingly, General von Manteuffel and his 5th Panzer Army was to capture Antwerp, while the 6th SS Panzer Army under Dietrich was to approach Lutich and capture this city. Therefore, the 21st British Army Group under Montgomery would then be encircled and could be destroyed during the second part of the offensive.

In this manner, so hoped Hitler, not only the Canadians, but also the Americans would withdraw from the war or, at least, reflect a greater interest in ending it quickly.

The "Wacht am Rhein" was prepared and 250,000 German soldiers awaited the attack order for the "phantom front in the Ardennes." Panzer divisions and panzergrenadier divisions were removed from the other theaters of war. All replacements went to the west, instead of – as was usually the case – to the east.

On the early morning of 16/12/1944 the phantom front opened fire. The sector in front of the 5th Panzer Army was illuminated with hundreds of searchlights, as the panzergrenadiers and tanks attacked. Thousands of tank, SPW and self-propelled gun engines roared. The battle in the Ardennes was on.

The American troops were collectively taken by surprise by this concentrated armor attack, many were shocked from sleep. "The Germans are coming!" was the dreadful call, a nightmare. No one had anticipated this: German divisions were not withdrawing, they were attacking!

When General Eisenhower learned of this attack in Versailles, General Bradley, the commander of the 12th Army Group, had just arrived to discuss future plans. A staff officer reported no less than five deep German penetrations in the fronts of the VIII and V U.S. Corps. All of the commanding generals, their chiefs of staff and Air Marshal Tedder were discussing what to do.

Up to this point in time the 7th AD was the only formation that could be transferred into the Ardennes and, at the end of this meeting, Bradley called his headquarters in Luxembourg and ordered the 7th AD to be set in march immediately.

When he hung up the telephone, Eisenhower's chief of staff, Major General Bedell Smith approached Bradley and remarked: "You had always hoped for a large-scale German counterattack, Brad! It seems that you have your wish."

"Yes, I wanted the Krauts to counterattack, however, I'll be damned if I wished for such a big one."

The battle in the Ardennes developed into a nightmare for the U.S. troops in and around Bastogne, which the German formations had encircled. In their further advance to the west, the Panzer-Lehr Division under Generalleutnant Bayerlein reached the area south of Rochefort, while the 2nd Panzer Division approached to within five kilometers of Dinant and, therefore, their objective, the Maas. The 2nd SS Panzer Division had also advanced quite a distance with its armored elements, before they ran out of fuel.

Ultimately they had to blow up their tanks and withdraw on foot. The lead elements of the 2nd Panzer Division were shot-up in front of Dinant and even the Panzer-Lehr Division had to withdraw on the first day of

Christmas. They no longer had the strength nor reserves to repeat their victory of 1940 on the same terrain.

If the German troops did not achieve the hoped for success, they did have an effect: they tied up the Allied preparations for an offensive in Germany and made it possible for the formations of Army Group G in Alsace – Loraine to recapture lost terrain.

What was hard to accept was the fact that this offensive in the Ardennes had cost those panzer formations which could have defied the Red Army, when they initiated their winter offensive out of the Vistula bridgeheads on 12 January 1945, an offensive that would bring them into eastern Germany up to the Oder.

Those panzer divisions which achieved such doubtful success in the Ardennes were missing from the Eastern Front and, therefore, the battle in the Ardennes was not only significant for the western region, but also for the eastern region, so it must be further discussed here.

Hitler had missed by a hair's breadth the great, perhaps even decisive for the war, success in the Ardennes. This offensive would have been crowned with success, had it led to the withdrawal of all U.S. forces out of Europe. This American step was not just German wishful thinking, but reality. When the German troops approached their objective, the Maas, the U.S. Secretary of War, Henry L. Stimson, went to the U.S. Chief of the General Staff, General George S. Marshall, on 27/12/1944 and spoke with him in his office. The main theme of this conversation was the nagging question of what must happen if the Germans succeeded in determining the fighting in the Ardennes in their favor. The consequence of such a defeat was that a number of new divisions had to be outfitted and sent to Europe, in order to replace the losses. However, whether Congress would approve such wide-ranging measures was uncertain. However, if no new divisions were approved then there would be nothing left to do but withdraw the remnants of the American Expeditionary Army from Europe. The upshot was that General Marshal was left with the following impression after a two hour conversation:

"If Germany defeats us in this great offensive and if the Russians are unable to initiate their offensive, then we must reappraise the entire war and establish defensive positions along the German border. Further combat like that against Aachen and in the Huertgen Forest was out of the question for us. We could no longer endure that. Moreover, we had to let the American people decide whether they were ready to continue fighting and create the necessary divisions needed for this purpose, or not." (See: Stimson, Harry L. and Bundy, McGeorge: *On Active Service in Peace and War.*)

On 4/1/1945 Hitler issued new instructions for the further conduct of the fighting. He ordered OB West to "conduct offensive strikes in rapid succession to defeat the Anglo-American formations and, therefore, to seize the initiative, which had, up to this time, been denied to the German leadership." (See OKW Combat Diary.)

On the early morning of 3/1/1945, however, the Allies began their major attack. The 1st and 3rd U.S. Armies attacked from the north and the south, in order to cut off the far-advanced German divisions.

At the same time the German divisions were attacking in the direction of Bastogne, which was, indeed, encircled and assaulted, however, it could not be taken and was finally relieved by U.S. replacement troops.

The 6th U.S. AD ran right into the German attack. They suffered heavy casualties and lost 40% of their tanks and artillery. On the evening of 4/1/1945 General Patton, commander of the 3rd U.S. Army, argued against the idea that Germany had already lost the war at Stalingrad in his combat diary:

"We can still loose the war." and he also noted: "This is the most important entry I have made at any time during the war." (See: Patton, George S.: *War As I Knew It.*)

After the first large American counterattack, which had the objective of encircling the German troops, had failed, another attack was to follow on 8/1/1945. However, it had to be delayed until 10/1/1945.

On 6/1/1945 Winston Churchill telegraphed Marshal Stalin and asked for help with the following words:

"The fighting in the west is very hard. I ask you to let me know whether we can count upon a Russian offensive on the Vistula or elsewhere in January."

Stalin replied that Churchill could anticipate it soon.

The Allied attack that broke loose on 10/1/1945 in the Ardennes only gained ground grudgingly at first. On the next morning it was already clear to the Germans that the Russians would be launching their feared winter offensive in the east in a short time.

On the following morning they broke out of the Vistula bridgeheads. Secretary of War Stimson was so relieved when he received this news that he said into his dictaphone:

"This is very good news, we were all a little nervous over Stalin's liesureliness, although we naturally believed that the Russians would keep their word." (See Stimson, Henry L. and Bundy, McGeorge: Op. cit.)

The Germans were forced to withdraw and when, on 16/1/1945, the assault divisions of the 1st and 3rd U.S. Armies met near Houffalize and formed the sack, there was nothing left in it but a cold Eifel wind.

By the end of January 1945 the great puss-boil in the Ardennes was again removed and, a little later, the Allied troops stood on the "Siegfried Line", as the West Wall was called.

The 1st U.S. Army was now concentrated on a small front between the Huertgenwald and St. Vith, while the 9th U.S. Army had taken over the front on the Roer. The 3rd U.S. Army under General Patton, the American Guderian, finally penetrated from the Luxembourg border to the Mosel.

Therefore, the old positions prior to the Ardennes offensive were reestablished. The Allies again had to pay a high price in blood, however, they avoided destruction and captivity.

The official losses of the three major formations in the Ardennes totaled:

1st U.S. Army: 4629 killed, 12,176 missing, 23,152 wounded.
3rd U.S. Army: 3778 killed, 8729 missing, 23,017 wounded.
XXX British Corps: 200 killed, 239 missing, 969 wounded.

These were heavy losses, however, they could be replaced. It was otherwise with the German formations. They bemoaned:

5th Panzer Army, 6th SS Panzer Army and 7th Army together: 10,749 killed, 22,388 missing, 35,169 wounded. Therefore, of the 250,000 German soldiers who participated in "Wacht am Rhein", 68,306 fell. That was over one quarter.

This offensive also had peripheral effects: The previously strained situation in the Army Group G area of operations on the front in Alsace – Loraine and between Saarbruecken and the Rhein was no longer a threat. The Allies, who had reached the foreground of the West Wall here, were pushed back in rapid counterattacks.

The battle in the Ardennes, which took six weeks, was the ruin of the Eastern Front. The last German Ardennes fighters were exhausted and all reserves were used up. Moreover, after the end of this failed offensive the divisions of the 6th SS Panzer Army had to set in march to the east to Hungary.

Hitler's plan failed, because the German Army was no longer the unified and well-equipped combat formation that it was in 1940, when it had easily scored the victory over France. Hitler had over-estimated his own strength, while under-estimating the forces of the western enemy.

It was necessary to hold on the Eastern Front and not on the Western Front. Time could only be gained on the Eastern Front. For this reason, the main effort of all combat operations had to lay on the Eastern Front. Then Churchill's and Eisenhower's secret wish could possibly have been fulfilled: that Montgomery's 21st Army Group would enter Berlin as victors far ahead of the Russians and, if possible, even reach the Oder. Then the arranged demarcation line, which ran 150 kilometers west of Berlin, would have to undergo a revision.

This was full of if's and but's, however, it was based on a realistic assessment of the situation, as Fuller describes:

"Politically the best possible solution was to give up the Western Front and concentrate all forces against the USSR. This would leave all of Germany and Austria in the hands of the Western Allies and would have struck a blow to the prestige of the USSR and the Red Army." (See Fuller: J.F.Ch.: *The Second World War 1939-1945.*)

Nevertheless, the Ardennes offensive was over. Germany's enemy was now back where he was six weeks ago, when he had gotten over the fortress of Aachen and the Huertgenwald.

"Eclipse" – A Secret Document at Dawn

During the Ardennes offensive a secret Allied document fell into the hands of the Abwehr that bore the code-name "Eclipse." Here were 70 pages of facts accompanied by a 50x45 centimeter map, which had marked significance. When Hitler received this document at the end of January, he personally read it before allowing his advisors to read it. "Eclipse" was classified "Secret Reichssache." On the map, Germany was divided into three parts. While U.K. (United Kingdom) was written in the northern and northwestern portion, in the south was printed in block letters USA. All of central and eastern Germany, however, bore the designation USSR. Berlin, the capital of the Reich, was likewise divided into three parts. The city was surrounded by its own borderline. Therefore, all doubts as to what unconditional surrender entailed were disbursed. The memorandum "Eclipse" showed the German leadership what was planned. The wishful thinking of causing a split between the Western Allies and their eastern ally was gone. Here were the hard facts, and in the foreword Hitler had to read:

"In order to impose conditions of surrender on Germany, the governments of the United States, the USSR and the United Kingdom agree that Germany will be occupied by the forces of the three powers."

This explosive document was signed in the headquarters of the 21st Army Group by Major General Sir Francis de Guingand, Montgomery's Chief of Staff. This plan gave Germany no more hope. If the Reich surrendered it could only be unconditionally, therefore, there was only one thing left for Germany to do: to fight until it was unconditionally defeated. "Eclipse" removed the last illusions.

Therefore, it was senseless to await the split between the two unlikely partners. The Alliance was still completely intact, and Yalta proved this.

On this map, the appendix to "Eclipse", the demarcation line between the Anglo-Americans and the Russians ran from Luebeck to Wittenberg along the Elbe, then it turned to the south up to the Eisenach area and from there to the east the Czech border. The Western Allies would also halt their troops after they reached the Elbe.

Meeting in Moscow – Planning

On 13/1/1945 Air Chief Marshal Tedder, Major General Bull and Brigadier General Betts arrived in Moscow. They were sent to the Russian capital as a coordinating team. Marshal Stalin greeted them amiably. Tedder was authorized by Eisenhower to present the Allied plans. After that, during the first meeting of the coordinating staff he explained the three-phased plan that was worked out by Eisenhower's staff:

Intent: Destroy all German forces located west of the Rhein in three major operations:

1. Major Operation: Major attack by Montgomery's 21st Army Group with the objective of winning the lower Rheinland from Nijmwegen to Duesseldorf by the 1st Canadian Army under General Crerar, the Reichswald and the Roer region by the 9th U.S. Army (which, therefore, would come under the command of the 21st Army Group).

2. Major Operation: Advance by the 1st U.S. Army under General

Hodges in the direction of Cologne – Bonn – Remagen and the 3rd Army in the direction of Koblenz.

3. Major Operation: Attack of the 3rd and 7th U.S. Armies against the German troops still holding the Saar region, with the objective: reach the Rhein on the line Stuttgart – Mainz. (The Kolmar Sack would be cleared by the 1st French Army.)

Stalin himself informed the mission that he – if the offensive he began on the previous day did not succeed – would order a series of further major operations, in order to tie down as many enemy forces in the east as possible. Therefore, this was to make it impossible for the German Wehrmacht to remove further troops from the east and transport them to the west, in order to commit them there. From this point in time on, this coordination staff would increasingly insure that operations in the west and the east were coordinated. It is due to them that the end of the war would be achieved in four short months.

At the same time, Operation "Veritable" was being prepared in the headquarters of the 21st Army Group, Montgomery believed he had General Eisenhower's approval for it. With this operation the British Field Marshal wanted to snatch away the initiative from the German enemy as quickly as possible. Because the operations in the Ardennes and before proved that the 1st and 3rd U.S. Armies were not strong enough to execute a breakthrough of the West Wall – at least Montgomery was convinced of this – he wanted to accomplish this mission. He wanted to reach the Rhein north of the Ruhr region, cross it there and establish a large bridgehead.

For this purpose he required the stocking of the 9th U.S. Army, which was subordinate to him, to four corps with 13 divisions.

An additional U.S. corps with three divisions was to be turned over to the British 2nd Army. Therefore, the 21st British Army Group would have 16 U.S. divisions available in their ranks. Montgomery informed the British Chief of the General Staff, Alan Francis Brooke (later Viscount Alanbrooke), that Eisenhower felt good about these plans. Field Marshal Brooke replied with a letter on 15/1/1945 that he was in agreement. He explained:

"We all agree that this attack must be made in the north. If accepted, your plan would secure the requisite force concentration at the correct location."

On the following day Montgomery's plan was discussed in SHAEF Headquarters. There it was decided that the number of American divisions that would be subordinated to Montgomery would be reduced from 16 to twelve and that the difference would be made up by having Bradley's 12th Army Group take responsibility for a sector of the 21st Army Group front and, therefore, have "a small role to play in the operation."

Montgomery agreed and declared to the assembled staff chiefs that it would be possible to initiate Operation "Veritable" on 10 February, "if the plan is approved and I receive six American divisions by 1 February." Operations "Veritable" and "Grenade" – a supporting attack by the 9th U.S. Army against Duesseldorf – "together would be a formidable undertaking, and most of us would not be at ease until we started." (See: Montgomery at the CIGS from 16/1/1945. Lord Alanbrooke's personal documents.)

On 18/1 Montgomery had a meeting with his U.S. counterpart, General Bradley, which led to agreement on all points.

Nevertheless, 48 hours later this complete agreement vanished, when Montgomery reported that he received information from the Supreme Allied Commander, General Eisenhower, on 18/1 that "there was still considerable disagreement and it is known that Bradley is again going his own way. Instead of a solid, clear and final plan there is indecision and patchwork." (See: Bryant, Arthur: *Victory in the West 1943-1945*.)

The Supreme Commander, General Eisenhower, proposed accomplishing a number of smaller missions. And at the core of his protest, Montgomery delineated Eisenhower's statements,

"that we will not – not – cross the Rhein before we deploy on the entire length of it from Nijmwegen to Switzerland. If we advance according to this plan, then we will need much more time to execute it."

During the following days there were a series of requests from various

U.S. commanders for the divisions, which were supposed to go to Montgomery.

And, indeed, considerable forces were deployed in the Kolmar and Strassburg area, which indicated that "Grenade", the attack of the 9th U.S. Army, had to be shifted to an unspecified time; however, because both operations depended upon each other, "Veritable" was thereby shelved. Montgomery pointed the finger at Allied discord, when he reported to the Chief of the General Staff of the British Armed Forces, closing with the words:

"I fear that the old stumbling blocks of indecision, wavering and refusal to take clear responsibility for military problems is again surfacing...

The main difficulty lay in the fact that there is no unified control, each of the three army groups has its own plan.

Patton issued today a motivating order to his 3rd Army, indicating that the next objective would be Cologne.

One must keep a sense of humor these days, otherwise one would go crazy." (See: Montgomery at CIGS, 22/1/1945.)

Eisenhower's general instructions for the continuation of combat were subjected to criticism, and the Chief of the General Staff of the British Empire, Marshal Brooke, declared:

"We question Eisenhower's statements in his report. When he writes that an operation west of the Rhein must be conducted so that it will include the entire course of the river, does he mean that it is to replace a concentrated breakthrough operation supported by a general attack."

These arguments from the British Chief of Staff led to the presentation of a draft to Eisenhower:

"All means for an offensive operation will be made available. This strike will be conducted with the greatest strength possible and after fresh reserve formations are trained, so that the attack momentum can be maintained. Forces will be committed to peripheral operations as long as they are not needed on the main axis. Only if the main strike is parried and the peripheral strikes continue to advance with they be utilized operationally.

If tactical considerations allow, the main strike will be conducted in the north, taking into consideration the overwhelming significance the Ruhr region has for the enemy.

The best results will be achieved if one commander takes direct responsibility for coordinating the operations of the land forces committed on the main axis." (See Ehrmann, John: *History of the Second World War.*)

The American staff chief accepted the British requirement that the main strike must be conducted in the north, however, they again raised for discussion their own plan of an "attack in the south", which would not interfere with a main attack in the north, however, it was to be strong enough to displace the German forces protecting the important Frankfurt area and, in case the main effort failed, provide an alternative attack direction.

In such a peripheral offensive, Patton would operate against the middle Rhein and twelve divisions would be subordinated to him without threatening the main offensive.

After both plans were illustrated many times, the British Chief of Staff and Bedell Smith, Eisenhower's Chief of Staff, finally approved them and informed General Eisenhower telegraphically. He accepted the final plan and he wrote to Bedell Smith:

"You can assure the combined Staff Chief Committee that I will accept the crossing of the Rhein in the north as soon as this operation proves necessary and that I will not wait until we are along the entire length of the river."

Nevertheless, he included a sentence that caused some concern:

"I will cross the Rhein in the north with as great strength and determination as possible, as soon as the situation in the south allows me to assemble the necessary forces and conduct the operation without undue risk."

Therefore, the British plan to relieve General Eisenhower and replace him as Supreme Commander in Europe with Field Marshal Lord Alexander failed, especially since the U.S. Chief of the General Staff, General Marshall, had said that he would never allow the Brits to thrust upon him their own Supreme Commander of all ground forces while he was in his duty position. (See Summersby, K.: *Eisenhower Was My Boss*.)

The assessment of Eisenhower by the British General Staff, as well as by the British in general, was expressed in Field Marshal Brooke's diary under the 6 March 1945 entry:

"Ike undoubtedly has an extremely charming personality and, at the same time, from a strategic standpoint, a very, very narrow mind. This is displayed at every encounter with him. His relationship with Monty is an unsolvable problem. He only sees Monty's bad side and not his good side."

The attack in the north became an accomplished fact. It would begin on 10 February and it would be started by Montgomery. His interpretation of the strength of the German formations in the west led him to say that the Germans could not long resist such a concentrated offensive.

The German and Allied Force Situation on the Western Front

At the end of February 1945, when the results of the Soviet winter offensive were becoming clear, the Western Front had to give up forces so that they could be committed in the east against the Soviet armored avalanche.

OB West had to deploy to the Eastern Front ten panzer divisions, six infantry divisions, ten artillery corps, eight rocket launcher brigades and other special troops. In this manner, the troops in the west were reduced to 55 weak divisions, some of which had not yet recovered from the Ardennes fighting. They were opposed by 85 fully equipped Allied divisions and an overwhelming superiority of air squadrons.

In all there were seven German armies on the Western Front. The 6th SS Panzer Army had to be removed and refitted. Even so, it would not be returned to the Western Front, but, after reconstituting, it would be shipped to Hungary.

From south to north the armies stood as follows:

In the Army Group G area of operations: The 19th Army in the Kolmar area on the Oberrhein. The 1st Army between the Rhein and the Mosel.

In the Army Group B area of operations: The 7th and 15th Armies between the Mosel near Trier and Roermond. The 5th Panzer Army was still located in departure positions, which they had taken up before the beginning of the Ardennes offensive.

In the Army Group H area of operations: The 1st Fallschirmjaeger Army on the Maas and the 25th Army in Holland in the Niederrhein area. This army group was newly established under the command of Generaloberst Blaskowitz.

The fighting around Kolmar, which had already begun on 20/1/1945, did not push through the 19th Army for the time being. The attacking 1st French Army was not strong enough to crack this block. When General Bradley ordered the XXI Corps under Lieutenant General Devers to also attack Kolmar, then this city fell on 3/2/1945. The large German bridgehead there was spilt up and the Allies reached the Rhein south of Strassburg on 9/2. The 19th German Army suffered 22,000 casualties here and also lost the majority of its heavy weapons.

At the same time, therefore, the preparations for the major attack on the Rhein were also completed.

The Allies now stood from north to south with the following major formations on the entire front:

Army Group North: Field Marshal Montgomery

1st Canadian Army	Lieutenant General Crerar
2nd British Army	Lieutenant general Dempsey
9th U.S. Army	Lieutenant General Simpson
1st Airborne Army	Lieutenant General Brereton

Army Group Center General Omar N. Bradley

1st U.S. Army	General Hodges
3rd U.S. Army	General Patton
1st French Army	General Lattre de Tassigny

Field Marshal Montgomery was immediately given five English and American-Canadian airborne formations, these were combined under the designation 1st Airborne Army under the command of General Brereton.

On 2/2/1945, when it became clear that the major Allied attack would occur in the north, OB West, GFM von Rundstedt, summoned all commanders on the northern Rhein front to his headquarters. During the meeting it became obvious that there was a difference of opinion as to where the attack would take place. While Generaloberst Blaskowitz proposed that he anticipated the British – Canadian forces to attack near Venlo, "where the English – Canadian armies could only expect the support of the Americans, because they anticipated an advance across the Roer in the direction of Cologne there any day", General Schlemm believed otherwise. The commander of the 1st Fallschirmjaeger Army declared:

"The enemy will attack on the Reichswald front and attempt to advance through Kleve toward Wesel and reach the Rhein there. This attack offers the advantage to the Allies that they need not cross the high water of the Maas. Moreover, they can bypass the West Wall with this attack direction, as it runs parallel to the Maas out of the Goch-Geldern area to Aachen. If an attack in this direction succeeds, then our enemy will be able to roll up the entire front from the northern flank."

In spite of the foresight of Schlemm, GFM von Rundstedt decided with Generaloberst Blaskowitz. He made the German reserves available in the south of the army area, not in the area behind the Reichswald. Indeed, he believed that the 7th Fallschirmjaeger Division would be able to stand east of Venlo and the XXXXVIII Panzer corps with the 15th PGD and the 116th PD in the Viersen-Kempen area.

The Attack Begins – Fortress Reichswald

In the early days of February the Panzer-Lehr Division received the order to hold the anticipated major attack of the 21st Army Group through the Reichswald toward Kalkar and Goch together with the 7th and 8th Fallschirmjaeger Divisions. The division immediately set in movement and reached the new commitment area on 6/2 with its lead elements. Here it first received a new panzer battalion with 60 Panther tanks. Even the panzergrenadier regiment received replacements.

The 901st Panzer-Lehr Regiment, which was still refitting in the Baden area, reached the village of Uedem via Tondorf and Marienbaum and took up positions on the Uedem stream. Between Keppeln and Schwashof stood the panzerjaegers, which held an important sector together with the fallschirmjaegers.

On 7/2/1945 the commander of the Panzer-Lehr Division, Generalleutnant Bayerlein, received the order to turn the division over to his successor, Oberst Horst Niemack, and take command of the LIII Corps, which became known as Corps Bayerlein by the end of the war.

On the early morning of 8/2/1945 at 0500 hours a barrage fire from over 1000 guns began between the Maas and the Rhein. Five hours later the British XXX Corps under Lieutenant General Horrocks attacked. In this corps were three British and two Canadian divisions. The objective of the XXX Corps was the Reichswald and Goch, which lay behind it.

Since the general attack direction was discovered by radio reconnaissance two days before the start of the attack, the Germans cut through the Rhein embankment from below Emmerich up to Pannerden. Therefore, high water flowed into the left Rhein combat area north of the Nijmwegen – Kleve – Kalkar Reichsstrasse.

When, at daybreak, the dominant ground fog began to dissipate several dozen batteries of rocket launchers opened fire. The first armored and motorized infantry formations appeared in front of the positions of the 84th ID, which alone defended the Reichswald, and shot the infantry out of their trenches. Fighting in the Reichswald expanded very quickly.

Over the constant Allied artillery fire could still be heard the engine noises from the Allied bomber and fighter-bomber formations. The first to appear were the fighter-bombers, who dropped their rockets and fired from their on-board weapons. After they flew away from the combat sector, the thick groups of bombers arrived, they conducted carpet bombing.

They were followed by enemy tanks and armored flame-throwers to smoke out the nests of resistance. A few anti-tank guns returned this massive fire and held the tanks off. The enemy was stopped by committing the last reserves.

As evening descended the Allied artillery still continued to fire. However, the attack stalled.

General der Fallschirmtruppe Schlemm, who was quartered with his staff in Dinxperlo near Bocholt, was awoken shortly before 0500 hours by the barrage fire. The barrage fire that came out of the west across the Rhein like a gigantic storm effected all formations in the area.

General Schlemm drove to the front in a kuebelwagen. He got his first impression of the weight of this barrage fire after driving for several minutes. The ground was thrown up to the front and fragments pierced the ground in such thickness that it increased the General's forebodings: This was the Allied offensive, and the enemy had initiated it – exactly as he had foreseen – in the Reichswald west of Kleve. He did not believe it was a diversion, as was suggested by one of his staff officers. This was the major offensive.

Reconnaissance reports had established movement in the Eindhoven area in the direction of Nijmwegen and, therefore, in the direction of the Reichswald. Immediately dispatched scout troops confirmed these reports.

On this 8/2/1945 the front of the 1st Fallschirmjaeger Army was adjacent in the north to the Rhein east of Millingen, it ran through Kronenburg to the Maas up to Gennep and then followed the Maas through Venlo to Roermond at the confluence of the Roer into the Maas.

Here it made contact with the front of the 15th Army on the Roer, while in the north the 25th Army defended the Rhein front up to its mouth.

After he returned from the front General Schlemm reported to Army Group H, Generaloberst Blaskowitz, in the afternoon of 8 February that the Allied offensive had begun in the Reichswald against the front of the 84th ID. At the same time, he reported that he had alerted the reserve troops of the 1st Fallschirmjaeger Army, the 7th Fallschirmjaeger Division, from the area east of Venlo, loaded them on vehicles and set them in march in the direction of Gennep. According to his report, he wanted to counterattack this division to stop the enemy from bringing up further forces and then throw him back.

That this would not be so easy to do considering the special organization of the XXX British Corps, which had a combat strength of 200,000 men, approaching the strength of an army, was clear, nevertheless, the Fallschirmjaeger General wanted to try.

However, the staff of Army Group H, in particular Generaloberst Blaskowitz, were not of the same mind that this was the major offensive. Of course they had not experienced the explosive effect of this attack first hand, but made their judgments from the "green table in their command post", as General Schlemm put it to the author.

There they anticipated the main attack near Venlo and, for this reason, Generaloberst Blaskowitz ordered the immediate transport of the 7th Fallschirmjaeger Division into assembly areas near Venlo. The Ic [Intelligence Officer] of Army Group H believed that only Canadian troops would be committed in front of the Reichswald. From this he deduced that all of the remaining British divisions had still not entered the battle.

Generaloberst[?] Schlemm knew better, however, he did not have the authority to do anything about it. On the basis of this, he took the stratagem that would be the most effective. He decided to stop the 7th Fallschirmjaeger Division half-way to its objective and awaited the events of the next few hours. This division now waited at parade rest near Kevelaer for commitment orders, for which direction, while the 84th ID was being bloodied in the Reichswald and bitterly needed their help.

Therefore, Generaloberst Blaskowitz had let his aversion to the "slipshod soldiers of the Luftwaffe" get the best of him, however, he finally got a better picture of the enemy's intent during the next morning, because the subsequent activities of the Allies could not be ignored.

On the afternoon of 9/2/1945 the statements of officers from no less than five Canadian and British divisions arrived at Army Group H headquarters that indicated that Montgomery had thrown all of his eggs into one basket, utilizing all forces available to him in this sector.

Again General Schlemm requested that the 7th Fallschirmjaeger Division be freed-up. This time the cries for help from all of the units on the edge of the Reichswald were so loud that they even reached OKH in Berlin.

The division rolled to the battlefield west of the Reichswald.

On the Allied side, by midday of 9/2/1945 not only was the 1st Canadian Army under General Crerar committed with subordinate elements of the 2nd British Army, but the entire XXX Corps under Horrocks was also committed in the Reichswald. Five infantry divisions, three armored brigades and eleven special regiments, including several commandos, were now involved in the fighting. They had received instructions to attack through the Reichswald as quickly as possible and continue the advance in the direction of Wesel.

In conjunction with Operation "Grenade" – the strike of the 9th U.S. Army on 10/2 across the Roer on Cologne-Neuss – the German troops located west of the Rhein were to be encircled by a large-scale pincer maneuver and destroyed.

The British 15th ID advanced as the lead attack element on the northern edge of the Reichswald and reached the western edge of Kleve by 10/2 at 1645 hours.

Now was the time for Operation "Grenade", however, General Simpson had conquered the last coffer-dam on the Roer on 9/2 and stood on the western bank of the long fought over river, however, he must have realized that he could not consider crossing the Roer. The water was too high. By opening the Urft Valley block, GFM Model had turned the lower course of the Roer into an insurmountable water barrier. General Simpson had to report to his headquarters that the Roer could not be crossed for a period of two weeks. In the meantime, any attack was senseless. Therefore, the 1st Canadian Army and the XXX British Corps had to conduct the attack alone.

On 8/2 the 84th ID repulsed the first enemy attack in its positions on the western edge of the Reichswald. By midday of the following day they had already fought against eight enemy divisions. The soldiers entrenched into the ground. They laid mine barricades and fired from panzerfaeuste. The individual battalions melted to companies within 48 hours. The two roads running through the forest were mined by engineers. U.S. tanks and fast personnel transporters were blown high into the air.

The center held, it was defended like a fortress. However, in the north the 15th British ID broke through.

In the center the tanks rolled through the forest trails and continuously ran into obstacles. Several anti-tank guns, a pair of hastily assembled assault guns and panzerfaeuste were sufficient to stop the enemy.

General Schlemm appeared at the front with the fighters. Indeed, he was able to insert elements of the 7th Fallschirmjaeger Division to support this shaky front, however, by the evening of 10/2 it was already clear that they could not hold off the enemy.

Now Generaloberst Blaskowitz had to consider giving up the XXXXVII Panzer Corps. With elements of the 7th and 8th Fallschirmjaeger Divisions also rolled the 15th PGD and the 116th PD into the combat area. On the adjacent sector on the Maas, the LXXXVI Army Corps under Generalleutnant Straube with the 180th and 190th Infantry Divisions secured near and south of Gennep. The 2nd Fallschirmjaeger Regiment of the 2nd Fallschirmjaeger Division was inserted between the 84th ID and the 180th ID near Siebengewald – Hammersum – Asperden. Oberst Vorwerck led the regiment. The two other regiments of the 2nd Fallschirmjaeger Division were still located in the 25th Army area between the Waal and Lek. The 2nd Fallschirmjaeger Regiment conducted its last commitment in front of Goch and in the area of this hotly contested city.

The enemy's attack momentum began to wither. Would the Reichswald become a hell like the Huertgenwald? This question haunted the British and American commanders during these days of bitter fighting.

Goch and Kleve were also bombed during the night of 8/2/1945. As General Crerar said to General Horrocks during a preparatory meeting, if he, Horrocks, needed air support he only had to ask, and when he asked whether Kleve should be bombed to secure a more rapid victory, General Horrocks replied:

"This was difficult for me, it is such a beautiful city, one of the wives of King Henry VIII came from there and there are many women and children in the city.

However, I finally said yes and I assured him: it will not please me to see the bombers flying over our heads on the night before our attack." (General Horrocks' diary.)

Kleve was bombed. The Church of Maria Himmelfahrt was the first target that was completely destroyed. The Schwanenburg and the market were destroyed by the high explosive detonations. Gressenich was leveled, Wesel and Dueren were bombed again.

However, the fighting continued. The fallschirmjaegers took up the defense and fought with an unparalleled bravery.

"Not in the course of the entire war had enemy units offered more bitter resistance, as did the German fallschirmjaegers during the fighting for the Rheinland", noted Field Marshal Montgomery in his memoirs.

General Schlemm moved his command post from Dinxperlo into a farmhouse near Xanten, in order to be able to reach his commanders on the main effort sector faster. On 13/2 he had to move his command post to Rheinberg, because the southern front took priority.

On 11/2 Kleve fell after fierce fighting, and the Allies occupied the ruins of the city. General Schlemm visited all of his formations when they needed him. The enemy was stopped by the circumspect leadership of the Fallschirmjaeger General and the steadfast bravery of the 180th and 190th Infantry Divisions under Generalleutnant Straube in the Reichswald and on its eastern edges.

On 14/2 the Allies reached the bank of the Rhein opposite Emmerich. The German lines were withdrawn to Uedem and Keppeln. Here, above all, were located the men of the 7th Fallschirmjaeger Division and several security battalions. The XXX Corps was to force the decisive breakthrough here.

On 17/2 the formations of the Panzer-Lehr Division also arrived in the Uedem area. They took up positions on the Uedem stream.

An initial enemy attack by elements of the XXX British Corps began on the morning of 19/2. Flame-thrower tanks rolled against the defensive positions of the 2nd Fallschirmjaeger Division, which was also transferred into this area and was subordinated to the 15th PGD. Individual fighters infiltrated to the front and frustrated the advancing tanks by firing panzerfaeusten. This attack, which was apparently conducted with the purpose of finding a weak position, stalled. However, it became clear that the major attack was still in the offing.

The major attack of the XXX Corps under General Horrocks began on the morning of 22/2/1945. Approximately 500 British tanks rolled against the German positions. The few German anti-tank and air defense guns, as well as the panzerjaegers of the Panzer-Lehr Division, tried to defeat the lead armored elements. The panzerjaegers of the 130th Panzerjaeger-Lehr Battalion of the Panzer-Lehr Division rolled into the armored wedge and shot-up several enemy tanks. Oberfeldwebel Stolz and Leutnant Schoenrath shot three enemy tanks each. A Canadian major, who approached the panzerjaegers with a white flag and requested to desert, was returned to General Crerar with a good reference.

On 23/2 the elements of the Panzer-Lehr Division had to withdraw in their combat area. They were ordered to close ranks with the formations of the LIII Panzer Corps under their old commander, Generalleutnant Bayerlein, which were attacking from the south and north, and to destroy the enemy forces located near Glehn. In this manner they were to stop the 9th and 1st U.S. Armies, which were crossing the Roer on the morning of 23/2. There the Americans had begun Operation "Grenade" with seven divisions in the first echelon.

The weak forces of the 15th German Army were thrown against this enemy force, however, they could not prevent the 363rd ID under Generalleutnant Dettling from being shot out of Juelich after fierce fighting. The 1st U.S. Army rolled into the city with tanks. Only on the eastern edge of the city were small stubborn battle groups from the 176th ID able to hold.

General von Zangen, commander of the 15th Army, did everything he could to stabilize the situation and prevent an enemy breakthrough. It was he who requested the 15th PGD and the Panzer-Lehr Division to help him prevent this disaster. Therefore, they were taken from the 1st Fallschirmjaeger Army.

On 27/2 the Panzer-Lehr Division began its attack. They stalled on the first day. The 901st Panzergrenadier-Lehr Regiment was decimated and had to withdraw to Toenisberg. General Bayerlein had to direct the LIII Panzer Corps toward Kapellen. This city fell on 26/2. However, immediately after that, the advancing panzer formations were attacked by Lightning and Typhoon fighter-bombers and six tanks were destroyed. Others were damaged by bombs bursting nearby. The attack stalled and on the evening of the same day the main group of the 5th U.S. AD of the XIII U.S. Corps under Lieutenant General Gillem attacked into the left flank of the LIII Panzer Corps. The corps had to withdraw and give up Kapellen.

A regiment of the 5th U.S. AD penetrated into this village directly in front of the Panzer-Lehr Division and it was only a question of hours until all of the 5th U.S. AD penetrated into Moenchengladbach from here and captured the city, if the Americans were not stopped.

On the evening of 28 February the formations of the Panzer-Lehr Division prepared to counterattack Schiefbahn. They were able to throw the enemy out of Schiefbahn. During night fighting against the U.S. tanks the panzerjaegers particularly distinguished themselves. Unteroffizier Eduard Job from the 3/PzJagLehrAbt 130 shot-up five enemy tanks here.

However, this success only gained 24 to 48 hours. On 1/3 troops of the XIII U.S. Corps took Moenchengladbach. On the same day Reydt also fell, and a day later Lieutenant General Simpson's troops reached the Rhein near Neuss. The center of the XIII Corps reached Krefeld and passed through this city untouched.

On the evening of 3/3 the left flank of the 9th U.S. Army made contact with the 1st Canadian Army north of Venlo. Therefore, the 15 German divisions still fighting west of the Rhein were caught in the pincers. A lead group of the 5th U.S. AD were able – since the German tanks were camouflaged – to cross a few dozen meters over the Rhein bridge near Oberkassel.

The lead tanks had already rolled up to the middle of the bridge when they noticed the enemy. Seconds later this bridge flew into the air with a thunderous explosion. Therefore, the advance of the 9th Army was stopped.

While the OKH was still trying to remove the three German divisions out of the Uedem – Keppeln area, the divisions of the XXX Army Corps under Lieutenant General Horrocks resumed their advance on the morning of 26/2 near Keppeln. The fallschirmjaeger and other formations had entrenched on the skull hill in front of Keppeln. They held off the British armored armada.

200 bombers attacked the hill and the entrenched positions and blew its top off. Then tanks attacked again with assault infantry. Again the attack was stopped as a number of enemy tanks were destroyed.

On 27/2, however, the German fallschirmjaegers had to withdraw from their positions, because they would have been cut off.

The withdrawal in the direction of Kervenheim was still not completed when the march in the general direction of Sonsbeck – Menzelen had to be given up due to the fall of Kalkar.

It was the assault guns of the XII Fallschirm Assault Gun Brigade, who were again committed in this situation and shot-up several enemy tanks, opening the way for the 7th Fallschirmjaeger Division. Since their first commitment out of the Goch – Gennep area the few assault guns from this formation had been in constant commitment. Early on 25/2 they had advanced up to Weeze into the flank of the enemy tanks, which were moving in the direction of the skull hill from Keppeln. After a short duel, the lead Sherman tanks stood in flames. Above all it was the platoon under Leutnant Heinz Deutsch that made themselves felt here.

Finally forced to withdraw by the enemy superiority, Leutnant Deutsch ordered his three guns to turn around after moving a few kilometers. They reached Kevelaer and advanced from here in the direction of the skull hill after the fall of the city and into the group of enemy tanks that had stalled south of here.

In the early morning hours of 1 March there was fierce fighting near Klappermanshof, in the vicinity of Kevelaer. Two Churchill tanks were stuck on the stretch, put out of commission by Deutsch himself. The other two guns of his platoon also scored hits.

1st U.S. Army infantry rolling to Germany.

Sherman tank on the West Wall.

Generalleutnant Gerhard Graf Schwerin, commander of the 116th Panzer Division.

The distance to Aachen is not very far.

GFM Walter Model, commander of Army Group B, at the 246th Volksgrenadier Division command post in Aachen.

General der Infantrie Gustav von Zangen, commander of the 15th Army.

Generalleutnant Harald Freiherr von Elverfeldt, commander of the 9th Panzer Division.

The church Maria Himmelfahrt zu Kleve after the bombardment.

Summon to resist at Aachen (People to arms!).

Oberst Gerhard Wild, last combat commandant o Aachen.

Negotiators demand Aachen surrender.

Temporary bridge across the Pruem near Luenebach.

The dead had fallen on the Ruhr bridge.

Between Juelich and Dueren: German wounded under guard by the 102nd U.S. Infantry Division.

Winston Churchill in Juelich. General Simpson in the foreground.

Generaloberst Johannes von Blaskowitz, commander of Army Group H.

GFM Walter Model, commander of Army Group B.

The Hotel Quellenhof in Aachen, the city commandant's command post.

U.S. troops advance through the bombed city.

View of the undamaged Remagen bridge.

7/3/1945: The Ludendorf Bridge is in enemy hands.

Patton's 3rd Army near Saarlautern on the Saar.

The 65th U.S. ID from the 3rd Army captures a town.

The new offensive on the Western Front is opened on 8/2/45.

Goch under the fire of U.S. armored formations.

Kleve was captured on 14/2/1945.

Xanten on 26/2/45: A soldier from the I Canadian Corps with German prisoners.

2/3/45: The Norfolks of the 3rd British ID in Kervenheim near Kevelaer.

U.S. infantry attack past a shot-up tank.

The 90th U.S. ID marches through the West Wall. There are also elements of the 6th U.S. Armored Division.

The 3rd U.S. Army reaches Luenebach near Pruem on 3/3/45.

Troops of the 3rd U.S. Army near Pruem in a German shelter.

Kranenburh was captured on 10/2/45 by British troops.

U.S. machine-gun troops support the air landing east of the Rhein on the morning of 24/3/45.

Allied paratroopers after landing.

Again the lead enemy tanks were stopped, and on the following day the assault guns advanced to again relieve the fallschirmjaegers who were already overrun near Kevelaer. Two Shermans and one Churchill were destroyed before Deutsch and his three guns had to withdraw through Wetten in the direction of Kappelen.

The enemy pursued cautiously. They had gained respect for the speed and maneuverability of the assault guns and the effectiveness of their long cannon. Leutnant Deutsch continued to maneuver against the advancing enemy tanks and open fire.

The fighting around Kappelen lasted until 4 March. For destroying thirteen enemy tanks in this battle Leutnant Deutsch received the Iron Cross I and was later awarded the German Cross in Gold.

The XII Assault Gun Brigade was indispensible for the 7th Fallschirmjaeger Division. They were the key to escape at the decisive moment, whenever the enemy was able to outflank the formation.

The lead formations of the LIII Army [Panzer] Corps reached the Rhein during the early days of March. Hitler had designated this as the last border, no German soldier was allowed to cross it. The corps was ordered to hold the bridgehead west of Wesel and, therefore, west of the Rhein. The LIII Panzer Corps command post was in Rheinland, which was already being fired on by U.S. tanks and enemy artillery on 3/3. The headquarters was withdrawn to the Rhein. On the morning of 4/3 Generalleutnant Bayerlein received permission to cross the Rhein.

This Fuehrer Order was issued on 1/3. It stated that "no staff officer was allowed to cross the Rhein to the east." The only exceptions to this order were to be issued be the OKW. The officers had to remain with their troops, in order to strengthen their resistance.

The XXX British Corps, which had passed through Marienbaum, Appeldorn and Niedermoermter Ward, halted its armored avalanche near Xanten. The fallschirmjaegers entrenched themselves in the houses west and northwest of Xanten. The defensive fighting around Xanten was conducted under the slogan "Jung Siegfried." The 1st Fallschirm Army Command under General Schlemm was fighting here since 2/3/1945. The entire Wesel bridgehead fell under his command. This included no less than nine

Rhein bridges. In retrospect, General Schlemm had this to say about this situation:

"I was responsible for nine Rhein bridges, and if I let even one of them fall into enemy hands it would be a catastrophe of immense proportions. They only thing to do them was to blow it up immediately. However, this was out of the question, because there was still a large amount of industrial material and cattle that had to be removed from the combat area across the river.

I assigned a capable engineer officer as bridge commandant for each of these bridges, they were to be prepared to blow them and remain in constant communication so that I could reach them immediately if I had to. Remnants of the 15th Army were streaming into the bridgehead from the south which – under instructions from Feldmarschall Model – would often come under my command.

On 3 March, when I ordered the destruction of the bridge near Homberg, an Oberst from the 15th Army tried to prevent the bridge commandant from blowing it up. I had to tell the gentleman that I would personally shoot him before he would allow the bridge to be blown.

If we waited until the enemy approached to within firing range of the bridges it would be difficult to blow them. I dispatched Feldgendarmerie Kommandos to the remaining bridge commandants to insure that the remaining bridges were destroyed at the proper time." (See: "In the Battle for the Reichswald" in: *The German Fallschirmjaeger* 1954; and a letter from General Schlemm to the author.)

With the American attack from Neuss to Krefeld on 2/3/1945 General Schlemm drove to Neuss, where he assumed that the Party leadership was in defensive combat on the southern edge of the city, because they had proposed to him they protect the city. When he arrived in the city, he discovered that it was not members of the Party leadership in the rifle trenches, but a formation of Hitler Youth in the strength of about 200 young men. He immediately ordered the young men be removed. However, before this could be accomplished the attack began, which did not bypass Neuss – as the army leadership had anticipated – but was directed at the southern portion of the city.

While the polizei and Party members had hurriedly withdrawn, the Hitler Youth defended their positions. This small unit was completely wiped out by the fire of the advancing tanks. Only a few were captured.

It was because of the enormous troop and equipment superiority of the Allies that they were able to reach the western bank of the Rhein near Wesel on 3/3. However, they engaged all resistance first with hours of artillery fire and then with the commitment of armored flame-throwers before they would advance further.

Nevertheless, the bridgehead was compressed narrower and narrower. When General Schlemm proposed crossing his exhausted troops to the eastern bank of the Rhein to establish a new defensive line, he was categorically turned down. The Wesel bridgehead was to become a fortress that was to be held with all means available. At the slightest chance, Hitler wanted to conduct a counterattack from here.

On the evening of 2/3, when the enemy penetrated from the south into the city of Krefeld and several attack wedges strived to capture the Rhein bridge near Uerdingen in a raid, the last combat ineffective elements of the Panzer-Lehr Division crossed the river to the east. To protect the access to the bridges, the commander of the 130th Panzerjaeger-Lehr Battalion committed three more Jagdpanzer IV's to block the entrance. These panzerjaegers were able to shoot-up the lead armored elements of the U.S. attack group so that they blocked the way for the following vehicles.

The elements of the 2nd Fallschirmjaeger Division, which were brought up at the last second, stopped the following U.S. infantry and threw them back.

Then the Allied artillery kicked in. The enemy fired airbursts here. Therefore, the German engineers were prevented from attaching the explosives to the bridge.

As darkness fell, the engineer troops were able to approach the bridge unnoticed by the Americans and fuse a number of explosive charges.

On the morning of 3/3, when the bridge was supposed to be blown, none of the explosives detonated. Now they had to look for another way to destroy the Uerdingen bridge at the last minute.

An officer from the II/PzLehrRgt 130 was able to obtain a truck on the far side of the bridge that was loaded with shells and aerial bombs. In the fire of the pressing U.S. advance guard they were able to drive this truck onto the middle of the bridge. It was then fired on by all of the German artillery. It was set on fire by a direct hit, which finally detonated the aerial bombs with an ear-shattering explosion. The Uerdingen bridge collapsed in the middle and the western section fell into the river. Therefore, in the last second, the smooth crossing of the Americans over the Rhein near Uerdingen was frustrated.

The U.S. forces turned to the north and now rolled on Moers. The panzerjaegers and tanks of the Panzer-Lehr Division that were left behind as rear guard near Hochfeld shot-up a total of 24 enemy tanks. During the following night, as the Panzer-Lehr Division's neighbor withdrew to Homberg, the Panzer-Lehr Division had to close with this movement on the morning of 4/3, if they did not want to be isolated.

The enemy now shifted the main effort of their attack against the bridge-head on the southwestern front, where the Panzer-Lehr Division was engaged in defensive combat. They were able to shoot-up the advancing enemy tanks and hold them at a distance by utilizing air defense guns in ground commitment.

On the morning of 5/3 the enemy committed stronger artillery forces. The U.S. 137th IR, which attacked with armored support, was repulsed, three tanks were left burning on the battlefield. The Panzer-Lehr Division withdrew to a line Rheinberg – Eversael and held here until 7/3/1945. Since the previous day, they were subordinated to the II Fallschirm Corps. Their right neighbor was the 116th PD, which again stood at the focal point of the defensive combat.

The bridgehead was reduced more and more by the energetic enemy attacks. The combat strength of the Panzer-Lehr Division melted down to two tanks. The combat strength of this elite division totaled 600 men. They held their sector from the southern edge of Ossenberg to the Rhein against a manifold superior force.

On 6 March English troops captured the observation post of the 1st Fallschirmjaeger Army on the Boenninghardt in a raid. The bridgehead on the western bank of the Rhein was reduced from an original 30 kilometers to half that size and then to a depth of only 12 kilometers. The enemy continued to fire all of his weapons into this bridgehead without pause. Losses were horrifying.

General Schlemm reported to Army Group B that the bridgehead had to be immediately evacuated if they were still to have a chance to defend on the eastern bank of the river.

Again he was referred to the Fuehrer Order that the Rhein and the bridgehead west of Wesel had been declared to be a fortress.

On 7/3 the OKH, nevertheless, dispatched an observer to the bridgehead, in order to report on the situation. General Schlemm gave this Oberstleutnant plenty of opportunity to be alarmed. In the evening the Oberstleutnant reported the situation to the Fuehrer Headquarters, and a little later General Schlemm had his permission to evacuate the bridgehead.

The evacuation was prepared for immediately. Meanwhile they had to hold the enemy off long enough to cross all of the troops over the Rhein.

One of the rear guards was the assault guns of the fallschirmjaegers under Leutnant Deutsch. They had destroyed one Sherman and one Churchill near Alpen on 6/4 [should be 6/3]. When an enemy armored group fell on the flanks of the fallschirmjaegers crossing the Rhein near Hause Loo, they were repulsed by Leutnant Deutsch's three assault guns. Then even Leutnant Deutsch's men received the order to withdraw across the river.

The fallschirmjaegers had crossed. On the early morning of 10 March the last assault guns rolled behind the rear guard. The clock showed 0400 hours, that was the time General Schlemm had ordered the detonation. However, men, who had held their positions until the very end, were still crossing the river. The engineer officer shifted the time to detonate the Wesel Rhein bridge to 0600 hours and, since foot troops and the last vehicles were still crossing the river, he delayed the detonation time another hour. Then he could wait no longer, enemy tanks were reported approaching.

At exactly 0710 hours on 10/3/1945 he gave the order to detonate. Four large explosives detonated simultaneously. The Wesel railroad bridge rose from its anchoring and fell, breaking into several pieces, into the river.

There were still hundreds waiting rescue on the western bank. They even opened fire on their own engineers, who had eliminated their last chance for rescue.

There were 3000 German soldiers captured in the Buederich area alone. The Wehrmacht report on 11/3/1945 noted:

"In order to utilize the better defensive lines on the right bank of the Rhein, our troops conducted an orderly evacuation of the Wesel bridgehead from the left bank."

With the withdrawal across the Rhein, the region to the east of the river had become the combat zone. The 7th Fallschirmjaeger Division established a defense from Haffen through Diersdorf to Bislich. The 8th Fallschirmjaeger Division took over the Rees area, where the army command post was situated. Volkssturm units closed north of Rees.

In the meantime, the luck of the attackers was holding at another location.

The Bridge at Remagen

On 5 March 1945 the VII U.S. Corps under General Collins reached the city of Cologne. The Rhein bridges here were all destroyed and lay in the river. Nevertheless, the U.S. troops were able to completely occupy Cologne by 7/3, without making it to the eastern bank of the Rhein.

At the same time, the III and V U.S. Corps advanced to the south and southeast toward the Rhein, in order to attack the German formations still located in the Eifel in the flank, while the 3rd U.S. Army attacked this sector frontally.

On the early morning of 7/3/1945 the 9th U.S. AD under Major General Leonard received orders to cross the Ahr near Ahrweiler and Sinzig and, thereby, make contact with the 4th AD of the 3rd U.S. Army.

The battle group under Lieutenant Colonel Engeman, which was the lead formation of the main battle group under Brigadier General Hoge rolled through Remagen and saw a bridge suddenly from the hills west of the Rhein which was not destroyed. This was the Remagen Ludendorf Bridge. Engeman reported over his radio and Brigadier Hoge ordered him to advance immediately and secure the bridge.

Engeman's tanks now rolled through the city and reached the bridge without a fight. Engineers dismounted and hurried to disconnect the explosive cables that they could find. Under the fire cover from a Pershing Tank platoon, which was led by Lieutenant Timmermann, the assault group rolled over the bridge and Sergeant Alex Drabik was the first U.S. soldier to set foot on the right bank of the Rhein at 1600 hours.

From the hills on the far side of the river a German flak battery fired without being able to prevent Battle Group Engeman from crossing. The tanks of Lieutenant Timmermann and Lieutenant Burrows were the first groups to establish themselves. The armored infantry secured the bridgehead on the eastern bank and took German soldiers, who had offered the last resistance, prisoner.

In the meantime, a small explosive was blown up which shook the bridge, but did no visible damage. The fuses to the main lines were cut.

General Hodges immediately received a reply over radio that they were able to secure an undamaged Rhein bridge. The commander of the 1st U.S. Army immediately ordered the 9th AD to roll, in order to establish as large a bridgehead on the eastern bank as possible. After that he made contact with the 12th Army Group in Namur. When he reported to General Bradley, who was at a meeting with the SHAEF officer Brigadier General Bull, he heard Hodges say:

"We have a bridge. Near Remagen, Brad", the commander of the 1st U.S. Army said triumphantly.

"That's the trick, Courtney", Bradley roared back. "We will throw every thing on legs there as quickly as possible."

Bradley ordered contact be made with the headquarters of the Supreme Commander, General Eisenhower, who was located in Reims. Ike discussed

103

meeting with his airborne troop corps and division commanders, who made it possible to cross the Rhein, when Bradley reported this good fortune. Eisenhower also said:

"I cannot believe my ears. We both, Bradley and I, had often discussed that this would be possible under very special circumstances. I almost shouted into the telephone: 'What do you have on hand? What can you get there immediately?'

Bradley said: 'I have four divisions, however, I wanted to first call you and see if it was all right to dispatch them.'

I replied: 'Listen Brad! We have anticipated that a number of divisions would be fixed near Cologne. However, now they are free. Cross at least five divisions over the river as quickly as possible.'

When Bradley replied I could hear how very glad he really was:

'That is exactly what I wanted to do, however, we have to ask ourselves whether this is consistent with the plans. I only wanted to make that clear.'

This was a moment of the war which I was glad to the heart."

On the German side this debacle hit like a bombshell. Unfortunately, there was not one division in the vicinity of the Remagen bridge which could eliminate the enemy who had crossed. 11 hours had passed before the 11th PD, which had crossed the Rhein near Cologne, in order to block the advance on Cologne, could be withdrawn and redeployed in the Remagen area.

On the following day, GFM Kesselring received instructions from the Fuehrer Headquarters to report there immediately. When he asked why, he was only told that the Fuehrer wanted to speak with him.

At midday on 9 March GFM Kesselring arrived in Berlin. At Fuehrer Headquarters he learned from GFM Keitel that Hitler wanted him to replace GFM von Rundstedt in the west. To his remark that the Italian Theater of War needed him, Generaloberst Jodl, who also attended this first meeting, explained to Kesselring that the Fuehrer would not accept this argument. Then Albert Kesselring met personally with Hitler in the afternoon of 9/3. He explained to him that the fall of Remagen demanded a change in the leadership in the Western Theater of War. He Kesselring, was to become the new OB West.

We learn more about this conversation from GFM Kesselring.

"Hitler said that, without laying the blame on von Rundstedt, a younger, more mobile General who has had experience fighting the troops of the Western Powers was needed or the situation in the west would not be mastered." (See Kesselring, Albert: *Soldier Until the Last Day*.)

Hitler described the general situation to Kesselring and explained that the decision in this war would be made in the east and that a collapse there would signify the end and the loss of the war. Therefore, he had recognized too late that all of his efforts in the west in the end brought nothing, only the weakening of the Eastern Front.

"In this situation", Hitler told the Feldmarschall, "there is only one thing left to do, bide time until the 12th Army was created and the new Duesenjaeger and other new weapons could be committed in large numbers. Grossadmiral Doenits will soon be equipped with new U-Boots and will be able to help us."

The mission Hitler gave GFM Kesselring at the end of this personal meeting read:

"Hold! – Hold at any price!"

The Feldmarschall at first was to command anonymously, because his name was to continue to be associated with the fighting in Italy.

From Berlin GFM Kesselring drove to the headquarters of OB West in Ziegenberg. There he was briefed on the situation by the OB West Chief of Staff, General der Kavallerie Westphal. GFM Kesselring made Hitler promise that Westphal, his former Chief of Staff in Italy, would remain his Chief of Staff in the west. Hitler wanted to relieve this troublesome General.

Westphal was able to name for GFM Kesselring the numbers of the 55 divisions committed in the west and their status, because he had made numerous trips to the front. He gave an unvarnished description of the situation to the new OB:

"Since the onslaught of the Soviet winter offensive, OB West has had to give up ten panzer divisions, six infantry divisions, ten artillery corps and eight rocket launcher brigades to the Eastern Front. The infantry divisions now have no more than 50 percent of their required strength and all panzer divisions are particularly weak in tanks."

When Westphal noted that the Feldmarschall was somewhat overcome by the situation report, he asked him what was wrong. Kesselring replied:

"The Fuehrer had briefed me differently."

Westphal referred to the status reports and declared that he requested his immediate relief if the commander did not believe him. He would gladly leave this posting and take up a front command.

"That is out of the question!," replied Kesselring. However, he still did not believe his Chief of Staff. He would not revise his impressions until, during the next few days, he drove to personally visit the various divisions. (See Kurowski, Franz: The Legacy – Siegfried Westphal as Chief of Staff to Three Feldmarschalls.)

During a trip to the front, in the area of the Allied Remagen bridgehead, GFM Kesselring met with GFM Model, the commander of Army Group B. When Kesselring sought to place blame, it is not clear as to how he referenced the names of Keitel and Jodl. Nevertheless, Model exploded and declared icily:

"I do not want to hear of these people anymore!"

However, back to the bridge at Remagen. How did it come to pass that it fell into the hands of the enemy? How come the explosives did not completely detonate. Who was to blame for this disaster that gave the enemy enemy an enormous bridgehead on the eastern bank of the Rhein and, therefore, departure positions for further advances into Germany?

The Germans at Remagen

On the evening of 6 March 1945 it appeared that the U.S. forces had no chance of reaching any of the Rhein bridges before they were sent crashing into the river.

Up to this time the LXVI Army Corps under General Hitzfeld was committed 60 kilometers west of Remagen, Hitzfeld, who had two exhausted divisions, was to conduct an attack against the Americans, who were attacking from Euskirchen in the direction of Bonn and already had mobile reconnaissance formations underway to the Rhein and Remagen.

Army Group B and the OKH believed that the enemy would conduct their main strike there against Bonn and that the enemy forces appearing in the area west of Remagen would only provide the southern flank protection during this attack.

General Hitzfeld was in no position to conduct a counterattack. He saw his most important mission as establishing a new front west of Remagen. The greatest threat to him and his corps was not the American main attack, but the eventual capture of the Remagen bridge by mobile U.S. armored formations.

The Ludendorf Bridge was 325 meters long. It rose from four steel columns on the eastern side of the Rhein near the Erpeler Ley, which the trains had to drive through coming from the west across the bridge. The tunnel, which traversed the Erpeler Ley, was 380 meters long.

General Hitzfeld tried to convince Army Group B several times that, above all, this bridge had to be protected. However, GFM Model stubbornly stuck to his order to counterattack through the Ahrtal.

An hour after midnight on 7/3 Army Group B subordinated the Remagen bridgehead to Corps Hitzfeld, without removing the existing combat missions.

At that time, the corps staff was completely unaware of the conditions in the Remagen bridgehead. General Hitzfeld did not even have any communications to the bridgehead. To see that measures were taken to establish communications the commander sent one of his officers, Major Scheller, to Remagen. The Major received the following instructions from General Hitzfeld personally:

"1. Return to Remagen immediately. Set up an eight man radio station to establish communications with the bridgehead.

2. Form a narrower bridgehead around Remagen with the forces available there, as commandant of Remagen. Expand the bridgehead with formation as they arrive there during the coming days.

3. Survey the technical aspects of the bridge so that the bridge can be blown up.

4. Report to the corps on arrangements made.

5. If necessary, take it upon your own responsibility to issue the order to blow the bridge; at the latest if the enemy makes it to the western side of the bridge."

The corps wanted Major Scheller to try to secure their right flank with the bridgehead.

Scheller was also informed that this bridge was the only bridge left standing in the corps area. This meant that Scheller was to blow the bridge as soon as the corps had crossed the bridge.

It was 0245 hours when Major Scheller parted from his comrades. He told the Corps IA: "This is a Knight's Cross mission!"

At this time there was a bridge security company under the leadership of Hauptmann Willi Bratge in Remagen. There was also an engineer company quartered there. This company was led by Hauptmann Karl Friesenhahn. The latter was bridge commander, while Bratge took command of the bridgehead area.

Defensive weapons stationed in Remagen included: two platoons of four-barreled 2 cm FlaMW on the bridge. On the top of the Erpeler Ley, which rose up on the eastern bank, and in Remagen were also 2 cm FlaMW and several heavy guns. There was a heavy and a light battery and a railroad flak battalion with 2 cm. 3.7 cm and 10.5 cm guns. There was also a light flak battery.

The units under Hauptmann Bratge were equipped with rifles, a few light machine-guns and panzerfaeusten. The bridge security company had a strength of 36 men at the beginning of March. Hauptmann Friesenhahn's engineer company was 120 men strong. The air defenders had a head-count of 200 men. In addition, as flak helpers, there were 180 Hitler Youth. There was also a 20 man Luftwaffen rocket battery.

In the vicinity of the bridge were units of the Volkssturm, 500 men strong. Therefore, the bridgehead had less than 1000 men available with insufficient weapons. There were no heavier weapons available to defend against enemy armored attack.

When the situation became critical at the beginning of March 1945, Generalleutnant Botsch, the Chief of Staff of the 15th Army, received orders to form a battle group. General Botsch, as an old troop commander – he had commanded the 18th Volksgrenadier Division – reported to Army Group B that he needed an entire division and a reinforced regiment to defend Remagen and establish a bridgehead. GFM Model was in no position to give him the required troops. He notified them that only a heavy flak battalion would be made available for Remagen.

Because Botsch received a report from the Army Group that the enemy had appeared between Cologne and Bonn, he transferred his command post half-way between Bonn and Remagen. The command post was supposed to be established in Bonn, however, Botsch was practical and placed it in Dottendorf, 24 kilometers north of Remagen, therefore, it could quickly operate in either direction.

Although General von Bothmer, the combat commandant of Bonn, criticized this command post placement, General von Zangen, the commander of the 15th Army, agreed.

On the afternoon of 5/3 General Botsch visited Remagen, where he learned that not only personnel from the Reich labor camps had been withdrawn there, but there was also an air communications company in Remagen. Several flak units, which were supposed to be located west of the Rhein, had arrived on the eastern bank. Generalleutnant Botsch hammered into Hauptmann Friesenhahn and the commander of the Volkssturm battalion, Major Moellering, what to do in case the enemy was to appear suddenly. The General was still responsible for the blowing of the bridge. Hauptmann Friesenhahn, as the engineer officer, was asked under which circumstances he could guarantee the destruction of this bridge. He replied that it alone depended upon how long the army group needed the bridge for the withdrawal of its troops.

When Generalleutnant Botsch left Remagen he was convinced that the city and the bridge were in good hands. On the evening of 5/3 he reported on the situation in the Remagen area telephonically to GFM Model and when Model asked him directly how he saw the situation there, Botsch said:

> "It is similar to Bonn. I have a bridge security company and a Volkssturm battalion at both bridges, however, there is much too little flak and heavy weapons."

Model asked the Generalleutnant to wait on the telephone. He hurried to his Chief of Staff and requested a heavy flak battalion for Remagen from the air defense officer of the army group. Then he returned to the telephone.

> "Listen, Herr Botsch, after you get a flak battalion and another alert company will you have enough?"

General Botsch protested:

> "I need heavy weapons and a reinforced regiment for Remagen."

"I cannot give you that", replied the Feldmarschall as he replaced the receiver.

Subsequently General Botsch discussed the question of the technical preparations for blowing the bridge with the army group's engineer commander, General Wirtz.

General Wirtz told him that it was necessary to place three to four explosive charges on the eastern side.

General Botsch later informed Hauptmann Bratge and Hauptmann Friesenhahn about this.

On 6 March the 15th Army – as already described – suffered a heavy setback. That army had 75,000 men available divided into seven divisions. In addition they had Battle Group Botsch.

It was the 9th U.S. AD, which tore through the weak German front on 6/3 and by evening reached the edge of Meckenheim. Therefore, they stood only 18 kilometers west of the Rhein. The attempt of the army commander, General von Zangen, to order the two divisions of the LXVI Army Corps under General Hitzfeld to close the gap torn in the center of his defensive front failed.

Major Scheller, who was ordered by General Hitzfeld to the bridgehead at Remagen, arrived there on 7/3/1945 and informed Hauptmann Bratge that he was the new bridge commandant. The radio troops he was to bring had to stop to refuel on the way, then they were prevented from continuing by strong enemy fire, so Scheller arrived at Remagen without them. Therefore, as before, Remagen still had no communications with corps.

Scheller learned that the detonation of the bridge had been postponed, but the explosives for the main detonation had been already installed. All of the preparations to quickly detonate the eastern bank, as ordered by General Wirtz, were completed by Hauptmann Friesenhahn. The fuses were laid to the installed explosives. Only 500 kilograms of TNT, which had been promised, had not yet arrived.

Nevertheless, as Scheller was to learn later, there was only 300 kilograms of Dolorit available. This was only a quarter of the necessary explosive charge, because Dolorit was weaker than TNT.

While Hauptmann Bratge was still briefing Major Scheller, enemy tanks appeared on the western bank of the river, in front of the bridge. When Bratge proposed securing the right bank of the Rhein with the available troops, Scheller replied that his mission was to defend the left bank of the bridgehead.

In the next few hours he tried to obtain the necessary forces. He stopped forces that were crossing the railroad bridge in front of the advancing enemy. However, they were not in unified units, only individuals were obtained in this manner.

At 1200 hours Major Scheller issued orders to make the bridge ready for destruction. Enemy troops were reported as being only two kilometers west of Remagen.

Lieutenant Colonel Leonard Engeman, battle group leader of the 9th AD's advance detachment, had received orders from General Hoge on the morning of 7/3 to roll in the direction of a city at the speed of ten miles an hour, the city was Remagen. The armored infantry company under Lieutenant Timmermann and A Company of the 14th Armored Battalion under Captain Soumas set out at 0630 hours. They were already taking fire from Fritzdorf after advancing only 1.6 kilometers. This resistance was broken by the massive commitment of American machine-gun fire. They continued on to Overich.

Here a German Landser was firing a panzerfaust. The half-track he fired at immediately was set ablaze. A platoon of tanks under Lieutenant Grimball moved forward and cleared the way. The first German prisoners were captured and sent off in the direction of the division rear.

A village appeared in front of them. Out of the windows of the first houses fluttered white bed sheets as white flags.

When they reached Niederich, a group of Landser quickly retreated. The pursuing U.S. vehicles fired after them with automatic weapons. They reached Birresdorf. It was only a half kilometer further to Remagen.

Platoon Leader Lieutenant Burrows saw that the Germans were withdrawing across the bridge and reported this to his company commander with the words: "that was an objective for us, Lieutenant!"

"Okay", he said, "move the mortar platoon into position. Prepare to fire on the bridge and report to Lieutenant Colonel Engeman by radio, he will want to throw in his tanks and dispatch artillery."

The order was overtaken by events. Several minutes later the commander appeared, followed by Major Deevers, the commander of the 27th Armored Infantry Battalion. They now saw for themselves that the bridge was intact and that there were still soldiers and civilians with cows and horses crossing the bridge to the east.

Major Deevers now summoned the commanders of A and C Companies, Timmermann and Lieutenant William E. McMaster.

"Tim, Mac, conduct a reconnaissance up to Remagen and give me your report immediately."

A courier accompanied the two officers over the 500 meters of hills on a footpath to Remagen. They were not fired at. However, they saw much activity on the other side and the great gaping entrance to the tunnel. Engineers were working there and what they were doing was very clear. They hurried back and reported to Major Deevers.

In the meantime, Major Ben Cothran, General Hoge's Operations Officer, had also arrived. He reported to the division commander over voice radio that the enemy was preparing to blow the intact bridge. Major General Hoge replied breathlessly:

"Speed, speed and more speed! I think it will be pretty good for all of us if we can snatch the bridge intact. Get going!"

The first mobile U.S. units stormed Remagen. Opposite the labor camp the German Unteroffizier Gerhard Rothe was in position with a group from the bridge security company. When the attackers appeared in front of his group, Rothe assaulted with his men over the hill, in order to separate the machine-gun vehicles from the attackers. However, the enemy had already opened fire. Unteroffizier Rothe reported to Hauptmann Bratge that the enemy had penetrated into Remagen. He had been shot in the leg. The Americans continued to advance.

At this time Major Scheller was still located on the left bank of the Rhein, trying to organize the defense of the bridgehead. At 1400 hours the first enemy tanks of the 9th U.S. AD took up suitable firing positions and opened fire on the bridge. The first shells cracked into the bridge planks and tore them apart, without causing any serious damage. In this manner, the Americans wanted to prevent the German engineers from setting additional explosives.

A little later these tanks rolled toward Remagen. In the lead was Timmermann's company. Lieutenant Fred Rango, who was the only German speaker, learned here from the civilians that the bridge over the river was to be destroyed at 1600 hours. He immediately reported this information back and received orders to immediately report it to Lieutenant Colonel Engeman.

It was already 1430 hours when Major Scheller and Hauptmann Bratge returned to the eastern bank. The combat commandant's command post was also transferred to the eastern bank. They moved it into the tunnel behind the bridge.

Exactly 45 minutes prior an artillery commander appeared before Major Scheller and requested that he wait to blow up the bridge, because his artillery battalion would arrive at any moment to take up new defensive positions.

Major Scheller agreed, his main mission was not to blow the bridge, but to secure the withdrawal of the LXVI Army Corps across the bridge.

By 1430 hours not one man from this corps had crossed the bridge. The stream of withdrawing infantry formations was blocked.

At 1435 hours Hauptmann Friesenhahn fused the explosives in Remagen itself, which was to render the access-ramp to the bridge impassible. Then he withdrew his engineers back across the bridge, trailed by American machine-gun fire. He and his men reached the tunnel on the eastern bank in good condition. Here Hauptmann Bratge implored him to also fuse the main explosive charges. It was at 1450 hours that Hauptmann Friesenhahn refused to fuse the main charges, because Major Scheller reserved this for himself.

Scheller had decided to wait a little longer. "The corps had to arrive soon and cross the bridge before it was blown", he thought.

By 1520 hours still not one soldier from the LXVI Corps had arrived. Scheller now ordered the detonation. Hauptmann Friesenhahn issued the necessary instructions and awaited the "thunderous explosion of the main detonation" in the tunnel at 1540 hours. However, only a weak crack occurred. The main detonation had failed. It was incomprehensible, the fuses were last inspected at 1500 hours and found to be completely in order.

"Emergency explosives!" ordered Hauptmann Friesenhahn.

The engineers now made an attempt with the remnants of the industrial Dolorit explosives. However, the resulting explosion only raised the bridge a little; it fell back to its original position undamaged. It remained standing. Major Scheller had fulfilled his duty one-hundred percent by ordering the detonation. It was not his fault that it did not work.

The reason for the failure of the main detonation could not be clarified. Several witnesses said that the main cable was severed by rifle fire. There was also the possibility of sabotage, however, no proof was ever found for this assumption. The possibility that the main explosive charges were destroyed by artillery or tank fire cannot be ruled out.

In Remagen the U.S. soldiers prepared to cross the river. They were not particularly enthusiastic about making the jump across the river. Several had even suggested that the Germans were faking and that they would blow the bridge into the air as soon as enough of them had gotten on to it. Major Deevers ordered Lieutenant Timmermann to cross the bridge with his company. Timmermann, who was born in Germany, gave the order to attack and General Hoge, who quickly hurried to the sight, watched from the hill opposite the Erpeler Lay as A Company set out. When Timmermann's men made it to the middle of the bridge, it raised up a little. Steel creaked, some powder smoke rose into the air. Several GI's hit the ground, others covered their faces with their hands and waited for the end. However, nothing more happened. The bridge was still standing.

"Everybody, behind me!" shouted Timmermann. The weapons in their hands opened fire. Two vehicles rolled forward. The lead tanks under Lieutenant Grimball stopped to fire from the bridge at the two bridge towers, from where machine-guns were being fired. The tank shells slammed directly into the towers under the machine-guns. The machine-guns were silenced. The men advanced further. The American Shermans opened fire in the rear. Timmermann assaulted against a dark trench from where shots were still being fired. There was still a pair of Landser firing from the two bridge towers, until they were shot out of them.

Major Scheller and Hauptmann Bratge, who were located forward near the first machine-gun positions, saw the U.S. tanks rumble across the bridge. To their right and left sprang other forms, rushing forward. Machine-gun fire slammed against the walls of the tunnel, several salvoes penetrated into the tunnel. Women and children and the elderly, who had fled into the tunnel, began to scream.

"Stop! Stop! This is senseless!" screamed one of the men. However, Major Scheller ordered Bratge to assemble the soldiers for a counterattack. The first tank shells were already detonating in the tunnel. The racket developed into chaos. Accompanied by two lieutenants Scheller rushed to the tunnel entrance. He saw that the enemy had already crossed 17 tanks over the bridge, while others were still rolling across.

When Hauptmann Bratge saw that the Americans had already placed the far side of the tunnel opening under fire and that the civilians there were waving white handkerchiefs, he stopped fighting. Major Scheller was no longer to be seen. Bratge ordered a cease fire and also made a white flag ready, then he emerged from the tunnel weaponless and with his hands raised.

The enemy also stopped firing, and suddenly stillness descended over the bridge and its immediate vicinity. Only the groaning of the wounded and the whining of the children in the tunnel could still be heard.

A light air defense battery continued to fire from the Erpeler Ley and machine-guns were still firing from the roof of the Hotel Waldburg, which did not have any effect, because they were too far away.

A platoon of light U.S. tanks rolled up the hill under Lieutenant Demetri and fired on the hotel.

From his forward command post Lieutenant Colonel Engeman called General Hoge at 1700 hours and reported the conquest of the Remagen bridge and that his battle group was already across and had established their first bridgehead on the far side of the tunnel. Major General Hoge drove back to Birresdorf and called General Leonard.

In the meantime, engineers neutralized the un-detonated main explosive charges. Therefore, the Americans had won an undamaged Rhein crossing and began to thrown their divisions across.

However, what happened to the LXVI Army Corps, which Major Scheller had waited for so long – so long – at this bridgehead?

Major Scheller looked for the corps. He wanted his report to get out as soon as possible so that countermeasures could be taken as soon as possible. In Remagen and to the east he found no communications. He looked for a vehicle so that he could get to a functioning communications site, however, he did not find one. (Several days later, Major Scheller was courtmartialed by the Germans and shot.)

On the morning of 7/3/1945 the LXVI Army Corps had been pushed back a considerable distance by the attacking American divisions. The corps command post had been located in Brueck for a couple of hours, however, it had to relocate to Degenbach in the early morning of 8/3 and, on 9/3, it had to withdraw to Broehl. There it was overrun by U.S. armored formations and the commander, General Hitzfeld, had to fight his way back to the Rhein through the forest with his staff on foot. He crossed the river with his staff near Andernach during the night of 10/3 and set up his command post near Altwied. The troops of his corps crossed the river on rafts and ferries.

Therefore, the front on the left of the Rhein collapsed.

On the morning of 8 March, when Hitler was informed of the fall of the Ludendorf Bridge, he suffered a tantrum and declared that the blame could only be laid with his officers, and they had to be found and tried for History's sake. He ordered the establishment of a flying court. This was set up on the same day. Hitler ordered General Huebner to sit it. Oberstleutnant Penth and Oberstleutnant Ehrnsperger from OKH were ordered to accompany him.

By this time, U.S. troops of the 9th AD, the 9th and 210th ID had already crossed the bridge and established a deep bridgehead. Engineers had already built a temporary ponton bridge across the river.

Nine hours passed on 8/3 before the 11th German PD was organized in the Remagen area.

GFM Kesselring now had to try to destroy this strong enemy bridge-head. As the new OB West, Hitler though he had the right personality to change the fates in the west.

The Battle for One Bridge

After General der Kavallerie Westphal had briefed his old and new commanders and they were convinced of the status of the divisions by making trips to the front, the GFM and the Chief of Staff drove to the 15th Army headquarters. There General der Infanterie von Zangen gave a report on the situation in the 15th Army area of operations. General von Zangen then briefed on the status of all measures that he had taken to remove the Remagen bridgehead. They admitted that the strength of the enemy on the eastern bank of the Rhein in the Remagen bridgehead was two U.S. infantry divisions and one armored division, with their subordinate and attached artillery formations.

Kesselring's visit to the Luftwaffenkommando West command post on 10/3 was just as unpleasant as his visit to the 15th Army. General der Flieger Schmidt maintained that the air situation was catastrophic.

On the late afternoon on this depressing day GFM Kesselring drove to Emmerich, in order to hear the bad news from General der Fallschirmtruppe Schlemm at his 1st Fallschirmjaeger Army command post. Both men knew each other from Italy. General Schlemm gave an unvarnished report that the enemy had occupied the western bank of the Rhein and was conducting air attacks with strong air forces.

Subsequently Generaloberst Blaskowitz, the commander of Army Group H reported to OB West about the situation on his front and finally General der Infanterie Blumentritt, the commander of the 25th Army reported on the heavy fighting expected to develop in his area.

When GFM Kesselring left the command post in Emmerich he was a little more confident. The troops and their commanders were in order and good shape. Kesselring had complete trust in the leadership of the fallschirmjaegers and in these troops themselves.

He finished up with visits to Army Group G in the Rheinpfalz and also to the 7th and 1st Armies. GFM Kesselring described the situation in this area as follows:

"Strong enemy concentrations in the Remagen area and in front of the 1st Army on either side of Saarbruecken. – Indications of strong main effort building by the American 3rd Army in front of the right flank of the 7th Army and in front of the 1st Fallschirmjaeger Army. Continuous attacks by the 1st U.S. Army south of Trier."

In his precise way, the Feldmarschall said of the rest of the frontal sector:

"The enemy is neglecting the Holland front (in the 25th Army area of operations), the Rhein axis forward of the Ruhr region (5th Panzer Army) and the Oberrhein front (19th Army).

Enemy intentions: Exploit the windfall success at Remagen and separate northern and southern Germany by rapidly attacking out of the Remagen bridgehead to the east and establish contact with the Soviets.

Subsequent: Attack past the west Rhein bastion of Saarpfalz, in order to destroy Army Group G and secure the Rhein crossing as the departure base for operations against southern Germany.

Subsequent: English attack to force a crossing of the Rhein in the fallschirmjaeger army area and establish a bridgehead which would give operational possibilities in three directions." (See: Kesselring, Albert: *Soldier Until the Last Day.*)

When Kesselring was again summoned to the Fuehrer Headquarters on 15/3, he briefed Hitler on this assessment. During this meeting with Hitler he was able to obtain permission to withdraw the right flank of the 1st Army from the West Wall.

This portion of the army was to transition to the defensive on a new line. Therefore, GFM Kesselring initiated the withdrawal of Army Group G.

The Course of the Operation

On the morning of 9/3 GFM Model appeared at the headquarters of the LIII Corps in Oberpleis. Generalleutnant Bayerlein met the commander of Army Group B and, as was his wont, GFM Model got right to the point.

"Bayerlein, your corps is committed on the Remagen bridgehead. I will give you 24 hours to assemble the Panzer-Lehr Division, the 9th and 11th Panzer Divisions and attack. Your formations must be rolling on 10 March!"

General Bayerlein tried to attack with all formations at the same time. However, Hitler had just issued an order to attack "immediately and with all available formations." However, this split the offensive strength of the corps and frustrated all attempts to collapse the bridgehead.

Battle Group Hudel, a panzer formation under the command of Oak Leaves winner Major Helmut Hudel, took over the assembled battle group of the Panzer-Lehr Division on 9/3 and rolled against the bridgehead. The formation consisted of 16 Panzer V's, ten Panzer IV's and ten Jagdpanthers, of which 20 were operational.

Major Hudel paved the way through the swarming enemy scout troops into the departure position. As soon as he had reached Assembly Area Erl, Generalleutnant Bayerlein ordered him to attack from there on the following morning at 0800 hours.

His mission was to split the bridgehead and then roll over it. The fact that he would be unable to accomplish such a mission with his few tanks was even clear to Bayerlein. However, that was the order that he had received and it was not changed.

It was difficult for Battle Group Hudel to reach the deployment area on time. The march route was damaged by Allied bombing attacks and, moreover, there were troop units and refugees all over.

The attack was called off by GFM Model, because the day ended with the complete destruction of Battle Group Hudel by fighter-bombers and artillery fire.

GFM Model ordered the establishment of an encirclement ring around the bridgehead and to await stronger forces, which was what Generalleutnant Bayerlein had proposed on 9/3.

Therefore, the chance to hit the enemy at their point of maximum confusion had been lost. The individual battle groups had to reach the encirclement front as they were committed against the U.S. formations coming out of the bridgehead.

The enemy attacked here without pause. He reinforced himself more and more and, on 10/3, was able to occupy Honnef in the north of the bridgehead and, on the following day, Linz in the south. Only in the east, where there was thick forest in which several battalions were inserted with anti-tank guns, air defense guns and panzerfaeusten, was the enemy prevented from advancing quickly.

On the morning of 11/3 Battle Group Hudel was given to the 11th PD and transferred to the southern flank of the LIII Panzer Corps in the direction of Dattenberg. Here, at the last minute, they were able to help some engineers, who had taken over the Rhein defense. The enemy attack to the south, which was conducted against these troops with tanks, was stopped by Hudel's tanks, who shot up the lead enemy vehicles, which stopped the follow-on vehicles and forced them to return to their departure positions.

From the few tanks, which were rolling in the platoons and companies of Battle Group Hudel, was formed Panzer Brigade Buttlar, which was commanded by Generalmajor Buttlar.

Dattenberg was held by Battle Group Hudel. South of this location ran the boundary to the LXVII Army Corps and its 26th Volksgrenadier Division.

When, on the morning of 13/3, the enemy attacked here with strong armored forces, they were able to achieve a deep penetration into the front of this division. This also led to the threat of Battle Group Hudel being isolated. They now had to withdraw their left flank.

In the meantime, Hitler ordered the bridge to be placed under heavy long-range artillery fire, because the enemy was preparing to breakout of the bridgehead. However, even the artillery could not collapse the solid bridge. On the morning of 17/3 bomber forces were flown against the bridge.

One aircraft was able to drop its load very close to the damaged bridge column. The column collapsed and the bridge at Remagen fell into the river. However, this success no longer influenced the crossing operations, which had expanded the bridgehead up to the Reich autobahn near Wullscheid by this time. In the protection of this bridgehead, the American engineers were able to construct a treadway ponton bridge across the Rhein. The corps engineer commander, Colonel J. Young, began the construction after the VII U.S. Corps had made it completely across the Ludendorff Bridge and was able to provide the engineers protection. Colonel Young bet General Collins, the commander of the VII Corps, that he could complete a bridge in less than 12 hours. The bet was over a pair of cases of Champagne, which the corps commander had been carrying since France. Colonel Young won this bet. The bridge stood in 10 hours and 11 minutes.

Additional U.S. Action in the Shadow of Remagen

The 3rd U.S. Army under General Patton, which, during the weeks of February, had prepared to destroy the German formations north of the Mosel, had already penetrated into Trier on 3 March. A strong bridgehead was established over the Kyll by formations of the XII U.S. Corps under Lieutenant General Eddy. After that General Patton turned two armored wedges loose to breakthrough. He committed his VIII Corps with the 65th, 87th and 89th Infantry Divisions in an attack to the northeast. At the same time, his XII Corps with the 26th and 71st Infantry Divisions and the 11th AD attacked along the northern bank of the Mosel. The direction of attack was to the northeast. These six fresh American divisions received special units, including armor. The 7th German Army, which they opposed, had to withdraw between Koblenz and Trier. In order to cover the rear of the 1st Army, which was located to their south, they had to establish a new defense on the Rhein. The Allied air forces attacked without pause so that the 3rd U.S. Army would reach its objective.

On 9/3 the VIII U.S. Corps reached Andernach and, therefore, the Rhein. Ten days later both corps joined up with the southern flank of the 1st U.S.

Army. The German 5th Panzer Army could only withdraw remnant formations across the Rhein. Therefore, the Allies had reached the western bank of the Rhein from Emmerich in the north to Koblenz in the south. The only corner-stone of the defense now standing was the 1st German Army in the western foreground of the river, while the Americans continued to expand the large bridgehead near Remagen every day.

The northern flank of the 1st German Army was widely torn by the repeated attacks of the 2nd U.S. Army. The gaps could only temporarily be patched by troops of the 7th Army. This was the departure area from which General Eisenhower could order the destruction of the German troops still located in the Saar region. The lead elements of these German formations still stood 130 kilometers west of the Rhein. They were now to be destroyed in the third phase of Eisenhower's three-phased plan. Eisenhower assigned the 7th U.S. Army under Lieutenant General Patch to attack out of the south toward the German Saar bastion. In addition, three fresh divisions came from the USA, indeed they were not combat experienced, however, they were 100% equipped. Therefore, the combat strength of the attacking army and the neighboring troops totaled 15 divisions. Moreover, there was also a subordinate French infantry division and the 3rd Algerian Division. On 15 March, as the bridgehead near Remagen was being consolidated, the attack against the Saar troops was initiated. The attack occurred in the south and the elements of the 1st Army located there withdrew to Bitsch and Hagenau, in order to be able to hold the West Wall. The request of the army leadership to deploy several fresh divisions or to release them from their defensive commitments and allow them to withdraw gradually to the Rhein, was turned down by Hitler. Here also the will of the Fuehrer was to treat the western Rhein as a fortress.

The 1st German Army could not hold the West Wall. Between Saarbruecken and Zweibruecken the 7th U.S. Army achieved a deep penetration. At the same time, the 3rd U.S. Army under General Patton attacked out of its Trier bridgehead to the south and southwest. Their objective was to fix in the rear and cut off the Saar defense between Merzig and Saarbruecken. Two additional attack groups were assembled by Patton near Zell and Cochem to cross the Mosel, breakthrough the weak forces of the

7th German Army and, together with the 7th Army, complete the destruction of all German troops between the Mosel and the Rhein.

The daytime attacks of the American air formations continued without halt, their fighter-bombers had a devastating effect when they flew in deep attack over the German positions and batteries and dropped their high-explosive rocket bombs.

Patton's armored wedges boxed their way through to Ludwigshafen, while the 7th U.S. Army penetrated across the Pirmasens – Landau road to the north. The two German armies west of the Rhein had only two bridge-heads and two river crossings. One lay near Germersheim, the second near Karlsruhe.

The remnants of the two German armies rolled and marched to the east. On 25 March these last bridgeheads were also taken by the enemy, after which the remnants had to fight their way through and take up the defense as a rear guard across the river.

The Allies had reached the Rhein along the entire length of Germany.

Besides Remagen, a bridgehead was also established on the eastern bank of the Rhein near Oppenheim. Patton ordered his 5th AD to cross the river. This was during the evening hours of 22 March, and Patton called his superior on the telephone:

> "Brad, all of the world must know that the 3rd Army was able to cross before Monty in the north!"

On the morning of 23/3 the new situation was discussed in the Fuehrer Headquarters in Berlin. Hitler declared this second bridgehead near Oppenheim as the worst thing that could have happened and asked what panzer forces were nearby to strike at this bridgehead. He learned that there were only five Tiger tanks in Sennelager. They could be thrown at the crossing site. All of the rest of the formations were committed in combat and could not be removed.

Therefore, the foresight of the staff of the 1st Army came to fruition. General Foertsch, the commander of the 1st Army, who had commanded all troops in the Rheinpalz since 21/3, received orders through GFM

Kesselring on 23/3 to evacuate the bridgeheads of Speyer, Germersheim and Maxau, which were still on the western bank of the Rhein. The General executed this withdrawal operation by 25/3, salvaging what he could.

When Hitler wanted to relieve General Foertsch and his Chief of Staff, General Hauser, OB West stood up for them and told Hitler:

"The 1st Army command under its commander, General der Infanterie Foertsch, and its Chief of Staff, General Hauser, has distinguished itself in its decisiveness and authoritativeness."

During the night before 23/3 the Americans completed their crossing of the Rhein near Oppenheim, giving the enemy the possibility of operating in the rear of the 1st German Army, which was still located west of the Rhein, and also for new operations in central Germany behind the Frankfurt basin.

As Remagen was the swan song for Army Group B, so was the Oppenheim bridgehead for Army Group G.

On 30 March General der Infanterie Obsfelder took command of the 7th German Army. To him fell the decisive mission of at least delaying the advance of the 3rd U.S. Army into central Germany and the attack of the 7th U.S. Army into southern Germany. They could not prevent this, because their strength was too weak, they lacked panzer troops and artillery.

At this point in time, the 7th German Army stood forward of Hersfeld and Fulda and in the Spessart. The 1st German Army was withdrawn to the Miltenberg – Eberbach – Heidelberg positions on 30/3. Therefore, the construction of the Tauber Positions was threatened.

On 17/3, after the destruction of the Ludendorff Bridge, there were no further decisive attacks against the Remagen bridgehead. Several local attacks brought some success, however, they were eliminated by the enemy within 24 hours. The U.S. troops attacking out of the bridgehead reached the Wied on 17/3, throwing mobile forces across and establishing another advanced bridgehead near Waldbreitbach.

The 3rd PGD and the 340th Volksgrenadier Division, which were committed against the bridgehead, were, indeed, able to hold the enemy, however, they were unable to compress it. On the contrary: at midday of 20 March, as soon as the 11th German PD was removed from the front, the enemy penetrated into the German positions, attacked through them and, therefore, tore through the encirclement belt. Battle Group Hudel could no longer take part in the fighting here, because it also was removed during the evening and marched to the north.

The 5th Panzer Army, which was now commanded by Generaloberst Harpe, because General der Panzertruppe von Manteufel was ordered to the Eastern Front, was able to hold its positions.

On the morning of 22/3, when it became clear that the enemy intended to breakout, GFM Model ordered the assembly of all freed-up panzer formations in the area south of the Sieg. From there they were to launch a concentrated attack to the west to stop the further advance of the enemy. Again it was the lack of fuel that delayed the execution of this order.

In the meantime, the Panzer-Lehr Division under the command of the XII SS Panzer Corps was being refitted in the greater Duesseldorf area. On 21/3 even it was ordered to commitment in the Corps Bayerlein area of operations. By the evening of 23/3 the combat effective elements of the division reached the area south of Eitorf, with the division command post in Irlenborn. There, on the evening of this day, also reported Battle Group Hudel, after executing its previous mission. After this commitment they had only six tanks left. 15 Jagdpanthers from the 654th Panzerjaeger Battalion were subordinated to it as reinforcement.

The Road to the Ruhr Pocket

On 22/3/1945 the 1st U.S. Army launched its first probing attacks out of the Remagen bridgehead to the east. These attacks ran into elements of the 15th Army, which had been in heavy defensive combat for days. All of the German artillery in front of the bridgehead suffered from chronic ammunition shortages.

The sector around Wied was lost to the Americans on the first day of the attack. The southern flank of the 15th Army was forced back into the Dasbach-Bendorf line.

On 23/3 the U.S. attacks relaxed somewhat. In the meantime, the bridge-head was expanded to a breadth of 48 kilometers and stretched from Bonn to Neuwied. Its greatest depth reached 16 kilometers. The front ran on a line Siegburg-Breitscheid-Isenberg-Hoer-Grenzhausen-Vallendar.

Army Group B now ordered the 15th Army to remove the 11th PD and the Panzer-Lehr Division and form a heavy panzer group out of the 506th and 512th Heavy Panzer Battalions (King Tigers and Tigers), as well as from the 654th Panzerjaeger Battalion. it would be led by combat commandant Hudel, who had already proven to be a trustworthy battle group commander. Hudel, who was awarded the Oak Leaves to the Knight's Cross of the Iron Cross as commander of the I/Pr 7, was one of the most experienced panzer commanders and was well known by all of the soldiers in the battle group.

In the 5th Panzer Army area of operations on the northern flank of the bridgehead it remained quiet. There the enemy appeared to be only holding.

OB West reported to the armies in his area that the enemy had established another bridgehead on the eastern bank of the Rhein in the Army Group Center[?] area of operations near Oppenheim. He ordered Army Group B to immediately set the 11th PD in march to Frankfurt, where it would be subordinated to Army Group G. The division set out on the early morning of 24/3 to the south.

On 25/3 artillery fire in the bridgehead area increased considerably. Enemy air activity also increased. After that the American armored formations initiated the breakout in several strong battle groups. First there were deep penetrations on the seam between the LIII Corps and the LXXVI Army Corps as well as in the LXVII Army Corps sector.

The immediate commitment of the panzer reserves of the Panzer-Lehr Division and Battle Group Hudel could no longer stop the indicated breakthrough in the direction of Altenkirchen. It was the VII U.S. Corps that began its attack here and advanced on Altenkirchen with the 1st and 104th Infantry Divisions and the 3rd AD as the spearhead.

Therefore, the enemy was not moving to the north – as assumed – but was striking directly to the east.

The mission of Army Group B was still to hold the Rhein front as well as the bridgehead front, even though enemy contact with the neighboring army group indicated a withdrawal to a prepared line to avoid the threat of being outflanked.

The likewise inflexible order to construct a unified front before the Remagen bridgehead was also no longer necessary after the breakout of the enemy. Therefore, GFM Model ordered the 5th Panzer Army to remove the 12th Volksgrenadier Division and the 176th ID from their front and deploy them to Army Group B.

The gaps in the front of the 15th Army were to be closed by counterattacks in such a manner that a unified front was reestablished. If this was accomplished, then they would gain time to insert the two divisions removed from the 5th Panzer Army into the gaps in the defensive front of the 15th Army and finally unify the front.

There was still no indication that the Allies were to attempt to force a crossing of the Rhein in the 5th Panzer Army area of operations.

The deep enemy penetrations in the 15th Army area of operations could not be closed, especially since the two corps had very little artillery support and no panzer formations available.

Taking advantage of this, the enemy attacked through with strong armored formations to the east. The general direction of the 1st U.S. Army with the VII Corps was the Herborn – Marburg area and Giessen on the Lahn. The two German formations from the 15th Army, the LXXIV Army Corps south of Altenkirchen and the LXVII Army Corps northwest of Limburg, were threatened by armored wedges and had already been partially attacked through by them.

The LIII Corps Bayerlein was unable to maintain contact with the LXXIV Army Corps during this fighting, but was pushed further back to the northeast and now stood south of the Sieg.

Meanwhile, the tanks of the 3rd U.S. AD attacked to the east on the morning of 26/3. They bypassed the forward positions of their own 1st and 104th Infantry Divisions, rolled forward and, by the end of the day, achieved a ground gain of 20 kilometers. Road blocks, that appeared in front of them, were shot up and overcome by the following artillery or, if they did not close in time, by the tanks.

Army Group B reported to OB West that the enemy had broken out of the Remagen bridgehead to the east and requested new instructions. Since they were not forthcoming, the old order concerning the Rhein defense was adhered to, even though it had already been overtaken by events. On his own, GFM Model decided to remove the 5th Panzer Army, which was still located on the Rhein, and regroup it for another commitment.

The morning of 26/3 saw the continuation of the attack of the 1st U.S. Army with the VII Corps, which gained the Altenkirchen area. The 3rd U.S. AD attacked here into fierce German resistance. German tanks and artillery stopped the American attack. It did not resume until they committed their fighter-bomber formations, which shot-up and destroyed a number of tanks and vehicles.

While the main body of the VII U.S. Corps was stuck west of Altenkirchen, two armored battle groups bypassed to the right and left of Altenkirchen. The 104th U.S. ID, which followed close on the heels of the 3rd AD, cleared out the German nests of resistance, which did not hold up the armored advance.

On 27/3 the American breakthrough was a fact. By the evening of this day the divisional battle groups of the 3rd AD were able to cross the Dill and reach the Herborn. After quickly refuelling and resupplying with ammunition, the individual battle groups continued their advance. The main battle group reached Dillenburg.

The remaining divisions of the 1st U.S. Army, which were advancing to the northeast and southeast, reached their objectives by evening of this day.

Meanwhile, on 28/3, the lead formations of the 1st and 3rd U.S. Armies met near Giessen. Therefore, all of the forces from the 15th Army located in the area between Lahn and Main and the adjacent 1st Army of Army Group G were encircled.

After this success the U.S. attack wedge, which had broken out of the Remagen bridgehead, advanced 144 kilometers. From the Sieg in the north to the Main in the south, all of this area was now in American hands.

At the same time, in the north, the 21st Army Group under Field Marshal Montgomery was also advancing to the east. The 9th U.S. Army, which was still subordinated to Montgomery, formed a strong and rapidly advancing pincer army in the north, opposite the 1st U.S. Army in the south. They were destined to outflank the Ruhr region, penetrate far to the east and encircle and destroy German Army Group B. (For more on the attack of the 21st Army Group across the Rhein and further to the east see the next chapter.)

On 29/3 the leadership of Army Group B recognized the fact that they could not avoid being encircled. Indeed, the 5th Panzer Army with the XII SS Corps still held a security line along the Ruhr, from the Moehnetal block up to the confluence of this river into the Rhein and there was still a Rhein front from Leverkusen to Duesseldorf and Duisburg. However, since the situation worsened dramatically on the southern flank, and it was also known that the enemy was turning to the north after reaching Marburg, and, therefore, turning into the rear of the troops on the Rhein, the situation was critical for troops remaining on the Rhein.

The army group leadership learned from OB West, GFM Kesselring, through restored telephone communications, that the enemy was advancing with the 9th U.S. Army through Duelmen in the direction of Muenster and that the 1st U.S. Army was penetrating some elements in the direction of Fulda and others in the direction of Kassel. The 3rd U.S. Army was also underway with strong formations in the direction of Kassel.

Nevertheless, the senior leadership refused to withdraw the order for OB West to hold on the Rhein. After being oriented on the situation, a Fuehrer Order was finally issued, it said:

> "Each withdrawal, each surrender of a village is forbidden under pain of death. In every large populated area a responsible commandant is to be assigned who will be responsible for carrying out this order."

The entire Ruhr pocket was, therefore, declared a fortified place.

On 29 and 30/3 the U.S. troops attacked to the north between Marburg in the west and the area 50 kilometers south of Fritzlar in the east. The VII U.S. Corps formed the western flank. The III U.S. Corps attacked in the center and the XX U.S. Corps rolled on the eastern flank. The attack direction was from west to east: Winterberg, Korbach, Warburg and Kassel.

The command post of the 15th Army was still located on the Biedenkopf, on the northern bank of the Lahn. A little later, this command post was cut off and General von Zangen sat in a trap with his entire staff and the army communications battalion. They lacked communications with Corps Floerke under Generalleutnant Hermann Floerke and with Army Group B. General von Zangen ordered:

"Fight through to Army Group B!"

At first the encircled group was unable to leave their stretch of woods southwest of the Biedenkopf, because it was swarming with U.S. troops and they would be immediately recognized during the day. However, here in the forest they were able to reestablish communications with Army Group B after several attempts. The LXVII Army Corps, to which communications was also established, reported that its command post was in the Vogelsberg area.

In the late afternoon, with the fall of twilight, General von Zangen personally reconnoitered the American deployment route. He established that the U.S. columns were rolling at a great distance from each other over the road and ordered that groups of five to ten vehicles should insert themselves in these intervals.

He also ordered his own march column, which consisted of 100 vehicles, to wait in a well-camouflaged position in Breidenbach until a gap appeared in the passing U.S. columns that was large enough for the vehicles of the army staff to roll in between.

It was the 3rd U.S. AD, which now "covered" the movement of the German vehicles in the direction where they would be able to breakout and find security. East of Wiesenbach the German vehicles turned off, took cover behind a wall from the approaching American vehicles and, after assembling, reached Altenhundem on the morning of 30/3, after a dangerous night drive. Here radio communications were reestablished with Army Group B. By this coup de main only one truck and one motorcycle was snatched by the enemy, everyone else made it through.

During a conversation with GFM Model the afternoon of 30/3 in Altenhundem, General von Zangen informed him of the construction of the eastern front of the Ruhr pocket. He explained his intentions of attacking LIII Corps Bayerlein through Winterberg to the east and, in this manner, stopping the enemy advance in the direction of Paderborn, reaching the Edertal block south of Korbach and establishing contact with the 11th Army there, which was advancing from Kassel in the opposite direction.

Generalfeldmarschall Model named General von Zangen, the commander of the 15th Army, the senior commander in the eastern half of the Ruhr pocket. He was to establish his command post in Schmallenberg. The 5th Panzer Army under Generaloberst Harpe would take charge in the western pocket.

U.S. Battle Groups on the Road to Winterberg and Paderborn

The VII Corps of the 1st U.S. Army was ordered by Lieutenant General Hodges on 28/3 to attack out of their departure positions near and to the north of Marburg on the following morning directly to the north toward Winterberg and with a strong attack wedge, led by the 3rd AD, continue on to Paderborn.

This attack on Paderborn was to be executed in four battle groups. And the experienced commanders Doan, Hogan, Kane and Welborn were to command one battle group each. The heavy armored units would be led by Lieutenant Colonel Richardson and Lieutenant Colonel Hogan. The two commanders received their detailed instructions from Colonel Howe, the chief of the battle group reserve of the 3rd AD on the evening of 28/3, as to how they were to advance on Paderborn, which still lay 150 kilometers to the north.

The chief of the battle group reserve ordered Richardson:

"Drive like the devil! Occupy the plateau around the Paderborn airfield. – And you, Hogan, cover Richardson's left flank, echeloned slightly to the left. The battle group under Lieutenant Colonel Welborn will take over the protection of your right flank, Richardson, so that you can concentrate on the advance."

They would meet the 2nd AD from Simpson's army coming from the north in the Paderborn area.

On the morning of 29/3/1945 at 0600 hours Battle Group Richardson broke out. The lead vehicle was a half-track equipped with a machine-gun. A few jeeps followed close behind for route reconnaissance, and behind them rode three Shermans that would be used to break enemy resistance and remove anti-tank obstacles.

Behind them rumbled an armored battalion of 17 Shermans and three heavy Pershing tanks with 9 cm cannon. In case of a surprise German attack mounted infantry could dismount and provide the tanks security if they were to be attacked by panzerfaeusten.

Shortly after midday, when the lead group rolled up to an anti-tank obstacle, the heavy Pershings rolled forward, shot-up the blockade and rolled it flat, so that all of the vehicles could pass.

With the fall of twilight the men of Battle Group Richardson had covered 120 kilometers. That was the absolute day's record for the entire war.

When Battle Group Richardson reached Brilon they received instructions by radio from their division commander, Major General Rose, to first clear the enemy from this city. However, Lieutenant Colonel Richardson did not agree with such peripheral operations, since the map indicated that they were still a 50 kilometer drive from Paderborn.

Continuing to the north – it had, in the meantime, become dark – he had established that the several groups he had dispatched to Brilon now left a huge gap behind the lead group. The lead group continued to roll on. It was night and the march had to be conducted slowly. Guides had to be dismounted from the vehicles to lead them. In this manner, one of the following companies caught up and suddenly one of the follow-on platoon's vehicles rolled into the last vehicle of the advance group and severely damaged it. Then a second accident occurred as a tank ran over another vehicle. Lieutenant Colonel Richardson clambered out of his command vehicle to untangle the chaos. Thus he learned that this follow-on company had "found" a wine cellar in Brilon and had proceeded to tank up on the stuff. The tanks smelled like wine cellars. One unit apparently stayed behind in Brilon in order to "destroy the wine." The battle group commander ordered that, in spite of the coolness of the evening, all hatches were to be immediately opened to clear the heads of his men. Then he ordered his adjutant to return to Brilon with a group and "kick the drunkards in the ass and get them moving again."

The two battle groups, which had taken over the flank protection and with whom there was radio contact, had also advanced well, even if they were echeloned somewhat to the rear. On the following day the battle group reached the edge of the Paderborn area. We will report on the further combat as soon as we describe the advance of the northern pincer arm.

The German Breakout Attempt from the Ruhr Pocket

On Good Friday, 30/3/1945, almost all U.S. forces in the area of Army Group B attacked the defensive front. During the previous night Generalleutnant Bayerlein received instructions on the situation from GFM Model at the Army Group B command post. The GFM declared to the corps commander that the Army Group B formations faced a decision in the Ruhr region and in Sauerland and that the enemy had penetrated out of the area south of Marburg to the north, while the English forces and the U.S. divisions subordinated to them were ready to advance on Muenster. All of this indicated that these two pincer arms were to meet between Lippstadt and Paderborn, to form a pocket far to the east of Army Group B.

Moreover, the GFM ordered:

"I order you to attack with available forces out of the Schmallenberg area to the east, south of the Edertal block, and make contact with a battle group committed from the northeast and together burst the ring of encirclement."

On the morning of 30/3 at 0300 hours, when Generalleutnant Bayerlein left the army group command post he first drove through Kirchhundem into the Schmallenberg area. He ordered the corps command post be established in Milchenbach. On the trip to Winterberg the commander ran into elements of the Panzer-Lehr Division battle group, which was rolling out of the Wuppertal area, on a road intersection at Gleidorf. This battle group with a staff from the II/PLD 130 under Major Ritgen was composed of soldiers from the Panzer-Lehr Division and also members of the Panzer-Lehr Division rear area services, who had, in the meantime, become combat veterans. To Major Ritgen was subordinated one panzer company and one panzergrenadier battalion of the 902 Panzergrenadier Regiment. A little later Ritgen also received the 130th Panzerjaeger-Lehr Battalion with 18 new Panzerjaeger IV's. They were unloaded in Bad Driburg.

During the breakthrough of Schmallenberg Major Ritgen was stopped by GFM Model and given direct orders.

"Feldmarschall Model ordered us to attack with the available troops, without waiting to reorganize, to the east on the evening of 30/3, in order to first gain the Hallenberg – Medebach road and, therefore, sever one of the three main enemy lines of communications." (See Ritgen, Helmut: *The History of the Panzer-Lehr Division 1944-45.*)

Major Ritgen formed three weak attack groups from his battle group, each with a panzergrenadier company and attached tanks and panzerjaegers. He reconnoitered the terrain east of Winterberg at 1300 hours and assembled there as ordered.

After receiving a situation briefing from Generalleutnant Bayerlein in his command post in Milchenbach, GFM Model issued the attack order. First the village of Kuestelberg was to be captured, in order to complete the assembly for the continuation of the attack to Medebach.

At 1900 hours Generalleutnant Bayerlein arrived at Battle Group Ritgen, after leaving the Panzer-Lehr Division forward command post. They had assembled south of Winterberg and received the order for the night attack directly from Bayerlein. In the meantime, 12 additional panzerjaegers from the 130th Panzerjaeger-Lehr Battalion arrived at the Panzer-Lehr Division and were used to reinforce the attack strength.

135

Oberst Horst Niemack, who led the Panzer-Lehr Division in this commitment, rolled in the lead with an assault company and ordered the entire Panzer-Lehr Division to attack. Again an attack was being launched like in the old days. The tanks reached Hesborn and Liesen, southeast of Winterberg. They ran into strong U.S. armored formations near Medelon and were stopped. When the follow-on units caught up, including the additional panzerjaegers, the attack resumed and Kuestelberg fell to the Panzer-Lehr Division.

The enemy artillery fire here hit the remnants of the 130th Panzerjaeger-Lehr Battalion, which was led by Unteroffizier Hans Scholde. Direct hits were scored. The crews abandoned ship and vanished into one of the Kuestelberg cellars.

On 31/3 the weather cleared and the fighter-bombers hit the Langenwiese – Schmallenberg rollbahn, the advance of the Panzer-Lehr Division stopped. Oberst Horst Niemack was severely wounded and was flown out of the pocket by order of GFM Model. Oberst Paul von Hauser, the commander of the 901st Panzergrenadier-Lehr Regiment, took over at the division command post of the orphaned division.

The attack had reached Kuestelberg, Liese, Hesborn and Medelon and occupied these villages. The road intersection north of Hallenberg was blocked. Then the Medebach – Diefeld thoroughfare was blocked two kilometers east of Kuestelberg. The enemy could no longer advance on these roads.

During the night before 1/4/1945 the first troops of the 176th ID under the personal leadership of Generalmajor Landau arrived in the combat area and took over the Diefeld sector.

The American counterattack on 1/4 forced the Panzer-Lehr Division to withdraw to the edge of the forested region east of Winterberg. Medebach, Rhadern and Hillershausen were the next stations. Lightnings eliminated the few remaining flak batteries in deep attack. West of Alt-Astenberg the main body of tanks of the Panzer-Lehr Division was also eliminated through deep attack.

The breakout from the Ruhr pocket and the attempt to attack through the northern encirclement flank and cut off the lead formations from their supplies had failed.

During the night before 2/4/1945 the attack divisions – which could only be described as ruins – withdrew again to Winterberg.

On 4/4/1945 even Winterberg was evacuated. The LIII Army Corps command post was transferred to Lenneplaetze.

On 5/4 U.S. troops attacked the Panzer-Lehr Division north of Winterberg. Fierce fighting raged between the Kahlen Asten, with its 841 meter high Erhebung des Sauerland, and Silbach. The main weight of this fighting lay on the shoulders of the 902nd Panzergrenadier Regiment. Oberstleutnant Ritter von Poschinger fell at the head of his regiment. With him also died Oberleutnant Rasmus, the commander of the 4/PGR 902. The entire 4th Company of the regiment was almost wiped out. Major Klein took command of the regiment on the battlefield. He led it through Altena and Hemer into the Iserlohn area.

The Panzer-Lehr Division had melted to 20 tanks and panzerjaegers and ten tracked vehicles. That was all that remained of the largest and best equipped panzer division in the great German Wehrmacht.

On 7/4/1945 Generalleutnant Bayerlein met with the commander of Corps Group von Luettwitz, General der Panzertruppe Freiherr von Luettwitz. It was clear to both generals that the situation was hopeless and any further fighting here in the west would result in only senseless sacrifice. On 9 April Werl was lost, and two days later the Allies reached Dortmund.

4

IN THE 21st ARMY GROUP AREA
OF OPERATIONS

Preparations for Operation "Plunder"

On 2/3/1945 at 1100 hours an RAF C-54 aircraft took off from Northolt Air Station and set a course for Brussels. On board were the British Chief of the General Staff Field Marshal Brooke, Winston Churchill, Churchill's daughter Mary and Air Marshal Sir Arthur Coningham. The objective of the flight was Coningham's headquarters in Brussels. From there, after eating lunch, they flew on in two Dakotas to Eindhoven, where Field Marshal Montgomery awaited his important guests. From Montgomery's headquarters they drove to the railroad station, to where Eisenhower's command train stood.

After eating dinner they all took part in a staff meeting. Montgomery summarized the meeting:

"The offensive was progressing famously, throughout there were indications the Germans were falling apart."

On the afternoon of 3/3 Churchill and Brooke were driven in Field Marshal Montgomery's two Rolls Royces to Maastricht to the headquar-

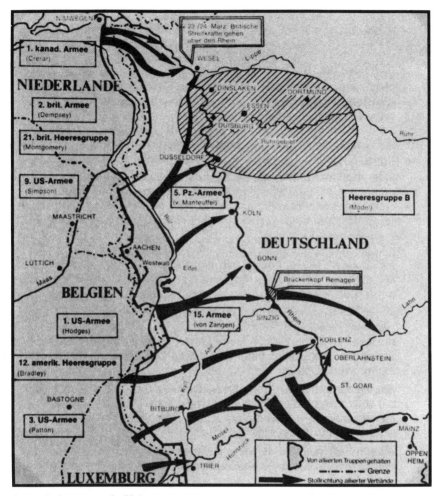

Before the leap across the Rhein.

ters of the 9th U.S. Army, whose commander, General Simpson, briefed the situation after a short meeting with Churchill.

From here they continued on to Aachen. On the way they made a stop at the West Wall, which had fallen into British – American hands after such fierce and costly fighting near Aachen. The group wanted to view several bunkers and machine-gun nests.

During the trip from General Simpson's headquarters, Simpson discretely noted that he had to use the "washroom." However, Churchill asked how far it was to the Siegfried Line and when he learned that it was only approximately a half-hour away, he replied that he did not need to use the toilet just yet. They would stop on the Siegfried Line.

Aachen, which the group examined next, was considerably damaged, it cheered the group to "finally see German houses in ruins, instead of French, Italian, British and Belgium."

After that they went to Juelich, and on the following morning they continued on to the 1st Canadian Army under General Crerar. They continued on through the Reichswald and through Goch to Gennep, where they inspected the 51st British ID. Winston Churchill was very annoyed when they did not want to allow him any closer to the front. Nevertheless, even this hurdle could be overcome.

In Reims they were driven to the large agricultural school near the railroad station, where General Eisenhower's headquarters was located. Eisenhower and Bradley were already awaiting their guests and described for them the situation on the large map in the map room. Major General Bedell Smith, as well as Spaatz and Tedder, arrived at dinner-time.

On the return flight on 6/3 Churchill declared that he wished to be informed in detail about the preparation for and the beginning of the crossing of the Rhein.

On 15 March 1945 Winston Churchill was again with the Allied commanders of the two army groups. In the left bank Rhein asparagus town of Walbeck, Montgomery and Eisenhower met with Churchill. After a meeting lasting several hours with the commanders participating in the Operation "Plunder", Churchill emerged confident. On a front of about 50 kilometers stood 29 divisions of the 21st Army Group (with the subordinate 9th U.S. Army), ready to attack across the Rhein. On the other side of this axis, on the eastern bank of the river, the Allies recognized that the 7th Fallschirmjaeger Division and the 84th ID were defending this same sector. While the Allies had approximately 300,000, there were only about 10,000 German soldiers opposing them.

At this meeting it would be established that the attack would be conducted by four divisions. Moreover, an already worked out plan for a large-scale airborne commitment – Operation "Varsity" – was presented. This would be conducted on the morning after the commitment of the four divisions and the German defenders were splintered.

The 6th British Airborne Division and the 17th U.S. Airborne Division were designated for "Varsity." The start of the "Plunder" attack was the night of 24/3/1945.

The Leap Across the Rhein

On the early morning of 23/3/1945, when General Patton jubilantly called Eisenhower to tell him that the Rhein had been forced near Oppenheim, the 21st Army Group also stood ready to leap across the Rhein. Monty's forces consisted of the 1st Canadian, the 2nd British and the 9th American Armies. There was to be no bridgehead established here, however, Monty wanted to conduct a strike on a front of 42 to 48 kilometers across the Rhein and then assault to the east and northeast in a single avalanche.

In addition, there was no less than 250,000 tons of war equipment and bridging equipment brought up and, on the evening of 20/3, prepared on the western bank of the Rhein.

The airborne operation lay in the hands of the commander of the 6th British Airborne Division, Major General Bols, who was to land in the Hamminkeln area and lead the general commitment from there.

At 1700 hours on 23/3 the British barrage fire began. 3480 guns fired on a frontal breadth of 44 kilometers. And while these fires continued, British and American bombers dropped their bombs. It was exactly 1800 hours when another hail of bombs rained down on Wesel. At 2100 hours the RAF flew a special mission, as ten individual bombers reached Wesel one after the other, each dropping only one bomb. These were the heaviest bombs dropped during World War II. Each of them had a weight of approximately 10,000 kilograms.

Wesel – according to enemy propaganda – was to have sheltered 80,000 defenders. The fact that this was Utopian did not change the fact that the Allies had it in for this city. Thus Wesel was the only city in Germany to be completely leveled, down to the last house.

Therefore, Dr. Joseph Goebbels' announcement over the radio that Wesel would be defended by 80,000 German soldiers received its reply.

Therefore, the Allied commanders saw in Wesel a main corner-stone of the German defense and had already decided in January that this city would be the site of the main crossing of the Rhein. This also strengthened the Allied desire to smoke out this city.

On 1/2/1945 twelve bombers attacked Wesel during the day. Then strike after strike followed. On 16/2 a strong group of Lancaster bombers attacked the ferry crossing at Rees. Two days later the bombers returned. Bombs now fell on the inner city. From the main street to the large market to the railroad station. Two large bomber groups dropped their high-explosive bombs. After that a third wave arrived. They dropped phosphorus bombs and entire phosphorus canisters. Fire rained from the heavens and set everything ablaze.

The Rathaus lay in ruins. The nearby Registry Office was pulverized and the enormous Maggi-Werke building complex was one sea of flame. In the midst of the ruins the delayed fused bombs detonated. And so it continued, on Monday, 19/2, the air raid sirens roared again. At 1500 hours the first bombs fell on the railroad bridge. Flak fired out of all tubes, in spite of the cease-fire order from the command. The batteries in Blumenkamp, near Lackhausen, Friedrichsfeld and Voerde, the heavy 10.5 cm battery near Drevenack and a similar battery in Marienthal fired at the enemy. The railroad guns shot down three bombers before they had reached the edge of Wesel. They exploded in rolling fire balls.

And during the last bombardment on 23/3/1945, which was committed at 1600 hours and mainly was directed at the harbor area on the Rhein, where approximately 650 soldiers were in their positions, everything was covered. An entire cataract of bombs was dropped on the Rheintor bunker, however, the bunker withstood it.

Two hours later, at 1800 hours, the second wave hit and, as soon as they dropped their bombs, the enemy artillery opened fire. In the command post of the Wesel Combat Commandant, Generalmajor Deutsch – a massive bunker on the northern glacis – Generalmajor Deutsch stood at the situation map. He looked at the thick enemy attack columns aimed directly at Wesel. The General raised his voice in order to be heard over the rumbling of the artillery fire:

"Gentlemen, 500 meters in front of us our soldiers stand on the defensive front on the Rhein. As soon as the Allied attack begins, I hope, they will all still be there. I will stand by my soldiers. The order of the day is, whatever my men must endure, so must I."

"There will be no defeat, Herr General", replied the Wesel Kreisleiter. "We will stop the enemy here on Germany's river, like the Fuehrer has ordered."

"Don't be silly, Herr Kreisleiter! With what will you stop 300,000 soldiers?" asked the General. Then he turned to the communications officer, who entered the room and approached him.

"What is it, Holhaus?" he asked.

"A radio message from the enemy, Herr General!"

"Give it here!"

Generalmajor Deutsch took the page and glanced at it. Then he turned to the men and gave them their last orders.

"Listen, gentlemen. The wording of this message will interest you: 'We demand the surrender of the city of Wesel without a fight. When our soldiers cross the river, do not fire. You will be guaranteed honorable captivity and treatment according to the Geneva Convention.

"If Wesel is not prepared to surrender, the city will be devastated further and our bombers will do their duty."

"We must accept this surrender, Herr General", said one of the staff officers.

"Now I know that no one lives in Wesel anymore. I know that the city is 100% destroyed. What, I am asking you, can the Allies do that is new? Where was the Geneva Convention when their bombers destroyed the civilian populace? There is really only one thing left for us to do: defend Wesel until the last cartridge."

We will review the defensive measures. The main nest of resistance in the Rheintor bunker. Fallschirmjaeger and flak units are grouped into positions and individual trenches. There are panzerfaeuste in bunkers.

The fallschirmjaegers of the 7th Division are to the north under Generalleutnant Erdmann. They are defending the region between Bislich and Bienen. South of Wesel the 84th ID is holding from Wesel through Flueren to Voerde. According to outpost reports, the Allies have assembled. We must anticipate that the crossing attempt will be made at the fall of darkness."

A courier arrived at the command bunker. "Herr General, the first amphibious vehicles have just approached the banks of the Rhein."

Generalmajor Deutsch stood up. He grabbed his machine-pistol that was laying on the table next to him.

"Gentlemen, it is time! The staff will remain here to coordinate all combat operations. You Bracke, can come with me if you wish."

"I want to come, Herr General", replied the 84th ID adjutant, who Generalmajor Deutsch had assigned as his personal adjutant.

"Out men, to the Rheintor bunker!"

The soldiers followed the General. And while these men set out to defend the Rhein, there was a single pistol shot in the underground command room of the Kreisleiter's bunker. The Kreisleiter, who had spoken of the glorious and successful defense of the Rhein until the very end, shot himself in the head, instead of fighting in the Rheintor bunker.

The Attack Begins

At 1700 hours on 23/3/1945 the Allied artillery, which were deployed on a breadth of over 40 kilometers on the far side of the Rhein, began the barrage fire. Flames flared out of the barrels of 3480 guns, clouds of powder smoke rose into the air. 3480 shells flew across the Rhein and slammed into the far bank and the German positions. They were directed by forward observers and air reconnaissance and guided to their targets.

Again the Allies probed the positions of the German Rhein defense with their notorious "Creeping Barrage." By 1710 hours all of the guns had found the correct salvo tactic. Salvo after salvo hammered the ground on the eastern bank and behind it, plowing the ground up. This lasted until 1800 hours, then the artillery fire was replaced by a heavy bomber attack. Again heavy and super-heavy bombs rained on the ground.

Then the guns resumed and, at 2100 hours, another ten RAF bombers appeared to unload their 10 ton bombs over Wesel. Then the artillery fired again, and in the cover of this steel curtain the Allied attack groups moved up to the Rhein.

It was exactly 2030 hours when combat units of the 51st Scottish Division – the Gordon Highlanders – boarded the "Buffaloes" near Mehr and Haffen and near Rees. 40 soldiers jumped into these flat armored vehicles, which now, after a salvo of smoke grenades had shrouded the gloominess of the Rhein, were launched and quickly crossed the Rhein

Opposite Wesel was the 1st British Commando Brigade – the King's Own Scottish Borderers – who a few minutes later boarded landing craft and rushed across the Rhein.

When the boats had covered the first third of the river, fire was opened on them from the eastern shore. The shots could barely be heard over the din of artillery. Nevertheless, one of the 2 cm four-barreled air defense guns scored a direct hit on one of the landing boats. The shells tore off everything hanging over the side wall, then hammered staccato against the side. One of the armor penetrating shells pierced. With a great explosion the landing boat flew into the air and came down like a fire ball. The rest continued on toward the other bank.

It was exactly 2059 hours when the first boats reached the right bank of the Rhein. They were met here by only weak machine-gun fire. The fire of Allied air defense guns and anti-tank guns from the other bank had earlier silenced most of the recognized German machine-gun positions.

After landing, the 7th Battalion of the Scottish Borderers attacked directly through between Reeserward and Grietherbusch. A machine-gun was silenced with hand-grenades, a German position was overran. Shots rang out through the night. The few German rifle trenches were overcome in hand-grenade combat.

An hour later the crossing was begun near Wesel. Here the first British assault troops had reached the eastern bank below Wesel at 2215 hours.

They then marched along the bank, outflanked the known positions and reached the assigned landing places, where the Buffaloes were signalling to land.

To the south, in the Dinslaken area, the combat troops of the 9th U.S. Army crossed the river from Emmelsum to Voerde. Therefore, the Americans were committed approximately 2000 meters further to the south as had been previously planned. Therefore, the crossing sites of all of the combat troops lay between river kilometers 798 and 842.

Fallschirmjaegers from the 8th Fallschirmjaeger Division held the defensive positions near Rees. They were able to hold the positions between Reeser Eyland and the northern corner-stone of the landing near Hause Pottdeckel. The German fallschirmjaegers were fighting with their last ounce of strength and withstood the overwhelming enemy pressure. Here fought the few formations of the 1st Fallschirmjaeger Army. Their four fallschirmjaeger divisions, which were completely exhausted and had lost a portion of their heavy weapons, stood shoulder to shoulder with the remnants of the three infantry divisions. They had entrenched in the ground and were firing their MG 42's at the attackers, forcing them to go to ground immediately after landing.

The German divisions, which no longer existed, faced 29 divisions and seven independent brigades on the front. They [Germans] had no artillery and air support.

The two Allied regiments, which crossed the Rhein near Wesel, reached the city center by midnight. Instead of the 80,000 soldiers that they had expected to face, there was only Generalmajor Deutsch with 650. Of these, two-thirds were Landesschuetzen and men from security battalions. One fallschirmjaeger assault troop offered the enemy the fiercest resistance. Moreover, there was Generalmajor Deutsch.

From his command post in Hause Galland he defended with his staff. Attacked by British armored flame-throwers and infantry, the men fell one after the other. When the rest finally refused to go to their death and wanted to give up the hopeless fighting, General Deutsch took his machine-pistol to Fluthgrafenstrasse against the enemy. He conducted the last fire-fight with the enemy. When he rammed his last magazine into his weapon and continued to fire at a group of advancing enemy soldiers, he was hit by shots from an enemy machine-gun and fell to the ground. The Wesel combat commandant died two hours later in an Allied forward first-aid station, where the enemy had taken him.

On Saturday morning, 24/3/1945 at 0200 hours, Wesel was in Allied hands. At 0900 hours British troops made contact with the neighboring units from the 9th U.S. Army near Friedrichsfeld – Emmelsum, they had advanced faster than the Brits, because there was not much of a Rhein defense at this location.

The 21st Army Group had forced the Rhein between Voerde and Rees and took up positions on the eastern bank.

The first wave of the attack – besides the already mentioned 51st Scottish Division – consisted of the 15th Scottish Division, the 1st Commando Brigade and the 30th U.S. ID. The latter was committed in the Friedrichsfeld – Spellen area. The 79th U.S. ID crossed the Rhein in the Loehnen – Mehrum – Stapp area.

The enemy had established a 50 kilometer foothold and established an enormous bridgehead that could not be removed. Therefore, the battle in the west was finally lost and it is time to turn to the Russian front.

On Saturday, 24/3/1945, Operation "Varsity" was begun. It was 0945 hours when the first wave of this enormous air fleet reached their target area north of Wesel. Exactly three hours and 10 minutes after they took off, the first tow aircraft, that had taken off from airfields in central England, loosed their transport gliders for their descent near Wesel.

These troops, which descended without pause on the right bank of the Rhein from 0945 hours to 1100 hours, were flown in 1572 aircraft and 1326 transport gliders to their commitment area. They were a total of 40,000 completely equipped and trained soldiers, the combat elite of the Western Allies.

889 fighter aircraft provided air security for this formation over German territory. An additional 2153 fighters and fighter-bombers secured the jump zone and hermetically sealed off this area from the east. Everything was figured out to the smallest detail.

While the majority of these two airborne divisions were dropped in the

Hamminkeln area, two regiments of the 17th Airborne Division landed in the Dinkslaken area, east of Reichsstrasse 8.

The objective of this monster air landing, immediately after the assault troops had crossed the Rhein, was to expand the bridgehead to the east and roll over the thick German defensive lines from the rear, thereby catching the defenders in a pincer and remove any possibility of withdrawal.

This plan worked. Particularly in the Mehr – Hiesfeld sector, where the German defensive lines were actually located in the middle of the pincer and destroyed.

The fallschirmjaer, who were located on the eastern bank of the Rhein, saw the white cloths of the paratroopers descending by the thousands. They saw the released transport gliders descend to earth noiselessly.

The field artillery group of the 6th British Airborne Division had it particularly rough, as they set down for a landing in the Hamminkeln – Bruenen – Lackhausen area. Guns, ammunition and equipment were loaded into 416 gliders. Of these, only 88 made it undamaged. Flak and rifle fire, as well as machine-gun fire, took their toll on the rest.

During Operation "Varsity" the "Curtiss C-46" was utilized in a paradrop for the first time in the history of warfare. 36 fully equipped paratroopers were carried in each of these aircraft.

The transport glider pilots were led by Colonel Chatterton. Colonel Chatterton had the Horsas gliders specially constructed for such an air land-ing operation. In the Colonel's glider, besides his personal staff, also flew a special correspondent for the "Sunday Express" during this attack. It was James Wellard. In an observation position in the lead aircraft, James Wellard photographed the scenes and made notes on his first impressions of this grand show. He voice taped his observations and, thus, on the following morning, Sunday, 25/3/1945, the English were able to read first hand about the largest airborne operation of all time. Here is Wellard's report:

"It is 1100 hours in the morning and as far as the eyes can see to the east at an altitude of 1200 feet Germany is covered in flames and smoke. What now appears around me in the sky, what is going on on the ground and water, is like a futuristic painting of Armageddon. For the Ger-mans on the eastern bank it is the last battle.

This day is the concentrated repetition of D-Day. The sky is full of aircraft. Transports, twin-engine American Dakotas, four-engine Halifax and our new "C-46" can be seen. This air armada is swarming in two enormous columns across the sky. I saw the first wave of airborne troops jump. From each aircraft popped many white balls, which expanded with paratroopers suspended like puppets.

German flak engaged the first wave. In spite of the destructive artillery and fighter-bomber fire, there were still flak batteries operational, and they fought bitterly.

The dirty-grey clouds of explosions from the German 8.8 cm shells sprinkled the sky. Red, yellow and green tracers rose from the enemy air defense guns toward our aircraft.

Suddenly I saw a Dakota fall. Two more dived, trailing thick smoke. One of them fell with flames flickering from it.

Now the second wave is approaching us. I am looking through my spy-glasses from my observation position, I see an enormous number of aircraft, each towing two gliders at the end of long nylon ropes. These are the smaller American Waco gliders.

Then the large British Horsas come, towed by Halifax bombers. They rise and fall in the air like seagulls. They come by the hundreds. Suddenly they loose their tow cables and quietly spiral to earth like an enormous bird of prey.

Thank God the German flak has now almost stopped firing. We are looking below us to see whether the gun crews have fled their positions in the face of this enormous spectacle, this army coming from the sky. However, it is not so! They have been exhausted, but they still lay in their shot-up and bombed out positions.

As we slowly fly over the Rhein, circling between Xanten and Wesel, throwing a glance at the burning Bislich, I see that the German resistance has collapsed for miles. We see only a few German shells impact on the western bank in between the alligator boats.

It is almost peaceful on the banks of the river. There is no more resistance being offered. Our ferries are rushing here and there, bringing men and equipment across the river.

Further to the east it is otherwise. There the German villages lay buried under a thick cloud of smoke. Our artillery has obliterated the towns. We are flying to Wesel. This city is leveled, from the air it looks like a pile of ashes left over by a fire. If there are Germans left in Wesel, they will have to be dug out.

Another wave of transport gliders is landing in the north. For miles the fields are sprinkled with white, orange and red parachutes. The transport gliders bringing ammunition and guns continue to descend. Everything is fantastic and difficult to describe."

This was what Winston Churchill wanted to experience; and in spite of all attempts to stop him, he would.

Winston Churchill on the Eastern Bank of the Rhein

Before the Rhein crossing began, several correspondents had already reported on Churchill's visit to this front. Churchill wanted to make sure that "this majestic operation which Montgomery had thought of initiating in the north was not passed up." (See Bryant, Arthur: Op. cit.)

After Churchill was prevented from visiting the troops before the beginning of "Overlord", he decided that this time he would go, and Field Marshal Montgomery prepared for him:

"In case the PM has decided to come over for the battle of the Rhein there is – I believe – only one thing to do: namely, request he stay in my camp. I will then be able to keep an eye on him and see that nothing happens to him."

On 23/3/1945 Winston Churchill sat in Field Marshal Montgomery's headquarters in Venlo.

On the next morning Monty informed his guest that the attack across the Rhein was taking place. Churchill burned to see the battlefield and set out at 0845 hours with Field Marshal Brooke and one of Montgomery's adjutants. 45 minutes later they reached an observation point 2 kilometers south of Xanten, from where they had a good view of the Rhein. Poor visibility dominated on this morning. Here is a report from the diary of Field Marshal Brooke:

"We were located between the positions of a battery that had supported the attack across the Rhein. These guns were still firing. They were now firing on German air defense positions to secure the follow-on air landing.

The British 6th and 17th American Airborne Divisions were to appear about 1000 hours and drop approximately three to four kilometers behind the Rhein, indeed, on the opposite side of this forest, which was a main obstacle.

The 6th Airborne Division took off from eastern England, while the 17th U.S. Airborne Division took off from airfields in Paris.

It was a wonderful sight. The entire sky was covered with transport aircraft. They flew directly over us and across the Rhein. Unfortunately they disappeared from sight before the paratroopers jumped.

Before they moved out of sight, we could see the German flak shells exploding under them. Shortly after that the aircraft returned with open doors and the remains of the parachute bands. A couple made the return flight in flames, their pilots floated to earth in parachutes.

After approximately one hour of endless streams of transports, the first transport gliders appeared.

We remained at this observation point for two hours and then mounted two armored vehicles. Then we drove to Xanten where we turned to the north and then through Marienbaum to the northeastern portion of the Reichswald to a small flat hill south of Kalkar. From there we had a good view of the crossing sector of the 51st ID, whose commander, Major General T.G. Rennie, had fallen during the morning river crossing."

That was a direct report. That this was not sufficient for Churchill was soon made evident to all. Next he undertook a flight over the front, in this manner he inspected the fortifications on the West Wall.

In the evening Churchill and Field Marshal Brooke received a report from Field Marshal Montgomery in which he informed them that all operations had achieved overwhelming success. In the south of the crossing area each of the crossing divisions had taken several thousand prisoners. The divisions themselves had lost only between 100 and 200 men.

In the northern sector the crossing and the gaining of the eastern bank was more difficult. The 51st ID had suffered heavy casualties, loosing 600 men and capturing a similar number prisoner.

Field Marshal Brooke noted:

"When I review this day I am convinced that the end is near for the Germans and I will not be surprised if they pack it in at any moment. I believe that a coordinated defense north and east of the Rhein will collapse in the next few days and that we will then be in a position to supply Monty's 8th AD through the air and allow it to operate throughout northern Germany."

This would turn out to be wishful thinking.

After services on Palm Sunday in Venlo, the delegation of the Prime Minister and the Field Marshal drove to Rehinberg, where they visited the headquarters of the XVI U.S. Corps under General Anderson. Eisenhower, Bradley and Simpson met them there.

After eating in a villa of a German mine director, they all drove to Buederich. A house stood on the bank of the Rhein which allowed a good view to the north up to Wesel and to the south up to the American ponton bridge. Here Churchill coined the words:

"My dear General, the Germans are defeated. Now we have them! Now they are finished."

The following are also Winston Churchill's words:

"The almost 350 meter wide Rhein flowed here at our feet. There, on the enemy bank stretched a flat, wide meadow. The officers accompanying us thought that it was free of enemy forces. Eisenhower wanted to move onto other things, and Montgomery and I were ready to follow his example, when I spied an infantry landing boat in the vicinity. I said to Montgomery:

'Why don't we go across and see what is happening on the other side?'

Somewhat to my surprise I heard the reply: 'Why not?' He first made a brief reconnaissance and then we set off across the river with three or four American generals and a half-dozen American soldiers. We landed on the other shore and spent a half-hour strolling unencumbered." (See Churchill, Winston: *The Second World War.*)

After that the group drove to the blown railroad bridge to Wesel and clambered around the iron construction. Thus they experienced enemy artillery fire, which was falling in the neighborhood. The German shells at first hit approximately 1500 meters to the side. However, when a later salvo went directly over their heads onto the western bank and a few shells even hit in the vicinity of where they had parked their vehicles, Montgomery decided it best they withdraw. They reached Montgomery's headquarters in Venlo after a two-hour ride.

On the eastern bank of the Rhein there was no longer a unified HKL [Main Combat Line]. There were no longer sufficient troops to form even a thin combat line. However, the small battle groups which had established defenses in Dingden, in Ringenberg and Loikum and, above all, near Mehrhoog, fought bitterly against the ten-fold superior attacking enemy infantry and armored waves. When the British tried to reach the Ijsseldamm near Loikum with scout cars, these vehicles were destroyed by panzerfaeusten. 600 fallschirmjaegers and members of the Waffen SS defended the dam and even launched a counterattack. They advanced meter by meter. They pushed the enemy back with hand-grenades and explosives, with panzerfaeusten and machine-guns, across the smaller and then even the larger Ijssel south of Loikum.

On Sunday morning, 25/3, the fallschirmjaegers entrenched in the Hurnhorst bushes. It was exactly 1000 hours when the enemy directed their concentrated artillery fire on this forest. Shells of all calibers hammered the trenches of the fallschirmjaegers for three hours. At 1300 hours the Hurnhorst was like a cemetery. 400 dead fallschirmjaegers were later found in this small area.

The fallschirmjaegers defending in the Mehrhoog area were encircled, when a British attack regiment, supported by armored flame-throwers, advanced through Mehr in an attempt to establish contact with their own paratroopers, which had landed south of Mehrhoog.

Wherever the fallschirmjaegers combined into small resistance groups, there rolled the British armored flame-throwers, spewing their 30 meter long flame. Burned out farmsteads indicated these defensive positions.

The bitterest resistance was offered to the attacking enemy near and in Bienen by fallschirmjaegers from Battle Group Huebner of the 7th Fallschirmjaeger Division. Three times the defending fallschirmjaegers were able to throw out the attacking Canadians from Bienen to the Rhein near Grietherbusch. In this town where the Anholt – Bocholt road intersected with Reichsstrasse 8, the fallschirmjaegers under Hauptmann Huebner fought with exemplary bitterness. They held out in the town from 24 to 27/3.

The Canadians were already desperate, however, they attacked for a fourth time, penetrated into the town and captured several houses in man-to-man fighting. When the situation was hopeless, Hauptmann Huebner requested fire on his own location. Mortar units and artillery batteries fired on Bienen from positions on Millinger Meer, turning the town to ruins. Both friend and foe were buried under the ruins.

On Thursday, 27/3, Bienen was finally in Allied hands. From here, the Canadians advanced further on Praest and Millingen and there turned toward Emmerich.

The 51st ID also had to pay for its further advance with blood and tears. In the Rees area the German fallschirmjaegers also fought until Thursday. Two fallschirmjaegers held out in the Groin brick-works until the very end. Hauptmann Huebner entrenched in the houses of Aspeln. The houses were fired at with incendiary shells in an attempt to smoke out the 32 defending fallschirmjaegers.

In the village of Empel the fallschirmjaegers held out for three days. Here the last resistance collapsed on Thursday. Several hours after that the assault regiment of the 51st British ID entered Isselburg. On the 28th the British advanced on Bocholt with several tanks, they reached it on the following day and captured it without a fight.

On 30 March – Good Friday in the year 1945 – Emmerich also finally fell. The last lower Rhein village to fall was the border town of Elten on the 1st day of Easter. The area on the right side of the Rhein from Emmerich to Dinslaken was almost all in Allied hands. The attack of the northern pincer arm to encircle the Rhein area and ultimately the Ruhr pocket from the north could now begin.

Summary After the Assault Across the Rhein

A week after the Rhein crossing by the first four assault divisions and the air formations, the 21st British Army Group had assembled 20 divisions and 1500 tanks east of the Rhein. Only the 25th German Army still held in front of the left flank of the 21st Army Group. The remnants of the 1st Fallschirm- jaeger Army had to gradually withdraw – being numerically outnumbered.

Simultaneous with the attack of the 21st Army Group across the Rhein, General Eisenhower had encouraged utilizing the two bridgeheads of Remagen and Oppenheim by crossing the 3rd and 7th U.S. Armies over the Rhein between Mannheim and Mainz. To the south, the French 1st Army crossed the river near Speyer, while (as already described) the 1st U.S. Army moved out of the Remagen bridgehead to the east and bypassed Marburg penetrating to the north to attack the Ruhr area from the south.

The initial U.S. objective in this phase of the fighting was the gaining of a unified bridgehead across the Rhein, from the confluence of the Nekar to the Sieg. This bridgehead was to be expanded to Hanau, Giessen and Siegen.

General Patton was untouched by these operations, as he had realized the Oppenheim Rhein crossing with his 3rd U.S. Army. On 24 March he had reached Darmstadt. A day later his lead armored elements penetrated up to Aschaffenburg. Here the Main bridges fell into his hands intact.

On 26/3 the 7th U.S. Army forced a Rhein crossing near Worms and established contact with the 3rd U.S. Army near Darmstadt by attacking to the north and, therefore, widened the bridgehead to Mannheim.

On 31 March General Eisenhower directed a proclamation to all German troops and the civilian population to give up resistance and surrender. The hopelessness of the situation was described in this demand. In closing it pointed out that any resistance would only increase Germany's misery.

Now we will follow the northern pincer on their way to Lippstadt.

Field Marshal Montgomery Reports

On Thursday, 27 March 1945, when the 21st Army Group reached its deployment areas for the breakout to the east, Field Marshal Montgomery dispatched a telegram to all army commanders, in which he summoned them to his headquarters. He discussed the situation and upcoming operations with them. In conjunction with this he sent another telegram to the Supreme Commander of the Allied Forces, General Eisenhower, in which he described the measures he had taken. The telegram follows:

"Today I have issued the order for further deployment to the east to the army commanders. I intend to order the 9th and 2nd Armies to advance to the Elbe with all forces. The right flank of the 9th Army will advance directly on Magdeburg, the British 2nd Army on the left flank has Hamburg as an operational objective.

On the left flank of the 2nd Army the 1st Canadian Army will operate to clear up northeastern and western Holland and the coastal region.

I have instructed the 9th and 2nd Armies to advance to the Elbe immediately with all armored and motorized forces and with all speed. The situation appears to be favorable.

On Thursday, 29 March, my command post will redeploy into the area northwest of Boenninghardt. The operations of the armies will be closely followed, then I hope to move my command post through Wesel, Muenster, Wiedenbrueck, Herford and Hannover and finally set up my headquarters in Berlin." (See Ryan, Cornelius: *The Last Battle*.)

Therefore, Montgomery expressed the opinion that Berlin was the most important objective of the Western Allies. He still had in his possession a letter from Eisenhower which expressed no doubts about this:

"In my view there is no doubt that we must concentrate all of our strength and ability on a rapid advance on Berlin."

Montgomery followed this maxim in his planning, without knowing that, at the same time, General Eisenhower had already set in motion events that would change the further development of the war.

Eisenhower's Secret Diplomacy

On Wednesday, 28 March 1945, General Eisenhower sent a telegram to Moscow to Major General John R. Deane, the chief of the American military mission in Moscow.

This telegram bore the secret designation "SCAF 252" and contained a message from the Supreme Allied Commander in Europe to Marshal Stalin. Major General Deane was informed that this message was only to be given to Stalin personally. Furthermore, a reply was urgently required.

Major General Deane immediately made contact with the chief of the British military mission, Admiral Ernest R. Archer. Both concluded that this message would be passed on to the head of the Soviet government during a meeting, to which they and the ambassadors of their countries were invited to on 29/3.

Eisenhower believed that one should deal directly with the Red dictator, who held all of the power, when coordinating the advance of the troops in the west and east.

In the referenced telegram, Eisenhower informed Marshal Stalin that the operations in the west had now entered a phase which "had the greatest importance regarding Soviet plans for the continuation of the fighting."

The core of General Eisenhower's proposal was an encirclement of the German forces in the Ruhr area. By the end of April these forces would be destroyed. Then he intended to advance to the east, in order to join up with the Soviet divisions in Germany, thereby splitting the remaining enemy forces in two halves.

For this meeting with the Russians, Eisenhower named the line Erfurt – Leipzig – Dresden. His main strike forces would be committed in this direction. A secondary attack to meet with the Soviet troops in Austria would be undertaken in the Regensburg – Linz area. The German resistance in the south of the Reich would be broken by this peripheral attack. Eisenhower's message ended with the words:

> "Before I make the final decision, I believe it is very important to come to an agreement with you on the time schedule and attack direction. Will you inform me of your intent and if you approve my proposals?
>
> If we are to conduct the destruction of the German Army without delay, then I regard it as being necessary to coordinate our actions and establish a good liaison between our advancing forces." (See Ryan, Cornelius: Op. cit.)

Immediately thereafter, Eisenhower dispatched corresponding messages to General Montgomery and the American Chief of the General Staff, General Marshal.

General Montgomery, who not 48 hours before had sent the already described plans to Eisenhower, was thunderstruck when Eisenhower informed him that after meeting with the 12th Army Group in the rear of the Ruhr area the 9th U.S. Army again had to be withdrawn and given back to Bradley. The message ended with the words:

> "Bradley will be responsible for the clearing of the Ruhr area, he will also conduct his main attack on a line Erfurt – Leipzig – Dresden as soon as possible and make contact with the Russians."

Montgomery was instructed to attack in the direction of the Elbe. There the 9th Army would "perhaps" be tactically subordinated to him, in order to facilitate the river crossing.

In his three messages General Eisenhower did not say one word about one particular city that was previously designated as the main objective of the attack on Germany: Berlin.

When, on 1/4/1945, Winston Churchill was made aware of SCAF 252, he immediately wrote to U.S. President Roosevelt, however, in the meantime, a few other details and Stalin's reply became known. Indeed, Stalin was willing to accept Eisenhower's plans and had explained that these plans completely corresponded with Russian intentions. And Stalin had also mentioned the core word:

"Berlin has lost its previous strategic importance. Therefore, the Soviet High Command plans only to commit secondary forces in the direction of Berlin."

It was immediately clear to Winston Churchill that this was a foul Stalin trick, he declared in his letter of 1/4/1945:

"It is completely obvious that the Allied armies in the north and in the center must make all speed and march to the Elbe.

The former goal of our advance was Berlin. Now on the basis of his estimation of enemy resistance, General Eisenhower wants us to shift our deployment direction further to the south, toward Leipzig and even further to the south toward Dresden.

I have often said that Berlin still has great strategic importance. Nothing would have such great effect on the resistance of the German forces than the fall of Berlin. In this the German people will see the signal of their defeat. Otherwise the resistance of all weapon-carrying Germans will continue as long as the German banner waves over Berlin and the ruined city holds out against a Russian siege.

Undoubtedly the Russian Army will march into Vienna and overrun all of Austria. If they also take Berlin, then will not the Russians have the impression that they gave more to our combined victory?

Therefore, it is my opinion that, from a political standpoint, we must march as far as possible into eastern Germany and capture Berlin.

However, this also seems to me to be correct from the military standpoint."

This letter was passed from the U.S. President to General Marshal, who decided that he was in complete agreement with Eisenhower's campaign plans. The fact that he had to say this was clear, for on Saturday, 31/3/1945, the U.S. General Staff expressed complete trust in Eisenhower. He only requested that General Deane not be provided with the details of the SHAEF plans, so that they would not be handed over to the Russians. The U.S. General Staff informed Churchill:

"The only objective is complete victory."

The other side, naturally, could not say anything contrary to this.

At the same time that Churchill wrote this letter, Marshal Stalin ordered contact be made with the front, in particular with Marshals Konev and Zhukov. He immediately summoned them to Moscow to report to the Kremlin on 1/4/1945. There they had an important meeting.

The Northern Pincer Advances

After consolidating the large eastern Rhein bridgeheads, Montgomery's 21st Army Group attacked through the weak forces of the 1st Fallschirmjaeger Army. After that, Army Group H reported to OB West on 28/3/1945 that they shortly anticipated that the enemy would be able to attack deep into the rear of the 1st Fallschirmjaeger Army. Indeed, the front of Army Group H was still holding, however, since they lacked reserves, they had to count on the front collapsing.

Therefore, the enemy advance was open into central Germany as well as to Bremen and Hamburg. In both areas combat capable divisions, which had to hold, were encircled and destroyed.

Only by immediately giving up the two named areas was it possible to block the enemy breakthrough in the Army Group B area of operations, establish a Weser defense, which, up to then, did not exist, and withdraw all troops and equipment from the Netherlands and commit them for further defense.

For all the above named reasons Army Group B now requested to give the corresponding order as quickly as possible.

Hitler not only forbid these proposed actions, but he also categorically forbid the submission of such situation reports for all time.

On 29 March the 9th U.S. Army launched a further attack to the east. Their next objective was Hamm in Westphalia. For this purpose the XIX Corps was committed with three infantry and two armored divisions. After the capture of Hamm forces from this very strong corps were to secure the right flank of the army east of Datteln.

The divisions of the XIX Corps paved the way through to the formations of the 17th Airborne Division, which had landed in the sector beforehand. They were also selected to establish contact with the formations of the 12th Army Group, which were coming from the south.

The rest of the divisions of the 9th U.S. Army, which were still regrouping and had to first be assembled in their departure areas to attack to the east, were to maintain contact with the 2nd British Army on the left army flank. These were: the 17th Airborne Division, the 5th AD and the 84th and 102nd Infantry Divisions of XIII Corps.

The 2nd British Army had the mission of advancing to the northeast toward Muenster.

The XVI Corps was entrusted with covering the rear of the two advancing corps with its four infantry divisions.

The 8th AD, which was performing a special mission of establishing bridgeheads across the Dortmund – Ems Canal and over the Lippe – Seiten Canal, as well as across the Lippe near Datteln, was subordinated to the XIX Corps after fulfilling its mission.

The first strike of the U.S. divisions at the beginning of this attack to the east and northeast hit the German XXXXVII Panzer Corps. The 116th PD of this corps, which was supposed to stop the enemy, was deployed in defense on the line Polsum – Buer. Generalmajor von Waldenburg established his division headquarters northwest of Recklinghausen. When the enemy appeared here on the afternoon of 29/3 the II/PR 16 and the 156th Panzergrenadier Regiment counterattacked. The enemy forces already penetrating into Polsum were thrown back during the first strike. Several enemy tanks were shot-up.

When Generalmajor von Waldenburg learned that the enemy had already broken through north of the Lippe and was advancing on Muenster, he immediately ordered all division rear area services still located north of the Lippe to be removed and deployed to the division. In spite of the dominant fuel shortage this maneuver was accomplished. These elements were committed in the direction of Paderborn, because there were already indications of a pocket forming around the 116th PD.

Hamborn and Ruhrort, which were being defended by Division "Hamburg", had to be evacuated during the night of 29/3. The division withdrew to the Rhein – Herne Canal. They established themselves north and west of Oberhausen to defend against the anticipated enemy attack.

The fighting around Gladbeck ended with the surrender of this city. Additional U.S. troops made it into the Gladbeck area via Kirchhellen and Feldhausen. Here the 190th ID and Volkssturm elements defended. During the evening the division received orders to withdraw to Buer. This order was carried out during the night.

The 2nd Fallschirmjaeger Division, which was committed on the left flank of the LXIII Army Corps, stood with its left flank on the northeastern edge of Bottrop and along the autobahn. They received instructions to make contact with the 190th ID on the right, however they were unable to do so.

The 8th U.S. AD, in the meantime, had reached Dorsten and Feldhausen in the north and rolled into these villages. The initial attack was made and, at 2100 hours on 29/3, the mobile advance group of the 2nd U.S. AD, as the first formation of the 9th U.S. Army, rolled out of the Haltern area to the east. Their long-range objective was the Elbe. The 83rd and 95th Infantry Divisions received instructions to follow the armored division and overcome the German nests of resistance. North of the Lippe there were no longer any German combat formations in a position to stop this armored attack. Still further to the north the 17th U.S. Airborne Division reached the Duelmen area, while the British divisions rolled through Coesfeld and Ahaus.

The German 116th PD was attacked by the 8th U.S. AD. The Germans had to give up Polsum and withdraw to Marl. Buer and Westerholt, which were held by the 60th Panzergrenadier Regiment of the 116th PD, were lost. The enemy penetrated effortlessly through the thin defensive line manned by the exhausted division, to which the neighboring 180th and 190th Divisions had to send tanks to help, because there were strong armored forces attacking.

After receiving situation reports and listening to radio broadcasts, the commander of the XXXXVII Panzer Corps realized that the enemy was attacking to the east at a fast tempo north of the Lippe and, therefore, threatened the right flank and rear of the corps. This enemy attack severed the communications between the corps and the 1st Fallschirmjaeger Army. They could only contact each other over radio. Finally radio messages from the 116th PD indicated that the enemy was already operating in their rear and had reached Luedinghausen and the area north of Datteln.

Generalmajor von Waldenburg proposed removing his division, in order to transfer it to the Beckum – Lippstadt – Wiedenbrueck area to prevent the threatened encirclement of Army Group B in the Ruhr pocket. Moreover, with this transfer he wanted the 116th PD, as the only motorized troops, to hold open the way to the east to the Weser as the encirclement area formed. Because the corps still refused, the division withdrew all non-committed division elements into the area northwest of Bielefeld during the night before 31/3 on its own. (See Guderian, H.G.: The Combat of the 116th PD from 24/3 to 16/4/1945.)

On the evening of 30/3 Generalmajor von Waldenburg ordered his Ordonanz Offizer, Major Dunker, to form a regimental battle group from the Feldersatz Battalion of the 116th PD and march it into the Lippstadt – Beckum – Hamm area and prevent the enemy troops attacking there from the north and the south from meeting until the 116th PD could leave the Ruhr pocket.

Major Dunker immediately drove with his small staff to Neheim – Huesten, the location of the Feldersatz Battalion. It was 2205 hours when

Major Dunker left the division command post. At 0500 hours on 31/3 he arrived in Neheim – Huesten, where the staff completed the last details. Hauptmann Inboden, the battalion commander, oriented Major Dunker on the situation and declared that the 2000 man strong battalion had been marching on foot to Sennelager for 48 hours. They were equipped with hand weapons. The battalion staff was now completely located in Neheim – Huesten and was fully motorized.

At 0800 hours Major Dunker left with the battalion staff and drove to Werl, where he learned that the southern attack group of the pincer was already rolling from Brilon in the direction of Paderborn.

While Major Dunker tried to organize this regimental battle group and set up a defense in the Beckum area, the divisions of Montgomery's 21st Army Group advanced through southern Muensterland, while dispatching a strong attack wedge to the northeast toward Ems.

The British XXX Corps under General Horrocks, the encircler of the 1st Fallschirmjaeger Army on the Rhein, advanced on Lingen, while the XII Corps took Rheine as the next objective and elements of the VIII U.S. Corps already stood northwest of Muenster and then passed this city. Formations of the XIII Corps attacked out of the southwest toward Muenster. Tanks of the 2nd U.S. AD already reached Ahlen on 31/3 and the 83rd U.S. ID was threatening Hamm.

Wherever the German formations were grouped for a decisive resistance they were bypassed by the rapidly advancing U.S. armored formations and handed over to the following infantry. Such tactics increased the advance tempo to a breathless pace.

During the night before 1/4/1945 the German troops withdrew across the Rhein – Herne Canal. Advance guards stood directly in front of them. Division "Hamburg" still held their positions west and north of Oberhausen, up to the area northeast of Essen. There closed the 2nd Fallschirmjaeger Division, whose right flank made contact with the 190th ID north of Gelsenkirchen. (See Generalleutnant Lackner: Combat of the 2nd Fallschirmjaeger Division East of the Rhein.) The above named divisions remained in the defensive line until 7/4/1945.

The planned closing of the Ruhr pocket by troops of the 1st U.S. Army from the south and the 9th U.S. Army from the north was delayed by the strong German resistance south of Paderborn. Nevertheless, the fate of Army Group B was sealed by the order from OKW to hold on the Rhein. It was now a question of days, then the army group would be encircled, and, after that, their ammunition would run out.

In the early morning hours of 1/4/1945 – it was the 1st Day of Easter – the battle groups of the 3rd U.S. AD rolled on Paderborn. Battle Group Hogan attacked Salzkotten and occupied this city on the morning of 1/4. They secured this region and advanced troops in the direction of Paderborn.

Battle Group Kane rolled out of its assembly area in Forst Boeddecken to the northwest toward Geseke. There were 75 panzerfaeuste in Geseke, manned by the Volkssturm. The advancing tanks of Battle Group Kane were met at the east gate by women waving bed sheets. On their further march in the direction of Bueren one of their tanks was destroyed by an eight-eight flak gun. The crew of this air defense gun was shot by the Americans. Also shot were a German officer, who wanted to flee in his private vehicle in the direction of Boenninghausen, and a Luftwaffe soldier from Austria, who warned an air defense gun at the entrance to a village.

After this "clearing-up" of Geseke this formation continued in the direction of Stoermede. The half flak battery, which stood south of the reichsstrasse and was manned by RAD men, opened fire. They were quickly put out of operation by shots from the U.S. tanks. The 40 soldiers, which were here as an airfield guard, were taken prisoner.

There were no longer any German aircraft at the Stoermede – Eringerfeld airfield. They were all removed after the heavy air bombardment on 24/3.

Battle Group Kane continued its advance on Lippstadt from Stoermede via Langeneicke and Boekenfoerde.

At the same time these battle groups were coming from the south, there was a telephone conversation between Lieutenant General Collins, the commander of the VII U.S. Corps and Lieutenant General Simpson, the commander of the 9th U.S. Army, during which directives for both sides of the lead formations were given. Lieutenant General Simpson ordered the 2nd AD to conduct a direct attack against Lippstadt. For this purpose the division commander committed Battle Command B. This formation occupied the important road intersection at Beckum without a fight on the night of 1/

4. In the early morning hours Battle Command B rolled through Beckum. The 67th Armored Regiment from this divisions, the core of Battle Command B, and elements of the 41st Motorized Infantry Regiment quickly rolled further. They bypassed Diestedde and rolled through Waderlos. A German vehicle column was severed on the Lippstadt – Wiedenbrueck road and numerous vehicles were captured, along with 400 prisoners. From here elements of Battle Command B turned to the south and rolled against Lippstadt. The German defense located at the edge of the city was taken by surprise by D Company under Lieutenant Glass, they captured 103 prisoners and 30 trucks. In addition, three half-tracks and eight panzerfaeuste and guns were secured. Therefore, Lippstadt was in Allied hands. The anti-tank obstacles and road blocks now hindered the Germans as they attacked into the city and broke out.

The remaining formations of Battle Command B continued to roll and they established a strong defensive line along the Lippe from Lippstadt to Herzfeld. The five roads leading to the south of Lippstadt were closed.

At 1609 hours the troops of this battle group met the forward elements of the 3rd U.S. AD. Therefore, the pocket around the Ruhr area was closed and Army Group B was encircled. (See: After Action Report of the 2nd U.S. AD.)

The Final Battle in the Ruhr Pocket - Battle Group Albert Ernst

The formations of the 5th Panzer Army under Generaloberst Harpe were withdrawn from the Rhein front during the first days of April, first the rear area services, the non-combatant elements, then also the combat divisions. On 10/4/1945 they stood on a line northeast of Cologne through Luedenscheid to Plettenberg in defensive combat. The remnants of the 15th Army were withdrawn to a line Werdohl – Iserlohn – Hemer – Menden. In the still 50 kilometer long and 30 kilometers deep pocket stood the combat formations of Army Group B with their rear area service troops. The Chief of Staff of Army Group B, Generalmajor Carl Wagener, reported on the situation:

"From 12 to 13/4 the north, south and east fronts of the army group had withdrawn considerably. The last Ruhr bridgeheads were recaptured by Gruppe von Luettwitz. Dortmund was evacuated.

A deep armored breakthrough occurred in the 5th Panzer Army area of operations from Siegburg to Burscheid and in the 15th Army area of operations near Luedenscheid with its direction of advance toward Sorpetal block.

On 13/4 the eastern front appeared to be cracked. The LXXXI Army Corps was missing. Heavy road congestion, vehicle concentrations and numerous stragglers all indicated the beginning of disintegration. The pocket only had a diameter of 45 kilometers. There was only sufficient bread and ammunition for three days.

From the Wehrmacht reports Army Group B learned of the hopeless situation outside of the Ruhr pocket. Hannover, Braunschweig, Magdeburg, Weimar, Jena were all lost. The enemy was on the Elbe; the Eastern Front stood right in front of Berlin.

It was time for the army group to make its own decisions, regardless of orders. An American demand to surrender was not answered, because their demand for 'unconditional surrender' brought into question the principals of the Geneva Convention.

After testing all possibilities for future operations, the commander of the army corps came to a solution used by the Russians in many pocket battles in the east: Army Group B would disband and reorder as best as possible. The date for this was established as 17 April. On that day rations and ammunition would run out."

On 14 April the enemy changed its normal tactic of slowly compressing the pocket front from all sides and now launched a decisive breakthrough. One of the attacks was directed along the Ruhr west of Neheim up to the area north of Iserlohn and another from the south in the direction of Hahenlimburg and Hagen. These attacks split the Ruhr pocket into two parts on 14/4.

On the afternoon of 12/4 Generalleutnant Bayerlein visited the prisoner camp east of Hemer, in which 25,000 Allied prisoners of war from all nations were incarcerated, they had not received any rations for days. The camp commandant received instructions from LIII Corps to gather rations for the prisoners from the surrounding population.

When Bayerlein learned that the Americans had fired artillery into this camp in the afternoon, he drove there again and saw that one of the tents was destroyed by a direct hit and the 70 inhabitants were killed. He ordered a prisoner, a U.S. major, be released and requested him to drive to the 99th U.S. ID and inform them that they were shooting their own people.

Otherwise, this was the first contact with the enemy in the corps sector.

During a situation briefing, which Generaloberst Harpe, the commander of the 5th Panzer Army, conducted in Siegen, Hauptmann Albert Ernst, commander of a Tiger company in the 512th Heavy Panzer Battalion, to which additional weapons were deployed, received instructions from the commander to cover the withdrawal of the 5th Panzer Army.

The Tigers of this battalion had 12.8 cm cannon of over eight meters length. They were organized under the command of Hauptmann Scherf in Paderborn at the 500th Tiger Ersatz Battalion.

From the Doellersheim area, where these jagdtigers were inserted, they received orders on 10/3/1945 to quickly march against the Allied eastern Rhein bridgehead near Remagen. The attack failed and Albert Ernst and his six jagdtigers received orders to cover the retreat.

They were able to shoot pursuing enemy tanks at over 2000 meter distances as they rolled through Niedernepfen and Obernepfen toward Siegen. There – as anticipated – they were committed as the rear guard for the 5th Panzer Army. During the fighting to breakout from the Ruhr pocket the jagdtigers ran into Sherman tanks for the first time. The enormous 12.8 cm anti-tank shells tore up these enemy vehicles.

Battle Group Ernst now received a platoon of assault guns, several Panzer IV's and a platoon with four 3.7 cm four-barreled air defense guns. Therefore, the battle group had considerable striking power.

While Oberleutnant Rondorf took over the jagdtiger company, Ernst led the entire formation, as it rolled out of Siegen through Meinerzhagen, Kalte Eiche and Bruegge to Luedenscheid.

Arriving in Altena, Hauptmann Ernst learned that he was to transfer to Iserlohn on 8/4 by rail. Several of his tanks moved on the ground.

They were loaded at the Menden – Oege railroad station. Albert Ernst and his jagdtigers rattled through Hagen. They were sheltered in the forest near Buehrenbruch – Ergste. Here Hauptmann Ernst received orders to re-lieve Unna – which fell on 9/4.

On the next morning the tanks and assault guns rolled on Bundesstrasse 233. While it was still dark they crossed the Ruhr near Langschede. Sev-eral battalions of panzergrenadiers and infantry followed the panzer for-mation. American armored columns were seen from the Bismarckturm, they were moving on B[?] 1 in the direction of Dortmund. A strong group turned onto B[?] 233 and rolled directly at Battle Group Ernst. Albert Ernst moved the heavy weapons onto the hill. The jagdtigers and assault guns deployed on the crest. Four jagdtigers and four assault guns fronted to the north. The four 3.7 cm flak guns took up suitable flanking positions. A little later the U.S. armored formation rolled onto the terrain. They probed forward cautiously.

Through binoculars Hauptmann Ernst saw that the soldiers in the kasernes in Dortmund were already being marched off to captivity. There was was nothing more to relieve.

When the enemy approached close enough, Ernst ordered: "Free fire at your own targets!"

In this battle, during which the jagdtigers were able to fire with effect at distances of up to 4000 meters, the U.S. combat formation was dispersed. The two Sherman tanks in the lead fell after the first shots were fired. They were left burning on the plain. Other weapons were set ablaze, black smoke spiraled from the fires. The American advance came to a halt. They were quickly shot-up. Oberfeldwebel Totzek alone shot-up six Sherman tanks with his jagdtiger. In all, over 40 U.S. armored vehicles were lost here.

Shortly after that, fighter-bombers attacked the hill. The first aircraft flew into the fire curtain placed by 16 air defense tubes. Two Thunderbolt fighter-bombers fell in flames and exploded with a powerful detonation. The remainder turned back to the west.

A half hour later they appeared again. One of the four-barreled air de-fense guns was hit by a rocket bomb and destroyed. The rest continued to fight until they ran out of ammunition.

The fighter-bombers kept coming. One rocket fell through the open turret hatch of one of the jagdtigers, in which Leutnant Kubelka sat. The Tiger was destroyed along with the entire crew. Ernst's Tiger was paralyzed. Without flak ammunition they were lost on the hill, therefore, Hauptmann Ernst evacuated this exposed point. The combat formation withdrew and received orders on the following morning from LIII Corps to hold the Deilinghofen airfield for another 24 hours.

Ernst established his command post in Haus Hemer. His tanks and assault guns were rolled to the nerve center. However, Ernst was concerned about the prison camp (which was visited by Generalleutnant Bayerlein) with an estimated 30,000 prisoners, including Russians.

On the evening of 12/4, when the Americans probed here, Oberleutnant Rondorf shot-up two Shermans with his jagdtiger at a distance of about 4000 meters. At the same time, Oberfeldwebel Heinecke reported two tank kills.

On the evening of 12/4 Hauptmann Ernst was invited into the Hemer Buergermeister office. There Buergermeister Renzing explained to him that he wished to declare Hemer a hospital city, because there were many wounded here, as well as prisoners of war. Of course, Hauptmann Ernst had no influence in the matter. He had to defer to his standing orders.

On 13/4 Menden fell and during the morning the first shells hammered Hemer. A staff surgeon from the hospital begged Ernst to cease fighting not only because of the wounded, but also because of the thousands of prisoners.

Albert Ernst took a chance. He initiated surrender negotiations. He met Major Boyd H. McCune in the vicinity of Haus Hemer, McCune was the adjutant to Lieutenant Colonel Kriz, who, as the commander of the 394th IR of the 99th U.S. ID, was in charge of the fighting here. He succeeded in getting the 99th ID to stop firing its artillery and was assured that his battle group could leave Hemer.

According to the agreement made by the officers, Hemer was spared any more shooting. The 30,000 prisoners that streamed from the gates of the prison camp into the city to seek booty, were pushed back into the camp by the Americans. Some shots were fired and some prisoners were sacrificed. There was no other way they could get things under control, as Colonel Kriz reported to his former enemy and now friend Albert Ernst after the war.

Battle Group Ernst drove back over B 7 in the direction of Iserlohn. The city was already burning in some places, as U.S. artillery fell into it. Battle Group Ernst was again committed in Iserlohn and Hohenlimburg. On 15/4, when U.S. armored formations probed here, several Shermans were destroyed. Oberleutnant Rondorf alone shot three enemy tanks on this day.

This decisive defense and the strength of Battle Group Ernst created new prerequisites here for operations that had to be conducted, if the enormous number of refugees that were lodged in Iserlohn were not to be sacrificed to this last battle. When the U.S. artillery fired on Iserlohn on 15/4, Hauptmann Ernst drove to Flak Kaserne, in order to ask General Buechs, the city commandant to initiate surrender negotiations. There a man wanted to block his way, however, he reached his vehicle and drove back to his radio site. The news that he received here indicated to him that the surrender of individual formations was in full swing.

This time accompanied by two Tigers and one assault gun, he drove to Flak Kaserne to ask General Buechs to surrender. However, the General had already "checked out", as he was told by an officer when he asked after the commander.

Albert Ernst now acted completely independently. On the morning of 16/4 he drove in the direction of Seilersee to the Americans. There he came to an arrangement with the 394th IR. They agreed that the surrender negotiations would take place in the Iserlohn Rathaus.

Formalities were exchanged between Hauptmann Ernst and Lieutenant Colonel Kriz in the Rathaus. On Schillerplatz occurred the only official surrender of a city in the entire Ruhr pocket. Albert Ernst turned his pistol over to the American regiment commander. From him he received an invitation to visit the USA after the end of the war. Here the later head of the Kriz – Davis Company in Grand Island, USA describes his impression of the surrender in Iserlohn:

"It is difficult today to describe my feelings and the respect I had for Hauptmann Ernst. We had settled on an official surrender. This was the only one in which I personally participated. To my memory, the entire combat phase in connection with Iserloh was fought with this brave German unit."

However, the American commander wrote to Albert Ernst:

"The city of Iserlohn is deep in your debt. If you and your comrades had not surrendered the city of Iserlohn would have suffered tragic consequences. Beginning with Rommel's desert battles up to the invasion of Europe, you, as a German officer, played the greatest role in my commitment...

Yours
Bob."

In the early morning hours of 15/4/1945 Generalleutnant Bayerlein appeared once more at the remnant of the Panzer-Lehr Division, in order to say goodbye to his old comrades. He asked Oberst von Hauser to surrender the division at the first chance offered.

From hour to hour the ring compressed. The corps headquarters near Rafflingsen was already being fired on by the 7th U.S. AD. On the same day the remnants of the Panzer-Lehr Division surrendered. There were 2460 men and eight tanks and self-propelled weapons, 50 armored vehicles and a number of operational 8.8 cm flak guns left.

In all, there were 20 divisions encircled in the Ruhr pocket. GFM Model had signed relief papers for them all. At the same time, because these approximate 325,000 soldiers were marched off weaponless over many roads into captivity, the Generalfeldmarschall, three of his officers and two soldiers broke out of an American vehicle column near Ratingen and hid in a forest near Duisburg. Generalfeldmarschall Walter Model did not want to experience this end of Germany. On 21/4 there was a single pistol shot heard in the forest. General- feldmarschall Model, the commander of Army

Group B, which had been destroyed in the Ruhr pocket, committed suicide.

The Last Efforts in the West

Although no less than 18 Allied divisions were committed to clear the Ruhr pocket, all of the remaining divisions of the Western Allies immediately set in march to the Elbe. On the Western Front there now yawned a gap 320 kilometers wide. For GFM Kesselring, OB West, there was not the slightest chance of closing this gap.

In his command train, which took him from Ohrdruf to Blankenburg in the Harz on 3/4/1945, where he established the OB West headquarters, Kesselring tried to rescue whatever could be saved. The special train operated in the forest from Elbingerode to Drei-Annen-Hohne.

On 8 April Hitler declared the entire Harz a fortress and the 11th Army under General der Artillerie Lucht was tasked with the defense of this enormous "fortress." For the 12th Army, which was to conduct a relief attack (which will be described in the following chapter), Hitler had another mission. This army, which still completely did not exist, was to conduct an attack to the west from its assembly area in the Harz, establish contact with the formations of Army Group B located in the Ruhr pocket and pave the way for them to withdraw to the east.

On the basis of the situation, GFM Kesselring requested the deployment of troops from the 12th Army to the 11th Army in the Harz, in order to be able to hold this "fortress." On the basis of this request the "Potsdam" ID, which was in the process of being formed, was transferred to Halberstadt on 10/4/1945. The 12th Army established its headquarters in Blankenburg/Harz.

After the Harz was declared a fortress, Gauleiter and Reichsverteidigungskommissar Jordan requested GFM Kesselring attend an urgent meeting at his house in Schierke, in order to express the positions of the leaders of the the four Gaue in the Harz.

At the first meeting Jordan described the situation to the OB West and the criticality of the supply of the population. Kesselring explained that the

Western Front existed only on paper and that his ill-equipped formations lacked heavy weapons and would have to improvise the defense.

"Under these circumstances", Kesselring said, "holding and withdrawing is my last strategy and tactic. Every day we can hold out on the Western Front equates to a day of rescue for the thousands of men threatened by the Soviet attack." (See: Jordan, Rudolf: *I Survived and Suffered.*)

Jordan then informed the OB West that in a Harz defense the population, as well as the picturesque countryside would be threatened by the Anglo-American terror bombing, this would cost fearful sacrifice, even though there were no reserves of supplies for the civilian population in this region and none available for the Wehrmacht.

During the second meeting with the four Gauleiters, Gauleiter Jordan declared for these and all Party functionaries that the Harz could not be defended, because during a long siege a food catastrophe would occur. Moreover, the Harz was easy to bypass and vulnerable to concentrated air attack. GFM Kesselring, therefore, made the decision to abstain from defending the Harz. He allowed several cities and villages to be declared hospital cities and informed the enemy of this over the radio.

On 6/4/1945 the command organization in the west was again reordered. Because of the imminent splitting of Germany, authority was divided between a Supreme Commander Northwest and a Supreme Commander South. When this Fuehrer Order took effect, the OB left the Harz on 8/4/1945, in order to establish a new command post in southern Germany as the new OB South.

On 12/4/1945 GFM Kesselring lingered at Fuehrer Headquarters in order to see Hitler first hand. Hitler left no doubt that he would not give in. Kesselring often expressed his doubts and, therefore, proved to be a lot braver than many of the senior commanders.

Hitler told him – in complete confidence – about a new extremely explosive bomb that would soon be ready for commitment.

On 15/4/1945 Hitler issued an order that entrusted GFM Kesselring with the entire southern area, while Grossadmiral Doenitz took command in the northern region.

The time that this splitting of the Reich into northern and southern halves would take place was fast approaching. On 17/4 the lead elements of the American armored formations reached the Elbe 240 kilometers[?] east of Kassel. The 3rd U.S. Army had already advanced to the Czech border and Chemnitz in the southern sector. The 3rd U.S. AD, which belonged to the VII U.S. Corps, reached the Elbe in the vicinity of Dessau on 14 April.

The advance of the 1st U.S. Army into the Harz cut off 15,000 Wehrmacht soldiers. They continued to fight until 21 April.

The course of this fighting on the Elbe and the meeting of the Western Allies with the Russians will be discussed in the next section.

In the northern sector of the Western Front Montgomery's 21st Army Group quickly advanced on Bremen and Hamburg. The 2nd British Army reached the Weser on 6/4 and on 19/4 also stood on the Elbe near Dannenberg.

The XX British Corps had to literally shoot its way through a Luftwaffen battle group near Rheine before they could advance through Soltau into the Lueneburger Heide and from there to Harburg.

The troops of the 1st Fallschirmjaeger Army fought their last battle near Lingen. This was still a bitter duel that turned out to be bloody and costly for both sides.

The German fallschirmjaegers held in front of Bremen, supported by the XII Fallschirm Assault Gun Brigade, until 26 April. The fighting here was also bitter and conducted with blind fanaticism. The enemy was constantly repulsed in this small frontal sector and they lost a great number of tanks. Individual fallschirmjaeger battle groups fought until they were completely destroyed.

The front around Bremen held for three days against strong attacks. Fighter-bombers and bombers flew attacks in vain against this center of resistance. The German fallschirmjaegers literally crawled into the ground. They did not willingly give up one meter of ground without exacting a price. The strength of the Allies was also being exhausted.

In this situation Field Marshal Montgomery ordered the 51st ID under Major General McMillan to cross the Weser south of Bremen and attack the German HKL from the rear.

This double attack finally overcame the fallschirmjaegers. Bremen fell on 26/4/1945.

The formations of Montgomery's 21st Army Group stopped on the Elbe and began clearing up the area between the Elbe and the confluence of the Weser.

The fighting in the Harburg area was conducted with the same bitterness. Elements of the 9th German PD and the 15th PGD, which formed the southern flank of the 1st Fallschirmjaeger Army, were able to withdraw to Harburg and establish a defense there.

GFM Busch, the newly assigned OB Northwest to whom the 25th Army in Holland and the 1st Fallschirmjaeger Army were subordinate, was ordered by OKW to hold his entire area and not give up one meter of ground without exacting a price with these two armies and a new army formed from elements of the 1st Fallschirmjaeger Army and groups from all three branches of the Wehrmacht and designated as Armee Student. How the fighting in this final phase of combat in the Reich developed and what success these last measures enjoyed will be described in the closing section.

Now we will turn to the army that the Fuehrer had believed would tip the scales: the 12th Army.

5

THE 12th ARMY BETWEEN THE ELBE AND THE ODER

"Out of the necessity of the situation the 12th Army was improvised. It was created too late, it was assembled too late, the divisions were still incomplete and insufficiently equipped to commit this army.

Several of the divisions, which were to belong to the 12th Army, did not even reach the army assembly area – they were already committed to combat before that and defeated.

However, the catch-word for the 12th Army was "in spite of everything"! In spite of all of this, the troops fought as well as they could. They faced hopeless odds in costly combat. They were defeated and broken. They broke free again, won a battle and fought on.

The missions assigned to the army were, for the most part, impossible. In spite of this the clever commander of this army, General der Panzertruppe Walther Wenck, consistently found a workable solution within the limits of his tactical and operational possibilities. The turning of all German troops from the west to the east, long proclaimed by Generaloberst Guderian, was initiated too late." (General der Panzertruppe (Ret.) Maximilian Reichsfreiherr von Edelsheim to the author.)

The Situation and the Creation of the 12th Army

At the end of March 1945 Hitler ordered the OKW to create a new army in the area of the Elbe, in the Dessau and Wittenberge area, it was to be committed to the fighting in the west.

This new army, which at first only existed on paper, was recruited from the youngest year-groups, the 17 and 18 year-olds, as well as from the personnel from many weapons and RAD schools.

The army received the following mission, even before it existed:

"Assemble in the Harz, west of the Elbe. Attack to the west to relieve Army Group B. Establish a unified front by splitting the forces of the Western Allies and conducting wide-ranging operations."

Because the command of Army Group North was no longer needed for the command of the troops encircled in a narrow area in East Prussia in the beginning of April 1945, it was assigned command of the 12th Army. It arrived between 15 and 20/4/1945 by sea at Warnemuende.

Therefore, this command appeared on the scene after the situation already described had unfolded and Army Group B no longer existed.

The commander of the 12th Army, General der Panzertruppe Walther Wenck, who had suffered an automobile accident at Chiemsee, received a telephone call from Berlin on the morning of 6/4/1945.

General Burgsdorf was on the other end of the line. He informed Wenck that he was to report to Fuehrer Headquarters on the next day.

"The Fuehrer has named you commander of the 12th Army", Burgsdorf reported.

"The 12th Army?" Wenck asked. "What kind of an army is that, I have never heard of it!"

"You will learn all you need to know from the Fuehrer. It has just been created", Burgsdorf added before he hung up.

Wenck drove from Bavaria to Berlin and stood before Hitler on 7/4/1945. The General told the author:

"I found that Hitler's health had deteriorated even worse that before. His right arm and hand shook so strongly that he had to hold it with his left. His face was pale. However, he appeared to me to be more peaceful within.

After the usual situation briefing Hitler turned to me: 'Herr General Wenck, I name you commander of the 12th Army.'"

General Wenck then drove to Dahlem to OKW. Here he was briefed on the situation at the Western Front by Generaloberst Jodl, the Wehrmacht Chief of Operations. General Wenck learned that Army Group B was encircled in the Ruhr pocket and that there was a huge gap in the middle of the Western Front. Above all, there was a wide gap between the Harz and the forces encircled in the Ruhr pocket, through which the Allied armies of the western enemy were assaulting to the east.

However, he also learned about his new army: the divisions themselves were not complete and not fully equipped, but they would be committed in heavy fighting in northern and southern Germany.

These divisions, which General der Panzertruppe Wenck would face in the next few days and would lead, were raised by the last levy, however, they were good men, some first-class officers, combat experienced and highly decorated, were available as commanders.

The combat strength of these divisions averaged 10,000 men, therefore, they were undermanned by a third. Besides the assault gun brigades and several tanks from the panzer troop schools the divisions had no heavy weapons.

The 3rd Panzerjagd Battalion, which was ultimately deployed to the "Ulrich von Hutten" ID, was one of the few capable armored formations.

Only the "Clausewitz" Panzer Division was sufficiently equipped with panzer formations. At this phase of the history of the war and of the Germans, according to Walther Wenck, everything had to be done to facilitate the organization. Therefore, the commander of the 12th Army issued all instructions under the motto:

"1. Rescue as many men as possible, especially refugees, from the attacking Russians.

2. This war, which has now lasted almost six years, will be ended with dignity for the German people." (Walther Wenck to the author.)

A total of ten divisions were in the 12th Army, as described to the new army commander by Generaloberst Jodl. They bore sonorous names:

Panzer Division "Clausewitz"
Panzergrenadier Division "Schlageter"
Infantry Division "Potsdam"
Infantry Division "Scharnhorst"
Infantry Division "Ulrich von Hutten"
Infantry Division "Friedrich Ludwig Jahn"
Infantry Division "Theodor Koerner"
Infantry Division "Ferdinand von Schill"
An infantry division in northern Germany (this was not committed in the 12th Army area of operations.)
An SS panzer division in southern Germany, from elements of the SS Junkerschulen. (They were already committed to battle before the army was completed.)
3rd Panzerjagd Bn with two panzer companies each with 15 jagd-panthers and an SPW company with 20 SPW.

General Wenck was assured that the remnants of the 11th Army would also be subordinated to him. Wenck was to attack from the Harz to the west with his still non-existent army, in order to liberate Army Group B under GFM Model.

General Wenck did not find the staff promised to him in the Harz in Blankenburg, however, he was informed that he had to go back to Dessau, they would report to him there.

On 12/4/1945 Oberst Reichhelm reported there as the Ia of the army. Still later that evening the communications battalion reported, they were able to establish communications to the Magdeburg Combat Commandant, Generalleutnant Raegener. He reported that U.S. tanks had already penetrated up to the edge of the city. The first attack was repulsed and the enemy turned to the south and an advance commando was crossing the Elbe between Magdeburg and Barby.

General Wenck immediately dispatched reconnaissance to Magdeburg. They confirmed the situation as described.

It was the 9th U.S. Army under General Simpson that had reached the Elbe south of Magdeburg on 11/4/1945. On 12/4 the 2nd U.S. AD of this army had established a small bridgehead on the eastern bank of the Elbe about 16 kilometers further upstream. Major General Isaac D. White was set to assault directly to Berlin with his 2nd AD – "Hell on Wheels" – and had already worked out a detailed attack plan with his Chief of Staff, Colonel Brirard P. Johnson.

On the morning of 12/4/1945 almost every American newspaper bore the headline:

"THE NINTH 57 MILES FROM BERLIN!"

Even President Franklin D. Roosevelt, who was in Warm Springs at the time, read this line. A little later he was dead. The commander of the army in Germany learned of the death of his President during the following night. The new President was Truman.

The First Commitment of the 12th Army on the Elbe

The divisions of the 12th Army were located in the large area south of Wittenberge up to Grimma east of Leipzig. The Holste Operations Staff, which was in the Rathenow area, received the mission of defending the Elbe with the available troops and those they themselves could organize and subordinate.

The "Potsdam" ID was committed to the fighting with the 11th Army in the Harz after it was created and, with the exception of a weak regiment that was taken over by the "Scharnhorst" ID, was not made available to the 12th Army.

The creation of "Ulrich von Hutten" was almost completed on 12/4/

181

1945, while the "Friedrich Ludwig Jahn" ID lagged the farthest. General Wenck did not know when it would be ready for its first commitment.

The Burg Assault Gun School (near Magdeburg) was essentially a personnel and equipment replacement pool for the 12th Army. General Wenck had personally saw to their utilization. After he had seen the available equipment, the weapons and the soldiers, General Wenck ordered the creation of a partially mobile division from the Burg Assault Gun School, he named it "Ferdinand von Schill."

This division was essentially employable on 24/4, although the assault gun brigade was committed earlier.

On 12/4 the 12th Army still had no panzer formation available. They did not come into play until the 3rd Panzerjagd Battalion was deployed to the "Ulrich von Hutten" ID for mobile combat operations west of the Elbe on 17/4.

As a backstop for the particularly threatened Elbe sector near Magdeburg there was at first only the Burg Assault Gun School with their heavy weapons, particularly assault guns.

On 13/4 the 12th Army took over the sector of the Magdeburg Combat Commandant on the basis of a report, according to which the enemy was penetrating into the western portion of the city. The 12th Army now had to immediately participate in the fighting, no matter what its stage of creation. Its area of responsibility stretched from Doemitz to Leipzig.

Generalleutnant Martin Unrein, commander of the "Clausewitz" Panzer Division, after his division was only partially ready, received orders from the OKW on the evening of 10/4/1945 to transfer into the area directly north of Uelzen. The division was to be made available as an attack reserve, in case the enemy attempted a breakthrough of the German HKL south of Uelzen. Therefore, the division was subordinated to the 25th Army under General Blumentritt. The division command post was located at the Emmendorf labor camp north of Uelzen.

When Generalleutnant Unrein arrived at his new headquarters, he described the situation as follows:

"British troops were cautiously probing Uelzen from the southwest with tanks. Because the available defensive forces south of Uelzen were insufficient and because this important railroad junction had to be held, the 25th Army ordered the commitment of this 'loan' division on the morning of 11/4."

Generalleutnant Unrein organized 20 tanks, 10 assault guns and the SPW battalion with about 80 SPW's on the defensive front south of Uelzen. He himself was designated as sector commander by General Blumentritt.

The Allied attack from the south and southwest on Uelzen began on 12/4. Martin Unrein saw the advancing enemy tanks from his command post. One group rolled right at his assembly of tanks and assault guns.

With the order for commitment the thirty combat vehicles rolled against the enemy and opened fire. Three minutes later four British tanks lay burning on the plain. The assault guns advanced quickly, stopping only to fire. Almost all of their shots were direct hits. Enemy tanks lay burning with shot-up tracks and blown off turrets.

Now Generalleutnant Unrein ordered the SPW's to move. They rolled on both flanks, outflanked the enemy lead attack elements and inflicted great loss on the enemy. Within a few minutes the armored duel was decided in favor of the German combat vehicles. The English armored division had suffered heavy losses for the first time since the fighting around Xanten, according to prisoner of war statements.

The English did not attack Uelzen again. They later continued their advance 10 kilometers to the west of Uelzen in the direction of Bienenbuettel.

On the following day, 12/4/1945, Generalleutnant Unrein received orders to regroup; the tanks and SPW battalion were removed from the front on 12/4. Two panzergrenadier battalions and 10 assault guns were left there and subordinated to the infantry division that took over the positions.

On 12/4 the staff of the XXXIX Panzer Corps under General der Panzertruppe Decker arrived at Generalleutnant Unrein's command post. Unrein learned that his division and two others still being formed were to be subordinated to the XXXIX Panzer Corps and that they would be ordered by OKW to leave the Uelzen area as soon as possible to the south, advance through Helmstaedt deep into the flanks and rear of the 12th U.S. Army Group and make contact with the 11th Army fighting in the Harz.

General Decker explained that the corps would make contact with the 11th Army under General der Artillerie Lucht in the Harz after crossing the Weser – Elbe Canal.

Generalleutnant Unrein proposed to General Decker that, after his division was fully formed, which he anticipated would be on 17 or 18/4, he would advance through Wittingen and Salzwedel in the direction of Fallersleben and the Elm toward the Harz.

The OKW believed that this would be too late and ordered all available division forces to set out immediately.

The forces still located south of Uelzen were to turn to the south, after they had first destroyed the British forces located in the Hollenstedt area.

Generalleutnant Unrein decided to launch a night attack with a strong armored battle group under the command of an experienced Hauptmann. This battle group would be supplied with 20 tanks, 10 assault guns and 80 SPW.

During the night before 15/4 they set out from the area north of Uelzen through Osterholz toward Bollensen. Their far-ranging objective was: to advanced through Stadensen toward Hollenstedt.

How this night panzer attack occurred was described by Feldwebel Ernst Hollmann, a tank commander in the battle group:

"We quickly rolled through the streets. Several reconnaissance tanks led, and when they ran into the enemy in a town before Bollensen, we received the news over the radio. Our battle group commander gave the order to attack. We attacked in a wide wedge into the town. The first enemy tanks appeared ghostly before us. Further to the right, near the assault guns, the first shots were fired, and enemy tank cannon replied from the town.

Then a large shadow appeared in front of us: a tank! The gunner saw him just as I did. He made some adjustments and fired the first round. The impact hit in front of us. A second later this enemy tanks was in flames.

We rolled further, entering the town. Flames shot out of 20 tank cannon and ten assault guns. Flames rose from tanks and buildings.

Still more enemy tanks appeared. Six or seven appeared in front of us, they were turning toward my company.

We fired as quickly as we could. A heavy strike hit the turret of our tank and made us hard of hearing. However, the shell bounced off. The right side received the next hit. Behind a low building appeared an armored vehicle. Unteroffizier Greller, my gunner, had him in his sights. He allowed him to approached a little more, when the turret turned in our direction he fired.

Our seven-five shell tore the enemy turret from its mount at this short distance. The next shot set it ablaze.

'Attack through – Everyone follow me!' the battle group commander ordered over the radio.

We rolled further. A fence crunched under our treads. Tanks were still firing at other tanks. Our assault guns fired at the enemy from right and left.

The schuetzenpanzers with the panzergrenadiers arrived, in order to protect us from the attacks of the English infantry as they tried to counter our tanks with explosives. Now machine-guns were hammering. Hand-grenades detonated all around us.

Several enemy tanks were on the flanks in a flat depression. They surprised us by opening fire on a neighboring company. Twice I heard explosions tearing apart my comrades vehicles. However, we fought our way through, reached the eastern exit and continued to fire at the withdrawing enemy tanks.

The fighting, which had started at 0300 hours, lasted over an hour until dawn. When the sun came up there was nothing remaining of the English armored battalion that had been located here in the town of Nettelkamp. Burning wrecks lay about the town, in the meadows and in the depression. Only three German tanks were destroyed. Two assault guns were also included among the destroyed. However, the enemy had lost 41 tanks and armored vehicles during this night. It was indescribable how we felt about this night battle. Our hastily thrown together group had defeated a strong enemy force."

In the morning the battle group commander was severely wounded. On the afternoon of 15/4 a major took command in his place. The panzer group now had to assemble in Bollensen, in order to re-supply with ammunition and refuel. They no longer anticipated an enemy attack on Uelzen or to the east after this defeat.

On the same day at 1700 hours the battle group attacked in the direction of Borgenteich – Schmolau and Reddinghaus on the insistence of the OKW. Generalleutnant Unrein gave the battle group commander free reign, he only ordered the next objective to be the area 15 kilometers west of Gardelegen.

On the afternoon of 16/4 the battle group reported over the radio that they had already reached the Gifhorn – Salzwedel road, approximately 2.5 kilometers northeast of Brome, and blocked it during the morning. Several English vehicles were destroyed. With the fall of darkness the advance was resumed. The end objective was the forest 10 kilometers southwest of Calvoerde.

After receiving this news, Generalleutnant Unrein immediately assembled a second smaller battle group. It consisted of 10 tanks and assault guns, several SPW and an engineer company, as well as trucks with a supply of fuel for the entire battle group.

This second battle group drove with a liaison officer from the first battle group, who had made his way to the division command post, to the first battle group, they reached it and reinforced it.

On 17/4 this reinforced battle group suffered heavy losses during an attack on the Weser – Elbe Canal. Strong British armored formations opposed it. A bitter armored duel led to heavy sacrifice on both sides; a British defensive line that was echeloned deep in the depth prevented the breakthrough.

Feldwebel Ernst Hollmann's tank, with the gunner Unteroffizier Greller, destroyed another three enemy tanks here before a hit knocked of their right track. Greller was still able to destroy another enemy tank before a second hit into the engine compartment set the tank afire. Feldwebel Hollmann order them to abandon ship. They were able to reach security through the enemy machine-gun fire, even carrying the wounded driver.

The German battle group stalled after the initial success. In the early morning hours of 18/4 Generalleutnant Unrein received a report on the recent events. He ordered a third battle group be assembled under Major Benningsen, which even included the division staff. They consisted of 12 tanks and assault guns that had just come from the repair shop. A company from the reconnaissance battalion and the two panzergrenadier battalions, which were previously engaged in defensive combat in Uelzen, were also included. Two light flak battalions completed the group.

When the two panzergrenadier battalions were removed from their front south of Uelzen on the early morning of 18/4 and rolled into their new assembly area British troops attacked out of the Lehmke area toward Schlieckau, broke through the weak security of the infantry division committed there and forced the two battalions to give battle near Schlieckau. Therefore, these reinforcements were denied Generalleutnant Unrein's 3rd Battle Group, including their ten Hetzer panzerjaegers. They were to follow in the general direction of Brome – Fallersleben on the evening of 19/4.

The OKW ordered over radio the immediate commitment of the 3rd Battle Group, even though the promised reinforcements of artillery and air defense had not arrived.

In this manner the otherwise strong "Clausewitz" Panzer Division was piecemealed into commitment and experienced the last battles in the forest south of Bergmoor and near Haselhorst sometime later, where the lead panzer elements met their end in an anti-tank block, which had, in the meantime, been set up by the U.S. forces. Indeed, Haselhorst was able to be captured in a last bitter armored battle, however, artillery and air forces made life difficult for the men of the 3rd and 4th Battle Groups. Finally there would only be 10 officers and 60 soldiers left to the division commander in the Appenrode area. They would be taken prisoner within the next few days.

Therefore, the "Clausewitz" Panzer Division would not be committed with the 12th Army.

Fighting on the Elbe

On 12/4/1945 at 2000 hours the first American amphibious vehicles crossed the Elbe. Since the bank at this location was, in general, unoccupied, they met little German resistance. At midnight Brigadier Hinds, commander of the 2nd U.S. AD Combat Command B, crossed two armored infantry battalions near Westerhuesen south of Magdeburg. In the early morning hours there were already three battalions standing on the eastern bank of the Elbe.

Generalmajor White, the division commander, informed the 9th Army:

"We are there!"

When the engineers were able to erect a ponton bridge across the river, German artillery opened fire from the southwestern edge of Magdeburg onto this bridge, which was turned to ruins by morning.

In the afternoon of 13/4 a new bridge building operation was begun further to the south so that tanks could be brought up as quickly as possible and reinforce the battalions located between Elenau and Gruenwalde.

Exactly 25 kilometers further south near Barby the first elements of the 83rd U.S. ID under Major General Macons also reached the Elbe. Here Lieutenant Colonel Crabill, commander of the infantrymen of the 331st Regiment, immediately placed all arriving men into assault boats and crossed them. The first guns of the division artillery crossed the river on Pontons. By the evening of 13/4 the entire 83rd ID had made it across and later their engineer bridge was completed. At the entrance and exit of the bridge on both banks were placed signs:

"Truman Bridge – The Door to Berlin!
Courtesy of the 83rd ID!"

From here it would have been light work for the Americans to breakthrough to Berlin. However, during a discussion about the ifs and buts General Bradley believed that the further attack to Berlin would cost the U.S. troops 100,000 dead and wounded:

"A very high price to pay for an objective of prestige, especially when one considered that we would have to withdraw at the end of the fighting and turn the area over to the Russians."

General Eisenhower was satisfied with this reply, because he had stated his intent to stop on the Elbe in his exchange of correspondence with Marshal Stalin. (See: Time from 29/9/1961: How Berlin Got Behind the Curtain – A political decision which the soldiers did not reverse.)

On 13/4 the "Scharnhorst" Division received orders from the 12th Army to prepare a reinforced regiment for an attack into the Magdeburg area. Therefore, at the same time the Burg Assault Gun School was alerted by the Magdeburg Combat Commandant. The combat capable elements were organized into Battle Group Burg on 10/4 under the command of Major Alfred Mueller. Major Mueller, who had been awarded the Oak Leaves to the Knight's Cross as commander of the 101st Assault Gun Battalion on 15/12/1943, was predestined for this mission as the commander of the Burg Assault Gun School. His battle group was committed against the Americans on the eastern bank of the Elbe north of Magdeburg.

The first assault guns of this battle group conducted an attack on the morning of 14/4 on the northeastern portion of the U.S. bridgehead south of Magdeburg, which was under the command of Lieutenant Colonel Anderson. Seven of the committed assault guns reached the enemy infantry positions and fired on them with shells and machine-guns. They attacked through these positions untouched, because, other than a few bazookas, there were no anti-tank weapons available.

The U.S. infantry companies took flight. Lieutenant Colonel Anderson requested artillery fire on his own location in vain, when the first shells flew across the Elbe the assault guns had already passed this area.

Simultaneous with this attack several tanks rolled on the left flank of the German attack wedge. Infantrymen from the "Scharnhorst" Division followed. German soldiers attacked the division that had just arrived in the bridgehead from three directions. The enemy resistance was broken by precise assault gun fire, which shattered the American positions. The Americans were either captured or thrown back into the river. At midday Brigadier General Hinds was forced to order the withdrawal of the surviving troops from the hard-pressed bridgehead to the western bank.

For the first time during their trip through Germany the 2nd U.S. AD, "Hell On Wheels", was forced to retreat.

Therefore, the bridgehead south of Magdeburg was eliminated and General Wenck then planned to remove the bridgehead near Barby. This one was significantly larger and had already received artillery.

Generalmajor Goetz, the commander of the "Scharnhorst" ID, received orders to immediately advance to block the Barby bridgehead. He led the division, to which two assault gun companies were subordinated, at a fast tempo. With the fall of twilight on 14/4 the infantry and assault guns attacked. They reached the security lines of the 83rd U.S. ID and pushed them back to the main body.

During a nighttime fire-fight the assault guns proved to be very capable. They were able to destroy forward-based machine-gun and anti-tank positions and push the enemy back to the river. Generalmajor Goetz was unable to throw the enemy into the river and, therefore, eliminate the bridgehead.

The reason for this was that a portion of the division was denied him, in order to stop an enemy attack reported on Dessau. A further portion of the division, which still stood further to the south of Magdeburg, was also unavailable.

The "Ulrich von Hutten" Division was also set in march from the 12th Army on 14/4 and moved from its assembly location at Wittenberg through Graeffenhainichen into the Bitterfeld area. They had the mission of assembling there and conducting reconnaissance to the northwest, west and southwest. In this manner they were to try to establish contact with German formations still fighting in the reconnaissance area. They were to hold off the enemy forces, which were advancing from all sides, for as long as possible.

Generalleutnant Engel, the division commander, brought his division into positions forward of the Dessau – Leipzig autobahn and ordered them to construct positions. The division then awaited the enemy attack alone. The U.S. armored troops arrived on 15 April at the forward positions of this division. The anti-tank guns and air defense guns, in conjunction with several assault guns, stopped the enemy.

On the two following days the division held off all enemy attacks. The panzerjaegers, engineers, artillerymen and panzergrenadiers of this division fought here with valor for three days and nights. In spite of strong artillery and armor support, the enemy did not get through. Nevertheless, the German bridgehead was compressed more and more and finally split in two: one bridgehead near Jessnitz, the other near Bitterfeld. These two bridgeheads were to be held, by order of the army.

On 15/4 the enemy crossed additional forces over the river near Barby, the assault guns of the "Scharnhorst" ID were unable to stop them. Nevertheless, the American attack momentum was halted. This reinforced Eisenhower's and Bradley's decision to stop on the Elbe. If the 2nd U.S. AD were able to hold the bridgehead on the eastern bank of the Elbe, erect a ponton bridge and cross additional heavy weapons, then they would have, perhaps, continued their advance on Berlin. However, now Major General White had to utilize the 83rd ID bridge if he wanted to cross his tanks over the river. However, at the same time, because the first tanks of the 2nd U.S. AD crossed the Elbe over this bridge, General Eisenhower dispatched a message to the Chief of the U.S. General Staff in Washington from his HQ in Reims, in which he informed General Marshall that the advance of his central forces had achieved the Elbe and the first bridgeheads across the river. He now saw their next mission as being the destruction of the German forces in Bavaria and in northern Germany.

With regard to Berlin, Eisenhower declared in this message:

"It is highly desirable to undertake an advance to Berlin, because the enemy would assemble as many troops as possible at his capital city and because the fall of Berlin would have a strong effect on the combat morale of the enemy and our own people."

However, Eisenhower did not see this operation being conducted in the central sector, there where the assault on Berlin had its departure point, he only saw "a solid front on the Elbe", which had to be held. It appeared to him more important to "break the Alp fortifications."

When Lieutenant General Simpson, the commander of the 9th U.S. Army, requested permission to attack his troops toward Berlin, "because my men, who have crossed the river, dream of Berlin", he was summoned to a meeting at the 12th Army Group headquarters. There he learned from General Bradley what he could not tell him over the telephone:

"You must remain on the Elbe, Simpson! You must not advance any further in the direction of Berlin! I am sorry, Simp, however, this is how it has to be."

"Where the hell did such orders come from?" asked the commander of the 9th Army.

"From Ike", replied Bradley.

"And how am I to tell my staff and the corps commanders and, above all, the troops, who had made such efforts to reach Berlin as quickly as possible?"

That Bradley did not know. The commander of the 9th U.S. Army flew back to his headquarters, to prepare them for this thunderbolt.

How the troops accepted this order is described by Brigadier General S.L.A. Marshall during the Berlin crisis in 1961:

"In April 1945 I was with a battle group near Barby, below Magdeburg, when the oder to stop arrived. We had the only bridgehead on the eastern bank of the Elbe, it was only 88 kilometers from Berlin. For weeks this city had been our objective. We had dreamed of reaching it as quickly as possible. The main battle group consisted of Colonel Crabill's 331st Infantry Regiment.

My notes from this period record:

We conquered the bridgehead in a battle that began at midday. Only a few shots were exchanged. Crabill drove along the lines of boats, in which his people had boarded, and called to them:

'Lets not loose the opportunity of our lives! You are on the way to Berlin, boys! We can be the first to get there! However, you must hurry!

Don't loose sight of the objective! You do not need to build positions. Get to Berlin!'

Troops from the Scottish 15th ID cross the Rhein near Xanten.

A wounded paratrooper is brought back.

Terror bombing against Dortmund: The destroyed Westfalenhalle.

The dead have to be identified at the Dortmund main railroad station.

A USAAF B-17 during a bombing mission.

This B-17 was hit by flak immediately after dropping its bombs.

Major Helmut Hudel fought with his battle group in the Ruhr pocket.

Hauptmann Albert Ernst, commander of the Jagdtiger Battle Group, near Paderborn.

Jagdtiger from Battle Group Ernst near Iserlohn.

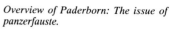
Overview of Paderborn: The issue of panzerfauste.

A Jagdtiger rolls to the Iserlohn market place.

Surrender.

Hauptmann Ernst reports to Ober: leutnant Kriz.

U.S. 8th Armored Division in Dorsten.

Iserlohn on the day of surrender.

29/3/45: German prisoners east of the Rhein.

Street fighting in Arnheim on 14/4/45.

Koeln and the destroyed Rhein bridge.

Koeln Cathedral was also hit.

Oberst Alfred Druschel fought with his S.G. 4 in the West; he fell on 1/1/1945.

Hauptmann Gerhard Stuedemann commanded the III/SG 77 in the east.

Feldwebel Hermann Bix, panzer commander during the battle of Danzig.

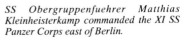
SS Obergruppenfuehrer Matthias Kleinheisterkamp commanded the XI SS Panzer Corps east of Berlin.

General der Infantrie Hermann Recknagel, commander of the XXXXII Army Corps, fell in defensive combat in the east on 23/1/45.

General der Panzertruppe Walther K. Nehring, last commander of the 1st Panzer Army.

General der Infantrie Hermann Niehoff, the defender of Breslau.

Generalleutnant Dr. Karl Mauss, last commander of the 7th Panzer Division, which was to liberate Elbing.

The 5th U.S. Armored Division of the 9th Army 12 miles west of the Elbe.

Russian troops of the 1st Ukrainian Front in Gleiwitz.

Oberst Stern, commandant of the French Officers' Prison Camp at Soest, is taken prisoner.

7000 German soldiers from Army Group B are taken prisoner near Iserlohn.

Troops of the 17th U.S. Airborne Division east of Wesel on 27/3/45.

1/4/45: Lippstadt is reached.

Army Group B command post: GFM Model with his staff officers and commanders: to the left is Oberstleutnant Werning. To the right of Model are Generals Lucht, Hitzfeld and Tolsdorff.

At the West Wall, from the left: Field Marshal Montgomery, Sir Alan Brooke, Churchill and Lieutenant General Simpson.

Tank destroyer troops take up positions in Silesia.

GFM Schoerner and Dr. Josef Goebbels in re-captured Lauban.

Searchlights as street obstacles.

And the regiment made it. In this manner we took the bridgehead.'

The enemy immediately launched a strong counterattack with infantry, artillery and tanks. They maintained the pressure for three days, however, our bridgehead held. And while the fighting around Barby was still raging, the order came to hold.

I drove in a jeep with Captain Robert E. Merrian to General Raymond McClain's headquarters, the commander of the XIX U.S. Corps, in order to hear an assessment on this order to hold. He told us:

'It is correct that we hold! This corps is stretched out too much. This also goes for the rest of the 9th Army. We are fighting to our front, on both flanks and in the rear. I don't think that we could carve out any large portion of Berlin before the Russians did. At best we may be able to get a couple of patrols into the city." (See: Marshall, S.L.A.: *We Couldn't Have Taken Berlin in 1945.*)

This statement from the commander of the XIX U.S. Corps was the standard comment expressed by General Bradley.

On the morning of 16/4 the 12th Army command learned that the Soviets had attacked from the Oder toward the capital in the west. Immediately they were concerned about the security of their rear area communications in case the Soviets broke through to Berlin and they took corresponding measures.

With his Chief of Staff, Oberst Reichheim, General Wenck drove to the five divisions that were now assembled in the army area in order to see for himself the state of their preparedness.

At this time the Americans were making further attempts to cross the Elbe or Mulde, unaware of the demarcation line that was to be established between the western and eastern Allies.

However, General Wenck ordered the first of his troops to be removed from the Western Front on 17/4. He intended to build a security line against the Russians with them. General Wenck intended to have the army make contact with Army Group Vistula in the north, in order to prevent a Soviet attack toward Mecklenburg and Holstein.

On the early morning of 17/4 the "Scharnhorst" Division attacked an assault gun company to the north and east toward the enemy bridgehead near Barby. Again the assault guns advanced slowly. Enemy tanks that were located in the forward assembly areas engaged in a duel with the quick assault guns.

A little later the Burg Battle Group attacked with all of its assault guns. However, even this attack did not succeed, because the enemy, in the meantime, was able to cross guns, tanks, anti-tank guns and air defense guns over the river.

General Wenck decided to also commit the "Theodor Koerner" ID against this bridgehead, although it was still being formed in Doeberitz. However, because this division would not be available until 20/4, the attack had to be postponed until 22/4/1945.

On the evening of 17/4 the scout troops reported that the enemy had not reinforced the bridgehead and that things were quiet there. Nevertheless, the 12th Army, as before, was convinced that after the enemy threw up another bridge they would deploy additional fresh forces to continue the attack to the east.

On 18/4 it remained quiet on the bridgehead front. The "Scharnhorst" Division maintained pressure on the American bridgehead.

The enemy pressure against the Mulde positions began to increase noticeably on 19/4/1945. By 21/4 all local attempts by the enemy to establish a bridgehead on the eastern bank of the Mulde had been repulsed. A German bridgehead near Eilenburg was lost during an enemy attack with strong armored forces. The defenders were able to stop the majority of the enemy armor with panzerfaeusten. The Jessnitz – Bitterfeld bridgehead, which was being held by the "Ulrich von Hutten" ID, was also lost. Here the young soldiers of this division had stopped enemy infantry and armored attacks for three days and nights. The young grenadiers allowed the U.S. tanks to approach to within 20 meters before they fired their panzerfaeuste.

On 19/4 three strong attacks occurred one after the other against both bridgeheads. Many times the defenders were overrun in their trenches by the attacking tanks. Jessnitz was lost. The survivors withdrew across the Mulde.

On the following day – it was the Fuehrer's Birthday – the last elements of this division, which had crawled into the ground in the Bitterfeld bridgehead, also had to yield to the enemy superiority and withdraw to the eastern bank of the river.

Over 30 enemy armored vehicles lay burning or destroyed in front of this bridgehead. The "Ulrich von Hutten" Division established a defense behind the Mulde.

During the course of 20/4/1945 the enemy ceased his attacks here, so that a line Mulde – Freiberger Mulde – Tschoppau including Chemnitz could be held.

Between the Elbe and the Schwarzen Elster a Russian cavalry corps was discovered by scouts, they were advancing on a broad front and they reached the Riesa – Elsterwerda rail line on 20/4 and crossed it to the northwest. They were now rapidly approaching the Muehlberg – Bad Liebenwerda road. Other Russian formations reached the line Elsterwerda – Herzberg, the Schwarzen Elster from the northeast and attempted to fight their way across the river. The defensive line there was reinforced by several troop units from Army Group Schoerner deployed by Generalleutnant Scherer. Nevertheless, the defenders had difficulty resisting these attacks.

This Russian advance to the Schwarzen Elster could not be prevented, because there were no further troops available. Therefore, it was necessary to withdraw the eastern front of the XXXXVIII Panzer Corps to the Elbe.

It was, above all, divisions of the 5th Soviet Guards Army that veered off from the Soviet army group north of Senftenberg and advanced on the Schwarzen Elster and then toward Torgau on the Elbe, while the 3rd and 4th Guards Tank Armies of the 1st Ukrainian Front continued to assault in the old direction. However, more will be said of this in the second part of this report.

Battle Group Burg – The Later "Ferdinand von Schill" Division – in Commitment

Battle Group Burg, which was committed under the leadership of Major Mueller by the Magdeburg Fortress Commandant to counterattack against the American forces located in the pocket south of Magdeburg, had its left flank on the autobahn near Hohenwarthe, while its right flank was near Rogaetz.

Besides striking the enemy bridgehead south of Magdeburg, the assault guns of this battle group also played a decisive role in the defense against an American attack near Zerbst out of the Barby bridgehead.

Over radio the XIX U.S. Corps, Major General McLain, had demanded that the Zerbst City Commandant surrender with his defenders. If this did not happen, then Zerbst would be leveled by aerial bombardment on the following morning.

The Zerbst City Commandant, a general whose name cannot be elicited, refused to surrender Zerbst, because this city east of the Elbe was also declared a fortress by the Fuehrer.

On the following morning the men of the Altengrabow Assault Gun Lehr Brigade, which was subordinated to the Burg Assault Gun School, saw the first groups of enemy bombers appear in the skies over the Elbe, however, they then suddenly veered off as the lead American armored elements rolled out of their bridgehead and attacked the front of the army group.

A bloody fight ensued, in which the assault guns, which had stood on all critical points on the Eastern Front for years, shot up the attacking enemy tanks.

Once again they heeded the call of the infantry from their trenches: "Assault Guns forward!" and again they appeared on the battlefield and opened fire. They pushed the enemy forces that had already advanced up to the southwestern edge of the city back and shot up the U.S. tanks that were to assist this attack to victory. The tanks lay burning on the battlefield.

However, immediately after this battle the adjutant of the Altengrabow Lehr Brigade, Oberleutnant Schuldt, saw from the brigade command post the attack waves of the U.S. Air Force as they dropped their bomb loads over the beautiful Renaissance city. He later told the author:

> "The city – viewed at a distance – collapsed like a house of cards and was set ablaze by the following incendiary bombs and phosphorus canisters. It was a picture of complete destruction. The unprotected civilian population suffered dreadful losses from the bombings.

Our brigade withdrew to the airfield immediately after this bombardment and was then set in march in the direction of Belzig in order to now be committed against the Soviets." (See Schuldt, Dr. jur. Rudolf: *In Commitment with the Altengrabow Assault Gun Brigade.*)

In the meantime, Battle Group Mueller received many units so that Major Mueller had to take it upon himself to supply this formation and reorganize it. Units that crossed the Elbe into the area between Magdeburg and Hannover were taken up by this formation and organized. Within a few days they had reached division strength. On 20/4, when the 12th Army established contact with this battle group, Major Mueller was summoned to the army command post at Dessau – Rosslau. Arriving there, General Wenck informed him of his promotion to Oberstleutnant and, at the same time, promoted the brave officer to Oberst on authority provided by OKH North.

Moreover, Battle Group Burg was renamed Division "Ferdinand von Schill." This ad hoc division was ordered by General Wenck into the Belzig area and committed next to the "Theodor Koerner" Division to defend against the Soviet attack east of Belzig. Therefore, the activities of the 12th Army in the west were finally ended, only weak security remained on the Elbe, while the army turned to the east to take part in the final battle for the Reich and Berlin.

We will now turn to the east of Germany, where several cities had been under fire by Russian artillery and Soviet bomber forces for months and had not surrendered.

6

THE FINAL BATTLE IN THE EAST

The Red Army on the Reich Border

By mid-summer 1944 the German eastern provinces were still a distance from any combat operations, if one discounted the sporadic sorties of Russian air attacks, which still had not reached any decisive dimensions.

The Russian major offensive "Bagration", which began on 22/6/1944 marked the beginning of the end for this period of quiet for eastern Germany. At the end of this operation the Red Army troops stood on the border of the Reich, it was now only a question of weeks until the next assault had to reach German territory, especially since a good portion of eastern Poland had already fallen into Russian hands.

Therefore, the Red Army could count on the active participation of Polish formations as we would see in Kolberg in the winter and spring of 1945.

The Polish Committee of National Liberation had taken over the government directly after the "liberation" by the Russians in this portion of the country and had reached an accord with the Soviet commanders which required Poland to offer as much military assistance as possible to combat the Germans. (See also: Foreign Documents to the Oder – Neisse Line in Eastern Handbook H.6.)

Die Zertrümmerung der Ostfront im Sommer 1944

14

Operation "Bagration." The Beginning of the end in the east.

The Polish forces, which had served in the Red Army since 1943, received reinforcements from volunteers and conscripts and from the partisans in eastern Poland, where the presence of Polish troops was considerably reinforced.

Since July 1944 the Germans had summoned all able-bodied men to work on the Eastern Wall. In addition, there were also foreign workers employed. They were shipped to the eastern border and behind the Narew front in four-week shifts to work on anti-tank trenches, rifle trenches and bunkers. The control over these workers from the Memel to Warsaw lay in the hands of the Gauleiter and Reichsverteidigungskommissar of East Prussia, Erich Koch.

There was similar construction work in the Generalgouvernement and in Warthegau. Here two lines were established, one behind the other, from Leslau to Wielun and the other from Kolmar to Lissa.

Along the old Silesian – Polish border fortifications were established as part of Operation "Berthold" and elements of the Silesian population were brought up for this work. (See also: Kaps, J.: *The Silesian Tragedy 1945-1946.*)

Reichsgau Danzig – West Prussia east of the Vistula and in the region of the Pomeranian and Obra positions there were similar occurrences.

All work on these defenses came under the Reichsverteidigungskommissar, the military commanders had only limited authority. This was indicated by the often unserviceable installations.

To all of the evils endured by the troops were added the inconsistencies of these fortification, which they were to occupy and stop the enemy's attacks.

However, the decisive failure for the hundreds of thousands and even millions of Germans was leaving the question of evacuating the civilian population from the combat area to the Reichsverteidigungskommissar and Gauleiter. The evacuation plans were not well thought-out by the party authorities, since propaganda had for weeks been spouting off about the fact that the enemy would be thrown back and that Germany's situation would change for the better soon.

Whoever during this retreat spoke of evacuation and did not believe in the promised salvation was a candidate for immediate execution.

The Russian Troops and their Situation

In mid-August 1944, the troops of the 1st and 2nd Belorussian Fronts and the 1st and 4th Ukrainian Fronts stood between the Narew and the Carpathians.

While the 1st Belorussian Front, which was advancing from Minsk across the Dnepr to the Vistula and had suffered considerable losses and could, therefore, not advance much further for the time being, stalled, the 2nd Belorussian Front reached the fortress of Ossowetz on the Lyck – Bialystok road on 11/8. General Sakharov was able to reach the Narew, which protected the southern border of East Prussia, by the end of August on a 150 kilometer front. Therefore, the pincer movement against East Prussia was initiated, it would lead to the isolation of this German province.

The 1st and 4th Ukrainian Fronts under Marshal Konev had, in the meantime, crossed to the western bank of the Vistula from the Sandomir bridgehead, which was taken by Rokossovskiy. He was advancing on the Krakau road up to Debica, 132 kilometers from Krakau and had overcome the Wisloka.

At the end of August it appeared that the entire central portion of the Russian western front had stalled and had deferred to the two flanks to achieve similar success as had the middle army groups.

The commander of the Leningrad Front, Marshal Govorov, and the commanders of his 1st, 2nd and 3rd Baltic Fronts, Bagramyan, Eremenko and Maslenikov, now attacked from the east and southeast with 100 divisions. These foot troops were supported by 4 tank corps and 28 tank brigades with a total of 2800 assault guns and tanks.

The German commander in this area, Generaloberst Schoerner, had approximately 30 large formations available.

The fighting in the Baltic Provinces began on 11/8/1944. By 13/8 General Maslenikov's troops assaulted through Pskow, broke through the blocking positions of the 18th German Army west of Lake Peipus and captured the university city of Dorpat on 25/8.

Simultaneous with this operation General Eremenko was able to force the Dvina and compel the 16th Army to retreat, reaching Kreuzburg.

General Bagramyan reached Tukkum on the Gulf of Riga on 1/8, severing the lines of communication between Army Group North and Army Group Center in this manner. On 8/8 his lead armored elements reached the town of Rossienai, 68 kilometers from the East Prussian border. From here on ran a good road to Tilsit.

The 3rd German Panzer Army under the command of Generaloberst Raus was committed into the left flank of this Russian attack wedge. This army attacked out of the area 80 kilometers northeast of Memel on 16/8 and was able to re-establish contact with the 16th Army on 20/8. This success gave Generaloberst Schoerner enough space to initiate the withdrawal ordered by OKW.

By 18/9 quiet dominated on this northern front, then Generals Maslenikov and Bagramyan resumed their attacks on both sides of the Dvina. In spite of the commitment of the III SS Panzer Corps under SS General Steiner, the attack gained ground. On 24/9 the Russian Leningrad Front had conquered all of Estonia, including the harbors at Reval, Baltischport, Hapsal and Pernau. Nevertheless, the German 18th Army was able to reach Kurland by sea with the main body of its troops.

The Russian attack continued. The Baltic islands fell to the attackers. Sworbe was held until 23/11 and the later evacuation of this peninsula, which formed the western exit to the Gulf of Riga, was accomplished without great loss.

On 10/10/1944 it continued. The commander of the 1st Baltic Front could report to Moscow that Army Group North was now permanently separated from Army Group Center.

The 16th and 18th German Armies held out in the Kurland bridgehead until the surrender, in spite of the Russian attacks conducted with overwhelming armor superiority.

When General Bagramyan had reached the Baltic Sea coast and, therefore, Kurland with its two German armies was cut off, General Chernyakovskiy had completed his preparations to attack East Prussia in his assembly areas on either side of the Insterburg – Kowno road. On 16/10 he initiated the offensive with a massive artillery strike, assembling a total of 75 batteries of all calibers for each kilometer of the attack area.

When the barrage fire ended, the 39th, 5th, 26th and 31st Soviet Armies attacked on a 140 kilometer front. They were supported by the tanks of the 11 Guards Tank Army.

The 4th German Army under General Hossbach, which was defending a 350 kilometer front with 15 infantry divisions, could not stand up to this attack. The Russians achieved a deep penetration in the area of Generalleutnant Matzky's XXVI Army Corps. The Wirballen border railroad station fell on 19/10 into the hands of the attackers. Therefore, the Red Army advanced here into German territory in the Eydtkuhnen area. From here the mobile armored formations pressed out in the direction of Rominter Heide. The first small German cities of Wirballen, Eydtkuhnen, Stallupoenen, Pilluoehnen, Rominten and Goldap were lost to the Red Army along with approximately 400 East Prussian towns.

The "Grossdeutschland" Panzer Division had to withdraw its troops to the left bank of the Memel on either side of Tilsit and, thereby, lost 2000 men during the crossing.

On 20/10 General Chernyakovskiy attacked the 11th Guards Tank Army across the Rominte toward Grosswaltersdorf. On the evening of the following day they stood, after an advance of about 20 kilometers, in the Nemmersdorf area on the western bank of the Angerapp. It appeared as if the enemy would achieve the breakthrough.

However, the troops of the XXVII Army Corps held in spite of strong enemy pressure. General Hossbach was able to remove several divisions from sectors of his extended front that were not being attacked and close the existing gaps with them.

The OKH had deployed the 5th PD and the "HG" Panzer Division. Both divisions counterattacked Gumbinnen, 12 kilometers northeast of Nemmersdorf. From Loetzen rolled a strong tank brigade and, because the XXVI Army Corps held unswervingly near Schlossberg and Ebenrode and stopped Chernyakovskiy's troops, the 11th Guards Tank Army fell into a pincer. They were thrown back in decisive combat to the right bank of the Rominte.

The Nemmersdorf Tragedy

During these operations the city of Nemmersdorf was re-captured. What the German soldiers found here defies any description.

The German tank drivers saw evermore frightening pictures as they pursued the enemy. In Scheunenwaende they saw lines of men, women and children stretched out.

The lead elements of the Russian troops had captured Nemmersdorf south of Gumbinnen on 20/10. When the German troops returned to this location several days later they found that the residents had suffered horrid deaths. When Hitler learned of this he immediately dispatched the military judge Paul Groch. Accompanying him were Stabsarzt Dr. Werner Rose and a press photographer. Several days later a medical commission arrived in Nemmersdorf.

Major Hinrichs of the Army General Staff was tasked with collecting the necessary evidence on the spot. The Volkssturmmann K.P. from Koenigsberg in East Prussia, who was in Nemmersdorf with his comrades on a reconnaissance mission, reported to Major Hinrichs the following:

"My Volkssturm company was ordered to tidy up Nemmersdorf. Shortly before the town, in the direction of Sodehnen – Nemmersdorf, we found destroyed refugee luggage. In Nemmersdorf itself we found entire columns of refugees. All of the vehicles were completely destroyed by Russian tanks and lay on the side of the road or in ditches. The baggage was plundered, torn open or destroyed. This column of refugees came from the Ebenrode area and Gumbinnen. I found a man's jacket in the ditch beside the road. Sticking out of the brest pocket I found a white paper. It was a letter envelope with the address: 'Schmiedemeister Grohnwald, Gumbinnen'.

On the edge of the town in the direction of Sodehnen – Nemmersdorf stood a large gasthaus on the left side of the road, the 'Weisse Krug'. A street ran to the left of it, leading to outlying farmsteads. At the first farmstead, on the left side of the street, stood a rackwagon. In it were four naked women, they had been strangled.

Behind the 'Weisse Krug', in the direction of Gumbinnen, is an open square with a monument to an unknown soldier. Behind this open square stands another gasthaus, the 'Rote Krug'. At this gasthaus stood a barn facing the street. On both barn doors were naked women in crucified positions, they were strangled.

We found an additional 72 women, children and a 74 year old man in their residences, they were all dead. Almost all were killed bestially. Among the dead we also found children in diapers.

In one room we found an 84 year old women on a sofa in a sitting position, she was totally blind. Her head was split in half to her throat with an ax or spade.

We had to carry these corpses to the town cemetery where they were left, because a foreign medical commission was to inspect the corpses. These corpses lay for three days without the medical commission showing up. In the meantime, a nurse appeared from Insterburg, she had lived in Nemmersdorf. She searched the village for her parents and found them. Both were dead, the 74 year old man, who was mentioned above, was her father. She then established that all of the dead came from Nemmersdorf.

On the 4th day the corpses were buried in two graves. Then the medical commission appeared on the following day and the graves had to be reopened. This international commission established that all of the women, including the girls from 8 to 12 years old and the 84 year old blind women, were raped."

(This report was in a protocol from Dr. Heinrich Amberger from Gumbinnen to the International Military Court of Justice in Nuernberg. See also: Documents on the Expulsion of Germans from East – Central Europe I, The Expulsion of the German People from the Region East of the Oder – Neisse, Volume I.)

What was experienced by the people of Tilsit during this time is described in another document.

"The enemy troops stood before Tilsit. However, the city held. The front was still 20 kilometers from us. On 25/10 we received the evacuation order. On 1/11 we left our farm. We left everything behind in the hope that we would be able to return. We set out on the path of suffering. Our town of Grossroden was evacuated after the Kreise of Braunsberg. We came to a town called Woppen. In the meantime, the Russians were held in front of Tilsit until shortly before Christmas. Then the Red Army broke through, refugees flooded into Woppen, who had already been under Russian control for two to three days before they were again liberated by German troops. They told us of horrors and then continued to flee in panic. There was a great fuss. My husband did not want to go any further.

The front continued to grow nearer, our troops retreated. The Russians were already in Paulen, a town only 5 kilometers from Woppen. Our troops built an artillery position right behind our farm.

On the evening of 20/1/1945 the battle began to rage. We cowered together in a corner. Shots flew overhead. During the night our soldiers broke into the house and told us that we had to get out if we did not want to fall into the hands of the Russians. We left at 0100 hours and drove in the dark. On the roads were refugees and Wehrmacht columns. However, the Russians were again held up and we advanced in the direction of Frisches Haff. Arriving at the water we rested for 24 hours. Thus we could see what was taking place on the ice. The ice covering was still not very thick. We saw vehicles sticking out of the ice, they had fallen through. I saw with my own eyes as an entire column of vehicles fell through. When we refused to go out on the ice we were told that the dam would be blown within an hour and, therefore, the town would soon be under water. We were forced to proceed.

We were told that we would not be on the ice for long. We were to go to Kahlberg, that was only 8 kilometers, then we would be safe. However, this was not the case. We drove for five hours and there was still not sign of the shore. After another hour we were attacked by aircraft. A fearful drama played itself out. The bombs tore hugh holes in the ice and entire columns of vehicles went under. We yearned for death, however, it would not occur here.

After this Russian attack we survivors drove on. Our vehicles rode over the ice all night until we finally reached land. We breathed a sigh of relief, however, then we learned that we were in another pocket.

We drove here and there in this pocket until 8 March 1945. On 9 March we were overrun by the Russians. The horses were taken from us and we were plundered. The women were raped and carried away. My husband was also taken away. I still have not heard from him to this day." (See: Documents on the Expulsion of the Germans from East – Central Europe I.)

The Russian breakthrough attempt had stalled and, on 25 October 1944, General Chernyakovskiy informed the Soviet Press that they should not anticipate any rapid progress by his troops.

Goldap, which was captured by the Red Army, was re-captured by General Hossbach's troops. On 29/10, however, Russian tank columns again rolled into this city and completely destroyed it.

During the night before 3/11 the 5th German PD attacked out of the north and the 50th ID from the south and threw the 31st Soviet Army back so far into the Rominter Heide that, on 5/11/1944, the Russian High Command had to admit that their offensive in East Prussia had failed. During this fighting the enemy had experienced a number of costly battles, loosing a total of 1000 tanks and 300 guns, a blood-letting that even they could not afford. On 5/11/1944 even Goldap was re-captured.

The Angerapp Line had held and the German panzer units, with Tigers and Panthers and several King Tigers, had destroyed the enemy armored fronts.

On the Russian side these "Eight Battles", as this fighting in autumn and winter 1944 in the north of the Eastern Front was called, were considered to be a success. The official history of the Soviet Union entitled "The Most Important Operations of the Great Patriotic War 1941 – 1945" reported:

"The combat operations during the Eight Battles were conducted in difficult forest and marsh terrain. In spite of this, our troops overcame the enemy defenses and progressed. The splitting of the enemy front on the northern border of East Prussia was achieved, because the main attack axis was shifted in time on the instructions of the High Command and the troops were regrouped quickly in the new direction.

The combat operations in the Baltic Provinces provided great experience in the organization of the inter-working between land and naval forces for the preparation for the conduct of troop sea landings, in order to attack into the enemy's rear...

The defeat of the German – Fascist troops in the Baltic Provinces was a great set-back for the Fascists and brought the Soviet Army closer to the final victory over Fascist Germany. The Soviet Army again demonstrated to the entire world the strength of the Soviet Union and the high combat morale and combat mastery of its armed forces." (See Zhilin, P.A.: *The Most Important Operations in the Great Patriotic War 1941-1945.*)

This first experience with the enemy on German territory showed that the Russian attackers did not take the civilian population into any consideration, but "brutally plundered them, raped the women and shot the remaining civilians. They drove thousands into temporary camps and then carried them off to the east."

The fact that the senior Soviet leadership not only tolerated but approved of these activities was shown by the fact that the soldiers of the Red Army during this phase of the fighting on German territory were allowed to take an unlimited number of 30 kilogram packs from the houses. They were not questioned on the contents of these packs and were allowed to take them from the front to Russia. Konstantin Simonov gave the author a few additional examples:

The eastern German population took flight, although a severe winter occurred in all of the eastern German provinces from January to March 1945, which froze them on the ice covered roads and required the greatest of effort.

The chances of escaping in many locations was extremely slim, because the Russian tanks were faster than the streams of refugees and there was always the threat that they would be encircled or caught in combat operations on the open road.

The high number of suicides in the time period before the Russian troops arrived indicated the hopelessness of the situation of the eastern German populace. (See: Documentation on the Expulsion of the Germans from East – Central Europe I, Pages 25 E and 26 E.)

7

THE GREAT OFFENSIVE

Red Army Plans

The "strategic offensive against Germany with five fronts" planned by the Red Army was to be conducted from one attack line which stretched from the Baltic Sea to the Carpathians. The STAVKA planned for the operation in two parts.

The first operation was directed against East Prussia, the second against the sector between the Vistula and Oder. German troop formations in East Prussia, as well as in Poland, were to be destroyed by these two operations. The way to the west was to be opened and the Oder was to be reached as a spring-board for further operations against Berlin.

In order to achieve this far-ranging objective, Marshal Stalin, after intensive deliberations in the STAVKA, committed the following formations:

To destroy the German forces in East Prussia: The 3rd Belorussian Front under Army General Chernyakovskiy and the 2nd Belorussian Front under Marshal Rokossovskiy.

Moreover, these operations were to protect the right flank of the Soviet fronts in the area of Poland.

The 1st Belorussian Front under Marshal Zhukov and the 1st Ukrainian Front under Marshal Konev received instructions to liberate Poland,

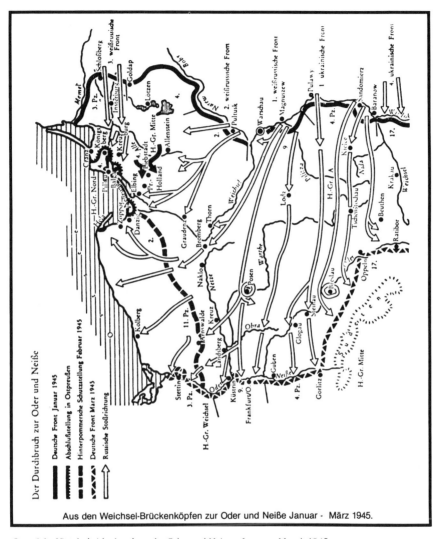

Out of the Vistula bridgeheads to the Oder and Neisse, January-March 1945.

conduct the attack to the Oder and secure the spring-board for the last attack against Berlin.

The right flank of the 4th Ukrainian Front under Army General Petrov received orders to support this attack.

Moreover, it was foreseen that in the Polish combat area a breakthrough would occur on a 490 kilometer front between Jaslo and Warsaw, the entire front would be split and the individual German formations would be isolated and destroyed.

A number of detailed orders and instructions were issued for these plans.

On 12/1/1945 the Red Army winter offensive began out of the Sandomierz bridgehead. Still on the morning of the day of the attack formations of the 1st Ukrainian Front broke through the German HKL on the entire sector in front of the bridgehead. The second German defensive lines were reached by the afternoon. As the day came to an end these were also broken through on a 35 kilometer front. The lead formations of the Red Army had penetrated 20 kilometers to the west on this first day of the attack.

The defending troops of the German XXVI Panzer Corps withdrew to the northwest in the direction of Kielce. This city was occupied by the Red Army on 15/1/1945.

The Soviet troops advancing on the left flank of the attack axis reached Krakau on 14/1/1945, after committing their second echelon. On the following day the main German forces in this area were also defeated.

North of the 1st Ukrainian Front, still in their assembly positions waiting for the signal to attack, stood the 1st Belorussian Front. They first attacked on 14/1/1945 out of the Magnuszow bridgehead. This front had received very strong formations, they were to conduct three attacks. First: an attack in the direction of Kutno, in order to break through the very strong German defensive lines there. The 61st Army under General Belov, the 5th Shock Army under General Bersarin and the 8th Guards Army under Colonel General Chuikov were assembled in this Soviet bridgehead on the western bank of the Vistula.

After these formations were able to breakthrough the German defense a portion of them were to be committed to the northwest in the direction of Blonie against the flanks and rear of the German Warsaw grouping, in order to destroy them and liberate Warsaw in cooperation with the right flank of this front.

The 2nd Guards Tank Army was assembled on the eastern bank of the Vistula, it was led by General Bogdanov. Besides them, the 1st Guards Tank Army under Colonel General Katukov and the 3rd Shock Army under

General Dimonyak stood ready to exploit the initial success of the first echelon troops in this direction.

The German front was also broken through here on the first day of the attack. A 30 kilometer wide and 12 kilometer deep penetration was torn into the German positions.

The second major attack was conducted by the troops of the 69th Soviet Army under General Kolpakchi and the 33rd Army under General Zvetaev out of the Pulavy bridgehead, south of the rail line to Krakau, in the direction of Radom – Lodz. A portion of these troops was led out of their departure positions from the right flank of this attack grouping to the northwest, with an attack direction on Szydlowiec, with the objective of destroying the German forces between Radom and Kielce. This in cooperation with the 1st Ukrainian Front.

The third attack group was formed on the right flank of this attack axis by troops of the 47th Army under General Perkhorovich and the 1st Polish Army under General Poplavski. Their objective was Warsaw, which was to be liberated by a wide envelopment maneuver with associated direct attacks by elements from the west against the Polish capital.

The advanced plans of the Red Army foresaw that the 1st Belorussian Front had to reach the Gabin – Lodz sector between the 10th and 12th day of the offensive, in order to then attack through Kutno toward Posen. From there it was still another 150 kilometers to Kuestrin on the Oder.

The 1st Ukrainian Front, which was attacking Radom, reached the Piotrkow – Tschenstochau – Miechow area on the 10th day of the offensive. Now the main forces of this front were ordered to continue the attack on Breslau, while partial formations were veered off to the northwest toward Szydlowiec. Therefore, a pincer maneuver was to be conducted by these elements and a southern formation from the 1st Belorussian Front against the German troops still located in the Kielce – Radom area, with the objective of encircling and destroying them.

This winter offensive was originally to take place on 20/1/1945. It was moved up to 12 and 14/1/1945 by the intervention of Winston Churchill on 6/1/1945.

The Execution of the Operation

The German HKL at the 1st Ukrainian Front was broken through along its entire breadth on the first day of the attack. In the afternoon the second defensive line was already reached and by the end of this day a gap 35 kilometers wide and 15 to 20 kilometers deep yawned in the German HKL opposite Sandomierz. During the pursuit of the XXVI German Panzer Corps on the following day, Kielce was reached and, on 14/1, the fresh troops of the second echelon entered Krakau. On 15/1 the main strength of the German Wehrmacht in this area was broken.

The formations of the 1st Belorussian Front, which were located north of the 1st Ukrainian Front and which attacked on 14/1, also broke through the German HKL on the first day of the attack and achieved a penetration 30 kilometers wide and 12 kilometers deep opposite Magnuszow, while the penetration near Pulawy was 25 kilometers wide and 18 kilometers deep.

The German reserves committed here were wiped out even before the main Soviet forces were committed to the battle.

On the second day of the fighting the penetrations were expanded by the new forces to a 120 kilometer wide and 30 kilometer deep breakthrough near Magnuszow and to a depth of 50 kilometers near Pulawy.

The mobile troops of this front, which were still in their assembly areas awaiting the order to attack, followed on the afternoon of 15/1 and the morning of 16/1.

The right flank of this front, however, did not attack until 15/1. These troops crossed the Vistula north of Warsaw and, on the second day of the attack, reached the Warsaw – Modlin road, which they crossed with their lead attack elements.

Rolling along the southern bank of the Vistula, they threatened the German forces still in Warsaw with a northern envelopment.

The Polish Army utilized this success of the main attack and attacked out of assembly areas they had since occupied southeast of Warsaw and advanced to the northwest.

When the main forces of the mobile group of this front reached the

Sochaczew area on 17/1, the German forces in Warsaw were cut off from their withdrawal route.

On the morning of 17/1 the lead mobile elements of the 1st Polish Army reached the northern and southeastern edges of their capital city. After heavy fighting Warsaw was captured on the evening of this day.

The 1st Belorussian Front advanced quickly. Their next objective was Tomaszow. The German XXXXII Army Corps, which was trying to avoid being encircled, was wiped out. On the evening of 17/1 the entire Vistula Front was torn on an almost 500 kilometer breadth. The commanders of the 1st Ukrainian Front and the 1st Belorussian Front received the order from Red Army Headquarters to immediately attack to the Oder, defeat the arriving German reserves and prevent them from establishing themselves in prepared positions.

At the same time, Marshal Konev received orders to immediately by-pass Krakau and advance on Breslau.

From 20 to 22/1/1945 the 1st Belorussian Front achieved a ground gain of from 120 to 130 kilometers. On 25/1 the lead formations of this front reached the German border fortifications and encircled approximately 60,000 German soldiers in Posen. The main strength of the 1st Belorussian Front, however, continued to attack in the direction of Kuestrin.

Marshal Zhukov now set out to reach the Oder as quickly as possible and establish a bridgehead on the western bank.

On 31/1/1945 his mobile formations reached the Oder north of Kuestrin, without regard to the security to their left or right and leaving the removal of the German nests of resistance to the follow-on forces, and immediately crossed the river.

By the evening of 3/2/1945 the entire length of the right bank of the Oder from Zehden to the south was in Soviet hands. The Germans held bridgeheads on the eastern bank only at Kuestrin and Frankfurt/Oder.

The troops of the 1st Belorussian Front established bridgeheads on the western bank of the Oder north and south of Kuestrin. Therefore, the offensive was successfully ended on this sector. The 1st Belorussian Front had reached its long-ranged objective – the Oder.

Rolling in the direction of Breslau, the 1st Ukrainian Front reached the German border region in the center of the attack axis on the evening of 19/

1/1945. Here the resistance of the German troops stiffened. Counterattacks attempted to stop this advance.

When the left flank of the advance of the Russian formations stalled, Marshal Konev diverted a strong armored formation on 21/1 out of the Namslau area to the south. The formation received strict orders to advance along the eastern bank of the Oder to the south and strike any German force groupings in the rear and destroy them.

In this manner, the German troops defending here were finally thrown back so that the left flank of the 1st Ukrainian Front was the first major Soviet troop to reach the Oder on 22/1. By 25/1 all of the Soviet troops stood on the river. From Koebeln in the north to Oppeln in the south this water barrier was reached. Several bridgeheads were thrown across the river and expanded in the course of the next few weeks, in order to serve as a spring-board for an assault on Berlin. There was still fighting around Krakau. The 17th German Army here was outflanked by the left flank of the 1st Ukrainian Front and the right flank of the 4th Ukrainian Front and had to withdraw to Krakau. After being threatened with being completely outflanked, they withdrew over the lower course of the Dunajec to the southeast toward Tarnow.

Then on 19/1 Krakau, the ancient capital of Poland, fell into the hands of the Soviets. Because the troops of the 1st Ukrainian Front were rapidly advancing on Breslau, the German forces had to give up the area southeast of Krakau they were still holding so that they would not be encircled.

On 17/1 the Red Army attacked out of the Miechow area to the northwest in the direction of Tarnowskiy Gory with their reserve troops and cavalry formations. Two days later they broke through the German HKL on the Warthe and reached the Oder near Oppeln with the right attack wedge on 23/1. The left wedge of this formation also advanced and reached the Beuthen area.

The German troops withdrew from this half-encirclement. On 28/1 Kattowitz fell. 24 hours after that there was no longer one single German soldier left in the Silesian industrial region. By 30/1/1945 the left flank of the Soviet offensive had also reached the Oder.

The Soviet Attack on East Prussia

At the same time as these operations, which were roughly outlined, the Red Army opened the attack on East Prussia with the 3rd Belorussian Front in the north and the 2nd Belorussian Front adjacent to the south. The objective of this attack was to isolate East Prussia and encircle the German troops located there. Then the East Prussian pocket was to be split into two halves by a direct attack in the direction of Koenigsberg.

The 3rd Belorussian Front received instructions to conduct the main strike out of the area north of the Masurean Lakes against the German formations located in the Tilsit area.

The 2nd Belorussian Front was to attack with its main forces out of the area north of Warsaw toward Mlawa – Marienburg and reach Frische Haff as soon as possible. Therefore, all of the German troops fighting in East Prussia would be cut off.

A southern wedge of this front was to advance in the direction of Plonsk and Bielsk. Its objective was to cross the Vistula near Modlin and then reach the assigned objective as quickly as possible.

The attack in the 3rd Belorussian Front area of operations was initiated on 13/1/1945. On 14/1 the 2nd Belorussian Front attacked.

The mobile divisions of the Red Army attacked out of the Pillkallen area after a strong artillery preparation and broke through the German HKL by evening to a depth of from seven to two kilometers. Between Pillkallen and Gumbinnen the German HKL was severely shaken.

On the second day the Red Army formations were stopped by counterattacks, causing problems in some areas. This fighting lasted five days before the troops of the 3rd Belorussian Front were able to attack through the deeply echeloned defensive lines and achieve a breakthrough on a 60 kilometer front, which was 45 kilometers deep in the center of the breakthrough.

Gumbinnen fell on 21/1/1945. On the following day Insterburg was captured by the Red Army, after that the northern attack group of the front overcame Tilsit, which had been encircled for some time. Therefore, important traffic hubs had now fallen to the Soviets and the way to Koenigsberg was open.

The 2nd Belorussian Front launched its main attack out of the Vistula bridgeheads of Rozan and Serok. On the early morning of 14/1 a strong Russian fire-strike was conducted on the German HKL here, as on the rest of the front, before the formations attacked and penetrated into the German defensive lines to a depth of from four to eight kilometers. By 18/1 the German defensive front here was broken through on a breadth of 100 kilometers and to a depth of 40 kilometers. The German troops withdrew to the west.

Both fronts advanced energetically during the next few days. The 3rd Belorussian Front overcame the Deime sector and on 26/1 stood on the line east of Koenigsberg – Friedland – Rastenburg.

The 2nd Belorussian Front bypassed the Mlawa area. Modlin was captured by the southern attack group. On 21/1 the right flank of this front reached the East Prussian border and advanced to Germany.

Turning toward Elbing, this front (the corresponding German designation for front is army group) tried to reach Frische Haff by the direct route. On 26/1/1945 Elbing and Tolkemit were captured. Therefore, the encirclement of the East Prussian front was complete. The formations on the left flank of this front advanced to the northwest to the Vistula, reached the river on the evening of 26/1 in the Grudziadz area and established a bridgehead on the western bank. The city of Thorn was bypassed and blockaded from the north and east. By the end of January the German forces in East Prussia were split into three groups. In the southwestern Heilsberger pocket, in the Koenigsberg pocket and in the Samland pocket.

On 8/2/1945 the 2nd Belorussian Front received the mission of initiating a new attack west of the Vistula and reaching the line Dirschau Vistula estuary – Berent – Rumelsburg – Neustettin, in order to continue the attack with newly deployed armies. In this manner, Danzig and Gotenhafen were to be captured. If this was successful, then the entire coastal region would be in Soviet hands and sea transport from and to the Reich would be interrupted.

At the same time the formations of the 3rd Belorussian Front fought in vain against the German formations defending in the greater Heilsberg area. Army General Chernyakovskiy, the commander of the 3rd Belorussian Front was mortally wounded on 18/2 near Mehlsack. On 20/2 Soviet Marshal Vassilevski took command of the front.

These two Soviet fronts did not advance any further in the next few weeks. The fighting in this area raged back and forth. On 13/3/1945 the enemy launched a new attack near Heilsberg with the objective of splitting and destroying the German defenders.

By 19/3/1945 the defenders in this area were compressed into a region 20 x 10 kilometers on the coast. Bombers and fighter-bombers from the Red air armies were in constant commitment. On 29/3 this German defensive group was destroyed. Approximately 50,000 German soldiers were captured. The number of killed and missing was higher.

Now the 3rd Belorussian Front was to attack Koenigsberg, while a portion of the forces of this front fought on the Samland Peninsula.

Red Army Operations in Eastern Pomerania

While the fronts of the Soviet central sector, as outlined here, still stood on the Oder, the Red Army initiated an attack against eastern Pomerania with the forces of the 1st and 2nd Belorussian Fronts, it was directed to the north toward the Baltic Sea.

The armored troops of the 2nd Belorussian Front attacked out of the deployment areas of Graudenz – Kulm – Zempelburg. The mobile formations of the 1st Belorussian Front directed their attack against Schneidemuehl, Deutsch-Krone and Arnswalde. They also had to repulse a strong counterattack near Stargard.

This fighting began on 10/2 and ended on 23/2/1945. From 24/2 to 4/3 the two fronts reached the Baltic Sea and from 5/3 to 13/3 the German formations withdrawing in the direction of Gotenhafen and Danzig were pursued. A small wedge from this attack group turned to the west in the direction of Stettinger Haff.

The final battle of this operation began on 14/3/1945 and was finished a week later, on 20/3. The German Army Group Vistula, which was involved in heavy fighting here, was defeated.

The 1st Polish Army joined in these operations and pressed on Kolberg.
After this brief description of the course of combat on the Russian side
a number of cities and locations were named that went down in military
history as fortified places and fortresses. Their defense and defeat, often
after weeks of fighting, will be described so that the sacrifices and losses of
the civilian populations in these fortresses can be calculated.

8

THE LAST BASTIONS IN THE EAST

The Sacrifice of Elbing

On 20 January 1945, the eighth day of the battle for East Prussia, the 2nd Belorussian Front attacked in the north in the direction of Koenigsberg. The intent of these two fronts was clear to the German defenders: They were to completely encircle Army Group Center and destroy it. And if the 4th German Army was not attacked in the center of this defensive front, then it would also be lost very soon.

Generaloberst Reinhardt, who recognized this Soviet intention, tried to convince Hitler of the threat. He telephonically requested the withdrawal of the 4th Army to the Masurian Lakes. Hitler refused and secured the deployment of reserve forces from Denmark and Kurland.

On the evening of 20/1/1945 Generaloberst Reinhardt again telephoned Hitler. He urgently described the situation and finally received permission from Hitler to withdraw the 4th Army into the lake positions. Nevertheless, permission came 48 hours too late to change the course of events in East Prussia.

The Soviet breakthrough battle, as described in the preceding chapter, advanced very quickly. On 21/1/1945 the Red storm troops achieved a breakthrough in the 2nd Army area of operations and, therefore, stood only 70 kilometers from Frischen Haff.

In the 3rd Panzer Army area of operations the enemy penetrated into Forst Eichwald. Enemy lead troop elements reached the neighboring area of Kurischen Haff.

Elbing and Insterburg were extremely threatened. Thick streams of refugees poured out of the Kreisen of Wehlau and Insterburg as well as from Elbing. All of the roads were jammed. Here is a report from Elbing. It was from nobody less than the Oberbuergermeister of Elbing, Dr. Hans Leeser:

"Kreis Neustadt in western Prussia was the kreis assigned for the evacuation of the people of Elbing, because the entire evacuation was to take place in view of a line of resistance on the Vistula, therefore, only the evacuation of the region east of the Vistula was foreseen."

During a meeting in Danzig of representatives from East Prussia and Pomerania Regierungspraesident Huth, the representative of the Reichsstatthalter in Danzig, tried to reach agreement on what measures to take. No one showed up from East Prussia. However, Regierungspraesident Dargel wrote a letter from Koenigsberg:

"We do not intend to evacuate the province of East Prussia. Therefore, I hold this entire meeting to be superfluous. However, if the intent is to transfer residents from the Reichsgau of Danzig in western Prussia to East Prussia, I am ready to participate.

In late summer 1944 we tried to evacuate the portions of the inner city of Elbing affected by the air war. The two schools there were both closed and women and children were removed from the city. In spite of the threatening situation these measures had only little success. After the front came to a standstill in East Prussia at the end of October 1944 and saw little fighting until the end of the year, a portion of the evacuated people returned voluntarily at Christmas."

Thus read the direct report.

With the beginning of the Soviet winter offensive the people of Elbing naturally were restive and concerned with what they were to do. Would these strong Russian attack forces be stopped before reaching the city?

Now many families voluntarily moved to the west. However, as they arrived in Koenigsberg, which was already filled, an organized flight was no longer possible. On 15/1/1945 the first train-loads of refugees were also rolling through Elbing.

The requests of the Elbing Oberbuergermeister to make available special trains and busses for the evacuation of Elbing could not be fulfilled by Danzig.

On Saturday, 20/1/1945, the commander of the Elbing Schutzpolizei appeared at the Oberbuergermeister's office. Major Schmidt informed the Oberbuergermeister that he had just received information about the commitment of enemy airborne troops in the area of the Vistula Valley.

If this report were correct, then the air landing had cut off the routes of flight for the residents of Elbing to the west. However, the air landing did not succeed.

When the Elbing Kreisleiter asked his Gauleiter for permission to issue Evacuation Level I, his request was turned down. Nevertheless, under the table all inquiries were made to leave the city as soon as possible.

Here again is Oberbuergermeister Dr. Leeser:

> "On 20/1/1945 I was informed that the order had been received to immediately evacuate all maidens from Elbing. On the same evening an order arrived from the Reichsstatthalter that on Sunday all industry would cease because of the lack of power.
>
> On Sunday, 21/1/1945, the Gaustabsleiter of the Volkssturm, the well known Knight's Cross winner and U-Boot commander, Kapitaen zur See Hartmann, called me and informed me that the military situation would change within the next few days. He had just come from a meeting in Marienburg, where the Reichsfuehrer SS had declared that he was now the new commander of Army Group Vistula and would put everything in order within a few days."

Kapitaen zur See Hartmann, one of the most prominent German soldiers – as were so many before and after him – was fooled by Himmler's slogans. Gauleiter Forster himself, who also attended this meeting in Marienburg, said:

> "Himmler had us fooled. He operated with panzer armies on a big map so that we had the impression that the situation would have to change shortly. In fact, these panzer armies did not exist." (See: Leeser, Dr. Hans: Documentation of the Expulsion of the Germans from East-Central Europe, Vol. I.)

On Monday, 22/1/1945, when the deputy leader of the Danzig/West Prussian Landwirtschaftsamte, Oberregierungsrat Dr. Koch, appeared in Elbing to speak of the supply of the "Elbing" bridgehead for two months with the Oberbuergermeister of the city, he was just as confident. Who would talk of so long a defense if he did not believe the front would hold? He said that the city's supply situation was sufficient if several tons of salt could be delivered into the city.

Therefore, the Danzig Gauleiter, as well as Oberregierungsrat Dr. Koch, had refused to grant permission to evacuate Elbing.

On Thursday, 23/1, the Oberbuergermeister received a call from the Kreisleiter, who had just received a call from Gauleiter Forster, and was informed that the situation had stabilized. There was no threat to Elbing. An evacuation was not necessary. Two hours later this would be confirmed by Major Altermann, the Ia of the Elbing Wehrmacht Commandant.

However, the refugees were still rolling through Elbing as before and more and more they were interspersed with Wehrmacht columns. It was a city Ratsherr who informed the Oberbuergermeister in the afternoon that the Russians had reached Preussisch-Holland. This city lay 20 kilometers distant front Elbing. The news was received by the Ratsherr from the leader of the NSKK Motor School in Preussisch-Holland by telephone.

A query from the Oberbuergermeister to the Ia of the Wehrmacht Commandant, Major Altermann, brought the assurance that this information was false. The commandant had just dispatched a battalion to Preussisch – Holland at midday.

While Dr. Leeser was making this inquiry, he suddenly heard over the telephone the voice of Oberst Schoepffer, the Elbing Wehrmacht Commandant. He had said to Major Altermann:

"Listen Altermann, Russian tanks have been reported near Pomehrendorf!"

Oberbuergermeister Dr. Leeser hung up the telephone. Pomehrendorf was only 8(!) kilometers from Elbing.

At 1700 hours the first shots from Russian tanks cracked into Elbing. A group of Russian tanks had detached from the main body of the advance detachment and rolled through the city firing their cannon and machine-guns. Dr. Leeser saw the tanks roll by the rathaus. Several stopped to fire into the houses.

Oberst Schoepffer immediately committed the anti-tank troops. They opposed the Russian tanks. Now the sounds of anti-tank weapons filled Elbing as they struck the enemy tanks.

These decisive tank destroyer troops destroyed the enemy.

Chaos followed this first Russian attack on Elbing. The strassenbahn still operated, the movie theaters still played and everything appeared "peaceful." And now this!

All of the bunkers were overflowing. There ensued a flight from Elbing even before the Kreisobmann of the DAF informed the Oberbuergermeister that the Gauleiter had declared Evacuation Level III. This indicated the complete evacuation of the city! Even the authorities were to evacuate as soon as possible. The Oberbuergermeister ordered the city government to leave the city in a fire truck.

At midnight the Oberbuergermeister was called by the Kreisleiter. He informed Dr. Leeser that he just learned from the Gauleiter that any authorities that leave Elbing were to be shot. The attempt of the Oberbuergermeister to reach these authorities was fruitless, especially since Evacuation Level III was declared.

Oberbuergermeister Dr. Leeser remained in Elbing with Oberverwaltungsrat Bergs and city men Moots, Quandt and Schroeter.

Because the Russian tanks did not advance in the next few days, the commuter and freight trains located at the Elbing railroad station were used as refugee trains. The ships in Elbing harbor were utilized for the same purpose. Finally, after endless requests, a column of trucks was also received from Danzig.

On Thursday, 25/1, when the Red Army was able to sever the Elbing – Marienburg rail line, it no longer was running. During the next night this enemy formation advanced to the Elbing – Danzig road and also blocked it.

Late in the afternoon of 25/1 the Navy reported that the unfinished but afloat torpedo boats in Elbing would be towed. They could carry 2000 people.

Thus, during the evening hours about 3000 people assembled on the Elbing docks. Unfortunately, they could only take 400 people.

As the rest wondered what to do, a strong Russian fire-strike opened up. The artillery fire also included "Stalin Organs", whose rockets slammed into the harbor and inflicted heavy casualties on those waiting.

During the night before 26/1 massive artillery fire was launched. Fires erupted in the city. They were extinguished by firemen and volunteers. Then the power went out, the electric station was hit. The flames spread more and more and within 48 hours Elbing was burning at all ends. A portion of the inner city was wiped out by the flames.

On Sunday, 28/1/1945, this strong enemy fire decreased. Oberst Schoepffer, who received the information that the 4th Army was advancing for commitment at Elbing and that the 7th PD was already being committed here from the west against the ring of encirclement, saw the hour of the city's liberation at hand.

The city commandant drove to the rathaus and requested Oberbuergermeister Dr. Leeser drive with him to the western edge of the city to greet the lead elements of the liberators.

They drove in a police car with several other men to the west. They ran into the lead elements of the 7th PD at the edge of Grubenhagen. These troops were greeted as the liberators of Elbing.

When they desired to drive to one of the 7th PD regimental command posts and through Grubenhagen the column received strong Russian fire from the Wansau camp. They had to turn around and return to Elbing across the Nogat. The firing had increased in the meantime. The Buessing bus factory was in flames.

After the gas and electricity went out, the central water supply system followed. There were only a few springs available for water. The majority of the water had to be obtained by melting snow.

With the loss of water the entire city stank and became a source for disease. Because even the civilian physicians left the city only Dr. Tschirner was left to treat the sick and wounded. Even the apothecaries were closed. Here a volunteer Polish pharmacist distributed the most important medicines secured by the man in the rathaus.

Grubenhagen was occupied by the soldiers of the Red Army on 26 and 27/1. Here again, as one woman reported, outrages were performed.

The 4th Army was unable to reach Elbing and relieve it. The few tanks of the 7th PD were still fighting on the edge of Elbing and shot-up the Russian tanks which were advancing only cautiously. Nevertheless, this division was separated into various combat groups and committed at various locations, so that they could not conduct a unified commitment.

Several lines are quoted from the history of this well-known panzer division of the German Wehrmacht:

"On 24/1/1945 the division was engaged in heavy defensive fighting east of Graudenz, on 25/1 in the Marienwerder area. On 26/1 the wheeled elements of the division crossed the Vistula over a bridge of ice near Marienwerder, while the tracked vehicles swung back through Graudenz.

The assembly of the division on the western bank of the Vistula was not inconsiderably delayed, because the tracked elements were stalled due to lack of fuel near Krebs. Consequently, the division did not reach Dirschau until 27/1, where the march groups had to be immediately thrown into combat east of the city. They were committed near Lichtenau, northeast of Dirschau. Other elements were near Einlage, west of Lichtenau, northeast of Dirschau. Other elements were fighting near Einlage, west of the Nogat on the Elbing – Danzig road, approximately ten kilometers west of Elbing, in order to attack in the direction of Elbing, which was threatened with encirclement.

During the next few days the main body of the division was attack reserve and as such counterattacked on 9-10/2/1945 with its armored elements to the north toward Elbing, which had been encircled in the meantime. This attack did not succeed, contact was not established with the encircled defenders of Elbing, however, during the night before 11/2/1945, some of the defenders were able to breakout of the fortress to the west and were absorbed by the division." (See: Manteuffel, Hasso von: *The 7th Panzer Division in the Second World War 1939-1945*.)

However, back to Elbing and to the time of trial for this city, which had been declared a fortress.

On 30/1/1945 Russian armored formations advanced across the reichsstrasse and penetrated into the village of Grubenhagen. Therefore, Elbing was encircled for a second time. We now turn from the civilian sector (which will be again described later) to the military events in the city and its defense.

With code-word "1.600" Oberst Eberhard Schoepffer, the commandant of Elbing, issued the alert order for the city on 23/1/1945.

Three days prior the scouts dispatched by Oberst Schoepffer came back with the news that Osterode was burning.

The guns had to be set in position during a strong frost and a northeastern storm. Long columns of refugees filed through the streets of the city from Preussisch-Holland and Braunsberg. Koenigsberger Strasse, which ran through Elbing, was travelled by thick columns of vehicles both day and night. This led to chaos at the only narrow bridge across the Elbing river. Here the refugees continued to come. Here the sides of the roads were filled with beds and suitcases, with boxes and cabinets, typewriters, clothes and other things. On 25/1/1945, when the city was first cut off from its withdrawal routes, the chaos increased.

By the evening of 26/1 additional small groups of refugees, Wehrmacht stragglers and small troop units were entering Elbing. Everybody in a Wehrmacht uniform was collected by Oberst Schoepffer. So was a battalion from the famed 83rd Jaeger Regiment from Brieg that was led by

Hauptmann Homburg and Oberleutnant Eisenblaetter. In addition, there was also a squadron from this regiment under Rittmeister Graf Finckenstein.

Hauptmann Heinrich Homburg had led the II/JaegRgt 83 in the summer during the fighting of his 28th Jaeger Division so successfully that he was awarded the Knight's Cross on 25/7/1944. These fighters supplemented the defensive strength of Elbing.

On the evening of the first day of the alert, when seven Russian tanks penetrated into the city among the columns of refugees, they opened fire from their machine-guns and tank cannon. Two of these tanks were eliminated at the entrance to the city by panzerfaust rounds. The remaining five continued to roll toward the bulwark in the vicinity of Mudra Kaserne, where they were shot-up.

Oberst Schoepffer committed a good number of tank destroyer troops and placed them at the city's nerve centers, above all, in positions at the entrance streets.

The attempt to improve the protection of the trenches was hampered by the deeply frozen ground.

The defensive line designated by Oberst Schoepffer ran in the northeast on the line Mudra Kaserne – Laerchenwald – Gut Freiwalde – Vogelsang.

On 25/1/1945 Russian formations attacked here. However, the main strike came out of the southeast, out of the Preussisch-Holland area. All attacks were repulsed. The Russians were only able to gain ground south of the Drauensee through Rueckfort. Their strike on Fichthorst was successful and, therefore, the rail line to the west in the direction of Danzig was blocked.

Russian assault troops advanced between the Elbing and the Nogat and occupied the forest-like trails one after the other. When they reached the town of Zeyer, Elbing was completely encircled. In the north, from the direction of Tolkemit and Trunz, only a few assault troops advanced on Elbing. A column of refugees coming from Trunz reported that the women from Lehrer Horst and the nurses from the foreign workers' hospital there were horribly mistreated by Mongolian troops and had taken their own lives with poison.

Therefore, it was finally clear to the last civilians in Elbing what they could expect if the Russians were to get into their city. The Russian tank attack on the afternoon of 26/1 occurred as a complete surprise. Here US Sherman tanks were committed, which the Russians received from the PQ convoys by way of the northern sea route. These tank crews wore German uniforms and were supplied with captured German pay books.

Nevertheless, battle was joined in time. The few anti-tank guns and air defense guns opened fire on the fortress front and shot-up the first enemy tanks. A thick group of 16 tanks achieved a penetration into the German HKL. Here they were engaged with panzerfaust rounds. Two of these tanks were destroyed by amputees, who were convalescing in Elbing and had reported voluntarily.

The din of battle lasted several hours. When the last enemy tanks turned away, 42 destroyed Red Army tanks lay burning in front of the northern defensive line. The Red Army suspended its attack with tanks here. They deployed a number of heavy artillery batteries and additional siege formations around Elbing.

During the following night three small harbor steamers were able to leave the harbor fully laden. They fell under Russian fire at the bulwark, but suffered no damage. All three ships made it to Danzig.

On 27/1, when the Red Army attacked again with strong forces, they achieved a breakthrough. They penetrated into the city on the harbor road with tanks. The Mudra Kaserne was captured in a raid. Several tanks advanced up to Ziesenpark and established a foothold there. They were supported by their own anti-tank guns and about two companies of Red Army soldiers. They captured the Englischbrunnen Brewery and held it.

In the early morning hours Oberst Schoepffer launched a counterattack. In spite of heavy fire from the outside and the tenacious defense by the two Russian companies, they were able to reenter Mudra Kaserne. Nevertheless, the penetration into the city could not be completely removed.

The battery commander of a flak position in Laerchenwald shot himself in his command post during this night.

48 hours later, from their positions in the Englischbrunnen Brewery, the Russians tried to breakout before sunrise, because their situation ap-

peared to be hopeless due to the lack of supplies and because relief troops had not arrived to liberate this contingent.

The breakout to the north ran into opposition. It completely collapsed in the murderous fire of German MG 42's. The Russians were wiped out.

In the meantime, the stragglers located in Elbing were organized into a company by order of Oberst Schoepffer, in order to replace the losses suffered by the defenders during this fierce fighting.

On 28/1 a new Russian attack was introduced by a barrage fire lasting several hours. Heavy guns, including a battery of rocket launchers, "Stalin Organs", fired into the city. Then the Russians crashed against the suburbs of the city in the northeast. They were repulsed, suffering heavy casualties. The Russian tanks leading the attack were shot-up by panzer- faeusten. Nevertheless, the positions had to be gradually withdrawn to the line Stolzenmorgen – Pulvermuehle – Danziger Kaserne.

In spite of this difficult situation, there was still contact with the 7th PD, raising the hope in the fortress that this famous division, which had been led by Rommel in France and Manteuffel in Russia, would be able to liberate Elbing again. They did not know that this division had many missions and the liberation of Elbing was not considered all that urgent by the senior leadership.

Nevertheless, the elements of the 7th PD were persevering on the western bank of the Nogat, only six kilometers from the outskirts of Elbing, which facilitated the defense and allowed Oberst Schoepffer to transport his wounded under the cover of night, in order to give these wounded another chance to live after they could no longer be treated in the city.

Approximately 1000 wounded were sent in transports, secured by a machine-gun group, in the direction of the 7th PD. To the joy and surprise of all of the skeptics, they made it.

There was still telephone communications with Danzig until 3/2/1945. Often the Russians would not sever such lines so that they could listen in and determine the conditions in the cities.

A message from the Reichsfuehrer SS, Heinrich Himmler, reached the fortress over these lines in which he passed on an order from the Fuehrer to the defenders of Elbing:

"The German city of Elbing, a bridge from the west to the east, must be held at any price!"

On 30/1/1945 the tank alarm was again given. Two T 34's were rolling toward Elbing. However, these tanks did not fire. The tank commanders tried to make contact with the defenders over radios, which were built in Braunsberg. When they did not succeed, they rolled into the city.

They were captured tanks from a group of twelve that were to break into Elbing and support the city. Ten of the captured T 34's were destroyed by the Russians on the way when the trick became known and they saw the Balken Crosses identifying these tanks as the enemy.

The fighting around the suburb of Marienburg on the western bank of the Elbing was costly. The Elbing suburb had to be given up after fierce house-to-house fighting on 1/2/1945. Russian troops were firmly entrenched in the houses. Therefore, the walls of the kaserne became the HKL. Here Russian assault troops crashed during the next few days, breaking gaps in the walls and engaging the recognized machine-gun nests. On the evening of 6/2 the kaserne had to be evacuated.

Therefore, the defensive line now ran in the north along Gruenstrasse to Jahnkrankenhaus [hospital]. Oberst Schoepffer set up his command post in the Gymnasium [secondary school], which was located on Koenigsberger Strasse. The Russians now fired on the defenders without pause from hundreds of guns of all calibers and from "Katyushas." Elbing was a fortress and was being treated accordingly.

At 1230 hours on this 6/2/1945 the combat alarm sounded suddenly and a few minutes after that an old man crossed Koenigsberger Strasse toward the Gymnasium. He waved a white cloth over his head and was met at the Gymnasium and taken to Oberst Schoepffer. He passed onto him the demand of the Russian commander to surrender the city.

Oberst Schoepffer wrote only three words and signed it. These words were "I have acknowledged." The old man returned the same way, bringing the reply of the fortress commandant to the Russians.

An hour later the Russian attack began, this time it was accompanied and supported by strong armored forces. The assault troops penetrated into the Schichau docks and, after a short struggle with the marine forces located there, who could not stand up to the armored avalanche, captured it. The police guard located there was pushed back through the harbor railroad station to Ziesestrasse.

From the docks to the Gymnasium was only 600 meters. The defensive ring around the Gymnasium was 1200 meters at its thickest point.

When the enemy attempted a breakthrough toward Ziesestrasse in the area of the small chapel near the cigarette factory, they were blocked by an encircled battle group under an Oberleutnant from the fortress commandant's staff. The Oberleutnant was wounded.

He was taken into the basement of the Gymnasium and treated there. In the basement was a swarm of wounded soldiers, sick and civilians, including many young women with children.

The dry thud of the firing tank cannon could be heard from all directions. In between was the rattling of the machine-guns and the impact of detonations.

A group of wounded were taken to the Heinrich von Plauen School, where a hospital was set up.

The Russian artillery and armored formations fired on Elbing for 48 hours. There were over 2000 wounded in the basement of the Heinrich von Plauen School. They could not be properly treated. Except for extreme cases, medicine was not available.

Among the wounded were civilians, who had fled here. In the only operation room of this hospital four surgeons worked without stopping, while new wounded continued to be brought in that had to be treated immediately if they were not to die.

Stalin Organ batteries, which had been brought up after the enemy's demand for surrender had been turned down, fired their salvoes into the city. Their 16 round rocket salvoes slammed into the houses in the inner city and set them ablaze.

On 8/2 Oberst Schoepffer ordered a breakout attempt. Elbing was at its end. They had to turn the hospital over to the Russians if any of the wounded were to be saved. On the last evening of 9/2/1945 the breakout began, it rolled in a long column, with the wounded in the middle, through courtyards and backyards up to the Englischbrunnen Brewery. The engineers waited there, they had constructed a ferry to cross the Elbing. By 0500 hours all 2000 men, wounded and non-wounded, had made it across.

Therefore, they had reached their first position from where they would deploy for the breakout battle to the west.

When the soldiers of the 7th German PD heard the shouts of hurrah, they thought that the Russians were attacking. The artillery opened fire. Before they realized what they were doing, several hundred German soldiers had been killed by German defensive fire.

And at that moment, as the civilians, who had been following the soldiers at a distance, set out for the safety of the German lines, the Russians opened fire. The Russian shells slammed into the thick groups of fleeing civilians. Nevertheless, about 1000 people made their way to freedom. From this time on, the Russians placed the breakout route under strong artillery fire so that no one else could get through. The Russians entered Elbing on the morning of 10/2/1945. The defensive fire was silenced. 2400 wounded in the Heinrich von Plauen School fell into their hands.

Elbing had fallen into the hands of the victors and so did those Germans left behind. What happened to them was provided to the often referenced Documentation of the Expulsion of the Germans from East – Central Europe by Frau E.O., who had been taken prisoner by the Russians on 29/1/1945.

"On the morning of 29/1/1945 at 0630 hours I was taken prisoner by the Russians. During my first meeting with Russian soldiers my boots and overcoat were taken. I had my 15 month-old daughter Christa in my baby carriage; my seven and a half year-old son Horst held my hand. Men and women were driven out onto Richthofenstrasse. A train with approximately 1500 people pulled into the railroad station and remained there under the fire of Russian artillery until 1500 hours. We were mustered here, sorted by age and sex. They opened our mouths and looked at our teeth. The men were taken away. We never saw them again.

Only women and young girls of 15 remained. Now the rape of the young girls started. I watched as 15 year-old H.N. from Elbing-

Trettinkenhof was raped by Russian soldiers on the open railroad platform. The mother of H.N. defended her daughter with her life. The mother's name was M.N. During this muster all of our valuables, wedding rings, eyeglasses and valuable papers were taken from us.

After some time were we led off in the direction of Tannenberger Allee and sheltered in temporary buildings. The battle continued to rage. Russian supply units marched down Tannenberger Allee, passing in the neighborhood of the temporary buildings. We were then mustered again and sorted by age. I was then 39 years-old. One of the rooms of the temporary building was reserved for the rapes, which now resumed. First the young women were taken off. I was first taken by three Russian soldiers in the morning.

These rapes were repeated twice a day, each time by more and more soldiers, until the 7th day. The 7th day was the worst for me. I was taken in the evening and released in the morning. I was severely torn in my sex and had wounds on both sides of my thighs to my knees. I couldn't walk or lay down.

Then another three days followed like the first to the sixth. Then it appeared that the Russian soldiers were finished with us and we were taken from this hellish room naked. Other women took our places.

These abominations were often conducted in the presence of ten women and often in the presence of their children.

After that we were assembled and set on a death march of 21 kilometers to the city of Preussisch-Holland. We no longer had any shoes on our feet and it was mid-winter. I had one child in my arms and another in my hand.

During this death march the Russians threw hand-grenades into trains, killing the inhabitants. I had to watch as Herr Kilian from Elbing-Trettinkenhof was left for dead, as was the daughter of Herr Neumann.

I can confirm that the elderly Jordans from Elbing could no longer go on after being marched two days to and from Elbing – Preussisch-Holland. They sat down on the edge of the road and on the next day, when we marched back, I saw that they had been killed, shot in the back of their heads.

We were not given anything to eat, we were supposed to die, that was the purpose of these back and forth marches. Of 800 women, children and elderly only 200 survived. The dead lay on the sides of the roads or in road ditches.

The men were driven in all directions by the Russians. The Russian Army withdrew to the north and northwest in the direction of Danzig."

Thus is the report from Elbing, whose abandoned residents suffered a horrible fate.

The 511th Heavy Panzer Battalion Arrives

On 22/1/1945, after the Red Army had succeeded in isolating East Prussia by attacking their armored formations through near Elbing and reaching Tolkemit three days later, the German army groups were renamed on 25/1/1945. Army Group A was renamed Army Group Center, Army Group Center became Army Group North and Army Group North became Army Group Kurland.

Generaloberst Reinhardt now had to overcome a series of crises with his Army Group North in the next few days. In view of the catastrophic reports from this area, Generaloberst Heinz Guderian, who was entrusted with the duty assignment as the Army Chief of Staff since 21/7/1944, struggled with Hitler over the decision to free-up the XXVIII Army Corps, which belonged to the 3rd Panzer Army in the Memel bridgehead, for commitment to East Prussia.

The first unit of this army corps to receive orders for the transfer to East Prussia was the 502nd Heavy Panzer Battalion, which would be redesignated as the 511th Heavy Panzer Battalion.

The first ten Tigers reached the docks of Pillau on the railroad ship "Deutschland" on 24/1/1945. Several other smaller ships and the sister ship of the "Deutschland", the "Preussen-Sassnitz", brought the rest of the unit over.

The small battle group under Leutnant Nienstedt was set in march in the direction of Deimestellung immediately after unloading. The city of Labiau, which they passed, was all ablaze. The 2nd Company led by Leutnant Rinke was unloaded in a suburb of Labiau at a small railroad station and, on the following morning, 25/1/1945, conducted their first attack to the northeast in the icy cold. The few Tigers with elements of the 240th Reconnaissance Battalion of the 58th ID were able to make contact on the front. Unteroffizier Carpaneto's Tiger, which was trailing in the rear of his company, discovered an enemy tank formation and attacked it by himself. They were super-heavy Josef Stalin II tanks and the new T 34/ 85's. In a dramatic armored duel Carpaneto was able to destroy 15 enemy tanks and, therefore, the entire Soviet formation.

Nevertheless, the front here still could not be held. It was withdrawn in the direction of Neuhausen. During the withdrawal Unteroffizier Carpaneto fell on 26/1/1945 from a Russian anti-tank round. (Alfredo Carpaneto, one of the best Tiger commanders, received the Knight's Cross on 28/3/1945 for his extraordinary commitment against the super-heavy enemy tanks.)

When the tanks reached their positions near Neuhausen during the night of 27/1/1945, the dismounted crews heard the fearful screams and wimpering of the women in the villages occupied by the enemy. Interspersed were a few shots.

The panzer men had to listen to this inferno powerlessly. They could not attack immediately like they had wanted, because they were completely out of ammunition and needed to refuel. They worked feverishly through the night. Then the tanks rolled. Before they reached the town of Prawten they also heard several shots and screams here.

The tanks opened fire at the enemy tanks at first light. Several Tigers rolled around the town and fired into the air. They could not and would not fire into the houses in which there were probably German civilians.

The enemy fled; wherever they appeared they were suppressed. All of the Russian tanks located here were in flames.

People seeking help were loaded on the tanks and driven to Neuhausen. In Neuhausen as in Prawten the men of the 511th Heavy Panzer Battalion experienced the horror of the penetrating Russian enemy: therefore, they were convinced that they had to continue to fight in other towns, they had to fight until they ran out of ammunition.

The 505th Heavy Panzer Battalion, which undertook a breakout attempt with the 5th PD on Reichsstrasse 1 Koenigsberg – Elbing, because Koenigsberg had to be given up, did not succeed. In the afternoon it was established that this attempt had failed and the surrender of Koenigsberg was no longer in question.

On the evening of 6/2/1945 Oberfeldwebel Goering was ordered to commitment with three Tigers from the 511th Heavy Panzer Battalion on Reichsstrasse 1. This small battle group was still in commitment on 15/2 at Frischen Haff, helping the hard-pressed infantry here. They attacked when the Red Army assault troops had penetrated into the HKL and pushed them out again. Gradually a number of repaired Tigers arrived. These were organized into small battle groups of two to three vehicles. During a dark night Feldwebel Kerscher and Leutnant Rinke shot-up ten penetrating enemy tanks, including super-heavy JS II's and KV 85's. Feldwebel Koestler also participated successfully with a third Tiger during this night.

Besides the 511th Heavy Panzer Battalion, the 190th Assault Gun Brigade under the leadership of Major Kroehne shot-up 104 enemy tanks within a month of fighting here in East Prussia. The 507th Heavy Panzer Battalion under Hauptmann Schoeck and, after he was wounded on the first day of commitment, Oberleutnant Wirsching, shot-up 136 enemy tanks within three days of combat and was mentioned in a Wehrmacht report. However, the 7th PD, to which these units were assigned, had to withdraw through Grudusk and Mlawa to Graudenz.

The "Grossdeutschland" Panzergrenadier Division fought against a strong Soviet tank group on 22/1/1945, they were rolling toward Allenstein. Then they ran out of fuel and ammunition and Allenstein was lost.

On 23/1 the Red Army stood before Thorn and cut Army Group Center off from contact with the Reich on this day. The 2nd Belorussian Front had reached its far-flung objective. From now on troops and refugees could only make it to the west by sea.

Because the 2nd German Army was separated from the army group by this attack wedge, they fell under the command of the newly formed Army Group Vistula on 24/1/1945.

After the fighting around Elbing, as described in a previous chapter, came to an end, it seemed only a question of time when Danzig would suffer this same fate. However, before Danzig is remembered it is first necessary to discus the fate of Army Group North, in order to illuminate the discussion of the final battle for Germany.

Army Group North in Defensive Combat

On 27/1/1945 Generaloberst Dr. Lothar Rendulic took command of Army Group North in Zinten. At this time the army group's 4th Army under General der Infanterie Mueller stood with its back to the harbor on a line Braunsberg – Wormditt – Heilsberg – Bartenstein – Domnau – Brandenburg. The 24 divisions of this army were being attacked by about 100 Soviet divisions and a number of independent tank brigades organized under the command of the 2nd and 3rd Belorussian Fronts.

The defensive combat of Army Group North climaxed dramatically at the beginning of February. The "Grossdeutschland" Panzergrenadier Division sacrificed itself near Waldburg. Before this they were able to open the way to Koenigsberg – which was completely encircled. Together with the 5th PD from Koenigsberg this division opened a narrow lane and protected a harbor road there, which was constructed by the engineers. From the history of the commitment of the "Grossdeutschland" Panzergrenadier Division, during the defensive battles and withdrawal combat from 15 to 31/1/1945 and to the attack of this division to re-establish contact with Koenigsberg, the defensive combat near Jaeksheim on 30 and 31/1/1945 was particularly fierce.

The fighting in Dohnaschen Schloss, which changed occupiers several times, was dramatic, because German and Red Army soldiers were in the same palace at the same time.

The proposal of Army Group North, to breakout the defenders of Koenigsberg, because a breakout route was opened, was turned down by Hitler. On 8/2/1945 Frauenburg was lost, however, on 19/2/1945 the troops in Samland were able to establish contact between Pillau and Koenigsberg.

At the beginning of March the Heiligenbeil pocket, which was held by the 4th Army, was compressed into a very narrow area due to the gradual withdrawals in front of the strong Russian armored attacks, from there ran a narrow land connection with Koenigsberg. The pocket extended from Haff west of Braunsberg and from Heiligenberg 14 kilometers to the south and 20 kilometers to the east, from there it ran to Heide Maulen, 9 kilometers east of Brandenburg.

On 12/3/1945 Generaloberst Weiss, who was born in Tilsit, took command of Army Group North, while Generaloberst Rendulic took command over all of the troops in the Kurland pocket.

On the following day the Soviet attack on the Heiligenbeil pocket began with a barrage fire from rocket launchers and heavy artillery batteries the likes of which had never been experienced before. Fighter-bombers joined in enormous formations along the entire breadth of the front, dropping bombs and firing on-board weapons. Nevertheless, the Red Army was unable to breakthrough the German defensive front.

Once more the "Grossdeutschland" Panzergrenadier Division stood at the strong point in Brandenburg. Their Tiger battalion suppressed the enemy tanks that had penetrated into the HKL. Two of these Tigers survived this duel that brought an end to many Russian tanks. Nevertheless, Wermten, Waltersdorf, Rehfeld, Koenigsdorf and several other villages were lost here. Braunsberg fell on 20/3/1945.

On 21/3 the Russian barrage fire began anew. Heiligenbeil was the HKL. The city, which was engaged by Russian fighter-bombers and bombers dropping phosphorous bombs was set ablaze and completely burned down. The final battle took place at the railroad station. Here Germans and Russians lay only 100 meters apart. On 24/3 Heiligenbeil had to be given up. Deutsch-Bahnau was lost on 25/3, Rosenberg was occupied by the Red Army and, therefore, was lost for the crossing. The formations of the 4th Army crossed near Bulga and Kahlholz, after Hitler approved this withdrawal on 25/3.

The "Grossdeutschland" Panzergrenadier Division held out until the last ship departed on the morning of 29/3, thereby giving the remnants of the 4th Army a chance to escape. However, the main body of this army was bloodied on the battlefields during the following weeks.

The Fall of Koenigsberg

On the evening of 30/1/1945, when Generaloberst Rendulic prohibited the 4th Army from continuing its breakthrough to the west, he intended to hold the Heilsberg intersection. This was an old pre-war position that was supposed to protect Koenigsberg from attack out of the south and southeast. He wanted to extend this position to the north with the idea of establishing a large bridgehead in a wide half-circle around Koenigsberg, which would make contact in the rear with Frische Haff and Kurische Haff. The 4th Army was to maintain contact with Elbing and occupy the southern portion of this bridgehead up to Pregel and secure it.

The Red Army was advancing to the west, south of the Pregel through Friedland, and had pushed the weak 4th Army rear guard to the side. The 2nd and 3rd Belorussian Fronts met in the Heilsberg area after the southern attack group of the 2nd Belorussian Front attacked into the withdrawing 4th Army through Loetzen and Rastenburg. The 4th Army was being attacked from the south on either side of Wormditt. In this manner its western flank was bypassed through Preussisch-Holland and Elbing. During the course of the fighting around Koenigsberg the 4th Army was pressured as was the eastern flank of the 2nd Army near Elbing. They experienced their end, pushed back through Heiligenbeil and Balga, the last peninsula before the sea. Approximately 5000 men, half of them wounded, escaped this destructive Red Army offensive.

At the end of January, the 3rd Panzer Army could no longer hold the Koenigsberg hills north of the Pregel. The Russians reached the eastern front of the city, which was declared a fortress, and stopped there, because they imagined that Koenigsberg was a fortress bristling with weapons.

The Red Army shifted the main effort of their attack into Samland, with the intent of conquering this first.

However, Koenigsberg was cut off from its land connection with the west and Pillau was the next objective of the Red Army, because the supplies for Army Group North were landed there.

The 3rd Panzer Army in Samland tried to maintain contact with these elements on the lower Pregel and the Baltic Sea coast. They even dispatched some forces, up to a division, to breakout of the Memel encirclement, march through the Kurische Narrows and break through the Russian blocking position near Kranz.

By mid-February the 3rd Panzer Army was compressed into a 20 kilometer wide strip along the coast and, with its last strength, repulsed the repeated Russian attacks near Fischhausen, with which they were trying to penetrate into this land passage, in order to finally occupy Pillau.

The situation in the Koenigsberg fortress on 27/1/1945 was as follows: the Soviet assault formations, which were directed at the city, had flanked the city in a half-circle from the south to the east at a distance of approximately 2000 meters. From the north they were located near Karmitten directly north of the city on Fuchsberg, directly east of Baeckerberge in the northeast, forward of Dossitten and Arnau in the east, near Gutenfeld in the southeast and near Wickbold – Ludwigswalde in the south.

From the south in the opposite direction Koenigsberg was defended by the following formations: the 5th PD, the 561 Volksgrenadier Division, the 367th ID and the 548th Volksgrenadier Division. Far to the north, opposite the enemy located near Karmitten, was the 551st Volksgrenadier Division.

On 25/1/1945 Generalleutnant Schittnig was entrusted with the defense of Koenigsberg with the staff of the 1st ID. However, on the morning of 28/1 this command was replaced and General der Infanterie Lasch was named "Commander of the Fortifications near Koenigsberg and the Fortress of Koenigsberg."

Generaloberst Rendulic, the new commander of Army Group North, appeared at his command post in Moditten on the morning of 28/1. He explained to General Lasch that the Fuehrer had decided that he, Lasch, had to take over the Koenigsberg Fortress. Generalleutnant Schittnig would become deputy to his staff. Therefore, after several changes in command, the course was set for the battle of Koenigsberg.

During the night before 29/1 a Russian armored attack occurred out of the north on either side of the Cranz – Koenigsberg road. The 947th Grenadier Regiment [GR] of the 367th ID, led by Major Schaper, and the panzerjaeger battalion from this division under the command of Major Hartmann, repulsed this attack, during which time the Red Army lost 30 tanks, the majority to the panzerjaegers, however, some were also destroyed by panzerfaust rounds.

The enemy now suspended his attacks in this sector. The reichsstrasse could now be secured in the Fuchsberges.

By 29/1/1945 the Red Army had encircled Koenigsberg, after their formations had made it to Heide – Waldburg in the southwest and Haffstrom at Frische Haff and had advanced in the north across Reichsstrasse 1 near Metgethen.

The 548th Volksgrenadier Division, which was withdrawing north of Koenigsberg, withdrew to Fischhausen. They then established a bridge-head for the protection of Pillau.

Metgethen was captured in a raid by Soviet assault troops during the night of 30/1. During this night the Red Army reached Reichsstrasse 131 to Pillau and advanced from there during this night to the Koenigsberg sea canal.

On the evening of 8/2/1945 the staff of the 3rd Panzer Army was transferred to Pomerania. The troops in Samland and in Koenigsberg were now led by the XXVIII Army Corps as the new "Armeeabteilung Samland."

After liberating the western portion of Samland with this newly created "Armeeabteilung Samland", Army Group North planned to attack from the west to the east and re-establish contact with Koenigsberg in concert with a counterattack out of the fortress to the west.

The attack out of Koenigsberg was planned by General Lasch with the 1st ID, the 5th PD, the 561st Volksgrenadier Division and the remnants of the 505th Heavy Panzer Battalion and a few vehicles from the 511th Heavy Panzer Battalion, which were still in the fortress. On the other side for the breakthrough to Koenigsberg stood the 58th and 93rd Infantry Divisions and the 548th Volksgrenadier Division.

At 0530 hours on 19/2/1945 the two-sided attack began. The divisions, which were advancing in the direction of Koenigsberg, had to overcome strong enemy resistance. The fighting see-sawed for several days near the Galtgarben hills before the enemy withdrew. However, on 20/2/1945 the two attack groups met.

From the fortress the 1st (East Prussian) ID, an elite division, and the 5th PD attacked to Metgethen and recaptured this location. The 5th PD then advanced to Seerappen. During the following days the rail line to Pillau was also opened.

The enemy withdrew to the north.

How this attack took place and what the liberators found in Metgethen is described in the following section.

Loss and Counterattack

"Our attack", reported Oberfeldwebel Goering, a tank commander in the 511th Heavy Panzer Battalion:

"Was conducted from Koenigsberg through Metgethen with the objective of capturing the airfield at Seerappen. We were to make contact with the Samland troops here, the 511th Heavy Panzer Battalion was to be on the main axis. My Tiger ended up remaining in Koenigsberg, therefore, I was separated from the battalion.

I was to negotiate the mine-field lane with my Tiger first. There were four more Tigers behind me. However, in front of our battle group was a T 34 with a German crew dressed in Russian uniforms. Its commander was a Feldwebel who spoke perfect Russian.

At H-Hour the T 34 set out. It advanced without firing. While its commander ordered in Russian that the Soviet outposts withdraw, because the Germans were hot on his heels, the Tigers rolled right behind him. The Russians fled, some just getting out of bed.

In a brief but bitter fight the entire enemy anti-tank front was rolled up from the rear and destroyed. The Tigers rolled toward Anhieb through the Russian artillery front.

We reached the enemy HKL without suffering any losses. The supply vehicles and artillery were fleeing before us. In Metgethen we saw what the Russians had been doing since they captured it at the end of January. There were still refugee trains standing at the railroad station. They had been taken by surprise there, women and girls had been raped there and then murdered bestially. We found 32 murdered women in one bomb crater, they were also treated bestially.

The soldiers that held here wrote on the sides of the railroad cars: "REVENGE FOR METGETHEN!"

From now on the fighting was merciless. Wherever the tanks ran into Russian troops they were suppressed.

In the early morning of 20/2 the fighting continued. The enemy had reinforced in the meantime. Nevertheless, we reached the airfield at Seerappen. Three kilometers further to the north we ran into the Regitten farm. The enemy attacked us here in the flank. The battle stood on a razors edge.

This farm, with the Muehlenberg – noted as Hill 28 on the map – dominated the terrain for some distance.

During the next night the Russians attacked us here. Three times, one after the other, they were repulsed suffering heavy casualties. During the following day the farmstead changed hands six times. This decisive high ground could not be lost under any circumstances.

On the afternoon of 21/2 the Red Army committed fighter-bombers and bombers here. During the breakout from Koenigsberg we had captured Russian signal ammunition. We now made use of it and fired the color white. The enemy fell for it and dropped their bombs on the far side of the hill positions.

Unfortunately, the hope that we would be reunited with our old comrades was not fulfilled, they were in a bitter armored struggle near Medenau."

Thus is the direct report from Oberfeldwebel Goering, which gives us a detailed look into the combat operations.

On the Samland side the attack was even more difficult. There stood the Tigers in the motorized battle group under Major Frey. To this battle group belonged ten Tigers of the 511th Heavy Panzer Battalion, the 240th Reconnaissance Battalion and elements of the 158th Panzerjaeger Battalion of the 58th ID. This battle group was to set out as soon as the infantry was able to occupy the ridge-line between Wischehen and Kragau.

The grenadiers stalled in front of this strongly fortified high ground, that was spiked with many machine-gun nests. Only the II/GR 154 was able to fight its way through Kragau to Mosehnen. Here it stood alone against a superior enemy force and was encircled by hastily deployed reserves and destroyed almost to the last man. Among the dead was also the battalion commander, Major Schindel.

In the meantime, the Russians had fallen onto the Tiger assembly area. 36 mortars opened fire on the German tank assemblage. The heavy mortars, which were located on the back slope, could not be ranged by the Tiger cannon. The tank commanders tried to escape from the hail of shells in the narrow area by a difficult withdrawal maneuver.

However, finally Unteroffizier Supper from the 2/sPzAbt 511 rolled his Tiger, without orders, at top speed over the hill and to the farmstead from where the fire was coming. Supper fired on the enemy. Tanks burst into flames, mortars were blown into the air by direct hits. Nevertheless, it would have been all over for the Unteroffizier had not Feldwebel Albert Kerscher, one of the Knight's Cross awardees from this battalion, and others followed him.

Without stopping, the Tigers rolled further, shot at everything that appeared in front of their cannon and rolled over the entire enemy held farm. Arriving on the reverse slope, Supper shot-up the mortars. An ear shattering crack filled the air as an ammunition dump exploded. The other tanks followed. None of the 36 mortars here escaped their fate.

The Tigers had achieved a great success. Unteroffizier Supper was recommended for the Knight's Cross, which, unfortunately, he never received.

Here at the farmstead the panzer men saw another gruesome sight. They found the woman of the farm hanging out of a window. The farmer and his daughter were also found dead. Several other members of the farm had suffered the same fate.

Elements of the 58th ID continued fighting during the night through the high ground east of Kragau. On 20/2 the attack on Gross-Medenau also began. The fighting around this village lasted for hours. After the Tigers broke through a strong anti-tank obstacle and had destroyed the infantry and anti-tank gun crews with high-explosive shells Gross-Medenau could be taken.

The panzer men also found killed and mutilated civilians here. They lay from Saugling to Greis, on the edges of the town roads, in the houses and in the gardens.

This was no propaganda of the usual Goebbels type, the Reichspropagandaminister could not formulate this bestiality. This was worse than anything they had heard of before.

Finally they were able to establish a narrow land connection between Koenigsberg and Samland. Here the Tigers were committed in small battle groups, in order to screen the land connection and prevent it from being severed again. Fighting developed here that was among the fiercest of the Second World War.

Near the Sickenhoefen farmstead Feldwebel Kerscher scored a success. In initial combat against three enemy tanks he was able to shoot-up all three. After that he destroyed another two T 34's and a 17.2 cm gun. Then he was forced to take cover in a depression, because a number of enemy anti-tank guns opened fire on him from the hills. He could not get out of the depression alone.

Leutnant Rinke, who recognized this threat in time, now rolled with four Tigers and a few SPW's, which had arrived in the meantime, toward the hill bristling with anti-tank guns, while the remaining Tigers opened rapid fire against these anti-tank guns, forcing the crews to take cover from their high-explosive shells.

The Tigers reached the hill. They rolled side by side and opened fire on the anti-tank guns. All of the anti-tank guns that were located here were destroyed by Rinke and his Tigers. Kerscher now secured the left flank of this battle group. After that the Sickenhoefen farm was re-captured in a decisive advance. (Leutnant Adolf Rinke received the Knight's Cross on 17/4/1945.)

The following days were filled with additional commitments. Kerscher's Tiger was shot at by his own anti-tank guns. Fortunately, he suffered no damage. Then a Russian anti-tank gun paralyzed him.

When two enemy tanks broke through the German security line at night, Unteroffizier Baresch was awake. He rolled with his recently refitted tank. He saw the flames coming from the exhaust, they marked his target. He advanced on their right flank and came to a suitable firing position. Two rapid shots took care of both T 34's.

They did it! With only a few formations they were able to defeat elements from two Soviet armies. The Wehrmacht report from 26/2/1945 noted these events and the 58th ID division diary particularly praised the commitment of the Tigers. It said:

"The battalion, which was subordinated to the division during the fierce fighting to re-establish land contact with the Koenigsberg Fortress, played an important role in the division's success.

The excellent reputation, which the battalion had already won in earlier commitments with the division, was re-confirmed. signed Siewert, Generalleutnant."

Koenigsberg was saved from immanent destruction by this fortunate strike. During the next few weeks a deceptive quiet existed here, while hectic and dramatic fighting raged on other sectors of the front.

Nevertheless, now the fortress was denied the services of the 1st ID and 5th PD, which did not return to the fortress after establishing the land connection. Therefore, the 548th Volksgrenadier Division under Generalleutnant Sudau was transferred into the fortress. General Lasch protested fruitlessly against this weakening and against the "plundering" of Koenigsberg, which was now denied no less than 72 air defense guns, most of which were the heavy 8.8 cm cannon that were decisive in anti-tank defense.

Since none of his protests, nor those of the OKH, had any effect on the OKW, at the end of March General Lasch requested the new commander of Army Group North, Generaloberst Weiss, relieve him from his posting. The commander of Army Group North could not consent to this.

Meanwhile, 30 Soviet rifle divisions had surrounded Koenigsberg and the four exhausted German divisions in the city. The ratio of tanks was 100:1. The Red Army now deployed strong artillery here. The mostly heavy guns were to soften up the German fortress.

Through a German reconnaissance operation, which brought back prisoners, the leadership in the fortress learned that the main Soviet attack would occur between 5 and 7/4/1945.

The anticipated attack was launched on 6/4/1945. 30 Soviet rifle divisions, supported by two air armies and artillery in the strength of 1000 tubes, including rocket launchers, turned their attention to Koenigsberg. All communications were knocked out by this massive barrage fire.

After that, several rifle divisions, supported by tank formations, attacked Charlottenburg, where the 548th Volksgrenadier Division was defending. The enemy also achieved deep penetrations in the 561st Volksgrenadier Division's 1143rd GR adjoining area of operations. After all reserves were committed General Lasch requested the immediate commitment of the 5th PD from the army, they had originally been assigned to the Koenigsberg defensive forces. They were to win back the lost positions with the concentrated fire of their tanks.

On 7/4 the Red Army continued its attack. The penetrations of the previous day near Amalienau and Juditten were widened. As soon as the fortress commandant Ia made contact with the 5th PD, a new Russian penetration was achieved on the 1st ID front, which was on the left of the 561st Volksgrenadier Division. The subordination of the 5th PD, which was as good as secured, was rescinded. Due to the change in the situation, they now had to be committed in the 561st Volksgrenadier Division and 1st ID areas of operations to destroy the enemy forces that had penetrated there.

In the south of the city the formations of the Red Army were able to attack through in the 69th ID area of operations up to the mouth of the Pregel. General Lasch now proposed breaking out his entire fortress defense to the west. This proposal was also turned down by the army.

On the evening of 7/4 the HKL ran in the southern sector of Koenigsberg near the reichsstrasse – main railroad station – Habersberger – Friedlaender Strasse up to the old field-works.

In order to prevent the threatened crossing of the Pregel by enemy formations in the 69th ID sector, General Lasch transferred elements of the 61st ID into this area. They came too late. By the evening of 7/4/1945 there was only a tentative connection with the west.

On the early morning of 8/4 Russian assault troops attacked across the Pregel from the south. Therefore, the ring of encirclement around Koenigsberg was reinforced. On 8/4 the 61st ID withdrew into the city.

The deputy Gauleiter, Grossherr, who was still located in Koenigsberg, proposed to Gauleiter Koch, who was in Neutief preparing to withdraw to the west, that the military forces breakout to the west. The "fig leaf" justifying this flight of the Gauleiter, first to Neutief, was supposedly that there was no time to properly execute an evacuation of the civilian population.

General Lasch proposed to Gauleiter Koch breaking out with all forces, because it appeared to be the only way to save the combat strength of the troops for further defense in a withdrawal position. However, even the army leadership decided: "Fortress Koenigsberg is to be held."

Only assault troops and groups received permission to breakout and establish contact with the 561st Volksgrenadier Division, which stood to the west of the city. This division, in conjunction with the 5th PD, was to attack from the west, in order to facilitate the breakthrough of the assault troops. In addition, the army ordered:

> "The 5th PD must not cross the suburb of Juditten during this counterattack."

This meant that they would not be returning to Koenigsberg.

In order to give this breakout attempt at least a little chance of succeeding, General Lasch set the staff of the 61st ID under Generalleutnant Sperl with all of the non-essential battalions on the eastern Koenigsberg front, elements of the 548th Volksgrenadier Division under Generalleutnant Sudau and artillery elements from the 367th ID to breakout.

The breakout began after a several hour delay on 9/4/1945 at 0200 hours and soon stalled against the thick wall of siege troops. Generalleutnant Sudau fell in combat, Generalleutnant Sperl was wounded and the Deputy Gauleiter Grossherr, who fought bravely with his entourage during the breakout attempt, was also killed. All of the troop units that were able to break contact with the enemy, fled back to Koenigsberg. Even partial elements were unable to breakout. If one is to breakout, then it must be done with all forces and it has to be started at midnight, not at 0200 hours, in order to take advantage of the familiarity of terrain.

9/4/1945 brought the end for Koenigsberg. There was no longer a main combat line which could be defended. General Lasch made the bitter decision to surrender. In a radio message to OKH at 1730 hours he reported the

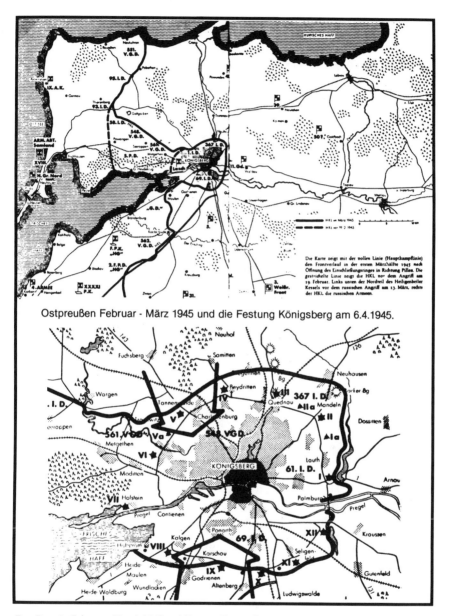

Ostpreußen Februar - März 1945 und die Festung Königsberg am 6.4.1945.

East Prussia February-March 1945 and Fortress Koenigsberg on 6/4/1945.

251

end of fighting in Koenigsberg. The Soviet leadership promised in the official surrender document that concern would be paid to the civilian population and, above all, also for the wounded and they would be treated as well as possible. The German soldiers taken into captivity were promised honorable treatment.

The exact opposite proved to be the case once the document was signed and the soldiers disarmed. The Red Army – as was often the case – turned the city over, after the hard fought victory, to 48 hours of plundering.

The Soviet Armed Forces Report on 10/4/1945 noted: "Troops of the 3rd Belorussian Front conquered the Koenigsberg Fortress on 9 April."

General Lasch was condemned to death in absentia by a court martial convened by Hitler. He was taken prisoner along with his soldiers. He returned from the USSR in 1955.

The end in East Prussia after the fall of Koenigsberg was only a question of days or a few weeks. General Mueller was replaced. His successor in East Prussia was General der Panzertruppe Dietrich von Saucken, who took command of the 2nd Army, which was compressed in Hela and into the mouth of the Vistula, and as the new and last commander in East Prussia was also to command the formations in Samland. These formations received the high-sounding title of "Army of East Prussia."

The Citizens of Koenigsberg Report

"On 24/2/1945 we were told to leave Koenigsberg. We were to assemble on the ruined square with small hand baggage within three hours and be taken by vehicles to Hafenbecken IV. We went to the assembly location. We left our houses and belongings behind. Unfortunately, we also had to leave our youngest daughter, who was working as a nurse at the main first aid station, with heavy hearts.

Out of her sense of duty, she could not leave the immobile wounded behind. Our parting was bitter, what fate awaited her we could only imagine.

In the harbor we were loaded onto coal ships. By darkness our ship reached Pillau. There were already thousands waiting there for sea transport. We were stuffed into a broken-down cattle transport. Due to high seas, this steamer could not leave for two days. It was escorted by a torpedo boat and two mine-sweepers.

We sailed in the direction of Neufahrwasser and we reached our goal at 0200 hours and thanked God that we had solid ground under our feet." (See statement of Eduard Schwarz, Kreisbuerodirecktor (Ret.) from Koenigsberg.)

These groups, who were able to get out before the fortress was completely encircled, stood is stark contrast with those who had to remain in the fortress. They had to endure the air attacks and artillery fire and waited for the indescribable events that would take place as soon as the Red Army stormed into the fortress.

A housewife from Koenigsberg, A.F., told her story in the Documentation of the Expulsion: "I lived on Oberteich. Our street was damaged by the first air attack in August 1944. Our house, a two family house, escaped damage and stood between burned out ruins. We remained in the house and I spent a couple of days in the cellar. The noises of combat grew nearer. There was a particularly severe fire strike one night. We heard a very loud crack. I was convinced that our house was coming down. This was not the case. In the morning I realized that the entrance to the other side of the house was destroyed when a heavy caliber shell hit the stairway. We decided to put up the family of Herr Dr. K., and share our hospitality with others in the cellar. We spent all of our lives in this cellar. The ring around Koenigsberg grew narrower. The large number of civilians in the city magnified the threat. The Party decided to forcefully evacuate them with all means. This last minute action cost many citizens their lives. In small fishing villages on the Frischen Haff concentrations of people awaited further transport, which could only come at great danger and with great difficulty. These masses of people were engaged by air attacks and on-board weapons fire.

In the city trench digging continued and the cellars in the ruins were cleared for defense. Daily living became more threatening, the firing increased.

The evacuation was conducted more energetically. The people now did not want to leave, because transport to the Reich was no longer possible. The local group leaders could not convince me it was better to go to the Reich. I made my decision not to leave Koenigsberg.

The fighting around Koenigsberg became more dramatic. The Russians flew air attacks day and night. The sirens no longer worked. However, at the sound of aircraft engines we could determine the approach of bomber formations. During the daytime came reconnaissance aircraft and fighter-bombers, which fired into the windows of the residences.

At the end of March 1945 Dr. K. had to leave us. He was ordered to transfer to F. The separation from him and his wife was not easy.

On the same evening my house was destroyed by bombs. The attempt to salvage anything from the ruins was hopeless.

During the last days the enemy also dropped pamphlets, in which they promised to keep families together. The soldiers were requested to put down their weapons and surrender.

During the night before 8/4/1945 a Party order arrived to move the civilian population immediately to the west, to Juditten. In my opinion this was suicide if the enemy was attacking the city from the west.

I remained behind with Frau Sch. There were no longer any men on our street. We found a local group taking shelter in the ruins of a bunker. The Volkssturm men were also there.

The local group leader did not want to accept us at first, however, all hell broke loose on the main traffic arteries. The Stalin Organs droned on incessantly, shells detonated all around us, in the air aircraft continued to drop their bomb loads and fire their on-board weapons.

Finally the local group leader vanished with his men. The Volkssturm and the deputy local group leader remained behind. It was Sunday, 8 April 1945.

On the following day, 9/4/1945, my wedding anniversary, the first Russians appeared. How many there were, I cannot say. Among us women was a Latvian, who was able to explain to the Russians that we were not women soldiers fighting with the Volkssturm.

When we came out onto the street there was still firing coming from the ruins. However, this last defensive fire soon grew quiet. We were led away and as we were moving off to our shelters we heard the cries of "Urri,

Urri! [watches, watches]" A Russian came toward us and took us down a side street and demanded our watches, which we no longer had.

We were not allowed to enter our street. An acquaintance, who was with us, led us to a pair of houses, where he lived. We entered them. The women cooked the midday meal in the cellar, while the men remained above.

After eating, we gathered in the living room above. When we were all together more Russians appeared, they demanded we follow them. We were assembled in a villa. We sensed danger. We heard of the first rapes. An old man, who we knew, was to be shot.

Finally they said: "Everybody out!"

We set out on our fateful path. We spent the first night in a destroyed kaserne. As we walked through the Fritzener Forest during the next few days we saw exhausted people on the edge of the trails, they were deciding their fate, to sit or lay down. We were not allowed to help them. We continued on until we reached T., where there were already many Germans assembled. Here occurred the first registration and the inspection of our baggage.

We spent the next night in a village that was filled with Russians. Here was danger for us women and girls. What occurred here is hard for me to describe. I was glad that my daughter was not with me. The hopeless cries of the children still ring in my ears today. Our men had to suffer these indignities helplessly.

On the next morning we continued further. It looked as if we were being returned to Koenigsberg. We were led to a kaserne complex into a great hall that was already filled with people.

Here we saw women and girls that had been separated from us, they faced a special fate. A mother surrounded by several small children was a rarity.

After several hours we were taken from the hall to the street in front of the kaserne gates. Koenigsberg had, in the meantime, surrendered. In the evening we were able to enter the destroyed and empty buildings.

Here began the first visits from Russian soldiers. Cries for help rose from building to building, from room to room and caused us anxiety and fear."

That was the fate of the civilians left behind in Koenigsberg.

The fate of the city had been sealed weeks before, in a place called: Kolberg.

Fortress Kolberg

Kolberg was declared a fortress in November 1944. The plan foresaw three defensive lines being erected in the outlying settlements at the beginning of February 1945 as ordered by the deputy commander of the LI Army Corps.

On 26/1/1945 the Kolberg fortress staff was organized and they set to work on anti-tank trenches and infantry positions. This planned position construction was not fully begun when the fortress commandant, Oberst Fritz Fullriede arrived on 1/3/1945. Only a portion of the anti-tank trenches and the infantry positions, as well as 16 temporary positions for 28 cm rocket launchers, was completed.

The attack of the 1st and 2nd Belorussian Fronts into eastern Pomerania to the north toward the Baltic Sea coast, which began on 10/2/1943 [sic, should be 1944] ended on 4/3/1945 as both army groups reached the Baltic Sea coast.

The main strength was transferred to the pursuit of the German troops withdrawing to the east toward Gdingen and Danzig, while a smaller axis advanced to the west in the direction of Stettiner Haff. This also included the 1st Polish Army, which had joined in these operations.

These troops advanced through Kauenburg and Stolp in the direction of Kolberg. When Oberst Fritz Fullriede, who as commander of a battle group in the greater Tunisia area had won the Knight's Cross and had fought as commander of the 200th Panzergrenadier Regiment of the 90th Panzergrenadier Division – the former 90th Light Afrika Division – in the Italian Theater of War, received the news that he was to be the defender of Kolberg, he was astonished.

Hitler, as reported in the Fuehrer Headquarters, in view of the historical battle of Kolberg against Napoleon, wanted to resurrect the memory of this battle and fight it anew. He declared Kolberg a fortress and hoped that Fritz Fullriede would prove to be as great a name as his forerunners, Gneisennau and Nettelbeck.

However, Fritz Fullriede had another objective, as he explained to the author. For him the defensive battle only made sense if it held out until the encircled refugees and the population was rescued by sea. He declared to his soldiers:

"You are not defending this city of Kolberg, but the population and all of the people living in the city. That is your mission!"

On 1/3/1945, when he arrived in Kolberg to relieve the former fortress commandant he met SS Oberfuehrer Bertling, who led all of the non-military agencies in the city, and SA Standartenfuehrer Pfeiffer, the commander of the Kolberg Volkssturm. The Oberbuergermeister of the city, Generalmajor (Ret.) Krapp, and Kreisleiter Gerriels were also still in the city.

The defensive forces Oberst Kolberg found in Kolberg were: the I Battalion of the Field Construction Regiment of the 3rd Panzer Army, with all regimental elements and the regimental staff, a Volkssturm battalion that was only partially equipped, a Volkssturm mortar platoon and an element of the Heinzel Flak Battalion.

On 2/3 eight light filed howitzers arrived in Kolberg without crews. They were also lacking their necessary limbers, however, these could be manufactured in Kolberg.

On 3/3/1945 the 51st Fortification Machine-gun Battalion arrived and, on 4/3, the last combat capable group from the Roemig Panzer Platoon followed.

Since the end of January 1945 there had been an unbroken stream of refugees passing through Kolberg to the west. In this manner, the population of the city rose from 35,000 to 85,000. The flow of these refugees in the direction of Stettin was only gradual, therefore the trains coming from Koeslin and Belgard were always jammed. Queries to the railroad administration in Stettin revealed that the trains could no longer make it through.

Thus, at the beginning of the encirclement of the city of Kolberg there were 22 refugee trains, in which there were also wounded, standing on the open stretch from Belgard to Kolberg.

Oberst Fullriede first met with the Party leadership of the city on 1/3. The Oberst requested the immediate removal of the civilian population to the west. This request did not get any response. His requests from 2 and 3/3 were also unanswered. On the evening of 3/3 at 2000 hours the fortress commandant requested the Kreisleiter immediately remove the refugees from Kolberg, because it was now time to move the refugees to Gribow, while there was still the chance.

The report from Battle Group Kettau from the evening of 3/3/1945 alarmed the fortress defenders. On the early morning of 4/3 Fullriede dispatched a scout troop, which ran into the enemy at 0400 hours near Rossenthin. At 0500 hours lead enemy armored elements and infantry formations, some mounted on tanks, reached Sellnow. Therefore, Kolberg was cut off from its source of water at the Koppendicks-Grund Water-works. At 0700 hours lead mobile troops from the Red Army reached the edge of the suburb of Gelder.

The Amtsleiter and Party leader were summoned to the rathaus at 0230 hours on 4/3. There they were sworn to secrecy. A finance minister had heard the report of an officer that the enemy stood on the Bergschanze.

On the morning of 4/3 Russian tank formations attacked Kolberg from the south. They were repulsed at the Gelder suburb by two eight-eight air defense guns, six mortars and elements of the 51st Fortification Machine-gun Battalion.

The enemy withdrew to Karlsberg and awaited the arrival of additional strong tank forces. These did not arrive, instead came three divisions of the 1st Polish Army: the 1st, 3rd and 4th Infantry Divisions.

The lead groups, led by tanks, rolled along the Treptower – Koerliner road in the direction of the city. The heavy 28 cm mortars, air defense guns and several tank destroyer troops repulsed this attempt to penetrate into the city in a raid.

Because the roads leading to Kolberg from Koeslin and Belgard were still open, additional refugees continued to stream into Kolberg at this time.

They had to be immediately led to the still open road to Gribow. Because enemy tanks were probing here, this was a dangerous undertaking that had to be secured by tank destroyer troops on bicycles.

On the evening of 5/3 Oberst Fullriede decided to counterattack out of the fortress with the objective of advancing on either side of the Treptower road to Neu-Werder and Neu-Geldern, as well as on the road to Karlsberg, to open up the refugee routes.

The attack began on the morning of 6/3/1945 at 0600 hours and reached the southern edge of Neu-Geldern in 35 minutes. In the afternoon it had advanced up to Neu-Werder and was now advancing on Karlsberg. However, this city could not be taken against the strong Red Army tank forces committed here.

Therefore, the Treptower road and the rail line to Treptow remained under enemy fire.

The road to Gribow and through Gribow to the west was held open by throwing the enemy back.

However, on the following day enemy troops were able to attack through to the sea west and east of the city. Therefore, Kolberg was completely encircled.

At 1535 hours a radio message arrived from the OKH at the city combat commandant, it forbid the further fighting to open refugee routes for the civilian population. The message ordered Fullriede to concentrate his forces in order to secure the removal of the population by sea.

On the evening of this day groups of Russian tanks advanced into the Gelder suburb. Here Battalion Hempel, which was composed of stragglers, blocked the enemy penetration. One company held off the Russian tank attack on Stettiner Strasse with Panzerfaust rounds. The kaserne located here remained in German hands. In spite of heavy casualties this assault wedge was able to advance up to the corner of Camminer Strasse and Treptower Strasse with several tanks and following infantry and entrench in the houses located there.

Ruegenwalde and Stolpmuende fell on 7 and 8/3/1945. Fregattenkapitaen Kolbe organized the boarding of the refugees in Kolberg harbor. They were taken from the docks in small boats to the refugee ships.

The 2,877 BRT "Westpreussen", the West Indian "Heinz Horn" with 3,994 BRT and the 4,592 BRT "Nordenham" took on refugees until there was no longer one square meter of space left. In addition, the 10,000 BRT "Winrich von Kniprode" arrived from the Hamburg – America Line. 9,500 refugees were transported by sea on the two previous days. On 9/3 Fregattenkapitaen Kolbe returned to Kolberg with sub-chaser UJ 119, in order to continue the evacuation operations directed by the Western Baltic Sea Admiralty.

There were still about 40,000 refugees in the city. On 8/3 the enemy shifted his main attack effort into the Lauenburger suburb. Tank and infantry formations advanced here under strong fire protection.

The enemy tanks rolled across the Persantewiessen along Koerliner Strasse against the anti-tank obstacles at the entrance to the city.

In the meantime, 20 heavy batteries were set up around Kolberg. In addition, rocket launcher and mortar units arrived. They fired a hail of shells onto the city. The harbor and the railroad station quarters were favorite targets, in addition to the recognized German defensive positions. The civilians as well as the troops suffered heavy casualties.

On 9/3 the Red Army achieved a penetration into the Lauenburger suburb. Attacks and counterattacks alternated at the cemetery and in the vicinity of the gas-works. The Pfeiffer Volkssturm Battalion repulsed a strong attack against the western defenses, which they held. Under the leadership of Leutnant Hempel a counterattack was conducted on Treptower Strasse. The enemy that had penetrated here were thrown back, the houses were cleared and 24 weapons were captured.

Naval artillery, which secured the commitment of the German destroyers and torpedo boats here, supported the defensive battle in this sector. The enemy suffered heavy casualties, especially in tanks.

The attack of the 1st Polish Army, which became more involved in the battle for Kolberg, was concentrated on the eastern and southern portions of the city on 10/3/1945. The rail line to Koeslin and Koerlin ran through here. The penetration into the Lauenburger suburb from the previous day was expanded by the commitment of fresh tank formations. The enemy tanks with mounted infantry were able to advance to Waldenfels Kaserne, penetrate into it and overcome the weak forces there.

Since the Georgen Church was the focus of the enemy artillery and was ultimately utilized as an enemy observation post, a scout troop advanced against this church on the night before 11/3 and set its tower ablaze. In the west and in the Battalion Hempel area in the southwest the enemy attacked constantly and was always thrown back in close combat. Of the seven bridges across the Persante four were already blown.

The fixing attack on the entire encirclement front became costly on 11/3/1945 as the Red Army and Polish soldiers entered the first houses. The accompanying tanks were shot-up. However, because there were no German anti-tank guns available and the few tanks from Panzer Battle Group Beyer were somewhat immobile and had to be towed into position to be used as guns, the Soviet tanks and assault guns were able to be used in direct fire on the defended houses.

After a heavy fire-strike on the morning of 12/3 a new enemy attack was launched on the Lauenburger suburb. The enemy achieved a penetration from the cemetery to the north across Koesliner Chaussee. The counterattack stalled in the strong enemy fire. At the fall of darkness, the eastern front of Kolberg had to be withdrawn to a new line along Wallstrasse. During the night a second defensive line was constructed behind it. On this day six additional enemy attacks supported by tanks in the west and southwest were repulsed. In the meantime, the Navy had joined in the battle for Kolberg and achieved a number of successes which allowed the defenders to hold out longer. Here is their report.

The Navy in Commitment

Beginning on 9/2/1945 the heavy cruisers "Luetzow" and "Admiral Scheer", supported by the destroyers Z 34 and Z 38 and torpedo boats T 8, T 23, T 28, T 33, T 35 and T 36, started firing on the Soviet positions in Samland.

However, after 26/2/1945 – the beginning of the Russian attack on inner Pomerania – a new battle group was committed to cover the German bridgehead opposite Wollin. It consisted of the "Admiral Scheer", Z 38 under KKpt [Korvettenkapitaen] Freiherr von Lyncker, Z 31 under KKpt Pual, "Paul Jocobi" and T 36. The combined fire of this battle group was to thank on 9/3 that this bridgehead was able to hold.

On 11/3, however, the destroyers Z 34 and Z 43, as well as the torpedo boat T 33 were at Kolberg almost constantly and placed the Soviet positions under fire. Whenever they had to resupply with ammunition, they took on refugees – as did the barges, siebelfaehren and other boats – from the hotly contested city. This was accomplished by the smaller boats slowly moving from Kolberg to the destroyers and then transferring the people over to the destroyers.

Thus the destroyer Z 34 under KKpt Hetz took on more wounded and refugees on 11/3/1945. Under the fire protection of Z 34, which was still engaging the Soviet positions with its 15 cm guns, 800(!) refugees and 120 wounded were boarded on this day, then the destroyer set sail for Swinemuende.

During this boarding four Russian IL-2 fighter-bombers attacked. They were followed by high-altitude Boston bombers. However, this time Z 34 was able to avoid being hit.

With 920 people on board this destroyer returned to Swinemuende, where it ran into an air raid.

This time it was a major attack by the USAAF with 700 B 17 and B 24 bombers, which dropped 1435 tons of bombs on Swinemuende. KKpt. Hetz reported:

"At 1100 hours, as I was approaching Swinemuende, an air raid alert was sent by all signal stations. Large bomber formations were reported in concentrated flight toward Swinemuende.

Deadly silence dominated the bridge. One could already hear the drone of heavy bombers through the high floating clouds. It was too late to turn about. There was panic flight of all types of craft from out of the harbor, they left at top speed in an attempt to flee the harbor and get into the open sea before the attack.

There was nothing we could do but continue on course. I decided to make for the bathing establishment, where the water was wider, and try to turn around there. Hopefully the aircraft would give me the time I needed." (See Report from Kpt. z. S. (Ret.) Hetz to the Author.)

Z 34 watched as the steamers and smaller craft passed it by. The destroyer approached the point where Hetz could turn it around. What happened next is described by the commander:

The minutes to the turn around point seemed like an eternity. Everyone on the bridge looked straight ahead so that they would not have to look their comrades in the eye. Finally I could give the command. The numerous times I made this maneuver in peacetime gave me the confidence of bringing the destroyer about with a few machine and ruder orders.

We made our way out at 15 knots. Just as we passed the light tower the bombs hit the city and harbor of Swinemuende. In the exact spot where we had just turned about rose a column of white from a heavy bomb hit. This released the tension on board and as we passed the jetty two refugee children appeared on deck, they were waving their hands and laughing. These laughs were the most pleasant I had heard in a long time."

On the morning of 13/3 Z 34 was able to unload its refugees and wounded at Swinemuende.

There will be more later about the commitment of these few German Naval units during the siege and breakthrough at Kolberg. First we must return to the fortress commandant and to the events of 13/3/1945.

The Last Seven Days

On 13/3/1945 the enemy attacked on the Maikuhle in the west as they did again into the Gelder suburb in the east. The attack on the Maikuhle ran into Volkssturm men and was repulsed. In the Gelder suburb Battalion Hempel threw the enemy back in hand-to-hand combat as they had before.

In the eastern quarter of the city, however, the Russian troops achieved a deep penetration. They were able to capture the desperately defended gas-works and were able to get a foothold in the engine-house after the defenders were shot out of here by tanks.

In a counterattack, for which two tanks were able to be made operational, this penetration was removed.

The Volkssturm defenders on the Maikuhle, who had suffered heavy losses, had to withdraw to a shorter line at the end of this eventful 13/3.

With the break of day on 14/3 the besiegers opened up a barrage fire from all directions with all available weapons. Besides artillery and rocket launchers even tanks and anti-tank guns participated in direct fire during this softening-up attack on Kolberg.

After that the Red Army attacked with everything it had. This attack led to deep penetrations on the Maikuhle. The kasernes in Gelder suburb were captured by the Red Army. An armored wedge pressed out of the Lauenburger suburb into the inner city. The rail junction west of the engine-house, which was already in enemy hands, experienced the attacks of Russian assault troops. They were blocked. The enemy infiltrated through the gaps at several locations and established a foothold in the houses. At 1400 hours, however, all penetrations were blocked and the front, if only temporarily, was re-established.

It was 1530 hours when an open radio message from the commander of the 1st Polish Army arrived in Kolberg, requesting Oberst Fullriede to surrender. Fritz Fullriede acknowledged receipt of this message over the open radio.

At 1600 hours a second request to lay down their weapons followed. This time Oberst Fullriede did not reply.

After that enemy artillery opened fire again, in order to launch an attack at the fall of darkness against the Waldenfelsschanze. The tanks that flanked this attack were shot-up by panzerfaust rounds. The fires burned with yellow flames. Detonations thudded. Then the attackers and defenders met. The hand-to-hand fighting lasted 150 minutes before the enemy suspended his attack and withdrew. He left hundreds of dead in front of the Waldenfelsschanze.

The penetration at the rail junction with subsequent advances up to the eastern railroad station during the night of 15/3 was first stopped at the edge of the eastern railroad station. In spite of an immediate counterattack, it could not be removed.

The defenders of Kolberg were compressed on the evening of this day into a narrow strip at the harbor. When Alarmbataillon Kell, the I/Festungs-Rgt 5, arrived at the docks, Oberst Fullriede ordered that they not be unloaded, because there was no place for them to defend. However, before this order reached the ship on the dock, two companies had already unloaded. Because these troops were not experienced in the kind of hand-to-hand fighting taking place in Kolberg, they suffered heavy casualties without bringing the hoped for relief.

These two companies attacked out of the area north of the railroad station in the direction of the inner city. Simultaneously a hastily organized battle group advanced from Gradierstrasse to the east, in order throw back the enemy that had advanced across Adolf Hitler Platz and recapture the lost Luisenstrasse.

The enemy was able to wrest the railroad area away. Only the northern and western edges of Adolf Hitler Platz could be recaptured, while the southern and eastern edges remained in the hands of the attackers. The achieved combat line now secured the boarding of the last women and children, who were brought to the ships from the docks by motor boats and taken on board. Still before the break of day on 16/3 these ships departed and reached Swinemuende unopposed.

On 16/3 the enemy again opened strong barrage fire onto the inner city, which was being held by Fullriede's soldiers. The last defensive positions and the last houses were set afire. However, once again the following enemy tank attack was repulsed, even if the Poles were able to assault several housing blocks. In the afternoon of this day the 3rd Company of Battalion Kell landed and established a new line of resistance in the direction of Moltkestrasse.

During the night before 17/3 Oberst Fullriede ordered all railroad men, OT workers and male civilians, as well as those who were unarmed, to be removed.

During this removal Z 34 and Z 43 again participated. Both destroyers returned to the docks of Kolberg after leaving Swinemuende and opened fire on the Russian artillery positions. The recognized batteries were destroyed in direct fire. The Soviet artillery fire that was directed at the docks was silenced.

On 16/3 the boarding of the last men in the city, who were not to remain during the final defensive phase, began. None of the ships left without being filled to overflowing. The MFP [naval ferries] had to take on 750 men. 250 severely wounded were taken on-board Z 34. Moreover, Z 34 and Z 43, as well as T 33, took on-board a total of 3,750 refugees and soldiers. All were to make it to Swinemuende.

Therefore, Oberst Fullriede had fulfilled his own mission, which he took on 7/3/1945. The mission of any fortress, to tie up strong enemy forces, could now be fulfilled until 18/3. By then the remnants of the defenders were compressed into an area 1800 by 400 meters.

On the afternoon of 17/3 Oberst Fullriede decided to withdraw the defenders of Kolberg by sea.

Before this last withdrawal occurred, the enemy launched an attack against the Waldenfelsschanze during the late evening of 17/3, this time it was lost. Therefore, the enemy could place the entire shoreline east of the Persante, the harbor entrance and the firing positions of the last German artillery under fire by tanks and anti-tank guns. However, because the withdrawal of the German remnants was being conducted under strong Russian fire, the enemy could not pursue – he was prevented by his own artillery.

The last security broke contact with the enemy and jumped into the last boats, which had already brought the other fighters to the awaiting ships.

On the morning of 18/3/1945 the shoreline and jetty of Kolberg were empty of German troops.

Oberst Fritz Fullriede evacuated nearly 75,000 people from the encircled city. His troops were removed from the encircled fortress to the last man. He arrived on-board Z 43 at 0630 hours on 18/3/1945 with the last man of his command.

On his own responsibility and without authority from OKH Fritz Fullriede, who fought with GFM Erwin Rommel in Africa, was able to make the impossible possible.

And in contrast to the fears of the officers at the Fuehrer Headquarters, the Oberst was not reduced in rank or condemned to death, but received the Oak Leaves to the Knight's Cross of the Iron Cross from Hitler's own hands on 23/3/1945.

On 3/5/1945 Fritz Fullriede took command of the 3rd Marine Infantry Division. As the commander of Battle Group Enderle he surrendered on 2/5/1945 and was released as prisoner of war by his enemies on his word of honor. On 4/12/1945 Fritz Fullriede was arrested as a "war criminal" and surrendered to Holland on 16/4/1946. Three years later he was released from Holland. He proved his innocence, however, he lost three years of his life.

We give Fritz Fullriede the last word on Kolberg. He reported to OKH:

"To the enemy fell a completely burned down and wasted city. The cathedral was burned, all of the Persante and Holzgraben bridges were destroyed. The railroad station and all of its tracks were destroyed. The loading installations on the docks had been inoperable for some time. This is what the enemy has gained with such heavy losses. However, it was also the price to get 75,000 people back to the Reich."

(According to a report from the Kolberg Harbor Commandant, Fregattenkapitaen Kolbe, 70,915 people were removed from the encircled city. In addition there were the soldiers, therefore, the number 75,000 seems reasonable.)

This is what Fritz Fullriede achieved with approximately 3,300 soldiers, of which 2,200 men were fighting troops.

They Must Be Left Behind

"The first Polish soldiers arrived in the cellar early on 18/3/1945 and demanded our watches, rings and other valuables with their machine-pistols. Then the Poles demanded that we leave the cellar. One told us we would be sheltered in the undestroyed houses.

However, it turned out otherwise. Heavily laden with three trunks, over-coats and furs, I left the cellar. We were not allowed to take the direct route on the street, but reached Viktoriastrasse through the holes in the walls and gaps in basements. This way took us an entire hour. From here we were led through the ruins of the city to Waldenfels Kaserne. On Kaiserplatz, the corner of Friedrichstrasse, we were searched by Polish soldiers. They relieved me of my large trunk.

In Waldenfels Kaserne my long boots were taken.

In the late afternoon we were led off in the direction of Belgarder Chaussee. We were to go toward Damgard. It was clear to me that the objective of this group was captivity." (See W.G. from Kolberg in: Documentation of the Expulsion of the Germans from East – Central Europe, Vol. 1 P. 245-46.)

It was as Herr W.G. expected. With some stops along the way, the Germans were transported to camps in Posen; from there the survivors returned in November 1945 to the completely plundered Kolberg.

9

ADVANCE ON DANZIG AND GOTENHAFEN

The Defensive Combat of the 2nd Army

The Russian high command set no less than ten combat capable armies against the 2nd Army defending in East Prussia. Among these troops were several tank armies, combat tested and determined to to put an end to Germany.

Marshal Rokossovskiy, commander of the 2nd Belorussian Front, led these troops rigorously. He always had strong air forces available to soften up the centers of resistance with bombing.

The right flank of the 2nd Army tried to stop the advance of the Red Army in this area, or at least delay it, with the divisions of the XXIII and XXVII Army Corps and the VII Panzer Corps.

On 27/1/1945 the troops of the 2nd Belorussian Front reached Dirschau. The 7th PD had just arrived there, they had crossed the Vistula near Marienwerder on the previous day with their wheeled elements and attacked the enemy, while the tracked vehicles could not negotiate the ice bridge, but had to move up to Graudenz, where they found a passible bridge.

Other elements of the 7th PD rolled toward Einlage, a village west of the Nogat, on the Elbing – Danzig road, 10 kilometers west of Elbing. (See the section on the Elbing Fortress.)

Indeed, these weak elements did attack Elbing from the west, however, they were insufficient against the superior Russian forces and armored vehicles. The 7th PD was again pushed back, without being able to relieve Elbing.

During the night of 11/2 the lead division elements were able to take up the elements assaulting out of Elbing.

Similar to the 7th PD, the 4th PD, which was committed in the Kurland pocket, was removed and, during the night before 22/1/1945, loaded onto the transport ship "Preussen" and convoyed to Danzig. This division had to leave its heavy equipment in Kurland, turning it over to the German formations continuing the fight there. On the way there was a submarine alert. The escort craft dropped depth charges in a hunt for the enemy.

A horrible picture met these men at the Danzig harbor jetty. Here people were just unloading from the refugee trains that arrived from Elbing. They saw desperate mothers and eighty frozen children, the result of this insufficiently secured evacuation.

The city of Danzig was full of refugees. Bombing attacks followed. Columns of refugees passed by the soldiers moving to the south. The Vistula road on the western bank led through deep snow drifts to Neuenburg. To the left of Danzig was open and unprotected terrain. As soon as the lead Russian armored elements arrived here they would roll through and then even Danzig, where refugee transports were still arriving, would be lost.

Graudenz and Bromberg were already encircled. The divisions of the 2nd Army were fighting a hopeless battle in the southeast. They tried to stop the widely separated attack wedges, which were rolling to the west on Berlin and to the north against western Prussia and Pomerania.

Generaloberst Weiss, the commander of this army, tried to withdraw his remnants in the direction of Danzig. However, he no longer had any fuel for half of his army. Tanks and assault guns, urgently needed for the battle against enemy armored formations, had to be blown up so that they would not fall into the hands of the enemy. The men of the 4th Armored Reconnaissance Battalion fought on the extended weak front in the south, on the Schwetz – Tuchel road. They had to defend against the strong flank of the 2nd Belorussian Front. Enemy tanks attacked along the Upper Silesian

– Gotenhafen coal route to the north. They turned to the west on the Schwetz – Tuchel road. Here stood the 1st Blocking Brigade under Oberst Georg von Unold, who would later take command of the 227th ID, when he would fall as its commander. (Knight's Cross on 20/3/1945.)

The 4th PD defended, divided into small formations, the entire area between Tuchel and Kamin. It was the mobile "Luchs Scout Troops" that immediately reported every enemy movement over radio.

The division leadership was able to obtain new Panthers for the panzer regiment in Konitz. The I/PR 35 of the 4th PD received six new Jagdpanthers that were destined for an assault gun brigade. Six commanders and crews climbed into these Jagdpanthers, which were the Jagdpanzer V with an eight-eight anti-tank gun L 71, one of the most capable tank cannon.

The 4th PD attacked to the south in front of Tuchel with their new tanks. The attack quickly gained ground, however, it then stalled suddenly in a deeply echeloned Russian assembly area.

To the right of the 4th PD the Russians launched an attack on Konitz. The 4th Reconnaissance Battalion was brought up on the right flank of the army to support the infantry formations located there. The mobile reconnaissance tanks counterattacked near Kamin and Grosszirkwitz, destroyed the penetrating enemy groups and were suddenly encircled themselves. The reconnaissance troops were ordered back to the division and rolled in the direction of Konitz, which was also being pressured by Russian tank groups. This maneuver became a deadly race, because the 4th Reconnaissance Battalion also had to pass by Tuchel.

When the 4th Reconnaissance Battalion arrived in the Konitz area, they saw flames rising up from the city. The Russians had won the race.

While the 4th Reconnaissance Battalion was making the trip from Konitz to Tuchel, in order to join in the final battle there, the formations of the 7th PD under Generalmajor Dr. Mauss attacked Konitz from the east. They were able to breakout of the East Prussian ring of encirclement here.

However, in Tuchel the armored battle was in full force. Strong enemy armored formations gradually pressed to the north. Arriving in Kelpin the eight-wheeled cannon vehicles of the 4th Reconnaissance Battalion with the 7.5 cm cannon joined in the fighting. Here the assault guns of the division panzerjaeger battalion also joined in the fighting. This was the time for Feldwebel Bix.

Bix had received one of the above mentioned heavy panzerjaegers. He was a platoon leader of five of these vehicles and was committed near Preussisch-Stargard, which was taken by the Russians.

When four Russian tanks advanced, the five German panzerjaegers fired their long cannon against the enemy tank groups. When they had shot them up, Bix ordered them to withdraw a little. He remained alone with the grenadiers while he still had sufficient ammunition.

A little later he sighted enemy tanks of unknown origin, as they approached to within 1200 meters he recognized that they were US tanks, which were supplied to the Russians over the Reykjavik – Murmansk northern sea route.

He opened fire. He fired round after round from the cannon. The tanks turned and when their right sides came into view Bix was able to shoot two more. Then his gunner reported that he had only five high-explosive shells left.

Suddenly Bix noted movement on the forward slope and saw that the Russians were bringing up two anti-tank guns into position.

He ordered the jagdpanzer to turn around and fired at the position. Wood and dirt flew into the air. The Russians had set up two dummies in position.

Now the Russians attacked with a third group of T 34's. Bix and his men withdrew a couple of dozen meters, where they found protection behind willow bushes. They let the T 34's approach to within 800 meters before they opened fire. The armored duel began. The battle lasted for ten minutes. The road on which the Russians were advancing was covered in thick black smoke from which the flashes of the Russian tank cannon flared.

The enemy tanks stopped, were acquired in the sights and shot. When the enemy withdrew from here, there were eleven destroyed tanks left on the road and in the field.

Suddenly a Russian truck column appeared on the road. The last high-explosive rounds were loaded and fired, and as they rolled back they ran into a T 34 that had broken through on the flank. It was shot at a distance of 80 meters.

On this day Hermann Bix and his panzerjaegers shot a total of 16 enemy tanks. Therefore, he was the most successful tank commander in the battalion. Leutnant Tautorus, his company commander, had also destroyed several enemy tanks.

When Kleschau fell, the 35th PR was ordered to support the counterattack on this city. The vehicles were organized into small battle groups of two to three. Feldwebel Bix took his leave from Leutnant Tautorus with three panzerjaegers. He was to help a Major of grenadiers conduct a counterattack and throw back the enemy that had penetrated here.

While he was underway he received a radio message that 20 enemy tanks were rolling on the main road to Danzig and that he, Bix, had to stop them. This he did and during the evening Hermann Bix and his three vehicles received orders to relieve an encircled volksgrenadier battalion that was being attacked by enemy tanks at a farmhouse.

The panzerjaegers set out at twilight in a driving snow storm. Columns of refugees forced them off of the road. They reached the location where two guides were waiting for him. Bix dismounted and accompanied them through the Soviet encirclement to the farmhouse.

The commander of this battalion showed him on a map where the enemy tanks were located. A little later Bix hurried back to his panzerjaegers and rolled with them to a skull-shaped hill. There they had a good overview of the enemy tank assembly position; when it became light the next morning the individual tanks could be made out.

They found an air defense position with four light FlaMW's on the top of the hill. After talking with the air defense Leutnant, Bix returned to his panzerjaegers and gave them their fire sectors.

When it was completely light they opened fire on the tanks that the panzerjaegers had in their sights.

After the second salvo three enemy tanks were already in flames. Additional T 34's rolled out from behind cover and drove down in front of the farmstead. They rolled right into the anti-tank guns then tried to escape to the back slope. However, there were met by a third panzerjaeger.

The armored duel lasted 20 minutes, then the enemy was destroyed or had fled. The grenadiers ran happily to freedom.

19 destroyed enemy tanks was the result. In the area of Feldwebel Bix stood eleven destroyed T 34's and KV I's. The rest were shot by commanders Schafferts and Igel.

On the following day the panzerjaegers and tanks of the 4th PD withdrew in the direction of Danzig.

When Buetow fell in mid-March and the Red Army broke through to the Baltic Sea near Stolp, Danzig became a bridgehead and a fortress. The mission of the division remnants of the 2nd Army and also for the 4th PD read: "Hold the ring around Danzig, if the hundreds of thousands of refugees are to be evacuated by sea to the west." Even Gotenhafen had to be held. The troop units of the 4th PD moved there after Karthaus had to be evacuated one night and they withdrew toward Seefeld, which was fully occupied by the Russians, then they reached Gotenhafen.

Meanwhile the remnants of the 2nd Army defended decisively against the superior masses of Russian attackers.

In Danzig itself the boarding of ships was conducted without pause, both day and night, while the Soviet air forces constantly bombed the city.

In front of Leesen, on the outskirts of Danzig, stood the 4th Reconnaissance Battalion with the panzergrenadiers of the 12th Regiment in defensive combat. The three anti-tank guns here shot six attacking enemy tanks before they themselves were eliminated. These men withdrew on foot through Emmaus into the Danzig citadel.

Bombs continued to fall on the city. The air defenses at Gotenhafen and Danzig and the heavy artillery in Danzig Bay shot-up Russian tank assembly areas near Koelln. Daily the few King Tigers and Jagdpanthers shot up 80 to 90 enemy tanks. However, the fighting here was approaching its final phase.

On the morning of 19/3 the attackers opened fire on Danzig from hundreds of tubes. The defensive lines of this division were withdrawn 2000 meters to the edge of the city. Generalmajor Betzel, the commander of the 4th PD, received a visit from General der Panzertruppe Dietrich von Saucken on this day, he had been the commander of this division. On 15/3 Dietrich von Saucken had taken command of the Danzig – Gotenhafen bridgehead. He learned here that his old division was holding bravely and decisively around the harbor from Hela, securing the base of the Admiralty of the Eastern Baltic Sea, which was of decisive importance for the supply of Army Group Kurland.

Above all, however, in view of the transport of refugees from Danzig, they had to win time to get the people out by sea.

General der Panzertruppe Dietrich von Saucken reports several facts on the overall situation in this area:

"Through our army ran, approximately along the Vistula, the boundary between Army Groups Rokossovskiy and Vassilevskiy. Both had committed strong forces against our bridgehead, which hindered the main effort of the Russian attack to the west. If the Russians, as we learned after the surrender, had committed three air armies against us, that meant they had important reasons to remove our bridgehead. We provided the shield for all who reached the west from the areas of Danzig, Pillau and Hela. Over a million Germans, children, women, elderly, wounded and sick, were protected by this shield. I took over command of the entire organization – because I refused to be subordinated to the Gauleiter.

In forested and sand dune terrain the supply had to be organized by staffs and distributed to the troops. The brave, untiring efforts of the engineer landing boats and the naval ferries cannot be praised enough.

The crews operated under enemy fire and unceasing attacks by the Russian air armies between the mainland and Hela. There the transfer was made from the transport boats to the large ships. It is difficult to describe the effort this trip required. Some numbers provide an example:

On 25/4/1945 5000 people left the Putziger Valley, on 26/4 there were 8000 people. On 27/4 seven ships took on a total of 24,000 people and brought them to Kiel and Copenhagen."

So wrote General der Panzertruppe (Ret.) Dietrich von Saucken to the author.

However, what was it like in Danzig? What happened to the remaining population? Who commanded there and what defensive forces and heavy weapons were available to the fortress commandants?

In the Fortress – The Horror in the Cellars

In the area of the cities of Danzig and Gotenhafen, which was declared a fortress, besides a few Volkssturm units, there were only convalescent companies, naval troops committed to the ground battle and some small Wehrmacht formations, whose combat strength was none too high.

The "Feldherrnhalle" Division of the "Grossdeutschland" Panzer Corps was removed from the city. The division was to be reconstituted in the Reich.

The XX Army Corps command under General Specht was in charge in Danzig. Specht, who as Oberst and commander of the 55th IR received the Oak Leaves to the Knight's Cross on 16/1/1942, was an energetic man with great Russian experience. He moved his staff at the beginning of March 1945 out of the kaserne on Weissen Turm in Danzig into the buildings of the Polish naval school in Adlerhorst. He officiated from there until 18/3/1945. He protested the removal of the "Feldherrnhalle" regiments, but he could not get them back.

When he received the order to turn Danzig and Gotenhafen into fortresses he lacked any prerequisites. He proposed withdrawing the troops to the Vistula line and holding the Vistula – Nogat delta and the terrain further to the east in cooperation with the troops located in East Prussia. His proposal was turned down and the Fuehrer Headquarters repeated that Gotenhafen and Danzig "were to be held until the last cartridge."

Around Danzig anti-tank trenches were dug and anti-tank obstacles erected.

When the enemy approached the Vistula – Nogat delta, the villages in this region had already been evacuated. The columns of refugees made their way to the west in icy snow storms.

However, the refugees that had come from the Neuteich and Tiegenhof areas only made it as far as the Mariensee area, where they remained until the advancing Russian armored formations drove them to Danzig. From there the people tried to escape this hell by sea.

On 17 March General der Infanterie Specht conducted a census of the people located in Danzig. The Gauleiter from Danzig estimated the number of people located in the Gotenhafen – Danzig bridgehead at 600,000 to 1,000,000.

The wounded collection point in Danzig had 16,000 wounded at the beginning of this decisive month. 4000 more were in smaller hospitals in the area of the double fortress and another 1000 wounded arrived daily from East Prussia and Kurland by sea, while approximately another 800 arrived daily from western Prussia.

A portion of them were transported by sea together with refugees every day. However, the influx far outnumbered the outflow, which increased the number of wounded in Danzig daily.

Holm Island and the Danzig harbor experienced scenes that mankind had never seen before. The refugees dragged themselves in icy storms in thick columns to Troyl. There lay the refugee ships. When the columns stopped, the over-exhausted people let their suitcases and rucksacks fall and waited until they would move again. Many of the people dragged their sacks behind them like sleds.

On 22/3/1945, when the Russians reached the sea through Gross Katz between Adlerhorst and Zoppot, the Gotenhafen – Danzig double bridgehead was separated. The final battle for both fortresses would no longer depend on each other.

On 18/3, when this occurrence was foreseen, General Specht moved his command post into the bunker on the tip of the Hela Peninsula. The headquarters of the 2nd Army followed him there a little later. Generaloberst Weiss had to turn over the command to General der Panzertruppe von Saucken.

On 24/3/1945 Marshal Rokossovskiy ordered the dropping of an enormous amount of pamphlets over Danzig. The contents of these read as follows:

"Marshal of the Soviet Union Rokossovskiy
to the garrisons of
Danzig and Gdingen.

Generals, Officers and Soldiers of the 2nd German Army!

Yesterday, on 23 March, my troops captured Zoppot.

Therefore, the encircled force group has been split into two parts. The garrisons of Danzig and Gdingen are separated from each other. Our artillery can range the harbors of Danzig and Gdingen. The ring my troops have around you is narrowing more and more every day.

Under these circumstances your resistance is senseless and will only lead to your destruction, as well as to the destruction of hundreds of thousands of women, children and elderly.

I demand:

1. You immediately cease resistance and surrender with white flags individually, in squads, platoons, companies, battalions and regiments.

2. To everyone who surrenders I guarantee life and personal property.

All officers and soldiers, who do not lay down their weapons, will be destroyed during the upcoming assault.

You will be completely responsible for the sacrifice of the civilian population.

The troop commander of the 2nd Belorussian Front, Marshal of the Soviet Union Rokossovskiy.

24 March 1945."

Since General Specht had forwarded this surrender demand directly to the Fuehrer Headquarters, the reply came from Fuehrer Headquarters. It read:

"Each square meter of ground in Danzig/Gotenhafen will be decisively defended."

Therefore, Danzig was condemned to death. The Red Army opened the final phase of the fighting around this city with a destructive barrage fire by all weapons they could bring to bear. After that, groups of double-engine bombers attacked the city. Their bombs covered the narrow streets of the city, levelling everything. This was followed by the fire bombs. Flames rose from the ruins of Danzig. And these attacks were repeated several times. All day long a constant wall of fire and smoke stood over the city.

In the harbor two ammunition ships received direct hits from artillery fire and burned after exploding. The Danzig Harbor Canal was blocked by the sinking of these two large ships, after which all ships that were still able to maneuver had to leave.

On 26/3 the harbor installations of Gotenhafen were also blocked, as a number of ships were sunk and explosions made the installations inoperable.

The fact that Danzig could be held for so long was because of the commitment of flak batteries here and near Gotenhafen. The eighty-eights shot-up attacking Russian armored groups before they could get into firing range.

One of the officers from the I Guards Tank Corps told the Ordonanzoffizier, Rittmeister Friedrich von Wilpert, that his 17th Brigade set out from Heiderode with 35 tanks, each of his battalions had 10 to 12 at the start, now they had only two left. The 16th Tank Brigade was completely wiped out.

When the first Russian assault troops penetrated into the city a tank destroyer company was formed from units of the 4th PD located in the city. It was equipped with panzerfaeusten, machine-guns and machine-pistols and charged with protecting the infantry from enemy tanks.

Several groups were moved on trucks to the threatened infantry positions on the access roads. There were already battle groups and units withdrawing on these roads into Danzig.

It was midnight when the destruction troops heard their first Russian voices. They also heard tank tracks and the rattling of the wheels of panjewagons. Soon the silhouettes of Russian T 34's appeared. The men with the panzerfaeusten worked their way closer to the steel columns.

Then the firing began. The fire streams of the panzerfaeusten blasted to the rear, propelling the warhead against the tanks. Two to three second passed then the detonation sounded. Seconds later, the tanks stood in flames. The detonations thudded through the night as the warheads penetrated into the T 34's.

The Russian night attack collapsed in this anti-tank fire by a handful of men. The tanks rolled back. However, now the guns and mortars began anew. The forward positions had to be given up several hours later. The tank destroyer platoons took over the abandoned positions. However, by midnight of 26 March it was clear that there were no longer any German soldiers standing to their right or left, they had to withdraw.

In the city the men now lay behind barricades and ruins. They fired at the advancing tanks from the gaps in the roofs of houses. Tanks flew into the air without the Russians ever knowing from where the firing was coming. During another commitment behind a street barricade the impact of a heavy shell killed a portion of a tank destroyer squad.

Danzig was in flames. The bridges collapsed and the last defenders withdrew across the arm of the Vistula into the suburb of Heubude.

While withdrawing they saw that the famous Krantor was in flames as were many other treasures of the city.

In Heubude they found a 7.5 cm anti-tank gun and a bunker with sufficient ammunition. From here they fired their last rounds at the Russians.

However, at the Danzig Olivaer Gate the 4th PD defended until the last. Here, on the morning of 27/3/1945 fell Generalmajor Betzel, who had just received the Oak Leaves to the Knight's Cross on 11/3. At his side was Hauptmann Kohl. Besides the many panzer men from the 35th PR, the commanders Hauptmann Kahle and Hauptmann Schalmat also fell here.

The Russians fought their way from here to the railroad station area under unimaginable artillery and mortar fire support. The switching station was bitterly contested. Near Langfuhr a single tank was able to stop the enemy for 24 hours. During the following night the city was evacuated west of the Mottau and the withdrawal over the last crossing to Heubude took place, where the tank destroyer commando stood ready.

Russian bombers destroyed the refugee assembly points and the first aid stations.

The last battle flared up on the irrigation fields near Heubude. Here fell a number of trusted chiefs and commanders, before withdrawing to Neufaehr. There the Vistula estuary bridgehead was formed and occupied. Engineers worked feverishly on the loading positions and brought more refugees and wounded to Hela and from there to the large ships, which then transported them over the Baltic Sea to Germany.

When the Oxhoefter Kaempe had to be given up, there were still about 100,000 people on the Hela Peninsula. The Russians did not attack here. During the surrender all of the Germans still located here, except for a handful who were able to escape in small craft by sea, were captured.

On 28/3/1945 The Russians had their hands on Danzig. Frau Klara Seidler from Danzig reports on the last 24 hours of fighting around Danzig and the first entrance of Russian soldiers into the city:

"Now all hell broke loose! Hails of bombs and artillery fire alternated. A hit tore the door off of our house. A sea of flame came toward us in the cellar. The earth shook, our house shivered, the lights went out. We left the cellar through a gap above us.

A burning portion of the building had blocked the cellar door. It was 1400 hours, in spite of this it was dark. Where to now?

To the Johanniskirche. It was overflowing, there was no room for anybody, nobody could get in. Again there was hail of bombs. We sought the slightest shelter and then ran for the long bridge. It also was covered in flames. We ran into a house and pushed our way through the heavily occupied doorway.

Another hit. Five people in the doorway were killed. We went out the back door into an ally-way. The large bunker there was full, so we had to climb to the upper bunker in the gloomy darkness. There was a frightful sight. The material here had ignited and people were burning like torches in the open. A burning gable fell toward us to the floor. We left everything, we only took our handbags.

We moved on. The streets were covered with suitcases, overcoats and people that were trampled, burnt, dead or dying.

There were many people running with us for their very lives. Finally we reached Hohenseigen. The buildings there in the gas-works were massive with slate roofs.

Two large air defense guns were set up on both sides. The gas-works itself was overflowing and we were directed above to an office room, where we lay on the floor under a table.

After several hits we were covered with glass. Then we went below into the basement.

There were 2000 women, children and elderly in this basement. A dim light was shinning. The air was stuffy.

We spent the long Sunday night there, as well as Monday morning. Other than a piece of dry break we had nothing to eat.

At 1400 hours the Russians had approached to within 100 meters. When someone asked whether we would surrender many voices cried "Yes!" in answer. What else was there to do?

The two flak positions now ceased firing and white flags were hung from the roof and front windows of the gas-works." (Thus is the first report.)

Approximately 30 minutes later 25 Russians entered the gas-works. They were wearing new uniforms and looked well-fed, and they also spoke German well.

The men now had to leave. Because they were all old and sick nothing happened to them. All of the women were told to go home, that the battle for Danzig was over.

Here is the second part of the report from Frau Klara Seidler.

"We hoped that the Russians would treat us graciously. However, we were sorely disappointed! The first Russians that came to our house tore the watch off of the wrist of Herr Bart, who was standing in the doorway. After that, a vehicle drove up to our door. Four Russian officers got out and asked us for something to drink. They were polite and friendly and even offered us cigarettes.

The four officers were our protection. The soldiers near us changed as soon as the officers were out of sight. By the fall of darkness, however, the officers moved on. We were now at their mercy.

In gangs of five to ten men the soldiers now came and plundered. We now kept hearing "Urri!" or "Frau komm!"

Frau F. heard this summons followed by pokes in the ribs and had to go away with six soldiers.

On the afternoon of this day, however, began the total destruction of Danzig. The Aris fired incessantly, the bombers dropped their bombs and phosphorus canisters. We packed a few rations and fled to the water.

We rested in a house that was still standing, however, we were so tormented by the Russians there that we rather would be in the flaming hell. With the soles of our shoes burning we ran to find a hiding place.

In Haeckergasse we finally found two empty houses next to a flak position. We crawled into them. However, our misery was even greater.

The second complement of Russians (perhaps the follow-on supply troops) were now set loose on us. No woman was spared. The women were raped in front of the men, who were held with machine-pistols pointing at their necks. We tried to hide, but the Russians still found us. A young woman with three small children tried to hide in a cellar just as a horde overwhelmed it.

The children cried: 'Mutti, Muttilein!' Then one of the Russians slammed the children against the wall. I will never forget that for the rest of my life.

On the following morning the last portions of Danzig were ignited. We had to get to open fields. We paved our way through Haeckergasse with a wagon on rubber tires through the piles of smoking ruins.

We found some water in the market hall. However, there were only corpses in this mass grave. Frau Jacobs, a grey wraith covered only in a horse blanket, said:

'The jewels and gold are in the cellar!'

Her property had long ago been turned into a pile of ruins.

We ran through this smoking desert to Ohra. Since there was still fighting there we turned down an ally toward Langfuhr. Half-way there we fell under fire and suffered some casualties. We turned to the Trinitatis cemetery. There we drank water from rain barrels.

Here again we were relieved of what valuables we still had by the Russians.

And then we again heard: 'Frau komm!' Whoever did not go with them immediately were brutally beaten and, in the end, forced to go with them anyway. The women were led off to the upper floors and there violated.

Frau Mielke, a 67 year-old, was also taken."

What Frau Klara Seidler experienced in the cellar of a half destroyed house, in which the GPU had set up operations with 20 to 24 officers and a pair of girls, was explained thus:

"The cellar rooms of this 'Court of the GPU' was filled with prisoners, mostly women and girls, however, also many males, from children to elderly. The commissars and female commissars interrogated the prisoners.

It was dark in the cellar. A hundred people were herded into a small room. Once a day, in the morning, they were led into the courtyard to go to the bathroom. The dead were left behind, none of them were removed. Once a Russian guard put a bucket with a burning carbide lamp under a woman because she would not go with him willingly.

Four rooms with two commissars and two female commissars were set up to interrogate the prisoners. The interrogation ran as follows: 'You belonged to the SS, SA or BdM.' If anyone denied this they got the horse-whip, then the interrogation was repeated and if there were further denials there were additional beatings and the court might sentence one to Siberia.

Frau Brueckmann, who did not want to see her 12 year-old daughter violated before her eyes, held Inge tightly in her arms. The Russians shot them both down.

Frau Papp's daughter, Frau Lemke, was overpowered by the Russians, as an older officer waited his turn at her. When she tried to go to the aid of her mother, the Russians shot her. Her mother was shot also.

Now a few words about conditions in Danzig from Frau Brigitte Pajain from Danzig-Langfuhr.

"It was 27 March 1945 at 0300 hours when an unearthly stillness lay over Langfuhr. We had been hiding in the cellar for three weeks, fearing the first meeting with the Russians. We were sure that they would be coming on this morning.

I looked down the street and saw the first Russian tanks move down Bahnhofstrasse.

And then searches of the cellar followed. They were looking for weapons and hidden soldiers. Soldiers entered the cellar at regular intervals.

It must have been at 0800 hours on this tragic 27 March that we began to breath a sigh of relief, when the first panje wagons stopped on our street. Before we knew what was happening, 20 to 30 Russians plundered through the house and cellar.

What we experienced I cannot describe. Numerous hordes of Russians robbed and plundered through the cellar. They had all been drinking and senselessly threw things around, tore open suitcases and cabinets looking for jewels and other valuables. Then the horrible time began for the girls. At this time I was nineteen and a half; when I saw women thrown into the cellar screaming and crying I fled to the courtyard. Russians, horses and wagons were swarming all over here. I saw a nun that lived in a small neighboring chapel. She took me with her and hid me by the alter.

When night arrived we had to leave. In the meantime, my mother had found me and covered me with kisses.

A horrible night followed. For hours I heard the cries for help from women and girls and the nuns. The Russians continued to enter the cellar, still looking for new sacrifices. At 0500 hours it finally grew quiet and I left my hiding place. The stifling cellar air forced us into the open. Above we faced an unforgettable sight. Our house was a sea of flames. Later the nun's house also began to burn. The Russians drove us out of the small chapel. We joined an endless line of people, they were being driven on by the Russians with shots and beatings. The men were separated, assembled and later sent to camps.

So now there were only women, children and elderly. Many of the refugees still carried their belongings with them, which they finally left behind piece by piece, because they were too heavy. The longer we marched, the more the children cried. The elderly were beaten by the Russians if they fell behind.

We made it to Oliva. Then we were commanded: Back! More people came. By darkness we were wandering through a forest. Tanks and guns rolled by us. We had to lay down where we were. Then many Russians came, our guards. They looked over our bodies and searched with lamps for new sacrifices. The screaming continued through the night.

I do knot know how many days this march lasted. To us it appeared to be an eternity. More women, children and elderly were being left behind. Silently we watched as the Russians would pounce on young girls, taking them away as candidates for Siberia. The helpless cries of these girls were horrible.

I will never forget how we were once standing in front of a row of Stalin Organs, which suddenly thundered over our heads.

One day we woke up without guards.

'Go home!', we were ordered. We wandered through the darkness and lay down in a barn. However, we did not find any peace. Russians came looking for women and girls.

Later we returned to Oliva and remained in a cellar for one week. It was overflowing. Day and night it was the same thing: rape and plunder.

During the last night a man found me. My mother tried to protect me with her last ounce of strength, so he beat her. Then he went to get a companion. We took advantage of this time to flee from the cellar.

On the way to Langfuhr I was separated from my mother and locked up in a cellar with 30 other girls. During the second night we were interrogated individually by an NKVD officer. I was at the verge of collapse and could not answer any of the questions.

Because of my serious wounds, I was freed with five other girls on the following morning." (See: Documentation of the Expulsion of the Germans from East – Central Europe, Vol. I, pages 302 – 305.)

10

COMBAT ZONE SILESIA

The Red Army Attacks

Shortly before midnight on 11/1/1945 a prisoner was captured in the 304th ID area of operations. He told the division Ic that the Red Army was going to attack out of the Baranov bridgehead on the following morning.

On the next morning at 0300 hours the Soviet artillery opened fire on this sector of the 4th Panzer Army front, it lasted one hour. When everyone breathed a sigh of relief, the barrage fire began again at 0800 hours and did not end until 1030 hours.

During this second fire-strike, Soviet assault troops attacked through an approximately 200 meter wide corridor, which was opened by the fire-strike.

Black powder smoke and thick dust from the fire-strike covered the battlefield for ten kilometers.

In the XXXXVIII Panzer Corps area of operations, on the southern flank of this attack, the enemy attacked through and, during the night before 13/1, Soviet Marshal Konev committed his tank formations here, in order to achieve an operational breakthrough.

Contact was lost between the 4th Panzer Army and the XXXXVIII Panzer Corps, as was contact between the 4th Panzer Army and Army Group A.

Burning Koenigsberg after the Russian bombing attack on 27/8/44.

The burned out Schlosskirche and the Blutgericht.

Volkssturm battalion anti-tank position on the road from Koenigsberg.

Street fighting in Koenigsberg on 7/4/45.

General der Infantrie Otto Lasch had to surrender in Koenigsberg.

Koenigsberg falls, the long road to captivity begins.

Dead in East Prussia.

General der Infantrie Hans Krebs initiated
the surrender of Berlin.

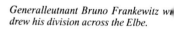
Generalmajor Otto Ernst Remer in Berl

Generaloberst Gotthard Heinrici, commander of the 1st Panzer Army during the
final battle (later the 3rd Panzer Army).

Generalleutnant Bruno Frankewitz w
drew his division across the Elbe.

Generalleutnant Martin Unrein led the "Clausewitz" Division during the last armored battles.

General der Panzertruppe Maximilian von Edelsheim initiated the surrender negotiations of the 12th Army.

Erich Baerenfaenger was a Generalmajor and leader of Defensive Sector A in Berlin from 1/5/45.

Hauptmann Hans Boelter fought with his Tigers in East Prussia.

Red Army soldiers penetrate into the city.

Destroyed T-34.

Hitler Youth from Battle Group Malotka with panzerfausten on 20/2/45 near Metgethen.

Remnants of the 5th Panzer Division and the Tigers re-capture Metgethen and find a hell there.

Refugees in East Prussia.

This refugee column was destroyed by Russians.

A Tiger participates in a defensive battle.

Panthers roll into an assembly area.

Red Army soldiers reach and block a rail line.

Russian tank that was destroyed by a panzerfaust.

Troops of the 3rd Belorussian Front enter a town.

After the battle of Koenigsberg: The old university and the cathedral are no more.

A farm is set ablaze during the retreat.

A withdrawal route in Samland.

Heiligenbeil: Wounded wait for transport.

Graves of soldiers in a cemetery in East Prussia.

The last levy: Men of the Volkssturm.

Hitler Youth Wilhelm Huebner received the Iron Cross II.

Berlin Unter den Linden: Refugees await transportation.

Red Army troops conquer Berlin.

Major Erich Mende, March 1945 in East Prussian as the commander of the 216th Grenadier Regiment.

Generalleutnant Georg Jauer, commander of the 20th Panzergrenadier Division in the east, tested in the defense.

Grossadmiral Karl Doenitz, the last German head of state. He initiated the withdrawal of the Navy from the east.

On the evening of 12/1/1945 the advancing Soviet tank formations had already outflanked the unprotected right flank of the XXIV Panzer Corps under General der Panzertruppe Nehring. Here stood the 17th PD, which suffered heavy losses in combat with the tank waves of the Red Army. The division's commander, Oberst Brux, was captured.

Generaloberst Harpe, the commander of Army Group A, ordered General Schulz, commander of the 17th Army, to personally get a picture of the situation in the XXXXVIII Panzer Corps area of operations. General Schulz found that the entire combat area was almost empty up to Krakau. The main body of the corps had fallen on 12/1/1945, they were either wounded or taken prisoner. Generalleutnant Freiherr von Edelsheim, the commander, tried to assemble the remnants of the 304th and 68th Infantry Divisions during the next few days. At first, he found nothing of the 68th ID, which was committed furthest to the north.

Generaloberst Harpe had already attempted to commit the reserves from OKH on 13/1, since enemy situation reports indicated that the advance from the Baranov bridgehead was still not over. After the start of the offensive in the northern portion of the front, they also had to anticipate an offensive in the south very soon.

The northern XXXXII Army Corps of the 4th Panzer Army was only fixed by the attack in the 291st ID sector. The corps committed a blocking formation under Generalmajor von Ahlfen in the Kielce area, where its army reserve was.

Late in the evening a query from the left neighbor about the army boundary received the reply that the major enemy attack out of the Pulawy and Magnuszow bridgeheads was anticipated on 14/1.

While it was still dark, the enemy artillery opened a barrage fire on 14/1 that was at least as intense as the one two days prior near Baranov. This barrage fire hit the 9th Army, specifically the 17th ID, the 6th and 45th Volksgrenadier Divisions. The 6th Volksgrenadier Division suffered heavy losses; its regimental and battalion commanders were almost all killed. The remnants of this destroyed division were taken up by the 19th PD during the next few days.

The 17th ID under Generalmajor Sachsenheimer fought on the front of the Pulawy bridgehead, where they and their neighbors, the 45th and 214th

Infantry Divisions, received the greatest weight of the attack. Approximately 100 tanks were shot-up by this division or destroyed in close combat. However, what was that against 800 Soviet tanks. Before this second attack of the 1st and 4th Ukrainian Fronts south of the upper Vistula, the 17th Army was withdrawn behind the Biala and the Dunajec by 16/1/1945.

The Soviet reserves, which followed out of the Baranov bridgehead, were diverted to the north, in order to outflank and destroy the XXXXII Army Corps and the XXIV Panzer Corps. With the same objective, the Soviet formations from the Pulawy bridgehead advanced to the southwest from Radom to join up with the aforementioned enemy forces. If these two formations met, then the two German corps would be encircled.

The 1st Belorussian Front, which attacked out of the Magnuszow bridgehead up to north of Warsaw, advanced north of Pilica with the 1st and 8th Guards Tank Armies toward Lodz. The 2nd Soviet Tank Army turned to the northwest in the direction of Plock, in order to outflank Warsaw and the German defensive forces located there.

The weak defenders of Warsaw broke out during the night of 17/1 and attacked north of Pilica, in order to make contact with the 9th Army, which was fighting there.

During the following combat, the 9th Army was pushed back to the north across the Vistula and into the area of operations of the 2nd German Army. Therefore, this army was missing from the battle for Silesia.

The enemy forces located directly south of Pilica did not press as hard, therefore, the XXXX Panzer Corps was able to escape with the remnants of the 19th PD (and mounted elements of the 6th Volksgrenadier Division) through Lodz to the west.

Army Group A removed the staff of the 8th Army, which was no longer needed in this area, at the last second on the evening of 16/1 and inserted it in Petrikau. On 17/1 they were ordered to transfer in forced march to Oppeln and organize the defense of Silesia there.

The situation on 16/1/1945 reflected the following:

Army Group A had suffered a complete defeat. The main body of the 4th Panzer Army and the 9th Army were defeated. Both army commands were leaderless due to the lack of or destruction of communications, command and control of the troops was lost. The enemy was dictating the course of further combat. There was a gap 300 kilometers wide in the great Vistula bend.

The Encirclement – Wandering Pocket

On 14/1 the command of the 4th Panzer Army and the staffs of the XXIV Panzer Corps and the XXXXII Army Corps realized that the encirclement was complete. On the afternoon of 14/1 the XXXXII Army Corps, which fought under General der Infanterie Recknagel, first received instructions to withdraw from the Vistula front. However, the lead armored elements that had broken through here had already driven over 150 kilometers deep into the west. The XXIV Panzer Corps, General der Panzertruppe Nehring, saw the problem to the left of the panzer corps to the XXXXII Army Corps. During the night before 15/1/1945, when a radio message from the 9th Army was intercepted which indicated that it had ordered a withdrawal, General Nehring faced a difficult decision. He said:

"In spite of the order to fight to the rear, I issued new orders to remain in the Kielce area for as long as possible, at least until the divisions of the XXXXII Army Corps, which were advanced far to the Vistula, could withdraw to the panzer corps.

This decision, which I made myself, signified fierce fighting for three of the divisions of my corps until the evening of 16 January.

During the night before 17/1 the withdrawal to the north was finally initiated and continued during the grey snowy nights of 18 and 19/1/1945; we were constantly attacked on all sides by the enemy, especially by heavy bomber and fighter formations." (See Nehring, Walther K.: *The History of the German Panzer Branch 1939-1945*.)

This "wandering pocket" finally fought its way back across the Warthe south of Lodz. With the corps marched the remnants of the defeated XXXXII Army Corps and the LVI Panzer Corps, whose commanding Generals Recknagel and Block fell during the fighting at this time.

However, back to the events in the Army Group A sector, which was redesignated as Army Group Center on 25/1/1945.

On 18/1 the following enemy situation was reported by the army group: The Red Army has achieved a penetration 300 kilometers wide and is attacking to the west in the direction of Germany. To the south of this breakthrough they have reached the Silesian border on either side of Chestochow.

In the north, in the 9th Army sector, where they had launched a major attack two days later, on 14/1/1945, the Red Army reached the Lodz – Kutno line.

These two breakthroughs had cost heavy casualties on both sides. However, while the enemy had deeply echeloned reserve formations, the defeated German divisions had no replacements.

The 4th Ukrainian Front was now attacking the Upper Silesian industrial region. The German forces were extremely exhausted by the concentrated Soviet attacks. The 4th Panzer Army and the 9th Army were no longer combat effective. The 17th Army, which had been fighting its way to the west since 17/1/1945, was able to maintain its combat strength. Armeegruppe Heinrici was the only army in Army Group Center that still had some reserves available.

On the urging of Generaloberst Schoerner, the Replacement Army was ordered to commitment on 18/1. This order was issued at least four decisive days too late.

The two infantry divisions committed from the west and two panzer divisions set in march from Hungary would not arrive with their lead elements until 20/1, they would not be fully available until the end of January.

The situation report from Army Group Center to the OKH on 18/1/1945 read:

"The mission of protecting the Upper Silesian industrial region will be secured by the hasty arrival of the 8th and 20th Panzer Divisions. The disposition of the 4th Panzer Army to the enemy in the area on either side of Posen requires the immediate commitment of new forces in the area between Breslau and Thorn, which, after blocking this attack, can attack against the front and flanks of the enemy."

The Commitment of Armeegruppe Heinrici

Armeegruppe Heinrici, which was located before and in the Tatra Mountains, secured eastern Slovakia and the region east of the Tatra Mountains with the villages of Leutschau, Deutschendorf and Kaesemark, in which German settlers lived, with the 1st Panzer Army.

The staff of the 1st Panzer Army moved from the eastern slopes of the Tatra Mountains on 27/1 to Sillein. At this time the XI SS Corps was subordinated in the Saybusch area.

On 29/1 the LIX Army Corps, which was adjacent to the north and committed between the Beskids and the Vistula and fighting back to a line Bielitz – Pless, came under the command of the 1st Panzer Army, which, on this day, was forced to evacuate the Tatra Mountains, because of the withdrawal of the 17th Army, and withdraw themselves to the line Berg Dumbier – Berg Banikov – Jelesnia.

The strong point of the 1st Panzer Army was shifted with the two subordinate army corps to the northern flank into the Upper Silesian area. For this reason, the army command post was moved to Friedeck, southwest of Teschen, on 30/1/1945.

On 16/1 the front in the XI SS Corps area of operations was already broken through in the center in the Jaslo area. This forced the two northern divisions – the 78th Sturm Division and the 544th Volksgrenadier Division – to withdraw. In this manner, they arrived in the LIX Army Corps sector, to which they were subordinated. The corps itself was withdrawn with the two southern divisions – the 320th ID and 545th Volksgrenadier Division – after a short halt near Makow in the Saybusch area.

The LIX Army Corps, which was holding in its positions on the Wisloka, was able to leave its sector facing superior enemy armored formations in snow storms and minus 20 degree cold and make it to a line Kety – Auschwitz on the western bank of the Sola River.

Because the situation in the XI Army Corps area of operations, which was to the northwest of the LIX Army Corps, was also dubious, Armeegruppe Heinrici had to pay special attention to this northern-most portion of its sector, even though this corps was not subordinate to it.

On 21/1 the XI Corps still held the Przemsza sector between Auschwitz and Myslowitsch, which belonged to the "B-2 Positions." This line was broken through by the Russians on 26/1, which rolled on to Kattowitz. The entire corps was forced back and found itself on the Pless – Sohrau line on 29/1. Because of the threat of a Soviet advance through Rybnik, which stood in the rear of the troops located between the Beskids and the Vistula, the XI Army Corps conducted a counterattack which struck the enemy located near Rybnik and secured the city.

Therefore, combat activity stalled here, which, because of the deeply cut mountains, was never all that great.

After the defection of the Hungarian Colonel General Miklos von Dalnoki to the Russians, the Hungarian army had to be removed from the front on 15/10/1944. They were never committed again.

Because the Hungarian army was removed from Armeegruppe Heinrici, it was re-designated as the 1st Panzer Army again. Its mission was now to stop the advance of the 4th Ukrainian Front between the western Beskids and between the Vistula and Oder. They were to protect the decisively important war production region of Freistadt, Ratibor, Troppau, Maehrisch-Ostrau, Teschen and Kaewein. Besides the iron and coal mines, here were also the iron and steel industries with the largest rollers in Europe at that time; to say nothing of the chemical works, the textile industries and the oil refineries.

East of the Oder, in the Lublinitz – Gross Wartenberg area, the 4th Panzer Army was in defensive combat. The staff of the VIII Army Corps under General Hartmann, which was already removed from Magnuszew on 17/1, arrived in Oppeln in the meantime. Hartmann received instructions from Generaloberst Schoerner to stop the Soviet advance across the line Lublinitz – Wielun to the Oder or at least delay it. On 18/1 the command post of the VIII Army Corps was located east of Guttentag. From there, General Hartmann dispatched reconnaissance. This reconnaissance found elements of the 4th Panzer Army Weapons School near Lubnitz and north of there the remnants of the defeated 168th ID on a defensive front oriented to the east. They were all organized into Battle Group Oppeln which was fought back to the Oder on either side of Oppeln by General

Hartmann on the evening of 23/1. The defense of the Oder positions succeeded thanks to the far-sightedness of General Hartmann.

The army group organized another battle group which, under the leadership of Oberst Krafft, stopped a Soviet advance with tanks and infantry
on either side of Wieruszew east of Kempen at the Prosna sector. During
the night before 20/1 Battle Group Krafft first had to withdraw to a line on
either side of Kempen.

At the same time, because Battle Group Krafft was defending the area
east of Breslau, Major Tenschert stood near Reichenthal on the deep southern flank with the 83rd Jaeger Ersatz and Construction Battalion. The battalion, which was located in Trautenau, was alerted on 18/1, loaded up at
the railroad station and transported to the Oberstradam railroad station on
the afternoon of 19/1. Here they received orders from the sector commander,
Major Henschel, to occupy the Berthold line in the sector of the village of
Glausche to the northern edge of Domsel and hold it against enemy attack.

The 600 soldiers, who were only equipped with light infantry weapons, therefore had a 10 kilometer wide sector to defend. The command post
was set up in the von Grunwitz farmstead. The Mainz, Melzer, Abischt and
Wolff Companies were placed in positions. The Soviet attack began here at
daybreak, it was conducted by tanks and motorized infantry. The forward
companies were overrun and destroyed. The Abicht Company was easily
destroyed, the rest were only able to save remnants, with the exception of
the Wolff Reserve Company, which was able to withdraw to Kunzendorf.

On the early morning of 22/1 the Wolff Company was located near
Niederstradam, when the enemy rolled up to here. Leutnant Wolff and his
men were able to destroy four anti-tank guns along with their Red Army
trucks, with one panzerfaust and several machine-guns.

On the early morning of 23/1 Battalion Tenschert withdrew behind the
line of the arriving 269th ID. Defending near Schollendorf the battalion
was outflanked by mobile Soviet troops and had their withdrawal route cut
off.

Generalleutnant Wagner ordered the breakthrough through Oels in the
direction of Breslau. The nighttime breakthrough succeeded. Battalion
Tenschert took up rear guard positions in Schmarse

At first light on 25/1 the march in the direction of Breslau was continued and the assigned defensive sector at Hundsfeld was reached. The defensive line was occupied near the Sakrau brewery. Therefore, Battalion Tenschert was now in the Breslau defensive zone.

The Defensive Mission of the 17th Army

The 17th Army, which defended from the Oder near Cosel through Dabrowa to Auschwitz on a front of 120 kilometers, was ordered to protect the Upper Silesian industrial region. Here were the last foundries that made weapons.

The army, which had been engaged in difficult withdrawal combat since the beginning of the Russian offensive, had the XXXXVIII Panzer Corps with the 68th and 304th Infantry Divisions, which were severely battered during this fighting. The 75th ID, which had only joined in the fighting near Meichow, was still intact. Half of the 97th Jaeger Division and the 712th ID would arrive in the new defensive positions by 20/1.

The 359th and 371st Infantry Divisions of the 17th Army were involved in the withdrawal combat south of the upper Vistula. The front of the 17th Army held for the time being. On 25/1 General Schulz proposed to Army Group Center obtaining permission to withdraw into a new combat line Bielitz – east of Pless – north of Rybnik – Cosel. Schulz had discussed this line with his southern neighbor, the 1st Panzer Army, and received their consent. This request was repeated on 26/1, pointing out that if permission were withheld the forces in contact with the enemy would be destroyed. However, the army group still did not give their permission.

On 27/1 General Schulz made a last attempt at GFM Schoerner to withdraw his army. The commander of Army Group Center now gave General Schulz a free hand to withdraw during the night of 28/1. Schoerner made this decision on his own, then he had to justify it to Hitler telephonically.

The line Bielitz – east of Pless north of Rybnik – Cosel was to be occupied. The I/Flak-Rgt 33 was set up in positions there with 8.8 cm air defense guns. The commander of this battalion was ordered to hold Rybnik against the probing enemy tanks until the reserves arrived.

The battalion shot-up the enemy tanks and when the 8th PD came from Ratibor in Hungary and the 1st Ski Jaeger Division arrived from the southeast from the Sohrau area, the enemy was already thrown back.

This still did not prevent the loss of Upper Silesia, because the enemy had already overtaken these forces in several outflanking operations. To the right and left of this sector the enemy reached the Oder between Oppeln and Steinau and crossed it in three places, in order to establish bridgeheads near Ohlau, between Brieg and Ohlau and, at the end of the month, also near Maltsch. With the exception of Breslau, there was no longer a defensive front here by the end of January.

The 269th ID joined in the fighting from Ohlau on 31/1/1945. They failed to hold the Goellnerhainer Berge. The division was gradually pushed back toward Breslau. The encirclement of the 269th ID was initiated as elements of the 3rd Soviet Guards Tank Army advanced toward Breslau on 10 and 11/2 and met forces south of the city that had set out from the Ohlau and Brieg bridgeheads. Generalleutnant Wagner was able to lead the artillery and wheeled elements of his division through the last gap to the south during the night of 12/2 and escape the encirclement of Breslau. (See in addition: Fortress Breslau.)

The 208th ID, which was ordered into this area in "blitztransport" from northern Hungary, was unloaded in Steinkirche on 3/2/1945 and led into the Wansen assembly area; with orders to attack in the direction of Fortress Brieg, establish contact with the fortress defenders and defend from the fortress to the southeast.

This attack began on 5/2, it gained good ground at first so that they were able to cross the Brieg autobahn. However, the attack stalled here and the division ultimately had to withdraw behind the autobahn. The closely pursuing enemy attacked to within 2 kilometers of Wansen. The 208th ID was removed from here; the division was set in march in the direction of Striegau, where the enemy was located.

The Soviet attack in the direction of Neisse, which began on 4/2, ran into Corps Group Jeckeln (with the V SS Corps) near Grottkau. Grottkau was lost. Enemy tanks advanced halfway to Neisse.

Then the 20th PD and the 45th Volksgrenadier Division arrived in this area one after the other and launched a counterattack. They threw the enemy back directly south of Grottkau and established a defense here on the line Oppeln – Grottkau – Wansen. This line was held until mid-March.

The 17th Infantry Division in Attack and Defense

"Every man in our division was inspired by the idea to help defeat the upcoming major attack of the Red Army and to stop them before our eastern border."

These words of the commander of the 17th ID, Generalmajor Sachsenheimer, proved to be true even if the strength of the division was insufficient to stop the enemy. The 17th and 214th Infantry Divisions stood on a 63 kilometer front, with 17 kilometers on land and 46 kilometers on water.

After the Luftwaffe discovered a large enemy deployment near Pulawy and the enemy batteries had fired on the HKL of the 17th ID, the attack was immanent.

The offensive also began in the Pulawy bridgehead on 14/1/1945 at 0530 hours with a several hour heavy barrage fire. After that, 11 rifle divisions, one cavalry corps and one tank corps attacked in the 17th ID sector.

The positions of the 55th GR, which had already been battered by the artillery fire-strike, were broken through by the Soviet rifle divisions crossing the river. The enemy reached the artillery positions and captured them. The main body of this regiment was destroyed. During a withdrawal Oberstleutnant Dr. Emmert, the commander of the 55th GR, was severely wounded.

Nevertheless, this division was able to destroy over 100 enemy tanks with anti-tank guns and panzerfaeusten on this day. However, what good was this against the 800 tanks and armored vehicles counted in the division sector on this day.

On 15/1 Generalmajor Sachsenheimer launched a counterattack on Zwolen, where he he knew Major Seifert was still holding on 14/1. Eight assault guns supported this attack, five broke down on the way, so only three fought in Zwolen until the Russian armored superiority became overwhelming. Major Seifert organized everyone for a breakout from Zwolen and he reached the division command post in Sucha on the evening of 15/1 with his battle group.

All of the remaining division elements also withdrew in a five-day battle, led by the division commander – without supplies and without sufficient control.

Still 1000 soldiers from the combat troops reached the saving Oder.

Generalmajor Sachsenheimer was subordinated to Armee Graeser with elements of the division staff, the communications, panzerjaeger and engineer battalions and they were hastily deployed in the Breslau area. Near Dyherrnfurth there was an important war plant which produced a highly poisonous nerve gas that was stored in underground containers. The plant was recaptured and the gas destroyed, so that it would not fall into the hands of the enemy.

In an attack lasting only one hour, the plant was reached. The accompanying "Technical Group" pumped the gas out, while the defenders held the attacking Soviets off. Six heavy air defense guns, which were brought along and set up in position behind a railroad embankment, were destroyed. Late in the afternoon "Battle Group Sachs" returned after fulfilling its mission.

The Battle for the Oder

After the fortunate withdrawal of the "wandering pocket" into the Glogau area, west of the Oder, the XXIV Panzer Corps and the XXXX Panzer Corps arrived in this area at the end of January. The divisions that arrived were: the 6th and 45th Volksgrenadier Divisions, the 17th PD and the 17th, 72nd 88th, 214th, 291st and 342nd Infantry Divisions and the von Ahlfen Blocking Formation, rear area services, air defense and Luftwaffe ground personnel.

The staffs of the XXXXII Army Corps and the LVI Panzer Corps were completely decimated. The commander of the latter, General Block, was killed. The commanders of the 17th PD, Oberst Brux, the 88th ID, Generalleutnant Graf von Rittberg, the 214th ID, Generalleutnant von Kirchbach, were all wounded and captured by the Soviets. Generalmajor Finger, commander of the 291st ID, was killed near Chestochow on 17/1/1945.

After reaching the Warthe near Sieradz, the XXXX Panzer Corps was tasked by the 9th Army to reach Wreschen and prevent the unopposed advance of the enemy into the northern area of the army. However, they could not think of stopping the enemy. They were first able to hold near Beuthen and Crossen. They held a Russian bridgehead near Odereck, north of Gruenberg. The bridge near Odereck was blown by German engineers in a surprise raid. After that, the Soviet bridgehead could be destroyed.

The staff of the XXIV Panzer Corps was also ordered to the Oder. General der Panzertruppe Nehring reported in his work "Wandering Pocket":

"After the 'Wandering Pocket' reached the safety of the 'Grossdeutschland' Panzer Corps on the Warthe, a message from OKH arrived in Walentynow (northwest of Ostrow) on 15/1:

XXIV Panzer Corps staff and the staff of the 16th PD will immediately convoy under heavy security to Glogau – Herrndorf. They are to report to the 9th Army there.'

The 20th PGD and all available panzer elements subordinate to the 'Grossdeutschland' Panzer Corps received similar orders, in order to delay the enemy deployment.

The march columns ran into enemy tanks in the vicinity of Krotoschin, however, they let them pass in the darkness. The march continued in the direction of Koeben and through Lissa toward Glogau, in order to reach Gut Herrndorf in the late afternoon. Here the 9th Army issued the order to organize and take over the defense of the Oder sector from Steinau, exclusive, through Glogau to Nausalz, inclusive."

The Soviet leadership had very clear objectives, as they drove their 4th Tank Army with very strong forces north of Breslau toward the Oder sector Parchwitz – Steinau – Koeben.

In fact, the Jauer Non-commissioned Officer School received orders to defend Steinau, however, this occurred on 20/1/45 and was too late to save this important Oder crossing with its railroad and road bridges. The troops did not arrive until 22 and 23/1. On the evening of 23/1, however, the first Soviet tanks approached to within firing range of Steinau and, on the morning of 24/1, the enemy tanks attacked through the outer defensive ring to the eastern bank of the Oder. The railroad bridge blew into the air. The blowing of the road bridge failed, because they lacked fuses for the explosives.

Of the nine Soviet tanks that crossed this bridge over the Oder with mounted infantry five were destroyed by panserfaust rounds. The rest returned to the eastern bank with the infantry.

The engineers quickly went to work with other explosives and finally blew this road bridge. Nevertheless, it was not completely destroyed, so that Soviet infantry elements were able to cross the damaged bridge to the western bank.

At approximately the same time, on 25/1, the Red Army also crossed the Oder with amphibious vehicles near Diebau, south of Steinau. North of Steinau Soviet engineers threw up several bridges, across which tanks moved to the western bank.

In Steinau itself the Non-commissioned Officers School fought their last commitment until the evening of 3/2. Elements of the 103rd Panzer Brigade under Oberst Mummert with elements of their 103rd Panzer Regiment attacked through to them. The costly combat still could not prevent Steinau from falling and the enemy from establishing a wide and deep bridgehead across the Oder. In the Wehrmacht report from 6/2/1945 this fighting leading to the destruction of the Non-commissioned Officers School was praised. The Jauer Non-commissioned Officers School had tied up strong enemy forces and had made it possible for the orderly withdrawal of the German forces still located east of the Oder.

By 28/1 the enemy had already reached Lueben. They were again removed from this village in a counterattack. Here the German soldiers found horrible things. In the cellar of one house 20 soldiers from the "Grossdeutschland" PGD were found shot in the back of their heads. They were executed by the Soviets.

The XXIV Panzer Corps was also committed against the Red Army's Steinau bridgehead. On 28/1 the 16th PD attacked from Glogau, however, they stalled in the Red Army's defensive fire near Gaffron.

The attack of the LVII Panzer Corps against the southern flank of this bridgehead between Parchwitz – Lueben did not succeed, it was forced into the defense by strong Soviet counterattacks.

By 31/1 the soldiers of the Jauer Non-commissioned Officers School fought their way out of Steinau to the 408th ID. The division fought until 8/2 in the greater area south of Lueben. On the afternoon of this day Generaloberst Schoerner appeared at the division command post in Vorderheide, however, he did not issue the hoped-for order to withdraw. This was issued by the LVII Panzer Corps a little later. The 408th ID withdrew to Langenwaldau. Since Russian tanks had already penetrated to here, the division command post was transferred to Baersdorf – Trach, after the Schwarzwasser bridge was destroyed. The withdrawal continued to Goldberg. A battalion commander in the 408th ID, Hauptmann Heinze, reported:

> "The city changed hands several times. The Russians ravaged the area brutally. The horrible picture awaiting the troops after they recaptured it cannot be described."

The attempt to eliminate the Red Army Steinau bridgehead failed. Fortress Liegnitz fought under Oberst Treuhaupt until it fell on 8 and 9/2.

Combat on the Northern Flank of Army Group Center

The 4th Panzer Army, which arrived in Glogau on 25/1, as ordered, after costly fighting in Poland, had taken over in the northern sector at the end of January. On 31/1 the northern army boundary ran through Glogau – Sagan, on 12/2 further to the north of there through Neustaedtl – Sorau and a little later at the confluence of the Lausitzer Neisse into the Oder north of Guben.

As the northern boundary of the 1st Panzer Army and the 17th Army was moved to the north, the northern boundary of the 4th Panzer Army was also moved further to the north. Their northern flank had already left Silesia and was now in the south of Mark Brandenburg.

When the Russians began their attack out of the Steinau bridgehead on 8/2, the 4th Panzer Army transferred its command post from Sagan to Bunzlau. They had to withdraw further from the enemy armored avalanche on 10/2 and they established themselves near Goerlitz.

Two Soviet tank armies and three infantry armies launched an attack. They broke through in the first wave. The 3rd Guards Tank Army advanced through Liegnitz to the southeast toward Breslau and quickly encircled the city. The two remaining attack wedges advanced into the south through Heynau – Bunzlau – Naumburg am Queiss toward Goerlitz with a secondary attack group advancing further south of Lauban, while the northern grouping headed through Priemkenau – Sprottau – Sagan – Sorau in the direction of Sommerfeld – Forst.

The long southern flank of the 4th Panzer Army on the Queiss was to be defended by the commandant of the Lower Silesian fortress sector, Generalleutnant Bordhin, and to the rear of this blocking position by Generalleutnant Friedrich, the Senior 312th Artillery Commander, on the Hammer sector on either side of Rauscha. Adjacent to the north of this line of resistance was the "Brandenburg" PGD, which was detached from its corps and had to fight its way back from Taudten – which was encircled by the enemy – through Heerwegen – Primkenau and Sprottau south of Sagan behind the Queiss.

On 12/2 the "Grossdeutschland" Corps assembled behind Bober and Queiss and transitioned to the defense. General von Saucken left the corps and went to East Prussia. General Jauer took over command from him. From his command post in Bautzen he commanded the "Kurmark" Division north of Frankfurt, the "Grossdeutschland" Feldwach Regiment near Kuestrin, the "Grossdeutschland" Replacement Formation near Guben, the "Grossdeutschland" Alert Brigade west of Forst and the "Brandenburg" Panzergrenadier Brigade east of Bautzen.

North of the "Grossdeutschland" Panzer Corps the XXIV Panzer Corps, General Nehring, marched out of the area 10 kilometers northwest of

Raudten, as ordered, back to the northwest. In the XXIV Panzer Corps were the 16th PD, as well as the 72nd, 88th and 342nd Infantry Divisions.

After these two corps had been established in the defense, General Graeser made the decision to attack with the XXIV Panzer Corps west of the Bober to the south and with the "Grossdeutschland" Panzer Corps, also to the west of the Bober, to the north between Sagan and Sorau and, therefore, cut off the enemy forces that were advancing on Forst from their rear area communications. In addition, the 25th PGD under Generalleutnant Audorsch was subordinated to the XXIV Panzer Corps.

The attack of the XXIV Panzer Corps began on 14/2/1945. By 18/2 they had achieved only a 10 kilometer ground gain south of Christianstadt. They did not achieve the hoped for link-up with the 20th PGD, which was attacking from the south. On 19/2 General Graeser had to break-off the fighting, since the enemy had brought up new reserves from the east.

Nevertheless, this attack did facilitate the withdrawal of the 4th Panzer Army behind the Lausitzer Neisse.

The XXIV Panzer Corps withdrew in the direction of Guben. General der Panzertruppe Nehring made this decision, because there was still a XXXX Panzer Corps (minus tanks) bridgehead located there. During the night before 21/2 the march in the direction of Guben was initiated. The 16th PD fixed the enemy with an attack against an enemy bridgehead located near Gastrose, 8 kilometers south of Guben, west of the Neisse and made it possible for its own corps to cross the river.

This enemy bridgehead was removed in mid-March by a night attack by the XXXX Panzer Corps. The XXIV Panzer Corps occupied defensive positions behind the Neisse. The Russian attack was stopped here. The "Grossdeutschland" Panzer Corps and all troop units adjacent to the south were also withdrawn behind the Lausitzer Neisse. The 4th Panzer Army now stood on a unified front on the Neisse from Rothenburg (north of Goerlitz) to its confluence into the Oder north of Guben.

The 1st Panzer Army in the Maehrisch-Ostrau Industrial Region

On the evening of 29/1/1945 the 1st Panzer Army took control over the XI SS Army Corps between the Slovakian – Polish border and Saybusch, as well as the LIX Army Corps between Boelitz and Pless. The attacking formations were repulsed near Saybusch.

The 4th Ukrainian Front established its main attack effort here to force their attack on 8 and 9/2 near Pless and breakthrough on 10/2. The two German divisions on the seam between the XI SS Corps and the LIX Army Corps were thrown back in the Schwarzwasser area.

When there was danger that the 78th Sturm Division would be attacked in their extended flank from the northeast, a small battle group under the command of a Hauptmann attacked the enemy on the evening of 11/2 at the Auschwitz – Maehrisch- Ostrau rail line near the Shiby railroad station. The battle group held the enemy off until the northern elements of the division were able to escape the threatened encirclement.

The Soviets also attacked in the LIX Army Corps area; an additional attack in the XXXXIX Mountain Corps area of operations, which was located on the mountain front between Bielitz and Rosenberg, was repulsed. Defending under this corps from the north to the south were the 545th and 320th Volksgrenadier Divisions, the 253rd ID and the 4th and 3rd Mountain Divisions.

On 10/2 the Red Army achieved a deep penetration near Bielitz and Saybusch. Saybusch was lost. The enemy had committed 36 infantry divisions and several tank formations against the nine divisions, which the 1st Panzer Army had committed between Sorau, Bielitz and Rosenberg.

The positions of the two mountain divisions were also attacked on either side of the Waag Valley. While the 4th Mountain Division was engaged in heavy defensive combat on either side of the Skorusina Berges 20 kilometers west of Zakopane, the Red Army tried to force a breakthrough toward Rosenberg into the Waag Valley in the 3rd Mountain Division area of operations from 11 to 15/2. On 14/2 the defensive efforts of the 3rd Mountain Division under Generalleutnant Klatt were praised in a Wehrmacht report. The Czech divisions attacking here were completely defeated.

On 16/2 the 1st Ukrainian Front launched a stronger attack out of the bridgehead between Ratibor and Cosel in the direction of Leobschuetz. It hit the 371st ID and the 18th SS PGD located there, which were turned over to the XI SS Corps. The enemy achieved a deep penetration near Gross Neukirch. By 18/2 this penetration was removed.

General Niehoff, who had recaptured the warehouse at Klein Ellguth (near Gross Neukirch) with his 371st ID, discovered that the Soviets had badly mauled many soldiers from the 18th PGD. Among the dead were many violated corpses of naked young girls.

In the 253rd ID area of operations, the enemy attack south of Schwarzwasser was expanded to a threatening penetration, it was finally removed.

The enemy was exhausted. The strength of his attacks significantly diminished on 22/2. Only small local attacks were now being undertaken, they were all repulsed.

The defensive line in the Saybusch – Skotschauhart Hills west of Schwarzwasser – Pawlowitz – Sorau held.

The 17th Army Counterattack

During the night before 2/3/1945 the 17th Army began its counterattack near Lauban. The conduct of this attack lay in the hands of General Nehring, because General Schulz was wounded at the front several days before by a bomb fragment. "Panzergruppe Nehring" was formed from the XXIV Panzer Corps. The plan foresaw the 6th Volksgrenadier Division defending in the center, while a left and a right attack group were to launch a flanking attack on either side of Lauban, meeting on the Goerlitz – Bunzlau road north of Lauban. The right attack group was to consist of the LVII Panzer Corps, General der Panzertruppe Kirchner. It included the Fuehrer Begleit Division, the 8th PD and the 16th PD, which was still reconstituting. The 2nd ID also belonged to it.

The left attack group, led by General der Panzertruppe Decker, consisted of the XXXIX Panzer Corps; to it were subordinated the Fuehrer

Grenadier Division, the 17th PD, the 6th Volksgrenadier Division and an infantry division.

The counterattack, which began during the night before 2/3, gained ground in both directions at first. However, then the Soviet resistance stiffened in front of the LVII Panzer Corps. In the area of operations of the left attack group, the XXXIX Panzer Corps, they advanced until the afternoon. Ober Bielau was recaptured. However, the Soviets defended bitterly in front of the forest and on the edge of the forest northeast and north of Ober Bielau. Generalmajor Maeder, commander of the Fuehrer Grenadier Division, which was to attack further through the forest and reach the road to Bunzlau, proposed to General Decker to avoid this difficult area, which had cost heavy casualties and much time, and to turn off to the east from the present line, in order to achieve a smaller, but more achievable solution. General Decker approved this decision; General Nehring, who was in charge of this operation, agreed and ordered Logau as the new direction. The fighting continued and 48 hours later the Fuehrer Grenadier Division crossed the Queiss and reached the 8th PD east of Logau.

Lauban was liberated, which was an important rail stretch for Army Group Center. The success was great. The 17th PD alone destroyed approximately 80 enemy tanks, mostly T 34's, on the first day of the attack. The 8th PD achieved approximately 150 tank hits. Here are the combat reports of two divisions that participated.

16th Panzer Division Counter-strike on Lauban

On 20/2/1945, when Generalmajor von Mueller received the Swords to the Knight's Cross with Oak Leaves at Fuehrer Headquarters, he requested withdrawing the battered 16 PD and having it reconstituted. This occurred in the Bautzen area. The first reinforced formation to roll out was Major Lippold's battalion with their heavy jagdpanzers. The first units were organized just as the order arrived to transfer into the Marklissa area. A Russian attack against Lauban had led to the loss of this city and, therefore the loss of the last railroad connection from central Germany to Silesia.

Elements of the 16th PD were ordered to launch a counter-strike from the south in the direction of Lauban.

The attack on 5/3 did not advance very far. In the early morning of 6/3 it rolled further after regrouping at night. Again the Soviet resistance stiffened. The division commander went to the front lines with his Ia to personally motivate the individual groups. Major Michael took over the "Jueterbog" Grenadier Regiment. The jagdpanzers under Major Lippold advanced and shot-up a number of T 34's in an armored duel. This gave the infantry new courage. Together with the engineers under Major Gerke, supported by the artillery under Oberstleutnant von Guaita, the lead elements penetrated into Lauban and threw the Soviets out of the city in house-to-house fighting. It was burning in some places. The situation in the city was horrible. Lauban was liberated, however, not for long.

Combat in the 6th Volksgrenadier Division Area of Operations

For the 6th Volksgrenadier Division under Generalmajor Bruecker, the fighting around Lauban began on 20/2/1945. During the first days of combat this division fought against the 6th Soviet Tank Army.

The enemy pressure against the 6th Volksgrenadier Division increased on 21/2. A deep armored breakthrough on the Hennersdorf – Schreibersdorf road reached Nonnenbusch. A number of villages were captured by the enemy.

During the night the majority of the armored groups that had broken through were destroyed by the grenadiers of the 6th Volksgrenadier Division in close combat. A tank destroyer formation from the Luftwaffe offered some assistance.

A counterattack by the newly arrived battalion under Hauptmann Schindel, the Rommelspracher Battalion and the Hetzer Company succeeded. Hennersdorf was recaptured.

The 6th Volksgrenadier Division had, in the meantime, fought its way through to the western edge of Lauban and made contact with the city commandant, Major Tschuschke, who was directly subordinate to the LVII Panzer Corps.

15 enemy tanks, which approached to attack to the south of the 6th Volksgrenadier Division's defensive line on the following day, were blocked by the Dallmeier Hetzer Company with only two of the Hetzers located there, seven of the enemy tanks were destroyed.

Leutnant Dallmeier's Hetzers were in constant commitment throughout the division sector. Attacks and counterattacks, the loss and recapture of villages constantly fluctuated. When the Oberleutnant, who held the northern corner of Gut Lauban, was killed, the enemy pressed on to the cemetery with eight to ten tanks. Therefore, Gut Lauban was lost. With only two Hetzers, Leutnant Dallmeier attacked the enemy and shot-up all of the enemy tanks that had penetrated near the Lauban cemetery. The last two Hetzers were lost to transmission problems on the way back. Since the 1183rd Panzerjaeger Battalion, Jaenisch, had to go to Goerlitz for repairs for several days, the division was now without anti-tank defenses. Luckily, a little later Oberst von Luck arrived from a panzer division located north of Penzig. He brought six Tigers and ten Panzer IV's with him. They were immediately committed.

A strong enemy penetration in the north of Lauban, which made it through to the nunnery at the Lauban Northern Church, was removed by a panzer brigade deployed toward Lauban. The fighting on the northern edge of Lauban lasted all day.

On 2/3 the division received news that a counterattack was launched with two attack wedges. The 6th Volksgrenadier Division closed with the attack of the Fuehrer Grenadier Division in the south on the evening of 3/3 at 1900 hours. This attack struck into the hastily withdrawing Russian columns. Therefore, the intent of the Red Army to breakthrough Lauban to the south and the southwest had failed. The battlefield was turned into a cemetery for the Russian tank army. The Dallmeier Hetzer Company alone shot-up 100 tanks. Of these, Leutnant Dallmeier registered 50 enemy tanks himself. On 3/4 Generalmajor Bruecker presented the Leutnant with the Knight's Cross.

The Situation in the 1st Panzer Army Area of Operations

After the defense against the Soviet February attack in the Maehrisch-Ostrau area, the 1st Panzer Army had to give up the battered 359th and 545th Volksgrenadier Divisions to the 17th Army. Therefore, the 1st Panzer Army now had only 12 divisions in its sector, of these, seven could only be considered "battle groups."

Moreover, on 24/2 the 1st Panzer Army sector was expanded through Cosel to Oppeln, whereby Corps Group Silesia, the LVI Panzer Corps with the 168th and 344th Infantry Divisions, an Estonian SS Freiwilligen Division and some Volkssturm units came under the command of the 1st Panzer Army.

Therefore, the 1st Panzer Army defended on a sector 300 kilometers wide, which extended out of the area south of Rosenberg into Slovakia to Oppeln. The 1st Panzer Army decided to preempt an enemy attack out of the bridgehead and to remove the bridgehead or at least reduce it by an attack. The main effort of this attack lay in the XI Corps area of operations, where all available assault gun elements would be committed. A regiment of the 4th Mountain Division had to be dispatched to Rybnik to defend there for the proposed attack by the 8th PD. The attack was to begin on 8/3/1945.

At the end of February the 4th Ukrainian Front prepared for a breakthrough attack in the Schwarzwasser area south of Skotschau, which was directed at the LIX Army Corps defenses under Generalleutnant von Tresckow. Generaloberst Heinrici ordered an HKL be prepared three to four kilometers to the rear, in which the formations of the LIX Army Corps could withdraw to during the night before the attack, in order to avoid the Russian barrage fire.

The Battle in Upper Silesia

The attack of the XI Corps against the Cosel bridgehead began on 8/3. This attack struck into the middle of the Soviet attack preparations. It succeeded in penetrating into the bridgehead in the south. Here fought the 1st Ski Jaeger Division and the 97th Jaeger Division with the 8th PD. They drove the enemy back. However, the northern attack wedge stalled. Soviet formations drove in between this wedge and the stalled elements of the corps and separated them from each other.

The Soviet counterattack against the German formations that had advanced into the southern portion of the bridgehead was repulsed on 11 and 12/3.

On the following morning Soviet fighter-bombers attacked the positions which were almost completely vacated the night before. Then the artillery fire opened up. When the Russian infantry attacked, they attacked into a vacuum. Nevertheless, the lead groups reached the HKL in the afternoon. The breakthrough failed. The Soviet tank formations prepared to exploit the breakthrough were not committed on this day. These measures prevented the simultaneous attack of the 1st and 4th Ukrainian Fronts. The 1st Ukrainian Front had to reorganize its forces. The tanks of the 4th Ukrainian Front remained in their assembly areas.

While it was quiet in the Cosel bridgehead on 13 and 14/3, the attack of the 4th Ukrainian Front continued north and south of Schwarzwasser. The 3rd Mountain Division, which had withdrawn from the HKL at the first enemy attack, counterattacked on 11/3 and won its positions back.

During the time gained in this manner, the 8th and 16th Panzer Divisions arrived in the area west of Schwarzwasser and east of Sorau on the evening of 11/3. They became the core of the defensive force, which continued to throw back the attacking enemy armor until 15/3. The HKL of the 75th ID on the northern flank of the LIX Army Corps was, nevertheless, broken through by Soviet armored forces, which then advanced on Sorau. The 8th PD blocked a penetration together with the 91st Mountain Jaeger Regiment. the offensive of the 4th Ukrainian Front stalled.

When the 1st Ukrainian Front launched its planned offensive on 15/3 between Cosel and Grottkau and its divisions slammed against the the XI Corps between Ratibor and Cosel, they achieved a deep penetration in the direction of Leobschuetz. Reserve formations had to be committed here immediately. The 254th ID had to be removed from the middle Silesian front of the 17th Army and the 16th PD from the front south of Schwarzwasser; both formations had to be sent to Leobschuetz.

The fighting around the Maehrisch-Ostrau area reached its climax when the 4th Ukrainian Front attacked again on 16 and 17/3. The 544th ID, the 3rd and 4th Mountain Divisions and the 253rd ID were engaged in fierce fighting southwest of Schwarzwasser, they repulsed all attacks. Northwest of Schwarzwasser, in the heavily battered 8th PD area of operations with the 68th and 75th Infantry Divisions and elements of the 4th Mountain Divisions, the enemy was also repulsed. The 8th PD under Generalmajor Hax was engaged in bitter fighting against a numerically far superior enemy. 65 enemy tanks were destroyed.

On 18 and 19/3 the enemy also attacked out of the Cosel bridgehead with strong forces. The objective of the attack was Leobschuetz. The first enemy tanks appeared directly east of Leobschuetz on the same day. Here they ran into the just arrived 16th PD, who threw the attack back. The 78th Sturm Division entrenched in defenses on the edge of the city.

By 20/3 there was a standstill on the entire 1st Panzer Army front. The enemy was frustrated during his second attempt to breakthrough into the Maehrisch-Ostrau industrial region. On this day Generaloberst Heinrici was summoned to take command of Army Group Vistula in the area east of Berlin. His successor as commander of the 1st Panzer Army was General der Panzertruppe Nehring.

The Defensive Combat of the 4th Panzer Army

The entire month of March passed in the 4th Panzer Army – with the exception of local attacks and reconnaissance attacks – without the anticipated major Soviet attack. In Fortress Glogau, which had been defended since 10/2 by Oberst Graf zu Eulenburg, it was coming to an end. General Graeser gave the fortress commandant permission to breakout on 31/3. Of the 800 German soldiers in the fortress only 50 made it back to German lines near Goerlitz.

On 15/4/1945, after the Red Army had committed the northern arm of the enormous pincer attack against the northern neighboring 9th Army of

Army Group Vistula near Kuestrin, the second phase of the barrage fire was began against the 4th Panzer Army early in the morning of 16/4. After that two attack groups advanced – one on either side of Rothenburg, the second south of Muskau up to Forst – forcing the breakthrough by 17/4. The northern attack group advanced through Spremberg – Cottbus against the southern front of Berlin. The southern group was successfully engaged and cut off by German counter-strikes on 19/4. The 20th PD and the "Hermann Goering" Fallschirm Panzer Division were located south of Goerlitz and had attacked the southern wedge on 17/4 and destroyed a large number of tanks. The two divisions fought until 19/4, nevertheless, the "Hermann Goering" PD took up the defense between Zodel and Ullersdorf. The enemy advanced further and reached Niesky, Weissenberg and Bautzen.

When the Red Army rolled through Bautzen to the west on 19/4, the "Hermann Goering" PD was in combat with a strong Russian tank force near Kodersdorf. The reported enemy tanks were first attacked by the division panzer regiment under Oberstleutnant Rossmann with 17 Panthers near Kodersdrof when the lead tanks of the formation of the I Polish Armored Corps had approached to within 50 meters. In 20 minutes 43 enemy tanks were shot-up here, the rest displayed white flags and surrendered. 12 undamaged tanks, three of them the type Stalin, fell into the hands of the panzer regiment. Outfitted with the Balken Cross, a few hours later they were taking part in defensive combat on the German side.

On 19/4 the battle group of the 17th ID under Generalmajor Sachsenheimer arrived in the area northwest of Goerlitz.

On the morning of 20/4 the 20th PD (on the right) and the 17th ID (left) attacked under the command of the LVII Panzer Corps to the northwest. The 72nd ID, following as reserve, joined in this attack. The long southern flank of the enemy was taken by surprise; Niesky was liberated, as was Stockteich. Operational freedom was re-established in the Goerlitz area, the Goerlitz – Lauban railroad was again open.

The next counter-strike built on this success. General Jauer, the commander of the "Grossdeutschland" Panzer Corps, was ordered to liberate Weissenberg and Bautzen. He ordered the "Brandenburg" Division to attack Weissenberg. The division attacked on 21 and 22/4 from the north and south, destroyed the Russian 29th Mechanized Division and recaptured

Weissenberg. 250 to 300 tanks, trucks, etc. of this division lay destroyed and burning on the battlefield.

The 20th PD attacked Bautzen from the northeast again under the command of Generalmajor von Oppeln-Bronikowski from 23 to 25/4, while the "Hermann Goering" Division attacked from the south. Bautzen was liberated.

If they were not able to delay the main enemy attack on Berlin, the 4th Panzer Army did secure the refugee routes to the west; and they did so until shortly before the surrender, so that hundreds of thousands of Germans were able to make it to the west.

The Final Battle of the 1st Panzer Army

On 22/3/1945 General der Panzertruppe Nehring took command of the 1st Panzer Army. The mission of the 1st Panzer Army in the final phase of the war read:

> "Continue to protect the Maehrisch-Ostrau area and maintain contact with the 17th Army by holding the area west of Leobschuetz."

On 13/4/1945 Vienna fell. During the fighting around Vienna the northern flank of Army Group South with the LXXII and XXIX Army Corps was pushed back to the north into the 1st Panzer Army. The Pliev Army penetrated through this gap toward Bruenn. South and southeast of Bruenn, however, the XXIX Panzer Corps, led by Generalleutnant Kaellner, with the 8th and 16th Panzer Divisions, was able to repulse the attack directed at Olmuetz. A large number of enemy tanks were destroyed by the two German divisions. Generalleutnant Kaellner fell near Socolnica during this fighting. Generalmajor von Mueller, the commander of the 16th PD, fell into the hands of Czechoslovakian partisans.

The XXIV Panzer Corps was to hold Bruenn under all circumstances, according to a "Fuehrer Order." The 16th PD rolled to the north. The "Feldherrnhalle" Division was committed in Bruenn itself, the 8th Jaeger

Division was committed on the eastern edge of the city and the 8th PD, whose commander, Generalmajor Hax, commanded the XXIV Panzer Corps until the arrival of General der Artillerie Hartmann, on the west of Bruenn.

General Hartmann took it upon his own decision to evacuate Bruenn on 26/4 to prevent the destruction of the defenders in Bruenn. GFM Schoerner, who visited Hartmann a little while later, approved the decision of the artillery general, who had his arm and leg amputated.

The end came quickly. In the north of the 1st Panzer Army front the 16th PD fought south of Troppau on 23/4 in loose contact with the 1st Ski Jaeger Division, the 4th Mountain Division and the FBD in the Troppau – Wigstadl area. The Red Army began an attack on 25/4 east of the Oder and they captured Maehrisch-Ostrau on 30/4. Therefore, the Maehrisch-Ostrau industrial region was finally in Soviet hands.

It was clear to the army command that the main mission now had to be the security of the refugee routes and their own troops. Mindful of the fact that the 17th Army was still deployed far to the east in Silesia, they did not allow all elements to withdraw to the west. Only the XXXXIX Mountain Corps, which was still fighting in the Beskids, had to immediately set out to the west, if they were not to be encircled. The XXX Panzer Corps (minus tanks), as the right flank of the 17th Army and an important link with the 1st Army, which with its few forces held the eastern edge of the foothills of the Altvatergebirge and faced complete encirclement by a double envelopment, shifted its HKL by withdrawing its right flank to Klein-Mohrau and the main body into the prepared Altvater Positions.

Near Maehrisch-Schoenberg the Red Army's lead attacking armored elements were repulsed by the XXXX Panzer Corps. The important road hub of Olmuetz was held by Generalmajor Hax and his 8th PD as well as local troops until the XXXXIX Mountain Corps under General le Suire was able to fight its way to the west. The forward-most elements of the "Branbenburg" Division, which were loaded up in Dresden on 1/5 and transported through Glatz, were also fighting near Olmuetz. Olmuetz was held until 8/5/1945. Generalmajor Hax was one of the last German soldiers to leave this city, which was under heavy artillery fire, on 8/5/1945 in his side car.

On 8/5/1945 the 1st Panzer Army stood in a wide arc from the area north of Bruenn to the Altvatergebirge, still protecting the long southern flank and the rear of middle Silesia.

From the Headquarters of Army Group Center

Army Group Center stood with the 1st Panzer Army on the right flank to its neighbor Army Group South out of the area north of Bruenn through Possnitz – Olmuetz to the Altvatergebirge. There closed the 17th Army, whose front ran from Altvatergebirge to the north through Zuckmantel, crossing the Neisse between Neisse and Ottimachau, through Strehlen to Zobten, which was still in German hands. North of the cities of Striegau and Lauban up to Goerlitz closed the 4th Panzer Army, which stood with its front to the north through Bautzen and the area north of Dresden into the Erzgebirge, west of Dresden. Since the loss of Strehlen on 25/3/1945, the 17th Army was no longer being attacked. If the main effort of the Soviet attack had lain on both flanks of Army Group Center, then the 17th Army in the center as the Silesian screen was threatened by the enemy, because they occupied the mountain passes. Therefore, they were able to screen the German refugees on their trek to the west almost until the end of the war.

Breslau under two commandants, Generalmajor von Ahlfen and General der Infanterie Niehoff, had tied up the entire Soviet 6th Army.

In order to save as many troops as possible it was necessary to hold several positions for as long as possible. In order to clarify this Generalmajor von Natzmer was flown to Reichsregierung Doenitz in Flensburg – Muerwik. He made the request that a cease-fire not be made until the majority of Army Group Center was able to get as far to the west as possible, so that they would not be captured by the Red Army, but by the troops of the Western Powers. Natzmer anticipated that this would be accomplished on 18/5. He was promised that they would not surrender before that date.

Therefore, the news that surrender was immanent hit Army Group Center like a bomb on 7/5. Now they could no longer anticipate getting all of their soldiers to the west. Whether or not a lengthening of the war would have saved the troops of Army Group Center depended on if the Red Army would have gotten into their rear at a later point in time, because after the surrender of Berlin on 2/5 they attacked to the south and were able to block the army groups withdrawal route.

The army group leadership did all they could. During the night of 6/5, when General von Natzmer returned from Flensburg – Muerwik, the troops were ordered to evacuate their positions during the night of 8/5 and to march through Freiburg – Salzbrunn toward Trautenau.

The withdrawal succeeded. Then Soviet tanks rolled out of many assembly areas, followed by infantry. They were again repulsed by assault guns, which were placed in suitable positions as rear guards. Approximately 15 enemy tanks were left burning.

Many groups were able to breakthrough to the US troops. The majority of the army group, however, fell into the hands of the Soviets. Generalmajor Richard Schmidt remained in Czech captivity for some time. General der Infanterie Toussaint, the last commandant of Prague, and Generalleutnant Hitzegrad likewise. They were not freed until 1961.

The fighting in Silesia was over. Over three million Silesians had to leave their homeland. The majority of the 400,000 soldiers in Army Group Center fell into the hands of the Soviets.

11

FORTRESS BRESLAU

77 Days: The Struggle, Grief and Death of a City

The Russian winter offensive, which broke loose on 12/1/1945, was already played out before. Indeed the Chief of Staff of Army Group A (later re-designated as Army Group Center), Generalleutnant von Xylander, had played it out with the army commanders, the corps commanders and the staff officers. This occurred in December 1944.

The Russian attack was played out as it actually happened.

The result of this war game was that the Soviets had crossed the Silesian border on the 6th day of their offensive.

The main reason for this was because Army Group A had to send so many divisions into the Hungarian combat area that they were reduced by half.

This was one of the greatest tragedies of the Russian winter offensive, and it occurred before it did.

The planned preventive measures, including Operation "Schlittenfahrt" (which considered the timely transfer of the 6th SS Panzer Army with its almost completely equipped panzer divisions from the west to the east) were rejected by Hitler.

The feared Russian offensive began on 12 January 1945 with 210 infantry divisions, 22 tank corps, 3 cavalry corps and 27 independent tank brigades.

The entire German force consisted on no more that 100 exhausted divisions.

The 1st Ukrainian Front under Marshal Konev attacked in the direction of Katowitz – Oppeln south of Breslau with its 53 infantry divisions, seven tank corps, one cavalry corps and four tank brigades.

Elements of the 1st Belorussian Front under Marshal Zhukov turned from Lodz toward a point north of Breslau.

Other elements of this army group had Glogau and Posen as objectives.

The attack began on 12/1/1945 at 0300 hours. First a "creeping barrage" was fired. At 1030 hours an eight hour barrage fire began. Then the tanks rolled forward in two flood waves, flanked by heavy assault guns. Behind these formations came the infantry, organized in three waves [echelons].

By nightfall the Soviets lost 200 T 34's and Stalin tanks, however, they also achieved a 15 – 20 kilometer deep penetration. This was more than they had dreamed of.

On 13/1 the OKW Wehrmacht report declared:

"We in the Reich capital trust that the development of the situation will play no important role in the surprise of the moment."

Two days later the entire Army Group Center front was deeply torn. Above all, Marshal Konev's mobile formations had advanced up to 115 kilometers during the next twenty-four hours. They had passed Chestochow. Oppeln and Breslau were in danger of being overrun.

In the north the troops of the 2nd Belorussian Front under Marshal Rokossovskiy attacked through to Frische Haff and sealed the fate of East Prussia. However, we will follow Marshal Konev further as he passed through Wielun with his right flank on 19/1. His left flank had already reached Krakau. The German border was crossed by his 3rd Guards Tank

Army under Colonel General Lelyushenko near Kreuzberg – Rosenberg – Guttentag. On 21/1 the Russian tanks stood near Gross Stehlitz severing the Breslau – Kattowitz road here. The 10th Panzergrenadier Division, which had defended with the courage of the desperate, was destroyed. Generalleutnant Schmidt was captured. On 23/1 the Red tanks stood near Oppeln, the capital of Upper Silesia. Here they reconnoitered their crossing possibilities over the Oder. On 24/1 they built on their success in front of the gates of Breslau and the Wehrmacht report noted on 24/1/1945:

> "In the combat area east of Breslau decisive counterattacks by our formations have thrown the Bolsheviks out of several villages."

For the first time, therefore, Breslau stood in the spotlight and would remain there until the last Wehrmacht report on 9 May 1945. On the next day enemy battle groups approached Breslau. They were stopped east of the city. What was happening in Breslau?

In the summer of 1944 Breslau was declared a fortress. However, is first fortress commandant, Generalmajor Krause, did not arrive until 25/9/1944. He found that the only troops directly subordinate to him were a local battalion and the 599th Landesschuetzen Battalion. Six fortress batteries and one each fortress communications and engineer company followed.

In spite of intensive work he was unable to organize these into a suitable fortress defense by the end of January 1945, when the enemy began knocking on the door of the fortress.

According to the commander of the "Eastern Fortresses", Generaloberst Strauss, in Frankfurt/Oder, five divisions had to be made available for Breslau. Three to the east, two to the west of the fortress. The main positions had to lie to the east of the Oder, in fact they had to be 25 kilometers distant from the Breslau Oder bridges. These positions were to be utilized only for combat in the foreground. There were not enough forces available to occupy this 120 kilometer long position in its entirety.

Reichsverteidigungskommissar Hanke, the Gauleiter of Silesia, also interfered in this hubbub.

General Krause requested that the more than one million residents of the city be evacuated during the winter. He suggested to Gauleiter Hanke that 200,000 women, elderly and children be transported by rail as early as possible. Otherwise, if Breslau became a fortress, it would death for the civilians. Gauleiter Hanke turned down this request.

Defensive Combat Before the City

On 19 January, when the Soviet tank armies were already approaching Breslau, the order for evacuation was given.

One could read attached to the walls of houses:

"Each house will be a fortress!"

With the beginning of the evacuation many clerics left the city and when the pastor of St. Elisabeth, Dr. Joachim Konrad, who remained behind, visited the Konsistorium on 23/1, the hausmeister told him that the church leadership had left for Goerlitz. Even Bishop D. Zaenker had already left Breslau.

On 17/1/1945 all of the Breslau replacement troops were alerted and formed into four fortress regiments.

A fifth regiment, the so-called "Regiment Mohr", was not formed until February. The fact that Breslau was not overrun in the first attack was thanks to the 269th ID, which fought under the command of Generalleutnant Wagner from 21 to 28/1 on either side of the Gross Wartenberg – Oels – Breslau road.

This division was the first buffer. With panzerfaeusten and hand-grenades, with plate mines and concentrated explosives the grenadiers attacked the Russian armored colossi. Panzerfaust rounds destroyed 76 enemy tanks within three days. The tempo of the Soviet lead steel elements slowed and gave Breslau a last chance to catch its breath of almost a week. The grenadiers of this division made this possible.

North of Breslau, the Russian tanks reached Maerzdorf on 26/1. Indeed, the bridge across the Oder here was blown, however, the thick ice held the heaviest Russian tanks.

On 29/1 the Soviets established a bridgehead south of Breslau near Peiskerwitz.

on 26/1 General Krause launched a counterattack to the north. Twelve tanks were subordinated to the four companies of Luftwaffen fahnenjunkers. Under the leadership of General Schulz this formation attacked and were able to throw the Russians back across the Oder.

During the night before 29/1 the 269th ID was finally transferred to the south in vehicles from Breslau, including busses. On 29/1 they arrived near Ohlau and also threw the enemy back across the river here. Near Trechen, closer to Breslau, Hauptmann Seiffert conducted a counterattack with a company from the SS Administrative Leadership School. This battle group brought its own doctor with it, a female who treated the wounded and operated under difficult conditions on the front line.

She was the first woman of Breslau to receive the Iron Cross II on 30/1/1945.

On 31/1 the 269th ID fought in the Ohlau area, where the Russians held a bridgehead. In this area, Generalleutnant Wagner felt obliged to request Feldmarschall von Kleist, who was retired to the Fuehrer Reserve in April 1944 and was living on his farm in Weidebrueck, to evacuate. The son of the Feldmarschall, who was home for convalescent leave, took command of a home guard battalion. (Generalfeldmarschall von Kleist was turned over from English captivity in 1946 to Yugoslavia, from there in 1948 to Soviet captivity. He died in 1954 in Camp Vladimir.)

By 23/1 over 100 light field howitzers were received in Fortress Breslau from the Borsigwerk in Markstaedt. The rest were destroyed shortly before the Soviets entered.

On 31/1 General Krause became very ill. Generaloberst Schoerner, commander of Army Group Center, appointed Generalmajor von Ahlfen as his successor.

In all, 40 Oder or Oder Canal bridges were prepared for demolition when Generalmajor von Ahlfen took command in the fortress. In order to coordinate the many individual engineer units Major Hameister was flown into the fortress from the Army Personnel Bureau. At the beginning of February two "Goliath" Platoons were transported by rail from the Koenigsbrueck Troop Training Area. Each of these platoons had 48 "Goliaths" (tracked vehicles, like small tanks, that could be remotely controlled to their objectives over any terrain with 75 kilograms of explosives.)

The 609th ID was formed by General Ruff. SA Obergruppenfuehrer Herzog took over organizing and leading the Volkssturm.

At the beginning of February there were still 200,000 people in the city, in civilian status.

During the night before 3/2 an engineer platoon arrived with flame-throwers, led by Hauptmann Seiffert and Oberfeldwebel Schultze, to attack enemy occupied Wasserborn.

Hauptmann Seiffert was unwilling to attack with two companies of combat inexperienced men.

However, he assaulted with the engineers, all combat experienced soldiers. Flames streamed out of the flame-throwers. Machine-guns hammered. The Soviets ran out of their shelters burning, throwing themselves into the snow. Hand-grenades and explosives went into action. The Russian strong point fell. Oberfeldwebel Schultze also fell.

The Russians still occupied a bridgehead near Peiskerwitz. Here, on 8/2, the Besslein Waffen SS Regiment attacked under SS Obersturmbannfuehrer Georg-Robert Besslein. This 1st SS Fortress Regiment – "the best regiment in the city", according to General Niehoff – attacked in the early morning hours. The men of the 1st Company under SS Obersturmfuehrer Franz Budka assaulted the initial enemy corner position. SS Unterschar- fuehrer Krause rolled over one sector of trenches and captured 70 Soviets. The enemy bridgehead was "erased."

On the following day Liegnitz fell. A German relief attack from the west stalled.

Another division, the 17th ID under Generalmajor Sachsenheimer, had also done much for the fortress. This division, led by one of the best soldiers, had fought its way through in heavy combat from the Vistula near Pulawy up to the Oder. Here they fought bitterly for two weeks in the Maltsch – Neumark area, in order to stop the enemy and, thereby, delay the encirclement of Breslau from the west. During the night before 14/2, after giving up several troops with heavy weapons to the fortress, the division undertook a breakout to the south.

The breakout succeeded, however, twenty-four hours later, on 15/2, Breslau was completely encircled. An enemy division advanced from the west toward Deutsch Lissa. Another enemy division advanced out of the Kanth region; a group of four divisions tried to capture Breslau from the south.

The fighting around the fortress entered its decisive phase. The Russians were attacking from the south. Soon a bitter street battle was raging in the southern suburbs of the fortress. The defenders fought desperately to defeat the penetrating Soviets. Flame-throwers, mines and bombs were ignited. Enormous clouds of smoke and dust rose into the air from the housing blocks occupied by the enemy. The Besslein Regiment fought from floor to floor and from house to house in Deutsch Lissa. The battle raged in hand-to-hand combat.

The fighting spread meter by meter into the city, which was, until then, under constant enemy artillery fire and air bombardment.

Hitler Youth and Volkssturm constructed barricades and anti-tank obstacles. Entire quarters were blown into the air by engineers working during the night, in order to create fields of fire and destroy the penetrating enemy.

On 13/2 the Wehrmacht reported:

"In Lower Silesia our formations launched counterattacks to frustrate the latest attempt by the Bolsheviks to isolate Fortress Breslau from its rear area communications. The enemy lost 60 tanks in a narrow area southwest of the city."

On 18/2 they reported:

"The enemy forces attacking against the southern and southwestern front of Breslau were repulsed in fierce fighting."

We allow Leutnant Leo Hartmann from the 311 Assault Gun Brigade – The Loewen Brigade – his say:

(The remnants of this assault gun brigade were given up to the fortress by the 17th ID.)

"We did not feel like we were in a besieged city. Even the street cars were running. The Russians tested their searchlights in the night sky. I went to the panzer company of the Breslau Panzerjaeger Battalion. The company commander was Oberleutnant Ventzke. We made plans for an attack."

The defenders were able to ferret out 100 tubes with 6000 rounds from the depots. This would serve well against the enemy armored attacks. On 14/2 the last evacuation was conducted. In all there were still 80,000 civilians left in the city.

The fortress command established itself in the cellars of the Liebichshoehe.

In the early morning hours of 18/2 Leutnant Kohne committed his first Goliaths against the bridge the Russians threw up on Reichsstrasse 5 in the Besslein sector on the Weistritz line. Three Goliaths rode one behind the other at 0600 hours. The Besslein artillery fired background and before the Soviets realized what was happening the first explosive tank stood in the middle of the double bridge stretch, the second stood right over a column and the third was located on the initial stretch of bridge.

Leutnant Kohne detonated all three simultaneously. The thundering crack sent thick clouds of smoke spiraling, and when they cleared the two stretches of bridge and one column lay destroyed in the Weistritz.

By 20/2 the Russians had approached to within two kilometers of the inner city from the south. They penetrated into the street car depot and were blown into the air by Goliaths. The southern portion of the suburb was now a pile of ashes. Several Soviet anti-tank gun batteries fired directly into the nests of resistance. Incendiary shells set entire blocks of houses on fire. The heat was unbearable. The Kuerassier Kaserne had to be given up.

On the late afternoon of 20/2 the 55th Volkssturm Battalion, under the leadership of Hauptmann Seiffert, attacked the Russians that had penetrated into the southern park. The Hitler Youth in this battalion fought like fiends. Over a hundred of the youths were killed or were wounded. The rest pushed the enemy back.

As Russian tanks rolled by the dozen toward the town of Neukirch the men from the Hanf Regiment fired at them with panzerfaeusten from the churchyard wall. The exhaust flames propelled the warheads, which bored through the steel and ignited the tanks. Russian heavy anti-tank guns were brought up on the two town roads. They were also forced from the roads by the panzerfaust rounds.

From 20/2 on Gauleiter Hanke attended the daily situation briefings at the fortress commandant's. He proposed flying in fallschirmjaegers. What he had in mind was a second Monte Cassino. On the other hand, the fallschirmjaegers could open up a breakout corridor to the south.

Thus, on 25/2 the I/Fallschirmjaeger Regiment 26 under Hauptmann Trotz was flown in. The II Special Purpose Fallschirmjaeger Regiment under Hauptmann Skau was also flown into the fortress on 5/3.

Naturally this was too little. Also, these important battalions were needed elsewhere.

Between the houses, on the open squares, in the installations along the Oder stood the fortress artillery, which threw its shells at the probing attackers. The enemy tried to capture the Gandau airfield and, therefore, the last supply point. When it finally fell, it was blown into the air. Kaiserstrasse was widened into a temporary rollbahn in the Kaiserbruecke – Scheitniger Stern sector. Bombing attacks lay more and more houses in ruins. Volkssturm, Hitler Youth and regular troops defended each meter of ground. Breslau resembled a Breughelian scene from Hell. On 26/2 the Wehrmacht reported:

"The defenders of Breslau and Glogau are defending in bitter street fighting so that the enemy is promised very little success."

General Niehoff Arrives!

On the evening of 5 March 1945 Generalleutnant Niehoff was flown into the Breslau Fortress. During a night flight to the city he saw the many fires and the smoking ruins, he also saw the front line under the Russian barrage fire. General Niehoff, General der Infanterie from 1/4/1945, who until then was fighting with his troops in the Ratibor area, was assigned this new posting at the suggestion of Generalfeldmarschall Schoerner. He had promised Niehoff:

> "If you can hold Breslau for three to four days, then Schoerner will open a corridor to you and meet you." (See Niehoff: "Thus Fought Breslau.")

Therefore, one anticipated that the attack groups established 50 kilometers south of Breslau were to break into the fortress ring from the outside.

By 7/3 the southern front of Breslau ran on a line of houses from Hancke Hospital – Steinstrasse – Heiliggeistkirche – St. Bernhardin Cemetery – Ohle – Niederung – Pircham. The soldiers were able to barricade themselves into the ruins here. In this street fighting the men of the Mohr Regiment shot-up 100 heavy Russian anti-tank guns within 14 days. This was also the working grounds of the panzerjaegers, Leutnant Leo Hartmann was committed here. He reported:

> "In the south, on the corner of Steinstrasse – Gallestrasse, in the 609th ID area of operations, we shot-up several anti-tank guns. When my own gun tore a track while crossing a trench, Major Schulz ran from a cellar through a wall of smoke to help us. Then we rolled on and shot-up the anti-tank gun, which was located between Cretiusstrasse and Helmutstrasse."

The men advanced against the penetrating Soviets in close combat. Faehnleinfuehrer Nordberg was one of the bold ones who formed an assault troop near Hancke Hospital. They suddenly faced a Russian assault troop and opened fire. When the Faehnleinfuehrer advanced with his plate mine, he was shot in the stomach and flew into the air with the fused mine. The mine exploded and the Russians were buried under a collapsed roof.

In the meantime, the enemy artillery hammered the city. Heavy shells bored through the roofs and walls before they exploded deep in the cellars – they were set with delayed fuses.

There, where the SS regiment was committed, banners greeted the Russians:

"Here fights the Besslein SS Regiment!"

Franz Budka and his Waffen SS company were committed in the ruins of Augustastrasse. The men sat under the burning buildings, they were shot-out of the Landesversicherungsanstalt buildings. The survivors fought with uncovered heads in heat reaching 50 degrees and higher. They constructed their hand-grenade catapults, as did the youths from the so-called "Hitler Youth Corner."

Traps were constructed in the cellars from explosives, oxygen and acetylene gas. As soon as the enemy entered these cellars the defenders would withdraw and blow them into the air.

Breslau was turned into a hell for the Soviets

"When we entered we were to cut the throats of all of the damned Germans", said the Russian soldier Gregory Olgonov. "And before that there were the women..."

The entire city was a burning torch. In spite of the winter weather the temperatures were as high as they had reached during mid-summer the previous year. Here fought fourteen year-olds next to their sixty year-old grandfathers.

The lines of wounded continued to flow into the hospitals and first aid stations. Oberfeldaerzt Dr. Mehling, who later died in Russian captivity, had to assign each surgeon and each assistant. In the three high bunkers on

Scheitniger Stern, in the Odertor railroad station and on Striegauer Platz the surgeons were fighting for every life. The severely wounded received their first treatment in the four deep bunkers and the ten hospitals and first aid stations. The Oberstabaerzte Dr. Hohsang, Dr. Joachim, Dr. Janschky and St. Steinbrink, the Stabsaerzte Dr. Gaida, Dr. Haag, Dr. Weil and Dr. Weiser experienced the horror day and night.

Under the leadership of Feldunteraerzt Dr. Greve 6000 wounded were flown out. It was a hell of a job to land and load the Ju 52's during the night under fire. During this loading fell the nameless soldiers who worked under an unknown Sanitaets- oberfeldwebel to save as many wounded soldiers as possible.

The Russian attacks in the south of the city died out. The Wehrmacht report from 25/3 was short and to the point:

> "The defenders of the fortresses of Glogau and Breslau again repulsed new enemy attacks."

On 26/3 the Soviets attacked again with strong armored forces. Again it came to a do or die battle. Again the assault guns and tanks from the "Breslau" Panzerjaeger Battalion were successful, as were the many panzerfaust operators. 64 tanks were destroyed.

From now on the attacks were more fierce and conducted with stronger forces. When the Russians tried to drive a wedge through the city, advancing along the western bank of the Oder, the German assault guns – at first only the guns of Hartmann and Unteroffizier Maier – rolled in the direction of the harbor. Maier and Hartmann each shot-up one of the heavy enemy assault guns. When a Volkswagen Kuebel rolled up with food for them, Leutnant Hartmann told the driver:

> "Go back. We are not hungry! It's ammunition we need!"

A third gun finally arrived bringing the needed ammunition. During the evening Oberleutnant Ventzke also showed up with a fourth gun. These four guns put the brakes to all breakthrough attempts and shot-up several enemy anti-tank guns. Shortly after Leutnant Hartmann promoted Unteroffizier Maier to Feldwebel, the gun of his comrade received a direct hit. Feldwebel Maier received several fragments in his lungs and died an hour later, in the hospital bunker at Odertor.

At this time, the suicide rate among the civilians rose. The sick and old vegetated in the cellars and bunkers. The attacks against the city now continued without pause. Fierce fighting occurred in the 75 kilometer long underground canal network. Russian attacks drowned in the drains. The German defenders were saved by flooding the lines.

The Russians attacked further on 27 April 1945. However, the core of the city still held out. Here fought men, old men and children. Here they were shot, fled and died.

On 28/4/1945 the Wehrmacht reported:

"The Soviet troops achieved additional deep penetrations into Breslau."

However, on 1/5/1945 they reported:

"The glorious defenders of Breslau continue to repulse all attacks by the Bolsheviks."

On the morning of 2 May General Niehoff spoke for the last time on the telephone with Feldmarschall Schoerner, who had promised him exactly two months before that he would come to help him within three days.

General Niehoff reported the fulfillment of his mission and his intent to surrender the fortress of Breslau in view of the untenable situation. Schoerner refused at first and demanded that he continue to hold out. However, he finally approved Niehoff's decision.

On 4 May a deputation of high church members visited General Niehoff to plead for surrender. They included: Weihbischof Ferche, Kanonikus Kramer, Pfarrer Hornig and Pfarrer Dr. Konrad.

The last visitor to General Niehoff during these fateful days was Gauleiter Hanke. When he was unable to convince the General to refrain from surrendering after exerting heavy pressure, the Gauleiter left the fortress in a Fieseler Storch. This aircraft was supposed to be used to fly the General and his operational headquarters out of the fortress.

General Niehoff decided to share the fate of his soldiers; and indeed he did, until the bitter end.

While it was still dark on 5 May, General Niehoff assembled his commanders for the last time and informed them of his intent to cease fighting. He issued his final orders to his commanders with a heavy heart. After he had finished, in a spontaneous outpouring of emotion they extended their hands to him and thanked him for making this difficult decision, which would put an end to the fiercest fighting in the Second World War: the sacrifice of a small element at a lost outpost, which had held out for 77 days in the face of an enormously superior force.

The Shocking End

On 6 May 1945 General der Infanterie Niehoff made his way through the mine-fields of the combat front to Colonel General Glusdovski, the commander of the 6th Soviet Army, which had besieged the city.

He proposed to him his desire to surrender and Colonel General Glusdovski proposed the following stipulations:

1. All of the troops under your command will cease combat activity on 6/5 at 1400 hours, Moscow time.

2. You will turn over all personnel, weapons, all combat equipment, means of transport and technical equipment undamaged.

3. We guarantee you that all officers and soldiers who stop resisting their lives, food and personal property and their return to their homeland after the end of the war. The entire officer corps can keep their blank weapons.

4. All wounded and sick will immediately receive medical help from our medical service.

5. The entire civilian population will be protected and guaranteed normal living conditions.

6. You personally and other generals will be allowed the use of personal vehicles in captivity.

The Commander of the 6th Russian Army
The Chief of Staff
signed Glusdovski,

General
signed Panov, MG
on 6/5/1945

General Niehoff regretted not inserting a special sentence for the security of his soldiers and Waffen SS. This sentence would have read as follows:

"I have to add to the conditions of the surrender of the fortress that the guarantees extended to me be extended to the officers and units of the Waffen SS, who participated in this defense."

During the night before 7/5/1945 the Russians entered the ruins, which they could not conquer for 77 days after they had encircled it.

Strauss waltzes blared from tanks. Then, in contrast to the stipulations of the surrender, the city was turned over to plunder. Burnings, rapes and murders started and lasted for an entire week.

They set the Barbara Church on fire during the night of 11 May and the Maria Magdalena Church on 17/5 and allowed them to burn to the ground.

The brave German defenders, however, were carted off to captivity. Many of them would never see their homeland again, including

Generalmajor Ruff, the commander of the 609th ID, who was hanged in Russia for alleged crimes perpetrated in Riga.

And so General Niehoff also remained in captivity for ten and a half years.

What was left of the 311th Assault Gun Brigade drove through Frankfurter Strasse on 7/5, past the destroyed Stalin tanks, into several years of captivity.

The wonder of Breslau was that this city with its few troops was able to withstand an entire army for so long.

Breslau fought this fight with a constant ammunition shortage and with 40,000 poorly equipped soldiers, Hitler Youth and Volkssturm men. They faced a fully equipped army with the strength of 150,000 men.

The losses in killed and wounded for the soldiers in the fortress and the 80,000 residents totaled 29,000 people; including 6000 dead.

The Red Army issued a final report on the fighting near Breslau that indicated 60,000 men were lost, killed and wounded, in the fighting around this city. A soldiers' cemetery was established by the Russians south of Breslau, there are 5000 Russian officers buried there.

A great enemy force was tied up in and around Breslau by this tenacity. The defenders of this city screened a great number of refugees on their flight to the west.

Oberst Tiesler, General Niehoff's deputy, also was captured. "Pappa Tiesler" died in winter of 1952 in the Urals. Oberstleutnant Mohr was the only one to follow the casket , as it was taken out of the camp on a panje wagon.

On 9/5 the last Wehrmacht report noted:

"The defenders of Breslau, who had withstood the attacks of the Soviets for two months, succumbed to the enemy superiority at the last moment."

12

THE SILESIAN CIVILIANS DURING THE COMBAT OPERATIONS

Summary

After the Soviet divisions resumed their attack to the west into Lower Silesia on 8/2/1945, they had also crossed the Oder at the same time north of Glogau, attacking out of the Steinau bridgehead, and reached the Goerlitzer Neisse after suffering heavy losses. Liegnitz fell into Russian hands on 10/2, Glogau was encircled on 12/2.

At the same time, therefore, a pincer operation was also begun on 8/2 by the Red Army from their Steinau and Brieg bridgeheads. This led – as already described – to the encirclement of Breslau. Jauer, Striegau and Schweidnitz were also conquered by the Russians in mid-February.

During the first and second halves of March, then, the Neisse near Gorlitz and finally the portion of Upper Silesia west of the Oder was almost completely occupied.

This Red Army operation corresponded to the flight of the Silesians in two main directions. Either to the west in the direction of Saxony, or to the south to Bohemia and Moravia.

In the German occupied regions east of the Oder and Neisse, combat operations almost ended at the end of March. The flight of the population from this region was in full swing.

For the people left in Liegnitz after 8/2/1945 there was no longer any time that they were not threatened with life and limb. Frau Selma Birke reports:

"On the early morning of 8/2/1945 we were woken by barrage fire. The last residents left their houses with handcarts. My daughter and I were the only ones to remain behind.

At midday there was a deep air attack, which resulted in killed and wounded. In the afternoon two or three other attacks followed and I went to the basement of our butcher, he had an air raid shelter that had room for about 30 people. We spent three days and four nights there.

On the morning of 9/2 the street fighting began in Liegnitz. In the late afternoon we suddenly heard shouts of triumph in a foreign language and we knew: the Russians were on our street.

A Ukrainian girl confirmed this and told us that we did not have anything to worry about. We and she would soon learn otherwise.

On 10/2 the cellar steps were lowered. Approximately 20 to 25 Russian soldiers and officers descended into the cellar and illuminated it with table lamps. They wanted watches and women. The first was my daughter; however, the chap that had pulled her from out of the corner saw a rosy-cheeked frau and he shoved my daughter aside.

And so the Russian thugs continued to look for watches, other valuables, women, young girls and even children.

On the morning of 12/2 the Ukrainian girl named Vera was taken by the soldiers to act as an interpreter. When she tried to protect herself from her masters, she was raped and violated. One father tried to insert himself in front of his two daughters. The Russians took him and two other men away. They never returned.

Day and night the Russians came down the stairs to the cellar. On the evening of 12/3/1945 three Russian soldiers appeared and told us that we had to pack and move out to the street. We remained next to our handcarts and, since no one returned to tell us what to do next, we spent the night sitting in the parlour. In the morning the Russians returned and were angry because we did not follow orders. We had to pack again.

Our objective was Langenwaldau, only six kilometers away. We arrived there in the evening of 19/3/1945 and were taken to a nearby farm. On the next day we learned that 28,000 people were being sheltered in this small town: in horse and pig stalls and in cattle stalls."

Frau Hedwig Rosemann from Breslau reported:

"We were Breslauers and had to leave our hometown on 22/1/1945 within two hours. We fled to Loewenberg to our parents.

On 13/2 we were ordered to leave Loewenberg and flee. The Russians were in the neighborhood. The roads were so jammed that we did not get very far.

We sought shelter in a stone cellar, we spent the entire night there. On the next morning at 0700 hours there was a pounding on the door of the house. The Russians were here. The wildmen rushed down the stairs.

The first screams of the women were heard. The women were thrown to the floor and raped."

Frau Frieda Schneider reported:

"The first troops were a few tanks that drove through the city. Behind them came the foot troops with long poles that they poked through all of the windows that they could reach. Then came others to rob watches and so forth and to plunder. The next to come fell all over the women, whether they be young or old! Taking up the rear were Polish workers, who had been in the city before. They burned the houses of the Party members.

We remained in the cellar for ten days. Here Frau Josef bore her son on 18/2/1945. Even she was not spared the raping, in spite of the fact that there was a little infant laying next to his mother.

No woman was spared. The Russians soon arrived in vehicles from nearby fronts to be serviced. And they were, day and night until 0300 hours in the morning."

Terror Without End

On 8/2/1945, when the Russians broke into Kanth near Breslau, there were also scenes of horror played out here. Frau G.F. from Kanth reported:

"At first the devils came during the night, Cossacks, Mongolians, Asiatics, most of them drunk. They trashed the houses. They brayed like beasts and achieved their manhood in Kanth, only 25 kilometers from the fortress of Breslau.

We had to suffer in this hell for three months. Laundry was smeared with filth and thrown from windows. We women were raped both day and night.

During the first night before 9/2/1945 I was raped by twelve of these beasts. I wanted to hang them, but I never got the chance, because there were always Russians in the house.

They murdered numerous people. On the second day they murdered our pastor, Dr. A. Moepert in his residence, because he tried to protect seven nuns from the rapings. They shot him in the back of the head with a machine-pistol. Women, who jumped out of window to escape these beasts, were shot from behind.

During one of the following nights the building burned down and we had to move from town to town. One night, it was, I believe, the end of February 1945, three women, including myself, were taken to a hospital. There were lightly wounded laying in about 15 beds. There I and Frau K. and Frau S. were thrown from bed to bed for these beasts. There we were raped by one bandit after the next and then thrown down the stairs. I could no longer speak or think. During the night I took 10 Quadronox pills, however, I regained consciousness again after three days. We were desperate. Fraeulein Maria Kuegler from Kanth had been raped so many times that she was all torn up in front and back."

In Namslau and Thiemendorf, in Lassen and Jeschen near Brieg, in Deutmannsdorf and Bossen near Bunzlau, in Freystadt and Ludwigsdorf and in hundreds and hundreds of villages and cities of Silesia the civilian population suffered this same fate. And after the German Wehrmacht surrendered unconditionally it was no different, the German populace was thrown from the regions east of the Oder and Neisse, out of Hungary, Rumania, Czechoslovakia and Yugoslavia.

However, back to the final battle in Germany, to the last days of a struggle that had extracted much sacrifice from all of the soldiers of all of the nations that fought in the war, but also sacrifice that the civilian populations could not avoid.

13

THE BATTLE FOR THE CAPITAL OF THE REICH

"Our Objective is Berlin"

On 1/4/1945 Soviet Marshals Zhukov and Konev arrived at the STAVKA in Moscow and were led into a conference room immediately after reporting to Marshal Stalin. There they met with Foreign Minister Molotov, the Chief of the Secret Police Beria, the Secretary of the Central Committee Malenkov and Member of the Defense Committee Mikoyan. The Deputy Minister of Defense Bulganin arrived shortly thereafter.

When they were all assembled here, Stalin arrived, accompanied by General Antonov, the Chief of the General Staff of the Red Army, and General Shchemenko, the Chief of Operations of the General Staff, with whom he was having a short discussion.

Stalin opened the meeting and declared to the assembled:

> "The little allies" (by this he meant the Western Allies) "intend to get to Berlin before the Red Army."

After that he read a report to General Shchemenko in which it was clear that Eisenhower's operations were supposed to be in support of the

Red Army, however, in actuality, they were directed at conquering Berlin before the Russians.

The fact that the Allied Commander in the West had sent him a telegram expressing the exact opposite was not mentioned by Stalin. He even revived a plan, long ago rejected by the Western Allies, to conquer the Reich capital by two or three airborne divisions, in order to beat the "little allies" to Berlin.

Marshal Konev took the floor first and said what his leader wished to hear: "We will capture Berlin! – Before the English and before the Americans!"

Both Marshals now tried to convince Stalin that they were in a better position to capture Berlin and destroy the hated Hitlerites. However, Stalin still did not make a decision. He ordered both Marshals to remain in Berlin and to work out a plan of attack with the General Staff during the next 48 hours. Each for his own army group.

On this 1/4/1945 Stalin also replied to Eisenhower's telegram and, in closing, referred to Berlin: "The Red Army will begin the attack on Berlin during the second half of May.

Berlin had lost its strategic importance. The city had become unimportant and the Red Army High Command will only commit second echelon troops against Berlin." (See: Ulam, Adam, B.: Stalin, the Man and His Era.)

On the morning of 3/4/1945 Konev and Zhukov proposed their plans for the new offensive and Stalin decided to execute Zhukov's plan. This read:

"Attack the 1st Belorussian Front out of its 44 kilometer wide Oder bridgehead. Six armies in the first echelon, including two tank armies as attack wedges. A total of 681,000 soldiers of the Red Army would conduct this attack on Berlin. 11,000 guns would initiate it with an hour barrage fire. I am convinced that my troops can cover the 100 kilometers from their departure positions to Berlin in one assault."

The 2nd Belorussian Front under the leadership of Marshal Rokossovskiy was to be adjacent to the north to the Baltic Sea coast, however, they would not participate in the attack on Berlin, but – after they had suppressed the resistance in East Prussia – attack through northern Germany to the west, in order to win as much ground to the west as possible. The Marshal had 314,000 soldiers available. In all, 13 armies were available for this final triumph of the Red Army, which would climax with the capture of Berlin.

The Assault on Berlin

On the early morning of 16/4/1945 the Red Army began the assault against Berlin from the Oder front. The 1st Belorussian Front initiated it with a fire-strike of such intensity that had never been experienced before. In all (according to the memoirs of Marshal Zhukov) not 11,000 guns, but 22,000 guns, including 400 rocket launchers, fired against the known German positions of the 9th Army. Russian bombers, combat aircraft and fighter-bombers attacked across the front in thick swarms and bombed everything in the way of the Red armored avalanche.

On the adjacent front line, the 1st Ukrainian Front opened its offensive out of the Gross Gastrose area up to the Sudeten. the main effort was in its large Oder bridgehead near Kuestrin.

The 9th German Army under General der Infanterie Busse, whose headquarters was in Fuerstenwalde, was at the center of the barrage fire. Their positions were plowed up by tens of thousands of shells.

When the Red Army attempted to cross the Oder southeast of Eberswalde, they were thrown back with the last ounces of strength. Even the fortress of Frankfurt an der Oder held out.

The Red Army assault battalions were able to attack through into the area west of Kuestrin and near Wrietzen, reaching the ridge-line west of the Oder Valley. Here the German divisions were pushed back between 3 and 8 kilometers before they were able to again entrench and bring the enemy armored avalanche to a halt.

During the evening hours of 16/4/1945 the German formations fought with their last ounce of strength on the hills west of the Oder. They withdrew only gradually. The enemy armored wedge, which approached the defensive positions of the Division "Muencheberg" HKL, was stopped. The division was well prepared by Generalmajor Werner Mummert, who as Oberst and regimental commander received the Swords to the Knight's Cross with Oak Leaves in October 1944, the defensive weapons were correctly placed. The enemy armor stalled here and they lost a large number of tanks.

On 17/4/1945, however, a wide gap yawned between the training formations of the CI Army Corps and the XI SS Corps, through which penetrated a thick armored wedge to the west. The CI Army Corps had to withdraw.

Generaloberst Heinrici, the commander of Army Group Vistula, released the LVI Panzer Corps under General der Artillerie Helmut Weidling on this decisive day. They were to close the gap in the CI Army Corps area of operations and prevent the enemy from rolling through it unopposed.

General Weidling inserted the 11th SS PGD under Brigadefuehrer Ziegler and the 18th PGD under Oberst Rauch into the front gap near Wrietzen. However, even these combat experienced divisions could no longer stop the enemy armored avalanche.

On 18/4/1945 the front collapsed. The enemy achieved breakthroughs not only in the CI Army Corps area of operations near Wrietzen in the north, but also in the 4th Panzer Army's V Army Corps area of operations in the south. The 9th Army under General der Infanterie Busse was pushed to the side and the main group of the LVI Panzer Corps had to withdraw before the overwhelming enemy in the direction of the Reich capital, if they were not to be outflanked and destroyed.

Generaloberst Heinrici requested Fuehrer Headquarters withdraw the 9th Army, which also lay in exposed positions and were threatened with being outflanked. Hitler refused to approve this withdrawal. He categorically demanded that not only would the 9th Army hold the Oder front, but also close the breakthrough gaps on the Neisse.

Strong Soviet armored groups attacked into the withdrawing troops of the LVI Panzer Corps. On 19/4 the Red Army captured Straussberg and, on the same day, crossed the Spree near Spremberg. The first Soviet long-range batteries opened fire on the Reich capital, which would get heavier and heavier from now on.

On 20/4/1945, Hitler's birthday, the armored troops of the 1st Ukrainian Front already stood deep in the rear of the 9th Army. General Busse received the divisions of the V Army Corps on this day for support and assistance. These were the 33rd and 36th Waffen SS Divisions, the 342nd ID and the 391st Security Division. The XI SS Corps, which was transferred by the 9th Army into the Fuerstenwalde sector to secure this northern flank of the army, had to defend against the 3rd and 69th Soviet Armies.

On 21/4, when the lead attack elements of both Soviet army groups met near Koenigswusterhausen, the entire 9th Army was encircled in the Guben – Huellrose – Koenigswusterhausen – Luebben area.

The army's Oder front between Frankfurt and Guben still held. The Frankfurt/Oder Fortress repulsed every Soviet crossing attempt during the first four days of this final Russian offensive. The 33rd Soviet Army first succeeded in crossing to the western bank of the river on 21/4. The front was withdrawn and the Frankfurt an der Oder Fortress was, therefore, isolated. Oberst Ernst Biehler had only 30,000 men available, which which he defended bitterly and successfully. He was promoted to Generalmajor and received the Knight's Cross on 9 May 1945.

On 23/4 the OKH approved the withdrawal of the 9th Army, however, at this point in time, it was already encircled on all sides and had to defend against the 3rd and 69th Soviet Armies in the east and against the 28th Soviet Army in the south. On 24 April even Oberst Biehler received permission to breakout of the Frankfurt/Oder Fortress. His troops broke out to the west suffering very heavy casualties.

General Busse finally succeeded in removing his army from the Oder front and withdrawing it into the Fuerstenwalde – Beeskow – Luebbenau – Luebben – Halbe to Zossen area.

By 25/4 the Red Army had inserted strong armored forces and motorized formations between Berlin and Zossen. The 9th Army was constantly being compressed into a narrower area by these measures and finally stood in the Luebben – Halbe – Zossen area surrounded by the enemy.

By the evening of 22/4 the Red Army Troops reached the Teltow Canal near Klein Machnow. Russian armored formations were penetrating from the northeast with their lead elements into the Weissensee and Pankow

Bezirkes. North of Spandau other armored formations reached the Havel and crossed it. The suburban settlement of Grossberlin became the defenders new HKL.

Soviet tanks were already firing against the anti-tank obstacles erected in Berliner Norden. The Russians were stopped in the Tegeler See region by a werkschutz battalion that brought hand fire weapons and panzerfaeusten to bear with success.

At midnight on 23/4 the enemy formations were repulsed in front of this position.

Major Komorowski and his Volkssturm battalion, which had an 8.8 cm air defense gun, stood on the western edge of the city near the Gatow airfield. They also repulsed the first enemy attacks.

On the evening of 22/4/1944 Hitler ordered that the former commandant of the city of Berlin, Generalmajor Reymann, be relieved. His successor was Oberst Ernst Kaether for a few hours, who served as the NSFO at Fuehrer Headquarters. However, a few hours after that, Hitler relieved him and decided that the command should go to himself, because he would remain in Berlin.

Because General Weidling had withdrawn without any particular necessity and had not reported to Fuehrer Headquarters for 24 hours, Hitler ordered that Weidling be arrested and shot.

Many had considered that General Weidling, after he stopped the enemy 1st Guards Army, should be named Berlin city commandant. The remnants of his LVI Panzer Corps formed the core of the defense of Berlin along with Waffen SS formations, Hitler Youth battle groups, police and air defense units.

The narrow defensive ring around the Fuehrer Bunker – called the citadel – was subordinated to SS Brigadefuehrer Mohnke. Within the next few hours and days members of the Waffen SS Division "Charlemagne" arrived and were incorporated in the defense. Brigadefuehrer Mohnke was directly subordinate to Adolf Hitler.

The "Muncheberg" Panzer Division of the LVI Panzer Corps was established in Defensive Sectors A and B on the eastern edge of the city.

The 11th SS PGD "Nordland" under Brigadefuehrer Ziegler defended in the southeast in Sector C, while Defensive Sector D, on either side of the Tempelhof airfield was defended by corps troops under the LVI Panzer Corps Artillery Commander, Oberst Woehlermann.

The remnants of the 20th PGD, minus their already lost tanks, stood in the southwest of the city and defended Sector E in the Grunewald area.

Police formations were committed in the center of the city to maintain law and order and to prevent plundering. They had to insure that chaos was prevented.

Spandau and Charlottenburg received a defense group under the designation Defensive Sector F, it was commanded by Oberstleutnant, then Oberst, Anton Eder. Oberst Eder fought with an unheard of tenacity. He was awarded the Knight's Cross on 26/3/1945.

Sectors G and H in the north of the city were assigned to the 9th Fallschirmjaeger Division under Oberst Herrmann and there was another battle group under the leadership of Oberstleutnant Seifert in the center of the city, which was designated as "Defensive Sector Z."

The "Muncheberg" Panzer Division, which had to withdraw during the night before 24/4 out of the suburbs into the southeast of the city in the direction of Tempelhof and who was pursued by strong Russian armored groups, held off the assault of the Russian tanks on the edge of the Grunewald and shot-up a number of them.

The French volunteers from "Charlemagne" fought in the area in and around the Neukoelln rathaus. 300 Hitler Youth helped them. The rathaus was held until 26/4. After a strong Russian tank group bypassed the rathaus toward the city for 900 meters, Hauptsturmfuehrer Fernet had to withdraw. He ran into the company under Hauptsturmfuehrer Rostand at Hermannplatz and held out here with the other company shoulder to shoulder until the evening.

On the evening of 25/4/1945 the Wehrmacht reported:

"During the battle of Berlin every foot of ground is being fought over. The Soviets have penetrated in the south up to the line Babelsberg – Zehlendorf – Neukoelln. Fierce fighting continues in the southern and northern sectors of the city. Enemy lead tank elements reached the area of Nauen and Ketzin to the west of the city. The northern bank of the Stettiner Canal is being held northwest of Oranienburg against heavy attack. The enemy is repeatedly attacking Eberswalde to make a penetration."

On the morning of 26/4 the enemy artillery formations, which had been brought up in the meantime, covered Sectors A and B in the eastern portion of the city with an enormous barrage fire. It hit the 18th PGD and Division "Muencheberg" hard. Nevertheless, the former, which was defending in the passage between Schlachtensee and Krumme Lanke, was able to prevent the Red Army from attacking through the Grunewald.

The 20th PGD under Generalmajor Scholtze fought here shoulder to shoulder with their comrades from the 18th PGD. The enemy finally broke through on the seam between these two formations on the morning of 28/4/1945. Dramatic and, for the 20th PGD, deadly fighting developed in the Potsdam area, the 20th PGD strong point. When the HKL was overran, Generalmajor Scholtze, who was leading at the front with his panzergrenadiers as he had learned to do in the west as the commander of the 901st Panzergrenadier Regiment of the Panzer Lehr Division, committed suicide. He did not want to fall into Russian captivity.

On the evening of this 28/4 General Weidling, who had now regained Hitler's trust, worked out a breakout plan that offered the only chance for success. Moreover, he also prepared the breakout order, which Hitler only had to sign. The men defending the Reich capital were to breakout in three battle groups. Hitler did not approve this plan, even though Weidling unmistakably informed Hitler that Berlin would not survive the next 48 hours. Also, when General Krebs stood up for the plan and requested Hitler make this last decision, he thought for some time and said:

> "If it is time for the end to come, then it will come in the Reichskanzlei. I cannot compromise. I cannot be captured. I will remain in Berlin."

Hitler still hoped that the 12th Army would be able to not only liberate the 9th Army, but also relieve Berlin at the same time. However, what was happening with the 12th Army?

The 12th Army in its Final Commitment

On 22/4/1945 General Wenck, the commander of the 12th Army, received reports that besides the "Clausewitz" PD the "Schlageter" Division, which had attacked out of the Uelzen area through Braunschweig to the south, had also been destroyed near Fallersleben.

On 23/4/1945 at 0100 hours, as the field telephone rang in the 12th Army command post, Walther Wenck picked it up himself. He had just returned from a trip to the front. He took a report from an OKW officer that stated that GFM Wilhelm Keitel was on his way to visit him and would soon arrive at the 12th Army. General Wenck ordered his Chief of Staff, Oberst Reichhelm, to prepare for Keitel's visit.

A little later Keitel's staff car arrived. The GFM got out and greeted them formally, General Wenck and Oberst Reichhelm returned the greeting.

Without any delay GFM Keitel began his briefing with the words: "We must liberate the Fuehrer!"

Then he noted that he had packed his briefcase improperly and requested a situation briefing, which General Wenck, supported by Oberst Reichhelm gave him.

After that GFM Keitel jumped up and declared to the officers and army commander present that the battle of Berlin had already begun and that not only Hitler's fate, but the fate of the Reich was on the line.

"It is your duty to attack and liberate Berlin!", said Keitel and Walther Wenck replied: "The army will attack, Herr Feldmarschall!"

The GFM now developed a plan of attack for the 12th Army out of the Belzig – Treuenbrietzen area toward Berlin. Keitel ordered the 12th Army to advance across the Wittenberg – Niemegk line toward Belzig – Treuenbrietzen and then attack toward Jueterbog from there.

There the 12th Army was to join up with the 9th Army, in order to relieve Berlin and liberate the Fuehrer by a further attack to the north.

Because radio reconnaissance had provided an accurate picture of the desperate situation of the 9th Army, General Wenck knew that nothing more could be expected from this army, on the contrary: this army had to be liberated if it were not to be completely thrown before the dogs. According to the situation map General Wenck could see that no great effort by the 9th Army to attack Berlin could be expected and explained that on the basis of this situation and the forces available only an attack north of the Havel out of the area east of Rathenow, which was still occupied by the Germans, offered any chance for success.

Nevertheless, the deployment of the 12th Army north of the Havel would take two extra days, because the XX Army Corps of the 12th Army first had to march through Genthin to the north. However, the assembly there would make up for the lost time.

"We cannot wait two days!" protested GFM Keitel."The situation in Berlin allows no wasting of time. The army must do everything in its power to execute the assigned order to liberate Berlin." Keitel got up and moved to the exit. He stopped in the doorway and turned again to General Wenck: "I wish you complete success!" he said and left. (See Kurowski, Franz: Armee Wenck: The 12th Army Between the Elbe and Oder.)

Now General Wenck and his Chief of Staff debated what to do. "We knew that it was not militarily feasible to attempt an attack to the east to liberate the 9th Army and save as many refugees as possible. We knew that this had nothing to do with the fate on one person, but the fates of hundreds of thousands." (General Walther Wenck to the author during a conversation.)

"If we were to wait for the possibility of attacking through to Berlin then the army would loose its chance of saving many of the refugees.

It must be realized that during the course of the combat, thousands of refugees would be able to make it from the lost eastern regions, from Silesia, from the Oder and Warthegau, from Pomerania and other places to the west under the protection of our army.

The soldiers saw the pictures of horror suffered by these people after the enemy had occupied their homes. And even if the situation was hopeless they would fight so that these people – the majority being women and children – could make it to the west.

Therein lay the reason for the heroism of the young soldiers from our Fatherland during April and May 1945." (See Wenck, Walther: Short Summary of the Final Battle Between the Oder and Elbe. – In Particular the 12th Army.)

On 23/4/1945 the army conducted a regrouping of the formations located in attack on the Elbe, because on the morning of this day the U.S. air activity over the entire 12th Army combat area had subsided. The "Ulrich von Hutten" Division under the command of Generalleutnant Engel had already turned some elements to the east to secure against surprise Russian armored attacks.

Gerhard Engel had regrouped one of his infantry regiments with subordinate artillery, panzerjaegers and assault guns to attack to the east. On the morning of 24/4, when a radio message arrived from OKW, according to which the 12th Army was to immediately to prepare combat capable elements in division strength to attack to the east, the "Ulrich von Hutten" Division was already disposed in this direction.

On the same day, this division received orders from the army to set in march to the east, leaving only weak security on the Elbe – Mulde front. They were to establish as strong a bridgehead as possible in the Wittenberg area.

We now give Generalleutnant Engel the chance to describe the fighting that immediately followed:

"In the early morning of 25/4 my two regiments, which I had marched to Wittenberg with artillery and assault guns, were already in contact with three Russian rifle divisions east and southeast of the City of Luther. Here was experienced the meeting engagement of two lead elements moving toward each other as it had seldom been during this war. Neither knew of the existence of the other.

In the course of half a day the two regiments threw three committed rifle divisions of the Red Army back 10 kilometers, liberated encircled German formations and established a bridgehead 30 kilometers wide and 15 kilometers deep around Wittenberg. This bridgehead was decisive for all subsequent operations. The army now had the room here for its hasty regrouping for an attack on Berlin. Above all, this large bridgehead was the prerequisite for the withdrawal of hundreds of thousands of soldiers and civilians." (See: Engel, Gerhard: A Record of the Combat of the "Hutten" Infantry Division from 12 April to 7 May 1945.)

The Russian attacks on this bridgehead were repulsed. The attacking groups of tanks, primarily T 34's, were shot up by the assault guns and the air defense guns. During the night before 27/4 the enemy pressure against this division was so strong that they had to break contact here with the enemy, if they were to remain available for future commitment. They were ordered by the army to break contact with the Soviets and move during the night to the assembly area near Belzig.

Gerhard Engel decided on an offensive solution.

Reinforced assault troops with panzerfaeusten, a few assault guns and tanks with mounted panzerfaust operators attacked at first light on 27/4 through the enemy encirclement ring. Enemy tanks were destroyed by the mounted panzerfaust operators. The Russians became nervous. This attack hit them right in the middle of their preparations for their own attack and breakthrough attempt.

The "Hutten" Division broke contact with the enemy and rolled along the Elbe into the deep forests north of Coswig up to Belzig, the assembly area.

The Russians had not been able to fix the encircled division near Wittenberg any longer and then destroy it after they had brought up additional forces.

In the early morning hours of 28/4/1945 General Wenck spoke with the Chief of Staff. On this day he wanted to try to attack in the direction of the 9th Army and simultaneously with Divisions "Schill" and "Hutten" in the direction of Potsdam, in order to make contact with the defenders of the city and Division "Jahn", which were in defensive combat in this area.

"If we can do this, Reichhelm", Wenck declared, "then we can return to the Elbe and surrender our army to the Americans. That is the last mission that we can fulfil."

A little later the XX Army Corps of the 12th Army attacked with Divisions "Schill" and "Hutten." In front of Division "Hutten", echeloned to the left, was Division "Schill." The attack was directed at the Lehnin Forest. The lead attack element of Division "Hutten" was the "Schill" Assault Gun Brigade, which formed the forward attack wedge on the left flank and also provided flank protection to the north.

"Assault guns march!" ordered Major Nebel over the radio. The "Schill" Assault Gun Brigade set in movement. A little later "combat readiness" was ordered. The commanders closed the hatches of their guns, the gunners looked into their visors for upcoming targets. Seconds later the lead attack elements opened fire. Any Russian tank that appeared in the open was shot. No cease fire was ordered here. It was "fire for effect!"

At a small town, in which the enemy had entrenched, Major Nebel ordered them to bypass. The spearhead of Division "Schill" rolled on. Whenever the order "Assault guns to the front!" was given, a few minutes later Russians would appear and be shot-up.

To the right of Division "Schill" advanced Division "Hutten." The attack direction was the Beelitz Sanitarium. From there they were to advance further in the direction of Potsdam.

Divisions "Koerner" and "Scharnhorst", which were committed on the wide right flank of the 12th Army and had survived heavy fighting on 27/4, also quickly advanced.

The armored reconnaissance of Division "Hutten" advanced north of Belzig into unsurveyable forested terrain toward the Russian resistance. The attack, which developed from the move, did not allow the Soviets any time to set up against this division. Thanks to the help of the attached assault guns, the enemy was thrown back to the east. Destroyed enemy scout vehicles indicated to Generalleutnant Engel that his division was still dealing with Russian reconnaissance forces.

The closer the division approached to the large forests southwest of Potsdam the stiffer the enemy's resistance became. Anti-tank guns appeared.

Enemy artillery sought to stop the lead groups with heavy fire. The crisis of the day arose and Generalleutnant Engel was faced with the question of whether to suspend the attack or to continue to advance. He decided on the latter.

At the second Soviet line of resistance northeast of Belzig Division "Hutten" was able to achieve the breakthrough with high-explosive ammunition and air defense tracer salvoes.

The heavy thunder of guns on their right flank indicated to Gerhard Engel that his neighboring division was also in heavy combat.

In the afternoon, however, both divisions succeeded in penetrating into the Lehnin Forest. Division "Hutten" now stood only 15 kilometers from its objective: the Havel crossing south of Potsdam.

For the decisive attack on 29/4, Generalleutnant Engel committed two regiments in the front line. One would be supported by the division assault guns, the other by two panzer platoons. These would be utilized as battering rams on the field and forest trails and to bring the infantry forward.

On the morning of 29/4 "Hutten" set out. The two regiments paved the way in heavy forest fighting. Gradually the enemy resistance had to be broken with empty weapons. Panzerfaust commandos shot-up enemy tanks set up in the forest aisles. The division radio vehicles, which rolled on both flanks, constantly reported on flank security and on the neighboring Division "Schill." In the evening they had already incorporated elements of Corps Group Reymann and were now also engaged in forest combat.

Fighting around the large autobahn interchange southeast of Potsdam flared up. Here the Red Army had already committed type "Josef Stalin 3" tanks, which were equipped with 15.2 cm howitzers.

While Division "Schill" secured the flank, "Hutten" turned against this strong armored enemy force on the autobahn interchange, which was known as the "Leipziger Dreieck." This objective had to be taken if contact was to be made with the encircled 9th Army.

Generalleutnant Engel ordered the experienced assault gun crews to advance.

The assault guns rolled through the bushes on either side of the autobahn and as soon as one of the "Josef Stalin 3's" would fire, the assault gun would fix the enemy in its sights, stand off at a safe distance and fire a shell at the junction between the turret and the lower vehicle. When this area was hit, the enemy tank was destroyed. Six of the super-heavy enemy tanks were destroyed by a handful of assault guns, not one of which were destroyed.

These assault guns decided the battle. They reached the location where they made contact with the 9th Army. Division "Hutten" occupied the Havel crossing and the northern and southern banks of Lake Schwielow and secured the flanks. Generalleutnant Engel committed his right regiment toward Beelitz. There Divisions "Koerner" and "Scharnhorst" were already engaged in bitter fighting. During this attack on 27, 28 and 29/4 Division "Koerner" of the 12th Army covered the eastern flank of the main army attack on Berlin and Potsdam. As often as the Soviets tried to breakthrough on the first day of the attack they were repulsed. This continued on 28/4.

The Malow Regiment, so called for its commander, Major Malow, who fell near Zerbst, advanced as part of Division "Scharnhorst." It had to maintain contact with Division "Hutten" as it advanced next to it. The new regiment commander led his regiment directly at the Beelitz Sanitarium, which was occupied by the Russians. Shortly before, a shell hit the staff of the II Battalion, putting it out of commission. Nevertheless, the battalion continued the attack.

In the afternoon of 28/4 SPW's attacked directly to the sanitarium, which now contained over 3000 wounded. The Russian outposts, which were left behind here, jumped into the open. They were overpowered. A Leutnant from Regiment Malow, with a bloody headband, jumped into the guard room and cut all of the telephone lines. Five minutes after that the entire sanitarium was liberated.

A little later General Wenck arrived, he found the chief surgeon and told him that all wounded and all duty personnel were to be removed as quickly as possible. He ordered all men able to march to be assembled immediately and to march on foot through the area cleared of enemy. Whatever vehicles the 12th Army were able to free-up were sent to Beelitz, ambulances and trucks and even hospital trains brought the wounded to Barby on the Elbe in an unbroken shuttle operation.

The attack, however, continued. They reached Ferch, south of Potsdam.

Thanks to the mediation of a representative of the International Red Cross, who happened to be in Beelitz by chance, the Americans allowed the first wounded arriving in Barby to cross the Elbe into their custody on 29/4.

A radio message from the 12th Army commander reached the defenders of Potsdam at midday on 28/4. It read:

"XX Army Corps had reached Ferch. Attack through to the 12th Army with all means available."

General Reymann acted immediately. He ordered his approximately 20,000 troops to set out immediately. They were able to make contact with the formations of Divisions "Schill" and "Hutten", which had penetrated into the Lehnin Forest.

While the "Schill" Assault Gun Brigade advanced against the Soviet encirclement ring and suppressed the enemy in their positions on the southern and southwestern edge of Potsdam, the elements broke out through the forest toward the sounds of the firing assault guns.

General Wenck ordered Reymann to break through the Alt Grabow lake passage and, thereby, defeat the inner Soviet encirclement ring.

Oberstleutnant Mueller led Division "Schill" through the forest toward Reymann's formations, which were breaking out. The assault guns under Major Nebel were in the lead. They shot-up the enemy tanks and anti-tank guns on the forest aisles. Then the two German groups stood opposite each other. The enemy withdrew to either side. The elements of Corps Group Potsdam that had broken out were immediately subordinated to Division "Schill."

From his headquarters in Pritzerbe, General Wenck immediately reported the breakout of all of the Potsdam defenders and the success at Beelitz. This news spread like wild fire. Even the 9th Army was cheered by this news as it gave them hope that they could be liberated.

In the meantime, General Wenck had again made contact with the 9th Army and informed them over radio that the area near Jueterbog was unsuitable for their planned breakout, because the enemy had significantly reinforced there. The chance was better south of Beelitz, since there were relatively weaker forces there. There alone could the breakout succeed and there would he hold against the enemy's pressure as it grew stronger with his 12th Army.

On the evening of 29/4 the enemy pressure on the 12th Army grew stronger. The three Divisions "Schill", "Koerner" and "Hutten", and last but not least Division "Scharnhorst" were fighting with their last ounces of strength. However, when the Russian infantry, which had been well-trained in forest combat, penetrated into the Lehnin Forest, the assault guns, which were securing there, had to gradually withdraw so that they would not be destroyed by enemy close combat troops.

Individual assault gun platoons launched forest attacks with limited objectives, in order to stop the closely pursuing enemy groups.

Individual groups of Russian tanks, which were making their way through the forest, were shot-up by camouflaged assault guns from close range.

However, the army still had to hold out for several days if the 9th Army was to be rescued. This required the last efforts of officers and men. "However, this sacrifice", declared General Wenck to his soldiers, "is our comradely duty and is self-evident. Each soldier will accomplish his duty in an exemplary manner."

A radio message arrived from Hitler at Gut Dobbin, where General Wenck and his command post were sheltered during the evening of 29/4 at 2300 hours. It read:

"1. Where are the Wenck lead elements?

2. When will they arrive?

3. Where is the 9th Army?

4. Where is Gruppe Holste?

5. When will they arrive? – signed Adolf Hitler."

The Meeting on the Elbe

While the 69th U.S. ID under Major General Reinhardt rolled on the Elbe near Torgau, the lead elements of an armored reconnaissance platoon under Lieutenant Kotzebue reached a farmhouse in the vicinity of the Elbe, they saw a white bed-sheet hanging out of a window. They saw similar signs on and in the rest of the houses.

Lieutenant Kotzebue ordered his troop to halt and approached the house with his rifle held at the ready, the house appeared to be quiet. He opened the door with the barrel of his rifle. His first glance fell onto a table, around which a man, a woman and three children sat. They were dead, Kotzebue determined that they had poisoned themselves.

They drove on toward the Elbe and they met a man on a horse in the town of Leckwitz on the western bank of the river. This was the first Russian that the 69th ID had laid eyes on. The man told them that his unit was located directly on the river. Lieutenant Kotzebue ordered his unit to continue on to the Elbe. On the western bank the soldiers of the 69th U.S. ID found a boat. Lieutenant Kotzebue boarded it with several men and sailed across.

"When they got out, Kotzebue saw that the banks of the river for hundreds of meters were covered with dead civilians – men, women and children. Tipped-over wagons stood all over, there were suitcases and pieces of clothing strewn everywhere.

Immediately after that the Americans met their first group of Russian soldiers. Kotzebue saluted, the Red Army soldiers did likewise. This was not a friendly meeting; they did not fall into each others arms or clap each other on the backs. They only stood there looking at each other. The date was 25 April 1945, 1330 hours. The Western and Eastern Allies had met near the small city of Strehla." (See: Ryan, Cornelius: *The Last Battle*.)

Two hours and ten minutes later L. Willaim, D. Robinson from the 69th ID ran into a Russian scout troop near Torgau on the Elbe, about 30 kilometers further to the north of Strehla. Robinson took four of the Russians back to his forward command post. This meeting was later declared to be the official meeting of the U.S. troops with the troops of the Red Army (because they did not have to deal with the mounds of dead). These were troops of the 1st Ukrainian Front that had run into the 1st U.S. Army. Therefore, Germany was split into two halves.

The troops at both meeting places were from the 5th Guards Army under General A.S. Zhadov. Indeed, it was Corps Baklanov, one of the three youngest corps commanders in this army, that had made it to the Elbe on 25/4/1945.

The Soviet Major General Russakov commanded his troops to be the first to reach the Elbe. The patrol that was met by Lieutenant Robinson was led by Lieutenant Silvashko.

On the next day, it was 26/4/1945, Major General Reinhardt, the commander of the 69th U.S. ID, and Guards Lieutenant Colonel Rudnik, division chief of staff, met with Major Rogov, commander of the 173rd Guards Regiment, and others.

Major General Emil F. Reinhardt was accompanied by his chief of staff, Lieutenant Colonel Lynch, and the commander of the division espionage and reconnaissance group[?]. There were also several other officers and the TASS representative to the U.S. Army, Major Zhadov. On the Russian side, members of the group at the meeting point included the Russian author Konstantin Simonov and several reporters from American, British and French newspapers.

"There were", according to Simonov, "approximately 38 people. The meeting took place in a manor house on the eastern bank of the Elbe. This was the quarters of the 2nd Battalion of the 173rd Guards Regiment." (See: Simonov, Konstantin: War Diary, Volume 2 1942 – 1945.)

On the next day the commanding generals of the two corps met, the Russian General Baklanov and the U.S. General Huebner, and at the end of this meeting the Russian correspondents and the reporters of the world press had the opportunity to cross the Elbe and visit the U.S. headquarters.

The first combined press conference was held in the "Press Camp" of the 1st U.S. Army in Naumburg. During the middle of the night the two

Russian correspondents got their first taste of the size of the world press, as approximately 150 Western Allied correspondents from all over the world swarmed over them.

However, back to the events in the 12th Army area of operations.

The 9th Army is Free

On 29/4/1945 General Wenck drove to all of the troop units of his widely separated army in a staff car. When he could no longer get through, he climbed onto his motorcycle, which accompanied his staff car. He found everyone to be confident that they could relieve the 9th Army.

On the morning of 30/4 Walther Wenck sent a radio message to the 9th Army: "The 12th Army is engaged in fierce defensive combat. The breakthrough is to be hastened. We are waiting for you!"

In the pocket, the 9th Army hastily equipped to breakout. And while the 12th Army waited for this breakout, Division "Hutten" received the members of the Swiss embassy, who flew out of Berlin. Generalleutnant Engel ordered they be turned over to the Americans between 1 and 4/5/1945.

"We were encircled with three army corps, approximately 40,000 exhausted soldiers and thousands of refugees", General Busse reported to the author after the war. "Our attempts to breakout the march capable battle groups to the west in the Baruth area constantly failed. The breakthrough to the 12th Army was to be our last attempt. We had to get out of the pocket."

From the combat diary of the 502nd Heavy SS Panzer Battalion (Tiger) we learn more of this breakout battle. This battalion was at the focus of the breakout. They reported:

"The 9th Army, to whose XI SS Corps we belonged and with whom we were encircled, organized for the breakout on 27/4/1945. They had learned of the most favorable breakthrough area from the 12th Army and knew where the troops from this army were waiting.

At 1900 hours on 27/4 Sturmbannfuehrer Hartrampf gave us the order and breakout objective."

And SS Unterscharfuehrer Ernst Streng reports further:

"We drove on. Slowly were drove our threatening colossus down the road, searching the forests on either side with our hands on the triggers. Four additional Tigers followed directly behind us. The strength of our panzer wedge was to create a penetration into the Russian ring of encirclement. The stream of tens of thousands filed behind us, pushed by our tanks to the left and right and widened to a breadth of 100 meters.

We rolled through the forest on a small trail. In front of us lay the Russian occupied Halbe.

'Tank obstacles and barricades!' reported the scouts on the Halbe autobahn exit. The General ordered: 'Attack the city immediately!' And then a short sentence followed: 'Our slogan is: Through!'

Our tank stood 30 meters in front of the road obstacle and in the narrow path we could neither withdraw nor fire. A German scout troop advanced. A bitter struggle flared up on a small front from house-to-house. The long road was covered with dead. There were wounded everywhere. The Russian fire increased in strength, in particular the mortar fire. Phosphorous shells exploded with blinding flashes. Houses were burning all over. Then we started to take tank fire. We received a direct hit. Within seconds our vehicle burst into flames. We opened the hatches, tumbled head-first from the openings and ran away from the vehicle, only to suddenly realize that it was an incendiary shell and that our tank was in no danger. Now we ran back to our Tiger, Driver Ott climbed aboard and started it up. We withdrew across an intersecting path.

Kuhnke, who was driving ahead, no longer answered. We learned that he was shot, however, he was still alive.

Then we finally passed Halbe and rolled on the right into a forest.

Hundreds of soldiers accompanied us and showed us the way through the forest, which led to a depression. This depression was under fire. A vicious fight took place here. Harlander's tank was shot. The commander was killed, the rest of the crew was able to abandon ship.

Shortly before daybreak the lead panzer elements ran into a Russian battery position, which they overran. The way was open.

We advanced a couple of hundred meters on the Berlin – Cottbus autobahn. Scouts reported that the bridge was open. It was secured and the lead panzer elements drove across and rolled into the Baruth Forest.

The lead elements halted again near the Massow forest house. An unending stream of German soldiers and refugees caught up to us. Here the extent of the bloody losses suffered at Halbe was realized. Among the dead this night was the commander of the XI SS Corps, Obergruppenfuehrer Kleinheisterkamp. Generalmajor Hoelz, the 9th Army Chief of Staff, was also killed."

That was the report from Unterscharfuehrer Streng.

The continuation of the march was ordered. On the afternoon of this 2/4 the lead panzer elements stood in front the railroad embankment and the Zossen – Baruth road, which ran right next to it. Here stood Soviet tanks and anti-tank guns, which fired flanking fire from the north and south into the march columns, tearing them apart.

Hartrampf attacked with the last Tigers along the railroad embankment and cleared up the situation by shooting-up the flanking tanks and anti-tank guns.

During the night before 29/4 they were able to capture the town and firing range of Kummersdorf in an assault. Here the many wounded could be laid out on the firing range.

The scouts advancing to the west reported a new enemy anti-tank barricade on the Trebbin – Luckenwalde road.

On the evening of 29/4 the breakout formations launched their final decisive attack. The Russian anti-tank obstacle was overcome in the first attack. As it became completely dark the breakout groups rolled, followed by the foot groups, north of Luckenwalde over the road and disappeared into the protective forests.

At midnight Berkenbrueck and the Foersterie Martinsmuehle were reached. In a final decisive jump the Russian encirclement ring had to be broken through and the breakout to the 12th Army forced.

The King Tigers reached enemy held Heinickendorf during night combat, the enemy resistance was broken. Driving further toward Dobbrikow the Tigers took anti-tank fire. Even Streng's vehicle was hit several times.

"A heavy hit shook our Tiger. It was still 400 meters to the edge of the forest. Our cannon roared against the forest. The detonations threw branches and tree trunks into the air. Another hit entered our inner combat compartment. Then a third hit followed.

We rolled to the left into a field. Then we drove again to the right. In the meantime, the other Tigers had been destroyed by anti-tank guns. The thousands continued to march.

When we ran out of fuel and looked for some more, the Tiger was hit from the left by a Russian tank cannon. I was wounded in my right upper arm and right upper thigh. My people carried me out of the tank and took over a Laebe. We soon caught up with the main column."

With the courage of the desperate the soldiers of the 9th Army broke out on the night of 1/5/1945. Now only the von Klust King Tiger of the 1st Company and Streng from the 2nd Company were operational. During this decisive breakthrough Streng's Tiger was hit again. This time it was set afire, however, it was extinguished. A little later it was able to destroy three T 34's in a duel. Then Streng's Tiger was hit by anti-tank gun fire. The fuel tank burned like a torch. This time, after a dozen serious hits, the tank could no longer be saved.

A little later the Tiger of Untersturmfuehrer Klust was also destroyed. Therefore, all of the Tigers that had paved the way for the 9th Army to freedom were eliminated. However, they had achieved the breakout. General Busse, who accompanied his men and cheered them on with the words: "Wenck is waiting for us!", and Generalmajor Wolf Hagermann, the commander of the 336th ID of the 9th Army, traveled with their men. Hagemann tore gaps with a series of machine-gun groups through which the men could break through.

On the morning of 1/5/1945 flares appeared in the sky in front of the totally exhausted men of the 9th Army, showing them where the 12th Army was located and when the panzergrenadiers of the 12th Army saw the return flares, they jumped up and ran toward their comrades from the 9th Army and broke through the enemy ring from the rear.

suddenly the men from the 9th Army saw the Russians in front of them separate. And then they saw German steel helmets, uniforms and faces; their comrades from the 12th Army!

General Wenck rode up on his motorcycle to his men in the trenches. He saw the soldiers of the 9th Army pass by, there were also refugees. And then he saw General der Infanterie Theodor Busse. The men broke through to the 12th Army in several columns, they were immediately protected and absorbed.

A battle group of assault guns and SPW units was formed under the command of Generalleutnant Engel, which attacked through the separated Russian formations on a 5 kilometer wide front, in order to create a wide enough passage for the following refugees.

A little later, at the 12th Army command post, General Busse said to his comrade Wenck:

"Our breakthrough is over. – My men are finished! They cannot fight their way through anything else."

30,000 men, including more than 5,000 refugees, found security behind the lines of the 12th Army. All wheeled vehicles were dismounted so that the refugees could be withdrawn out of the danger zone to the Elbe.

Now the divisions of the 12th and 9th Armies fought their way back together.

Surrender on the Elbe

The divisions of the 12th Army defended directly south of Brandenburg with their front to the north until 2/5. Then they marched back through Genthin and reached the Elbe between Jerichow and Ferchland. The assault guns repulsed the pursuing enemy at a series of halts.

On the morning of 3/5/1945 General Wenck entrusted the commander of the XXXXVIII Panzer Corps, General der Panzertruppe von Edelsheim, with the conduct of the surrender negotiations.

The group crossed the Elbe in an amphibious vehicle to the other bank with a written offer of surrender. When the vehicle reached the western bank it was surrounded by American soldiers. Major Kandutsch the translator told the American Captain from the battalion staff that it was the wish of the negotiation group to meet with the commander of the 105th IR.

At 1700 hours the small group arrived at the headquarters of the 102nd U.S. ID in Gardelegen and turned over its written surrender offer. When they learned that the reply could not be given until the next morning at 0800 hours, Oberstleutnant Seidel crossed back over the Elbe and reported this to the commander.

On the morning of 4/5/1945 the negotiations began in the Stendal Rathaus. At the same time, the Russians attempted to collapse the 12th Army bridgehead on the eastern bank, Russian artillery fired out of many tubes against the bridgehead, while the engineers from the divisions of the 12th Army prepared their crossing equipment.

In Stendal the U.S. leadership finally approved the utilization of the damaged Elbe bridges near Tangermuende and the three ferries near Schoenhausen, Tangermuende and Ferchland.

The crossings were permitted to be utilized by the surrendering soldiers of the 12th Army and the wounded under treatment of medical personnel. The Americans forbade the crossing of "all civilian personnel."

General Moore, who signed this surrender, added the two words "No Civilians."

Oberstleutnant Seidel, who was in Stendal in the early morning, had to return again across the Elbe to inform General Wenck of this clause. He had to repeat these words several times before the General understood their significance.

In the early morning hours of 5/5/1945 the crossing of the wounded and unarmed soldiers over the Elbe began. By using every possibility offered, as many civilians were crossed as possible. If they were discovered, the U.S. outposts sent them back across the river to the Russians. Ultimately tens of thousands of refugees were abandoned on the eastern bank of the Elbe!

During the night before 6/5 the engineers of the 12th Army crossed refugees in assault boats. Because of the Russian artillery fire directed at the eastern bank of the Elbe, the Americans were forced to pull back, so that they were not hit by their ally's fire. This opened the way for the refugees.

Divisions "Koerner" and "Hutten" held the pursuing Russians off until the last columns made it across the river. There was fierce fighting in the "Scharnhorst" ID area of operations. The Malow Battalion shot its last enemy tanks near Wust on 6/5/1945. 14 of these colossi were destroyed, the majority by panzerfaeusten.

This battalion held the western edge of Wust until 7/5/1945. They they withdrew to Fischbeck. Here the rear guard fought under Oberleutnant Denk and Leutnant Henning and fired up the last of their ammunition.

The Red Army was not able to breakthrough to the Elbe in the north, where the Divisions "Koerner" and "Hutten" had crossed, until that evening. In the Division "Koerner" area of operations, the division commander, Generalleutnant Frankewitz, was the last soldier of his division to cross the Elbe on the afternoon of 7/5/1945.

Division "Schill" blew up its last assault guns on the Elbe dam on this afternoon and then crossed to the western bank.

General der Panzertruppe Wenck and his Chief of Staff Oberst Reichheim, the Army Ia, Oberst von Humboldt, two ordonanze officers and several soldiers crossed in the last boat near Ferchland.

The combat of the 12th Army between the Elbe and Oder was at an end. Oberst Reichheim reported to the author:

"In all 100,000 soldiers were crossed in an orderly fashion over the Elbe into U.S. captivity. The number of civilians smuggled across was in the tens of thousands. Looking back it must be said that this last battle was fought out of soldierly duty and for the German people."

However, what was happening in Berlin during the last days of April and beginning of May?

14

THE END OF THE SECOND
WORLD WAR

In the Reich Capital

During the last situation briefing with Hitler on the evening of 29/4/ 1945 General Weidling informed him that the troops were no longer being supplied with ammunition and rations. He then said openly:

> "The situation is hopeless! – My Fuehrer, I must report that the battle for Berlin in all reality my be over by tomorrow."

Hitler turned questioning to Brigadefuehrer Mohnke, who was named the commander of all troops located in the center of Berlin. He replied: "It is as General Weidling says, my Fuehrer!"

Hitler now permitted the breakout of all battle groups that had run out of ammunition. The rest were to remain in their positions until their last rounds were fired and then they could withdraw.

On the morning of 30/4/1945 the Soviet 380th, 674th and 756th Rifle Regiments assaulted through the ruins of the inner city to the Reichstag building. Non-commissioned officers Yefgorov and Kantariya clambered up the dome and raised the red flag at 1425 hours. The fighting around the Reichskanzlei and the government quarter was still in full swing.

Hitler listened to the last situation report from Brigadefuehrer Mohnke in the meeting room of the Reichskanzlei. He reported that the Russians were still being held up at Potsdammer Platz and that there was still fighting around the Anhalt railroad station and the Tiergarten. Elements of the LVI Panzer Corps had stopped the 8th Soviet Guards Army under General Chuikov.

After that, Hitler signed his last Fuehrer Order, which gave General Weidling the permission to breakout. At 1430 hours Hitler bit into a cyanide capsule, while putting a pistol to his temple.

His wife, Eva Braun, who he married the previous day, died from the cyanide. Dr. Stumpfegger, Hitler's physician, established the deaths of both of them. They were taken out and laid three meters to the right of the bunker in the fire of Russian artillery, they were covered with gasoline and ignited, as Hitler had ordered.

On the afternoon at 1700 hours, Hitler was already dead for some two and a half hours, Reichsleiter Bormann issued a radio message from the OKW to the commander of the northern sector, Grossadmiral Doenitz, it was also signed by General Krebs. The radio message read:

"Grossadmiral Doenitz. – In place of the former Reichsmarschall Goering, the Fuehrer appointed you, Herr Grossadmiral, as his successor. Written authorization is underway."

During the evening General Weidling was informed of the recent events. Bormann and General Krebs now assaulted Dr. Goebbels until he clearly understood that General Weidling would initiate the surrender. On 1/5/1945 at 2000 hours the command posts of all of the formations fighting in Berlin were informed of Hitler's death and the planned breakout.

General Weidling sent a radio message to the Soviet commander and requested a cease fire and his acceptance of a surrender negotiating group.

Marshal Zhukov gave General Chuikov the permission to conduct surrender negotiations. An hour after midnight on 2/5/1945 Oberst Duvfing crossed the Soviet lines as the German negotiator and was led to Schulenburgring, where he later stood opposite General Chuikov. He only asked:

"Unconditional surrender, yes or no!"

Oberst Duvfing answered: "Yes!"

At midday on 2/5/1945 Soviet Marshal Zhukov ordered the cease fire. Generalissimo Stalin issued an order of the day to the Red Army in which the fall of Berlin was made known to all of the Red Army soldiers. The order of the day closed with the words:

"Today, on 2 May 1945 at 2330 hours, the capital of our homeland, Moscow, saluted the 1st Belorussian Front and the 1st Ukrainian Front with 24 artillery salvoes from 323 guns to honor their great success in the capture of Berlin."

After Hitler's death and the fall of the Reich capital the days of the Third Reich were numbered. However, what happened to the civilians in Berlin during the last days of fighting will be reported in a brief closing section.

The Hell Called Berlin

Even Berlin could not avoid the wave of murder and rape, vandalism and destruction.

The Russian soldiers now demanded their "price of victory, the women of the besieged ." (See Ryan, Cornelius: Op. cit.)

It was no longer the forward-most formations of the fighting troops that staged this massacre. However, the strength of the young Frau Ursula Koester could not prevent herself from being raped by four Russian soldiers.

Juliane Bochnick was discovered by the Russians and was able to escape. However, her girlfriend, Rosa Hofmann and her mother, who were raped, took poison.

When the Russians reached Reinickendorf they searched for valuables and women. The same thing happened throughout, in all of the suburbs and in the center of the city:

Women and girls were rousted from bed at night and, while the Russians "raped and plundered", many of them committed suicide. Within three weeks in Pankow Bezirk alone 215 suicides were reported. Most of them were women. Josef Michalke and Alfons Matzker, Jesuit priests at St. Canisius Church in Charlottenburg, watched as a mother and her two children were dragged from the Havel Canal. The woman had tied shopping bags filled with bricks to each arm, then had taken a child under each arm and jumped into the water.

Hannelore von Cmuda, a seventeen year-old girl, was raped several times by a horde of drunken Red Army soldiers. After that she was shot three times.

Frau Margarete Promeist, who worked as a lookout in a Berlin air raid bunker, reported that the Russians would come into the bunker for two days and nights and rape and plunder. "Women who tried to defend themselves were murdered. In one room alone I found the corpses of six or seven women with crushed skulls, all were still in the positions they were when they were being raped."

She herself was also raped.

"The women were driven together and brought upstairs to the rooms", reported Margareta Probst from Berlin-Kreuzberg. "We heard their screams all night long, they pierced our ears in the cellar."

When Frau Schulz was abused in front of her husband and 15 year-old son while other Russians held their guns on them, the broken father shot his son and wife after the Russians had left, and then he shot himself.

In Hause Dahlem the mother superior of the Sisters of Mercy had to endure a mother of three children being abused by the Russians all night long. When she returned home in the morning, she saw that her mother, her brother and three children had all hanged themselves. The abused woman then slit her wrists and bled to death.

With the end of the fighting in Berlin these things did not stop happening. There were further murders and rapes in Berlin.

"Reparations in kind" this was called. According to reports from the German Red Cross 845,000 civilians were displaced as reparations. Of them

220,000 died on the march to the work camps, that is 25 percent. However, people were also displaced from the German settlements in the east.

The women from Preussisch-Holland in East Prussia were loaded into cattle cars for displacement to the east. After 29 days the doors to hell were opened. Of the 100 stuffed into the individual cars, between 20 and 32 had died. (See Displaced – Women and Girls Displaced from East Prussia to Siberia, Landmannschaft East Prussia 1978.)

They died in the Taplau Penitentiary as well as in the Ruja coal mines in the Urals, near Kistin in the Urals as well as in the Boehmisch-Leipa area, in Aussig, where women and girls drowned in the water, as well as in Binnenwesthafen from Berlin, where a ship-load of children arrived from a home in Finkenwalde, 300 of them starved to death in the belly of the ship.

Bertrand Russel stood up against this bestiality, as did Victor Gollancz and the Czech Dr. H.G. Adler. R.W.F. Bashford, from the British Foreign Ministry, submitted a report on Germany, in which he wrote:

> "The concentration camps have not been eliminated, but they have been taken over by new authorities. In Upper Silesia prisoners, who are not too weak from hunger, must stand night after night in cold water up to their heels until they die. In Breslau there are cellars from which the screams of sacrifice are heard day and night."

Then there are the closing words of Victor Gollancz:

> "This expulsion will remain in the memory of humanity with undying shame." (See Gollancz, Victor: *In Darkest Germany*, London 1947.)

15

THE SURRENDER

In Italy and in the West

When the new government under Grossadmiral [GA] Doenitz learned of the surrender of the troops located in northern Italy over the radio on 2/5/1945, GA Doenitz was relieved.

Because English troops took Schleswig-Holstein on the same day, Generalmajor Wolz, the defender of Hamburg, received instructions from OKW on 3/5/1945 to send a negotiator to the English and prepare for the surrender of Hamburg. At the same time, he was to announce the arrival of Generaladmiral von Friedeburg on a mission from the Grossadmiral.

Grossadmiral Karl Doenitz, named as the last German chief of state after the death of Hitler, dispatched Generaladmiral von Friedeburg to Field Marshal Montgomery's headquarters in Lueneburg, in order to work out the partial capitulation of the northern German area. Konteradmiral Wagner and Generalleutnant Kinzel accompanied him.

When they reported to Montgomery on the morning of 4/5/1945, he [Montgomery] was not unwilling to accept this partial surrender, if Denmark and Holland were also included in it. Moreover, no more war ships were to be scuttled.

Von Friedeburg, who went to Flensburg, the seat of the government and the Grossadmiral, after meeting with Montgomery, flew again to Lueneburg on 4/5. He signed the surrender documents here for "all German forces in Holland, northwestern Germany, including all of the islands and Denmark."

On the British side, Field Marshal Montgomery alone signed. On the German side, besides Generaladmiral von Friedeburg, Generalleutnant Kinzel and Generalmajors Wagner, Poleck and Friedel all signed this document. This partial surrender was to go into effect on 5/5/1945 at 0800 hours.

From Montgomery in Lueneburg, Generaladmiral von Friedeburg flew directly to Reims to General Eisenhower's headquarters. A partial surrender was also offered to the U.S. troops. After this was accomplished, Grossadmiral Doenitz would be able to hold out as long as possible against the Red Army until all German soldiers could get out of the east and all refugees could make it to the west.

General Eisenhower categorically turned down this partial surrender. On the morning of 6/5/1945 Generalleutnant Kinzel arrived again in Muerwik to report to Doenitz that he did not succeed in Reims and that Eisenhower demanded unconditional surrender, to include that on the Russian front. The implementation of this demand, which would also signify the immediate cessation of all transport movement on land and sea to the west, would deliver up all of the troops still located in the east to the Russians. However, the troops could not be issued such a suicidal order, if they still had a chance of fighting their way to the west. Whether this was intended, is not clear. However, if Eisenhower's demand was met, it would boil down to this, coincidentally or on purpose.

Now GA Doenitz requested that Generaloberst Jodl fly to Reims, in order to explain to Eisenhower why a partial surrender was desired with the U.S. forces. If Eisenhower again refused, Jodl was to propose a complete surrender in two phases, whereby as much time as possible would be requested between the time of the cease fire and the time when all movement would cease.

Generaloberst Jodl was given full authority to sign such a complete surrender. However, only if a partial surrender was again turned down.

Moreover, he was to inform GA Doenitz of the text of such a complete surrender beforehand.

After a final meeting with GA Doenitz and Graf Schwerin-Krosig, Generaloberst Jodl flew to Reims on 6/5/1945. The negotiations there lasted all day. At 0000 hours on 7 May Jodl sent a radio message to Flensburg-Muerwik, in which he informed the GA of the following:

"General Eisenhower maintains that we should sign today. Otherwise the Allied fronts will conclude separate agreements with any persons desiring to surrender; all negotiations will be broken off. I see no other course than to sign, or there will be chaos. Request immediate confirmation as to whether I am authorized to sign the surrender. It will not go into effect immediately. Hostilities would then cease on 9/5 at 0000 hours. – signed Jodl."

Doenitz had gained another 48 hours and, therefore, an hour after this radio message arrived, he granted his permission for this complete surrender at Reims. At exactly 0241 hours the surrender documents were signed in Reims.

At 1245 hours on this day the Reichsminister Graf Schwerin-Krosig broadcast the cease fire over the Reich radio transmitter in Flensburg. The announcement of the unconditional surrender of the German Wehrmacht ended with the words:

"May God not abandon us in our misfortune and bless us in our difficult work."

In the surrender document was – corresponding with a Russian request – the provision for " a second signing of the surrender in Karlshorst ." It was to take place on 8 May.

Generaladmiral von Friedeburg, GFM Keitel and Generaloberst Stumpff signed this military surrender document.

The Karlshorst Spectacle

On the same day that the unconditional surrender of the German Wehrmacht was signed in Reims, Marshal Zhukov also received a report from his War Counsel Telegin in Reims and determined that the unconditional surrender would be signed in the building of the engineer school in Karlshorst.

The Russian diplomats that were to participate in this act landed with the first aircraft in Tempelhof on the following morning. They were led by the Deputy Soviet Foreign Minister Andrei Yanuarevich Vyshinskiy. 90 minutes after that another aircraft landed. It brought Marshal Vassiliy Sokolovski. It was notable that neither Zhukov nor Eisenhower appeared. Also arriving were: the British Air Marshal Tedder, General Spaatz and their staff officers.

Marshal Sokolovski greeted his colleagues and they all reviewed the honor guard while the national anthems played.

During this ceremony another aircraft landed. It brought GFM Keitel, Generaladmiral von Friedeburg and Generaloberst Stumpff with their officers.

Russian officers met this group and led them to waiting vehicles.

The vehicles drove through Berlin to Karlshorst, where the Germans were quartered.

The fest hall of the engineer school was gaily prepared for the signing. On the front hung the flags of the Soviet Union, the USA, Great Britain and France.

In the meantime, the French representative, the commander of the 1st French Army, General Jean Lattre de Tassigny, arrived.

A long table stood under the flags, it took up the entire width of the room. Here the representatives of the Allied powers were to take their places. There were three tables standing in front of them. The short table was for the German delegation, the medium for the Soviet generals and their allies and the other for all of the correspondents that were able to obtain entrance cards.

The surrender negotiations, that is the signing of the surrender, was to take place at 1400 hours. This was delayed for several hours and, when

Marshal Zhukov and his War Counsel Telegin finally arrived, followed by Vyshinski, Tedder, Spaatz and Lattre de Tassigny, it was already evening.

The Russian generals sat at the first small table, which was assigned to the Germans. When they realized their blunder, they became flustered, jumped up simultaneously and moved to the larger table. Then the newspaper photographers swarmed over everybody. At the large main table sat the men representing the Allies.

After the flashing of the photographers was over and a hush of anticipation descended over, Marshal Zhukov stood up:

"I hereby declare the meeting for the acceptance of the surrender of the German Wehrmacht to be open", he began, before it was established which government would take the authority.

After that Marshal Zhukov requested that the officer at the entrance show the German delegation in.

Keitel was the first to enter. After a few steps he reached the small table, he stopped at the middle and greeted the Marshal's staff before he sat down.

The signing began. First Zhukov, Tedder, Spaatz and Lattre de Tassigny signed. After that Zhukov stood up and said that now the German delegation must sign. When GFM Keitel made a motion to hand the document to him, "Zhukov stretched his arm in the direction of the Germans and said: 'you are to come here and sign!'" (See: Simonov, Konstantin: Op. cit.)

Keitel was the first to get up and go to the table to sign the document. After that Generaloberst Stumpff and Generaladmiral von Friedeburg went to sign. Again Marshal Zhukov got up and declared that the German delegation could leave the room.

The surrender was signed by all of the nations that had participated in the war, therefore, the war had ended.

Instead of a Postscript

The assumptions and speculation as to whether the Western Allies actually had a plan to conclude a cease-fire with the Germans so that the Germans could throw everything they had available to the east, in order to stop the Russian offensive, was never clarified.

Several statements from Field Marshal Montgomery indicated a vague possibility. This is strengthened by statements made by Winston Churchill, not only that "the wrong swine were defeated", but a powerful enemy was created, one who was extending its influence into other countries.

This was put in Churchill's own words in his work *The Second World War*:

> "When a war fought by a coalition comes to an end, the political aspects gradually take the upper hand. For example, the Americans were not interested in terrain acquisition. However, wherever the wolf is prowling, that is where the shepherd must protect his flock, even if he personally does not desire to eat meat."

The American staff chiefs at the time did not see this question as having decisive significance.

Nevertheless, they would play an important role in the fate of Europe; and perhaps they have given us a long lasting peace for which they had struggled for so long and hard.

• • •

The destruction of the German military power changed the relations between Communist Russia and the Democratic West. The common enemy, that had bound them together, was obliterated.

From now on Russian imperialism and the communist ideology would know no boundary for its lust for expansion and its drive for world domination.

This end, with the new threat to the gates of the Western Allies, was won with blood and tears. The Second World War had torn Germany into two parts, destroyed the Baltic States, cost millions and millions of people on both sides of the fronts and in their homelands their lives and left the Soviet Union as the greatest military power in Europe.

Casblanca and the following Allied conferences had changed the balance of power on the earth in favor of the USSR.

SOURCES AND BIBLIOGRAPHY

Ahlfen, Hans von: Der Kampf um Schlesien, München 1961
ders. und Niehoff, Hermann: So kämpfte Breslau, München 1959
Alman, Karl: Panzer vor! Rastatt 1964
ders.: Sprung in die Hölle, Rastatt 1966
ders.: Mit Eichenlaub und Schwertern, Rastatt 1971
ders.: Karl Dönitz — Vom U-Boot-Kommandanten zum letzten deutschen Staatsoberhaupt, Leoni 1983
Andronikow A. G. und
Mostowenko, V. D.: Die roten Panzer, München 1963
Antonow, A. S.: Die Panzer, Berlin (Ost) 1959
Arutjunow, A. S.: Die Ostpommern-Angriffsoperation Februar · März 1945; (Siehe dazu: Shilin, P. A.)
Barbaschin, I. P.: Die Oberschlesien-Operation (Siehe Shilin)
ders.: Die Wiener Angriffs-Operation (Siehe Shilin)
Bauer, Prof. Eddy: Der Panzerkrieg, Bonn 1955
Bedell-Smith, Walter: Moscow Mission, London 1950
ders.: General Eisenhowers sechs große Entscheidungen, Bern 1956
Bayerlein, Fritz: Die Panzer-Lehr-Division vom D-Tag bis zum V-Tag (i. Ms. durch General Bayerlein)
Bieroth, Dr. Ella: Der Zweite Weltkrieg — Die Schlacht im Hürtgenwald, Monschau 1968
Boesch, Paul: Road to Huertgen — Forest in Hell, Houston 1962
Bosch, Heinz: Der Zweite Weltkrieg zwischen Rhein und Maas, Geldern 1961
Bradley, Omar N.: A Soldiers Story, New York 1964
Brandenburger, Erich: Die Ardennen-Offensive im Abschnitt der 7. deutschen Armee (Freiburg/Brg. Sign. MS — B — 049)
Bullitt, William: How we won the War and lost the Peace, in: Life vom 30. 8. 1948
Busse, Theodor: Die letzte Schlacht der 9. Armee (ZS 1955)
Butcher, Harry: Drei Jahre mit Eisenhower, Bern 1946
Cartier, Raymond: Der Zweite Weltkrieg, München 1962, 2 Bd.
Carius, Otto: Tiger im Schlamm, Neckargemünd 1960
Churchill, Winston: Der Zweite Weltkrieg, Bern — München — Wien — 1985
Clay, Lucius D.: Entscheidung in Deutschland, Frankfurt/Main 1950
Crocker, George: Schrittmacher der Sowjets, Tübingen 1960
Dahms, Helmuth, G.: Geschichte des Zweiten Weltkrieges, Tübingen 1965
Denk, Josef: Mit der Division »Scharnhorst« im Einsatz, i. Ms. (an den Verfasser)
Dieckert, Kurt u. Grossmann, Horst: Der Kampf um Ostpreußen, München 1960
Dönitz, Karl: Zehn Jahre und zwanzig Tage, Bonn 1958
ders.: Mein wechselvolles Leben, Göttingen 1958
Edelsheim, Maximilian Frhr. von: Das XXXXVIII. PzK. beim amerikanischen Feldzug in Mitteldeutschland 11. 4. - 3. 5. 1945
ders.: Die Kapitulationsverhandlungen der 12. Armee mit der 9. US-Armee am 4. 5. 1945 in Stendal, beide i. Ms. (an den Autor)
Eisenhower, Dwight D.: Crusade in Europe, Washington 1946; deutsch: Kreuzzug in Europa, Amsterdam 1948
Ellis, I. F.: Victory in the West, HMSO London 1962
Eremenko, A. I.: Tage der Bewährung, Berlin (Ost) 1961
Engel, Gerhard: Division Ulrich von Hutten im Kampf i. Ms. (an den Autor)
Fey, Willi: Panzer im Brennpunkt der Fronten, München 1960
Fretter-Pico, Maximilian: Mißbrauchte Infanterie, Frankfurt/Main 1957
Friessner, Hans: Verratene Schlachten, Hamburg 1956
Fuller, J. C. F.: Der Zweite Weltkrieg 1939 - 1945, Wien 1952
Funck, Frhr. von und
Hübner, Anselm: Kriegstagebuch I und II der Panzer-Lehr-Division (im Original an Autor)
Görlitz, Walter: Der Zweite Weltkrieg, Stuttgart 1951/52
Grams, Rolf: Die 14. Panzer-Division, Bad Nauheim 1957
Greiner, H.: Die oberste Wehrmachtführung 1939 - 1945, Frankfurt/Main 1950
Guderian, Heinz: Erinnerungen eines Soldaten, Neckargemünd 1960
Haupt, Werner: Heeresgruppe Mitte 1941 - 1945, Dorheim 1968
ders.: Heersgruppe Nord, Dorheim 1970
ders.: Rückzug im Westen, Stuttgart 1978
Hausser, Paul: Soldaten wie andere auch, Osnabrück 1966
Hossbach, Friedrich: Infanterie im Ostfeldzug, Osterode 1951
Jacobsen, Dr. H. A.: Der Zweite Weltkrieg in Chroniken und Dokumenten, Darmstadt 1959
Kalinov, Kyrill: Sowjetmarschälle haben das Wort, München 1960
Keilig, Wolf: Das deutsche Heer 1939 - 1945, Bad Nauheim 1955
ders.: Rangliste des deutschen Heeres, Bad Nauheim 1955
Kern, Erich: Die letzte Schlacht, Preußisch Oldendorf 1972
Kesselring, Albert: Soldat bis zum letzten Tag, Bonn 1953
Kleine, Egon und Kühn, Volkmar: Tiger — Die Geschichte einer legendären Waffe, 1942 - 1945, Stuttgart 1987 (4. Aufl.)

Sources and Bibliography

Koller, Karl:	Der letzte Monat, Mannheim 1949
Korotkow, I. S.:	Die Zerschlagung der Ostpreußengruppierung der deutschen faschistischen Truppen (Siehe: Schilin, P. A.)
Krätschmer, E. G.:	Die Ritterkreuzträger der Waffen-SS, Göttingen 1955
Kühn, Volkmar:	Torpedoboote und Zerstörer im Einsatz 1939 - 1945, Stuttgart 1984 (4. Aufl.)
ders.:	Deutsche Fallschirmjäger im Zweiten Weltkrieg, Stuttgart 1986 (6. Aufl.)
Kurowski, Franz:	Deutsche Offiziere in Staat, Wirtschaft und Wissenschaft, Herford 1967
ders.:	Von den Ardennen zum Ruhrkessel, Herford 1963
	Die Geschichte der Panzer-Lehr-Division, Bad Nauheim 1964, Armee Wenck — Die 12. Armee zwischen Elbe und Oder 1945, Neckargemünd 1967, Heimatfront, Bayreuth 1960, Der Panzerkrieg (3. Aufl. 1986) München, Alliierte Jagd auf deutsche Wissenschaftler, München 1980, Bedingungslose Kapitulation, Leoni 1983, Generalfeldmarschall Albert Kesselring, Oberbefehlshaber an allen Fronten, Berg 1985, Balkenkreuz und Roter Stern — Der Luftkrieg über Rußland, Dorheim 1985, Die Schlacht um Deutschland, München 1981, Das Vermächtnis, Bochum 1982, Grenadiere, Generale, Kameraden, Rastatt 1968, Blutiges Dreieck, Rastatt 1969, Zu Lande, zu Wasser, in der Luft, Bochum 1968
ders. und Tornau, Gottfried:	Sturmartillerie — Geschichte einer legendären Waffe, Stuttgart 1977
Lasch, Otto:	So fiel Königsberg, München 1958
Liddell, Hart:	Die Verteidigung des Westens, Konstanz 1951
ders.:	Jetzt dürfen sie reden, Hamburg 1948
Lüdde-Neurath, Walter:	Regierung Dönitz, Göttingen 1950
Mabire, Jean:	Berlin im Todeskampf 1945, Preußisch Oldendorf 1977
MacDonald, Charles, B.:	The Battle of the Huertgen Forest, Philadelphia/New York 1946
Manstein, Erich, von:	Verlorene Siege, Bonn 1954
Manteuffel, Hasso v.:	Die 7. Panzer-Division im Zweiten Weltkrieg, Uerdingen 1965
ders.:	Die Schlacht in den Ardennen in: Entscheidungsschlachten des Zweiten Weltkrieges, Frankfurt/Main 1960
Marshall, S. L. A.:	We couldn't have taken Berlin in '45, ZS September 1961
Montgomery, Bernard:	Von der Normandie zur Ostsee, Hamburg 1949
Munzel, Oskar:	Gepanzerte Truppen, Herford 1965
Müller, Alfred:	Die Division Schill im Einsatz (i. Ms.)
Nehring, Walther K.:	Die Geschichte der deutschen Panzerwaffe 1916 - 1945, Berlin 1969
Parotkin, I. W. und Fokin, N. A.:	Die Weichsel-Oder-Operation (Siehe: Schilin, P. A.)
Patton, George:	Krieg wie ich ihn erlebte, Berlin 1950
Reichhelm, Günther:	Das letzte Aufgebot — Die 12. Armee im Herzen Deutschlands zwischen Ost und West vom 13. 4. bis zum 7. 5. 1945, i. Ms. (an den Autor)
Rendulic, Dr. Lothar:	Gekämpft — Gesiegt — Geschlagen, Heidelberg 1952
ders.:	Soldat in stürzenden Reichen, München 1965
Schaulen, Joachim von:	Hasso von Manteuffel, Panzerkampf im Zweiten Weltkrieg, Berg 1983
Shilin, P. A.:	Die wichtigsten Operationen des Großen Vaterländischen Krieges 1941 - 1945, Frankfurt/Main 1962
Stacey, Charles Perry:	The victory Campaign, The Operation in North-West Europe 1944 - 45, Ottawa 1960
Studtnitz, Hans-Georg v.:	Als Berlin brannte, Stuttgart 1963
Tedder, Lord Arthur W.:	Air Power in War, London 1946
Telpuchowski, Boris S.:	Die sowjetische Geschichte des Großen Vaterländischen Krieges 1941 - 1945, Frankfurt 1961
Simonow, Konstantin:	Kriegstagebücher Bd. 2, München 1979
Thorwald, Jürgen:	Das Ende an der Elbe, Stuttgart 1950
ders.:	Wen sie verderben wollen, Stuttgart 1952
Trees, Wolfgang:	Schlachtfeld Rheinland, Aachen 1976
ders. und Whitting, Charles:	Die Amis sind da, Aachen 1975
ders. und Hohenstein, Adolf:	Hölle Hürtgenwald, Aachen 1986 (7. Aufl.)
Trevor-Roper, H. R.:	Hitlers letzte Tage, Hamburg 1947
Unrein, Martin:	Berichte über den Einsatz der Panzer-Division »Clausewitz« vom 11. - 21. 4. 1945, i. Ms. (an den Autor)
Warlimont, Walter:	Im Hauptquartier der deutschen Wehrmacht, 1939 - 1945, Frankfurt/Main 1962
Wenck, Walther:	Kurzer Überblick über die Endkämpfe zwischen Oder und Elbe im April/Mai 1945, i. Ms. (an den Autor)
Westphal, Siegfried:	Heer in Fesseln, Bonn 1952
ders.:	Erinnerungen, Mainz 1975
Wilmot, Chester:	Der Kampf um Europa, Frankfurt/Main 1960
Zavlalow, Aleksandr:	Die Angriffsoperation der Roten Armee in Ostpommern, Moskau 1960
Zhukov, G. K.:	The Memoirs of Marshal Zhukov, New York 1970

Daten und Berichte über die Zivilbevölkerung in den von der Roten Armee besetzten Gebieten, sind sämtlich dem fünfbändigen Werk des Bundesministeriums für Vertriebene: Dokumentation der Vertreibung der Deutschen aus Ost-Mitteleuropa, dtv-reprint Bd. I bis Bd. V. entnommen. Die Herausgeber waren : Dr. Theodor Schieder, o. Prof. a. d. Universität Köln, Dr. Adolf Diestelkamp, Oberarchivrat im Bundesarchiv, Dr. Rudolf Laun, o. Prof. a. d. Universität Hamburg, Dr. Peter Rassow, o. Prof. a. d. Universität Köln, Dr. Hans Rothfeld, o. Prof. a. d. Universität Tübingen.

ABBREVIATIONS

Abbreviations

Abt.:	Abteilung	PD:	Panzer-Division
AK:	Armeekorps	PGD:	Panzergrenadier-Division
AOK:	Armeeoberkommando	PGR:	Panzergrenadier-Regiment
ArtAbt.:	Artillerie-Abteilung	PiKp.:	Pionier-Kompanie
AufklAbt.:	Aufklärungs-Abteilung	PLD:	Panzer-Lehr-Division
Batl.:	Bataillon	PzAOK:	Panzerarmee-Oberkommando
BatlFhr.:	Bataillonsführer	PzGrenBrig.:	Panzergrenadier-Brigade
BatlStab:	Bataillonsstab	PzJägLehrRgt:	Panzerjäger-Lehr-Regiment
cm:	Zentimeter	PzK.:	Panzerkorps
Div.:	Division	PzKp.:	Panzerkompanie
DivArt.:	Divisions-Artillerie	PzKGr.:	Panzer-Kampfgruppe
DivGefStand:	Divisionsgefechtsstand	PzLehrRgt.:	Panzer-Lehr-Regiment
DivKdr.:	Divisionskommandeur	RAF:	Royal Air Force
DivSt.:	Divisionsstab	Rgt.:	Regiment
FBD:	Führer-Begleit-Division	RgtFhr.:	Regimentsführer
FGD:	Führer-Grenadier-Division	RgtKdr.:	Regimentskommandeur
FHQ:	Führerhauptquartier	»Schere«:	Scherenfernrohr
Fhr.:	Führer	Sich Div.:	Sicherungs-Division
FJD:	Fallschirmjäger-Division	SkiJägDiv.:	Skijäger-Division
FlaMW:	Fliegerabwehr-Maschinenwaffen	SPW:	Schützenpanzerwagen
FschPD:	Fallschirm-Panzer-Division	sPzAbt.:	schwere Panzer-Abteilung
Fw.:	Feldwebel	StD:	Sturm-Division
GebAK:	Gebirgs-Armeekoros	Uffz.:	Unteroffizier
GebDiv:	Gebirgsdivisiom	US-ID:	amerikan. Infanterie-Div.
Gefr.:	Gefreiter	US-PD:	amerikan. Panzer-Division
GefStand:	Gefechtsstand	VGD:	Volksgrenadier-Division
Gen.d.Art.:	General der Artillerie		
Gen.d.Inf.:	General der Infanterie		
GFM:	Generalfeldmarschall		
Gen.:	General		
Gen.d.Pz.Tr.:	General der Panzertruppe		
GenLt.:	Generalleutnant		
GenMaj.:	Generalmajor		
GenOberst:	Generaloberst		
GR:	Grenadier-Regiment		
»HG«:	Hermann Göring		
HGr.:	Heeresgruppe		
Hptm.:	Hauptmann		
HQ:	Hauptquartier		
ID:	Infanterie-Division		
i.G.:	im Generalstab		
IR:	Infanterie-Regiment		
Jäg.Div.:	Jäger Division		
KAdm.:	Konteradmiral		
Kdr.:	Kommandeur		
KGr.:	Kampfgruppe		
KGrFhr.:	Kampfgruppenführer		
KommGen.:	Kommandierender General		
Kp.:	Kompanie		
Kpn.:	Kompanien		
Lkw:	Lastkraftwagen		
lMG:	leichtes Maschinengewehr		
Lt.:	Leutnant		
mech. Div.:	mechanische Division (russische)		
MFP:	Marine-Fährprahm		
MGBatl.:	Maschinengewehr-Bataillon		
mot.:	motorisiert		
MPi:	Maschinenpistole		
NSFO:	Nationalsozialistischer Führungs-Offizier		
ObGefr.:	Obergefreiter		
Oblt.:	Oberleutnant		
OKH:	Oberkommando des Heeres		
OKW:	Oberkommando der Wehrmacht